Twelve Dispositions

A Field Guide to Humans

by Coralie Koonce

Acknowledgments

I would like to express my appreciation to Maya Porter, Sonia Gutierrez, Linda Farrell, Aimee Crochet, Lucy Imrie, and George Imrie for their feedback, help, and support in the writing of this book.

Contents

Chapter 1
A Field Guide

The true test of civilization is not the census, nor the size of the cities, nor the crops, but the kind of man [and woman] that the country turns out.
~Ralph Waldo Emerson, American poet and essayist, 1803-1882

Field guides identify birds of North America, butterflies, fishes, wildflowers, and snakes both poisonous and non-poisonous, but one finds no such guide to the wide range of human attitudes and behavior patterns. It would be useful to identify these because we all imitate each other—it is how we learn to be human. Not only do we select certain individuals as role models, we also model generalized behaviors and mental manifestations from memes to worldviews. A field guide could make us more conscious of *what* we are imitating.

Most field guides are assembled by species, but this one has a different organizing principle. It describes behaviors in terms of twelve dispositions. *A disposition is simply the usual attitude or the tendency of a person or group to act or think a certain way.*

These dispositions spread through families and neighborhoods, schools and workplaces, becoming attached to larger social institutions and systems of ideas and belief. These, in turn, reflect, impel, and reinforce individual tendencies to behave in a certain manner. Eventually this process expands to entire cultures, civilizations, and eras. Historian John Harmon McElroy defines a historical culture as "a unique set of extremely simple beliefs, formed and communicated through behavior over more than three generations." [1]

Dispositions are habits of long-standing, millennia old. This field guide aims to describe them, *especially as they are embedded in institutions, ideologies, and other cultural inventions.* It is less about individuals and more about the cultures that grow from and then further shape individual dispositions.

Unlike most writings about ethics, this one says quite a bit about the dispositions that fall short—the negative models. Describing ethics on the wing is quite a bit harder than describing the color and markings of various thrushes, and it necessarily involves a certain subjectivity. I do make assumptions about what to imitate and what to avoid, judging that some dispositions are more likely than others to help individuals, cultures, and the species to survive and flourish. Nevertheless, this is a field guide rather than a treatise; more description than proscription. It is not about moral systems, Moral Foundations Theory, the evolution of morality, or traditional moral philosophy.

Humans generally have a "moral imagination" and ethical judgments are not solely the province of moral philosophers. As novelist John Dos Passos said, "The mind cannot support moral chaos for long. Men are under as strong a compulsion to invent an ethical setting for their behavior as spiders are to weave themselves webs." [2] Research shows very young children are already developing a sense of morality. [3]

Social psychologist Jonathan Haidt defines moral systems as "interlocking sets of values, practices, institutions, and evolved psychological mechanisms that work together to suppress or regulate selfishness and make social life possible." Ordinary people in daily life make many moral and ethical evaluations, intuitively judging the actions of family members, co-workers, neighbors, celebrities, politicians, even fictional characters. They/we give implicit or explicit ratings to institutions, groups, and belief systems such as Congress, Wicca, food stamp recipients, public education, or the One-Percent.*

Meanwhile, philosophy has several approaches to morality and ethics. Concerning the six higher dispositions, we are closest to *virtue ethics*, which depends on criteria which have recurred throughout civilization and across cultures in mythology, religious teaching, philosophical writings, psychology, and literature, values such as the following:

Respect for human life	*Restraining violent impulses*
Respect for all life	*Desire to "to be all one can be"*
Sincerity	*Using reason*
Justice	*Conflict resolution*
Concern for future generations	*Creative solutions*
Self-reliance and responsibility	*Service to others*
Good will towards others	

Ancient Chinese philosophers Lao Tzu, Confucius and Mencius concerned themselves with listing such virtues. Confucius added the understanding of changing conditions ("contingency"). He said that the failure to deal with reality and to call things by their proper names were major causes of social disorder. We see this 2,500 years later in an era of propaganda. Lao Tzu taught that virtue resided in returning to the natural order of things, in reverence for life and in simplicity. For Mencius, tendencies toward benevolence and wisdom (the higher dispositions) are innate; they are natural inclinations, suggesting that the lower dispositions are deformations or atavistic functions of the natural person.

Such criteria help determine how well each pattern of behavior serves individuals, societies, the human race, and Life itself. In general, the six higher dispositions support long-term survival and flourishing of human beings, while the six lower dispositions tend to retard human development both individually and collectively.

The twelve categories of dispositions are intended to describe patterns of thinking and behaviors and are *not* meant as pigeonholes for individuals, who are infinitely more complex. Each disposition is a potential in all of us, and we all show mixed behaviors. It is true that individuals or cultures can get stuck in a certain disposition that becomes habitual and dominant—the conventional wisdom. This is still only part of an overall pattern of dispositions. Nothing is written in stone. Individuals, collectivities, and ideas are constantly changing.

Lower dispositions range from behavior quite without moral sense to those limited more by social institutions and ideological beliefs. They display a lack of empathy and moral imagination; greater conditioning and manipulation by others; more behavior that is hard-wired and less individual consciousness or autonomy; and the relative inability of individuals and societies to acknowledge and channel their negative unconscious.

At best these dispositions do not help humans to solve problems or to develop their potential. At worst they express violence, hate, and pure selfishness. Despite the fact that these mindsets are very common, they do not tend to happiness for either individuals or societies. In fact they cause a great deal of suffering.

A great many of us *habitually* think and act from these flawed and maladaptive mind-sets. They are expressed in many of our institutions and in popular belief-systems which may even wear the cloak of morality. Ironically, habits of thought that deeply repel us in individuals are often the coin of the realm when they appear in our ideologies and belief-systems whether patriotic, political, economic, or religious. For instance, most people would denounce an individual who murders out of personal revenge, yet several countries and several parts of the United States continue to practice capital punishment. On the international scale, nation-states gloss over the collateral killing of civilians as leaders seek revenge for actions by another country's leaders.

Individuals who operate as decent family members in their personal life may be found at the lower dispositions in their public life, when in letters to the editor or on blogs they verbally promote war crimes and torture. (Ideas that are repeatedly verbalized or visualized become more acceptable in actual situations.)

Some institutions embody outworn values or become corrupted, yet keep going by their momentum. We also find ideologies that change over time, often for the worse. Ideas once beneficial are oversimplified and twisted out of recognition. Some acquire unmerited haloes.

As a field guide, this writing identifies all kinds of behaviors, both negative and positive models. Despite my emphasis on the lower dispositions, overall the outlook is positive. Recognizing prevailing human tendencies is a prelude to transformational changes.

*Some use the terms *morality* and *ethics* interchangeably although the two concepts have different histories and meaning. We might use as a rough guide this statement by Ian Walsh: "Morals are how you treat people you know. Ethics are how you treat people you don't know."

[1] John Harmon McElroy, *American Beliefs*, Ivan R. Dee, 1999

[2] John Dos Passos, *The Preparation of a New Society*, Houghton Mifflin Company, 1950

[3] Sandra Crosser, Ph.D., "Emerging Morality: How Children Think about Right and Wrong," *Early Childhood News*,
http://www.earlychildhoodnews.com/earlychildhood/article_view.aspx?ArticleID=118

Chapter 2
The Twelve Dispositions

*Heaven and hell suppose two distinct species of men, the good
and the bad. But the greatest part of mankind float betwixt vice and
virtue.*
~David Hume, Scottish philosopher, 1711-1776

This book describes six lower dispositions (0° through 25°) and six higher dispositions (30° through X°): twelve in all. Dispositions are latent tendencies, not specific behaviors. In general, these distinctions indicate the depth and breadth of empathy and the degree of ethical maturing expressed by individuals, social groups, and the ideas and belief-systems they live by.

     0°   Destructive
     5°   Reactive
     10° Power/Domination
     15° Confusion
     20° Competition
     25° Narcissism
     30° Family
     35° Community
     40° Humanitarian
     45° Reason/Principles
     50° Creative
     X°   Spirit

Keywords provide focus, but with neutral numbers, complex concepts do not become limited by associations with one or two words.

To repeat: dispositions do not describe whole persons. A personality identical with a certain disposition could only be a cartoon or a stock character in a melodrama. Although one or two dispositions may *dominate* an individual's behavior, most people demonstrate multiple attitudes, harboring jealous rage at one moment, sacrificing their own desires for someone else's good at another. The same is true of dispositions that express collectivities and ideas—groups, institutions, ideologies, cultures. They are seldom all of a piece.

Nor is this system a ladder from Total Evil to Total Good, which would be a gross oversimplification. You may note a moral progression from disposition 0° to 30°, but it is neither simple nor absolute. For instance, the victim is just as dead whether killed by an emotionless hit man (0°), a drinking buddy in a rage (5°), a case of mistaken identity (15°), during a war of nation-states competing for colonies or resources (20°), or in a struggle against a conqueror or tyrant (45°).

Mixed motives and behaviors abound: Sweet and loving B is also 10° possessive of those she loves, to the point that they feel smothered. Y habitually carries a chip on his shoulder but attempts to rise above 5° suspicions and combativeness once a week for one hour in church. Or consider Z, a man who is devoted to his invalid wife but often makes shockingly violent remarks about persons of another race or religion. Obviously, we can't easily sum people up.

An individual's habitual tendency to act or think in a certain way changes throughout life as each person matures and becomes—hopefully—not only older but also wiser. An adult operating at the emotional level of a toddler would be more loathsome than adorable. In addition people have aspirations and models that serve them as a lodestar although they may not fully understand or follow them.

There is nothing static about an individual's awareness. Realizations or conversions, as well as declines and falls, are always possible. It would be a shame to misuse this system in order to create new stereotypes and scapegoats, or to practice one-upmanship. Do remember that people are complex and people can change.

One hears many dicta about human nature based on a limited range of human experience, just the USA or this moment in time. I try to look as broadly as possible across cultures and history, at prehistory and even at our animal cousins. In one form or another, dispositions have existed for a long time.

Any examples you or I use of historical or contemporary individuals can reflect only an external, public impression of who they are. We do not really know the psychological depths of any public figure. Often fictional characters can better illustrate the development of ethical awareness (or its lack), since a work of fiction is pretty much a closed system.

Ancient Greek dramas presented the tragic hero whose single flaw of character brings him to ruin. The reverse side would be someone with personal flaws who may have creative talent or spiritual aspirations so great that they tend to uplift his general pattern. Many eminent people have had irregular love lives, substance abuse problems, or an inability to stay out of debt from gambling or extravagance. As examples, St. Augustine, St. Francis of Assisi, and Leo Tolstoy gave up early excesses to become spiritual models.

A more puzzling personality, Adi Da (born Franklin Albert Jones) seems to have moved in the opposite direction. He began as a brilliant spiritual teacher in the Eastern tradition, but as he accumulated followers he declared himself a unique avatar more enlightened than Buddha and Christ. In a well-publicized controversy, a number of ex-members accused Adi Da of sexual and physical abuse, false imprisonment, and fraud, as well as personal excesses.

US President Woodrow Wilson was another complex individual, with high ideals and scholarly attainments (45°) and a deep desire to further world peace (40°). Yet he retained the racist views (10°) of his Southern upbringing, and also promoted harsh measures against those citizens who disagreed with his policies (10° authoritarianism). Finally, Wilson's 25° arrogance and his inability to compromise undermined his own, deeply held dream of a League of Nations.

In some cases the low notes of a person's awareness are so strong and even criminal, that they eclipse his higher values. With added intelligence and/or power, personal flaws become more dangerous and operate on a greater scale. Examples are Osama Bin laden and Ted Kaczynski, both of whom espoused higher principles, but used 0° violence to advance them. [1,2]

Here's something else to keep in mind: Two expressions of a disposition are *not* equivalent. Certainly their effects can be different. While acting out murderous impulses, Ted Bundy and Heinrich Himmler operated on vastly different scales. Violence may occur at various degrees of awareness, for different reasons, from different motivations, and with different effects.

Psychoanalytic theory also describes the psychological mechanism of *sublimation*: "to divert or modify an instinctual impulse into a culturally higher or socially more acceptable activity." Sublimation is one step on a long path to completely extinguish negative emotional patterns such as rage and hatred. For instance, anger can be sublimated into chopping wood—or writing a novel.

Psychoanalyst Carl Jung introduced the idea of the human Shadow:

> Man is, on the whole, less good than he imagines himself or wants to be. Everyone carries a shadow, and the less it is embodied in the individual's conscious life, the blacker and denser it is. If an inferiority is conscious, one always has a chance to correct it. Furthermore, it is constantly in contact with other interests, so that it is continually subjected to modifications. But *if it is repressed and isolated from consciousness, it never gets corrected.* [3]

The Shadow manifests in a negative way when it is rigidly closed off and unacknowledged. Yet it also contains the seeds of our emotional and creative life, if we can but manifest them in a positive way. For example, the murder mystery is a highly popular genre, yet its readers include very few murderers among them. A great writer or actor may sublimate 0° (a potential in everyone's Shadow) by creating a fictional Raskolnikov in *Crime and Punishment*, or by portraying on film the brilliant serial killer Hannibal Lector. We sublimate our own destructive 0° tendencies by reading or viewing these conceptions, thus gaining greater understanding of our own Shadow and that of others.

One rule of thumb: *It is hard to understand someone else acting outside of one's own range of awareness, especially those operating at degrees beyond one's own immediate ceiling.* For instance, in following a spiritual leader, some pick out a relatively minor aspect of the leader's personality rather than the essence of his teaching. I saw this dynamic at work in a large spiritual community where some followers drank Pepsi Cola because they noted that their leader did so.

It may also be hard to understand individuals or groups acting at the lowest degrees, behaviors which the rest of us outgrew as toddlers. Or we may not wish to think about them because they remind us of the residues of our former selves. Yet they morbidly fascinate many of us in literature, films, and news stories.

While it may not make for pleasant reading, there are persistent negative potentials of our species that we cannot afford to deny or ignore. I begin with the lowest forms of awareness, the most dangerous to humanity. The object is not to assign blame but to try to understand. As the ancient Roman playwright Terence said, "I am a man: I hold that nothing human can be alien to me." Be assured, later on I will describe more heroic, creative, and noble dispositions.

Not only individuals but also diverse groups of all kinds and sizes show a wide range of behavior patterns. Group dispositions are formed of the dispositions of current members—some of whom may have stronger personalities or greater formal authority—as well as by policies and traditions laid down by previous members of the group. One can use the word *ethos* for the disposition of a group, large or small, defined as the characteristic spirit of a culture or community; the sentiment underlying the beliefs and customs of a group or society— their dominant assumptions and aspirations. Unfortunately, this obvious truth is often abused by those acting at lower dispositions who over-generalize about nationalities or ethnic groups in order to prove their own group's superiority or to create scapegoats.

Any teacher knows that each class has its distinct personality. So with other groups. One office has a dark cloud above it; another seems populated by smiling people. In a business or organization, the personality of the leader, like the captain of a sailing vessel, has a great deal to do with whether she or he runs a happy ship instead of one that is full of grumbling, back-biting, and turnover, even mutiny.

In a social club, company, church, or country, one naturally expects higher-consciousness individuals to lead the way as mentors and models. Yet too often a collective resonates with its lowest common denominator. People may elect or become burdened with a leader whose pattern of dispositions is lower than their own, who resonates with their own negative Shadows. A charismatic narcissist or power-hungry sociopath can charm a nation. Whether by hereditary kingship, a coup, or "a wolf in sheep's clothing," a country may come under the thumb of a brutal tyrant or a cluster of such leaders (*pathocracy*).

History is often taught to us in terms of a succession of leaders. Even in a nominally democratic country, such a personalized view of history (and of current events) reinforces the hold of authoritarianism.

A useful word from German—*Zeitgeist*—describes the spirit of a whole generation or time period: the prevailing intellectual, moral, and cultural climate of an era; the dominant disposition of an age such as the Elizabethan Age, Gilded Age, Progressive Era, the Sixties. Even before the telegraph and telephone, new ideas, cultural trends, and rebellions passed through populations and across borders surprisingly fast via travelers, traders, and couriers. With digital technology, memes spread almost instantaneously.

The *Zeitgeist* inevitably influences those individuals who live in that time and place, who in turn compose the *Zeitgeist*. We cannot separate out humans from the complex societies in which we live. Psychology underlies our ideologies, while ideologies—often imprinted by society's authority and now spread by modern advertising techniques—help shape individual psychologies. Temperament, social institutions, and ideologies all combine in forming dispositions.

[1] Usama Bin Laden, "The Way to Save the Earth," February 17, 2010, http://www.nefafoundation.org/miscellaneous/nefa_ublwaytosaveearth0210. pdf chapter 4 One could read this document as an expression of Bin Laden's higher aspirations.

[2] Jack Levin, director of the Program for the Study of Violence and Conflict at Northeastern University in Boston says "I think [Kaczynski's] motivation changed over the years. As a young man he may have been seriously concerned about the direction of American society and he may have felt strongly about the role that high-tech was playing and then decided he was going to try and reverse that. But I think later he became more interested in power and feeling important than he did in changing society." http://www.salon.com/news/1997/11/14news.html

[3] Carl Jung, *Psychology and Religion: West and East*, 1938

Chapter 3
The Problematic Concept of Evil

Epicurus's old questions are still unanswered: Is he (God)
willing to prevent evil, but not able? Then he is impotent. Is he able,
but not willing? Then he is malevolent. Is he both able and willing?
Then whence evil?"
~David Hume, Scottish philosopher, 1711-1776

Although this is a guidebook, and not a *Summa Theologica,* it is hard to avoid the word *evil.* And yet, does talking about evil help us to understand our fellow human beings? I submit that it doesn't, that the word tangles us up in three ways. First, we don't all agree on how to define evil. Second, we are not certain about how much free will anybody has to commit evil—and this is a special problem for those millions of Christians who subscribe to the notion of original sin. Third, there's that human propensity to see all the evil in the other guy, especially in that 'monster,' the psychopath.

The first problem, then, is that we are not all talking about the same thing. Is evil a force outside ourselves, a potential within all of us, the nature of particular people, certain behaviors such as murder and torture, the absence of good? The term 'evil' can apply to institutions or social customs that perpetuate wrongs through individuals who have no personal intention to commit harm, who think that they are doing the accepted, normal thing. Shirley Jackson's chilling short story "The Lottery" shows a town with a long-standing yearly custom to sacrifice one individual chosen by lottery. Yet all of us entertain ideas and live with institutions that perpetrate much greater horrors.

Some use the term 'evil' to describe opposing political systems, religions other than their own, or entire foreign countries. Ancient ideas that the material world is evil sometimes contributed to indifference towards injustice or to destruction of the natural environment.

Most readers are likely to come from the Abrahamic religions, which tend to see Good and Evil as moral absolutes. Many view evil as a supernatural force and some personify it. Recent polls suggest that at least one-third of American adults regard Satan as an actual living being.[1] These believers might falsely assume that if I use the term 'evil' I agree with their own definitions.

Another caution about moral absolutes is that the long view may differ from the day-to-day view in a particular culture and tradition. For instance, several societies have regarded left-handed people as unlucky, unclean, even as devil-worshippers. The word 'sinister' originally meant left-handed. Yet about one-tenth of us continue to be born as 'southpaws'. Lefties may have had an advantage in personal combat and still do in many sports; they are found disproportionately among divergent thinkers, creative people, and those with high IQs. Thus it now appears that they are more advantaged than disadvantaged. [2]

To make my own position clear: I find evil to be a lack of good rather than a force or entity. Instead of either moral absolutism or moral relativism, I prefer the philosophical position called moral universalism: that some moral values apply universally to everyone—at least everyone in similar circumstances—but *not* as absolute standards that apply regardless of culture or situation.

Free Will or Not—or How Much?

It is necessary for him who lays out a state and arranges laws for it to presuppose that all men are evil and that they are always going to act according to the wickedness of their spirits whenever they have free scope.
~Niccolo Machiavelli

A second thorny area concerns free will. A common assumption is that all human beings have equal free will, and can choose whether or not to do evil. This has consequences in law. Only a few centuries ago our ancestors defined free will more broadly, executing people who were clearly psychotic and children as young as eight (seven was the age of criminal responsibility). Some courts convicted and executed large domestic animals, especially pigs, for maiming or killing humans, thus implying that these animals had at least some free will.

Today we make more distinctions. Legal systems now recognize that young children and the insane are not responsible for their crimes, as when a toddler shoots a loaded gun found in his mother's purse. The age of criminal responsibility has risen, and since 1976 nobody has been executed in the United States who was younger than 16 at the time of their crimes. However in the matter of just who is insane, there is a great deal of legal debate.

But what if free will is not an either/or but rather a question of how much? This is very hard to adjudicate. How can one weigh the effects of heredity, of childhood abuse, of brain injuries, of social conditioning that sometimes resembles brainwashing? In general, the lower dispositions have less free will than the higher ones, and in fact this is a large part of the differences between them.

Original Sin or Bad Code?

For what is more contrary to the rules of our miserable justice than to damn eternally an infant incapable of will, for a sin wherein he seems to have so little a share, that it was committed six thousand years before he was in existence?
~Blaise Pascal, French polymath, 1623-1662

Original sin is a theological concept that the state of sin is innate in all humans because they are descendants of Adam and share his guilt from the first act of disobedience (eating the fruit of the tree of knowledge). As sinners, humans are thus utterly depraved in nature, and lack the freedom to be good on their own. Many assume this notion is in the Bible, but it originated in the writing of early church fathers such as Tertullian (160-220) and Cyprian (200-258) and was mainly developed by Augustine of Hippo (354-430) who now identified the original sin as concupiscence (sexual desire).

Some branches of Christianity, such as the Orthodox Church, never accepted the idea of original sin. However, 16th century Protestant reformers Martin Luther and John Calvin expanded the idea and made it a cornerstone of their faith.

One notes that converting from the more symbolic idea of the expanding human consciousness to the instinctive desire for sexual congress, is quite an intellectual leap. Not only that, but regarding the natural desire as sinful, while at the same time promoting reproduction, produces a contradiction that can create great psychological confusion

(15°) and distress.[3] This doctrine was used to justify the enforced celibacy of Roman Catholic clergy, although another motivation may have been that the Church saw the support of families and bestowal of inheritances as detrimental to Church power.

Philosopher W. Paul Franks says, "It is not likely that a broad free will defense will succeed if one ascribes to original guilt." The two ideas are not easily compatible, although many people seem to believe in them both.

Several theories could be seen as secular or scientific versions of original sin. In a comprehensive study of evil, *The Pathology of Man*, psychologist Steven James Bartlett treats evil as pathology—but one that is a normal human state. It is 'a flaw in the machine' and results from 'bad code' whether genetic, biochemical, or errors of thought. Some suggest that the rapid development of the human forebrain was a malformation rather than a sign of progressive evolution. In Kurt Vonnegut's *Galapagos* the narrator says that all of humankind's horrors and sorrows have been caused by "the only true villain in my story: the oversized human brain." [4]

Others refer to an ancient mistake of the human race, whether agriculture, civilization, or technology. Several anthropologists (e.g., Claude Levi-Strauss, Bill Schindler) claim that society has been declining since the Neolithic, 10,000 years ago. Jared Diamond states that adopting agriculture was "the worst mistake in the history of the human race." Indirectly, agriculture contributed to wars, which John Horgan notes began in earnest about 12,000 years ago, along with domestication of animals, farming, and villages near rivers. Now people had more resources worth stealing or defending, and all in one place. [5]

Increased reliance on agriculture became a trap, as described by British science writer Colin Tudge: "The farmers find themselves in a vicious spiral. The more they farm, the more their population rises and the more they are obliged to farm, because only by farming can they feed the extra mouths."[6] The agriculture trap has led finally to growth of world population to the point of outstripping Earth's carrying capacity.

However, rather than focusing on agriculture, Deep Ecologists see civilization itself (specifically industrial civilization) as irretrievably damned by unsustainability. Technology has also given us weapons that could destroy civilization, humankind, and/or the planet.[7]

Evil as Individual Pathology

For 150 years, science has known of the psychopath's existence; for at least 140 years, scientists have quarreled over the definition of this disorder.
~J. McCord and M. McCord, *Psychopathy and Delinquency,* 1982

It is too easy to exclude 'bad people' from the human race, especially those we do not understand. Confusion is reflected in the use of three imprecise terms for people who are said to lack a conscience: sociopathy, psychopathy, and antisocial personality disorder. Harvard psychologist Martha Stout says this confusion reflects "an unstable mix of ideas," and that "the absence of conscience does not really make sense as a psychiatric category in the first place."[8]

A recent flurry of genetic and neurological research has found that people with various psychiatric disorders show brain abnormalities and physiological differences. For instance, brain scans show that people diagnosed as psychopathic personalities have a much longer but thinner corpus callosum, a less responsive amygdala, and abnormalities in the right side of the brain.[9]

We don't know at what point in their development people develop these brain discrepancies. We do know that various kinds of stress can cause, trigger, or contribute to abnormal brain structure and neurotransmitter dysfunctions. For example, researchers found reduced size of hippocampus, corpus callosum, amygdala, and frontal cortex in women who were sexually abused as children.[10, 11]

In several studies of children and adolescent males with callous unemotional traits indicative of psychopathy, researchers looked for the respective roles of nature and nurture. These scientists estimated a heritable range between 30 and 67%. Another way to look at these findings is that the environment accounts for between 33 and 70% of the development of an apparently conscienceless person. These figures do not support the notion of a 'bad seed' or of an incurable condition.[12]

We could also reflect on the nature of conscience or lack thereof in historic contexts. No one would accuse President Harry S. Truman of being a psychopath, yet he ordered the atomic bombing of Hiroshima and Nagasaki. Many other leaders have initiated mass killing in warfare for what they considered good and sufficient reasons, thus murdering millions of times more people than all the Ted Bundys put together.

Stout points to one highly important aspect of an individual's environment: culture, noting that some cultures "actively encourage antisocial behavior including violence, murder, and warmongering." In America, in particular, "The glorification of killing [0°]…has been a lasting feature of our mainstream culture" and a pernicious influence on vulnerable personalities."

The term psychopath is more widely used than understood, acquiring overtones that owe more to Hollywood movies than to science. The term has become virtually synonymous with evil. Some even suggest that psychopaths are an entirely different subspecies or species from 'normal' people, perhaps a throwback to an earlier hominid. Others see psychopathic traits as part of a continuum. Meanwhile, evolutionary psychologists argue about whether they evolved as an adaptive strategy or as a byproduct of selection for dominance.[13, 14]

Despite popular beliefs, not all who are called psychopaths are criminals. It seems some are in managerial or power positions in society (dominant 10°). Psychologist Robert Hare says that many 'sub-criminal' or 'subclinical' psychopaths function as "lawyers, doctors, psychiatrists, academics, mercenaries, police officers, cult leaders, military personnel, businesspeople, writers, artists, entertainers, and so forth." This suggests a trait that is at one end of a Bell curve, not an entirely different kind of human being.[15]

Dr. Hare, who devised the Psychopathy Checklist (PCL-R) as a diagnostic tool, estimates that 1-2% of the population is psychopathic. 1% is a commonly accepted number. *If this estimate is accurate*, that would suggest that at least three million such individuals in the United States and 70 million worldwide presumably function without an inner sense of what is right and wrong. Keep in mind that the term *psychopath* is imprecise, and the map is not the territory.[16]

The Dark Triad

Diseases of the soul are more dangerous and more numerous than those of the body.
~Marcus Tullius Cicero, Roman orator and writer, 106-43 BC

Many psychologists speak of the 'Dark Triad,' a constellation of three distinct personality traits they believe form the basis of an anti-social human core. The Dark Triad combines Machiavellianism, narcissism, and psychopathy, which all share a callous, manipulative way of acting towards others. Machiavellianism describes a tendency to pursue one's own selfish aims without concern for others, and an interpersonal style that is unemotional and deceptive. High Mach individuals—who score high for this trait on a test devised to measure it—are exceptionally competitive (20°) and flexible, changing their own strategy to fit the circumstances. But unlike others who are good at playing the game, these individuals remain cool and detached from morality, ready to win at any cost.

Now some psychologists add a fourth trait, sadism, to form a Dark Tetrad of traits that constitute the most negative expression of the human Shadow. Sadistic people actually enjoy hurting others; they have an appetite for cruelty. [17]

Because such human tendencies exist, some psychiatrists such as M. Scott Peck (*People of the Lie*) and Michael H. Stone (*The Anatomy of Evil*) use the word 'evil' to describe *individuals* with certain psychiatric disorders or psychological traits. This is a gray area at best. Other psychiatrists argue that even introducing the concept of evil into psychiatry is unscientific and harmful to all mental patients. [18]

The problems that may result from combining an absolute morality with psychiatry were shown by Dr. James Grigson, a psychiatrist in Texas. He testified in 167 capital cases that the defendant was almost certainly likely to commit another murder. His authoritative testimony swayed juries, and about two-thirds of the defendants were executed. Widely known as "Dr. Death," Grigson had often given the defendant only a cursory examination—or none at all—but believed that people who had once committed murder could never be rehabilitated. [19]

Such determinations involve many ethical problems. What if we find that an 'evil' person was suffering from a brain injury or tumor that points to diminished responsibility? If some of these psychological disorders are partly heritable, and if abuse can actually change people's brain structures, then what becomes of free will—and culpability?

It is important to make the distinction between an evil act and the psychologically abnormal person we believe is responsible for it. Any theory that describes certain individuals or groups as *evil* easily lends itself to prejudice, hatred, and punitive justice. Here I prefer to describe behavior patterns and tendencies (dispositions) that we all share to some degree, agreeing with Jung that the shadow is a largely unconscious potential within every human being.

People tend to project their unacknowledged impulses and motives onto others, to avoid seeing their own Shadow. And so the concept of evil is most often used to apply to somebody else, to thrust them away, to justify one's own culture or kin or self as compared to others. Avoidance also happens on the group level, with collective Shadows. Most nation-states have grave misdeeds in their history. Jung speaks of the national Shadow, which denies our collective crimes and projects them onto various scapegoats.

We could regard the lowest dispositions as the collective human Shadow. Whether as individuals, nations, or other groups, to become more conscious of our Shadow is prelude to transforming ourselves, a gradual evolution through greater self-awareness.

By describing dysfunctional customs and beliefs, I hope to make it somewhat harder for vengeance to disguise itself as justice, sadism to mask itself as good order, or greed to cloak itself in freedom. I would encourage the world's citizens to scrutinize their leaders as they gain power and to take a long hard look at their own ideologies.

[1]"Beliefs by the Public and Religious Groups"
http://www.religioustolerance.org/chr_demo2htm
[2] Maria Kounnikova, "Sinister Minds: Are Left-Handed People Smarter?" *New Yorker*, August 22, 2013, http://www.newyorker.com/tech/elements/sinister-minds-are-left-handed-people-smarter
[3] Tony Jones, "Original Sin: a Depraved Idea,"
http://www.beliefnet.com/columnists/tonyjones/2009/01/original-sin-a-depraved-idea.html#ixzz2yEsBcxT

[4] Steven James Bartlett, *The Pathology of Man: A study of Human Evil,* Charles C. Thomas, 2005

[5] Jared Diamond, "The Worst Mistake in the History of the Human Race," *Discover Magazine*, May 1987, pp. 64-66, http://www.ditext.com/diamond/mistake.html

[6] Colin Tudge, *Neanderthals, Bandits, and Farmers: How Agriculture Really Began*, Yale 6 University Press, 1993.

[7] Arie McBay, Lierre Keith, and Derrick Jensen, *Deep Green Resistance,* Seven Stories Press, 2011

[8] Martha Stout, Ph.D., *The Sociopath Next Door: The Ruthless Versus the Rest of Us,* Broadway Books, 2005

[9] Barbara Oakley, *Evil Genes*, Prometheus 2007

[10] Bryan Kolb, Robbin Gibb, and Terry Robinson, "Brain Plasticity and Behavior," *Current Directions in Psychological Science,* **February 2003** vol. 12 no. 1, **1-5** http://www.psychologicalscience.org/journals/cd/12_1/Kolb.cfm

[11] Susan L. Anderson, Ph.D., Akemi Tomada, M.D., Ph.D., Evelyn S. Vincow, Elizabeth Valente, M.A., Ann Policari, R.N., C.S., Ph.D, and Martin H. Teicher, M.D., Ph.D., "Preliminary Evidence for Sensitive Periods in the Effect of Childhood Sexual Abuse on Regional Brain Development," Published in final edited form as: *Journal of Neruopsychiatry & Clinical Neurosciences,* 2008 Summer, 20(3): 292-301, http://www.ncbi.nlm.nih.gov/pmc/articles/PMC4270804/

[12] S. Bezdjian, A. Raine, L.A. Baker, and D.R. Lynam, "Psychopathic personality in children: genetic and environmental contributions," Psychol Med. 2011 Mar; 41(3): 589–600. Published online 2010 May 20

[13] Gary Federman, Dave Holmes, and Jean Daniel Jacob, "Deconstructing the Psychopath," *Cultural Critique* 72, Spring 2009

[14] Jarkko Jalava, The Myth of the Born Criminal, University of Toronto Press, 2015

[15] Robert D. Hare, Ph.D., *Without Conscience: The Disturbing World of the Psychopaths among Us,* Guilford Press, 1993

[16] Alix Spiegel, "Can a Test Really Tell Who's a Psychopath?" *All Things Considered*, May 26, 2011, http://www.npr.org/2011/05/26/136619689/can-a-test-really-tell-whos-a-psychopath

[17] Wray Herbert, "Everyday Sadism: Throwing Light on the Dark Triad," April 24, 2013, http://www.psychologicalscience.org/index.php/news/were-only-human/everyday-sadism-throwing-light-on-the-dark-triad.html

[18] Michael H. Stone, *The Anatomy of Evil*, Prometheus, 2009

[19] "Texas 'Dr. Death' retires after 167 capital case trials," *Washington Times*, December 20, 2003 http://www.washingtontimes.com/news/2003/dec/20/20031220-113219-5189r/?page=all

Chapter 4
0° Celsius or Frozen Souls

O poor mortals, how ye make this earth bitter for each other.
~Thomas Carlyle, *The French Revolution,* 1837

A news story from the Syrian Civil War shows a dramatic contrast between very low and very high levels of consciousness. A British surgeon, Dr. David Nott, volunteers to treat wounded civilians in war zones one month out of every year and he has done so for two decades. Nott says Syria is "more horrific than any other war zone I've worked in," adding that in most conflicts civilians are caught in crossfire, but in Syria they are in direct fire. He reports an unusual pattern of gunshot wounds in his sniper victims:

> One day we'd have pregnant women being brought in with gunshot wounds to the uterus. Not just one or two, but seven or eight, which meant to me they must be targeting pregnant women. And the following day, we would get people coming in with chest wounds to the right side of the chest. The next day it would be the left side and no other injuries. Then it would be groin wounds; everybody would come in with a groin wound.
> So it seemed to me that there was a death game going on with the snipers. [1]

Nott says wounded children also arrive in clusters. And the doctors themselves are often targeted. On the one hand is Dr. Nott, who tithes his highly specialized skills at great risk to himself in order to save human lives; on the other, bored and brutally cynical soldiers who use innocent human beings for target practice. Dr. Nott has arranged to set up a course to train other UK physicians to work in war zones. So far, at least 1,000 have volunteered. [2]

When acting at 0° people seem to care nothing for human life, or they have contempt for it. This is where the most profound kind of hatred resides, where some actually enjoy inflicting pain on other sentient beings, human and otherwise. For whatever reasons, empathy and conscience never developed at 0° degrees.

The Origin of a Word

> *To be modern is to tear the soul out of everything.*
> ~Yohji Yamamoto, *My Dear Bomb*

The word 'soulless' entered the English language somewhere between 1545 and 1555 at the start of the modern era. It was a time of unprecedented changes and social stresses in Europe. New inventions included the printing press, hoisting gear (cranes), spinning wheel, and improved guns. Commerce grew with a money economy financed by interest and debt. Explorations of Africa and the Americas were leading to an age of colonialism. The transatlantic slave trade began.

Europe endured continuous religious conflicts engendered by the Protestant Reformation that began in 1517. Other big and little wars were fought all over Europe and the Near East, also wars of conquest in the New World and a number of peasant revolts, harshly repressed. The ruthless Ottoman Empire was expanding into Europe. Russia was ruled by the violently unstable Ivan the Terrible. In the Italian states, the Medici and Borgia families intrigued on the grand scale, and Niccolò Machiavelli's *The Prince* exposed 16th century Realpolitik.

The mass hysteria of witch-hunting began, spurred on by an infamous book—*Malleus Maleficarum* (The Hammer of Witches)—which had achieved twenty printings by 1520. Thousands of political and religious executions occurred during the reigns of Henry VIII and his daughters Mary and Elizabeth. Excesses of the Spanish Inquisition gave rise throughout Europe to the 'Black Legend.' All these events and changes gave examples of heartless cruelty that only needed a word to describe them. Events in the roughly 500 years since then have added far too many examples of complete lack of empathy for others, fanaticism, and deliberate cruelty to humans and other living things. But are there really people without souls?

Soul: life, spirit, consciousness; the animating and spiritual principle embodied in human beings. It is a difficult concept. For the secular, our spirit animates us only while we are alive. For most religions, souls are immortal. Animism, our ancestral religion and still the religion of most tribal societies, grants soul not only to humans but also to animals, plants, and even to natural entities and phenomena such as rivers, mountains, and storms. Some branches of modern-day religions would give a soul—even an immortal soul—to nonhuman animals, but others reserve the term for human beings.

Scientists speak of mind rather than soul and most deny the existence of an immaterial soul. But whatever we mean by the word 'soul,' certain individuals are said not to have one. They are heartless and cruel, without nobility or humanizing qualities, and lacking sensitivity, warmth, or the capacity for deep feeling. Works of art or literature are sometimes described as soulless because they are dead, spiritless, and mechanical—like a machine.

A machine has no soul, although some science fiction writers have imagined a highly intelligent machine that might develop one—Data, the android crewman, or the holographic Doctor, both of the *Star Trek* series. Cybernetic enthusiasts who look forward to the Singularity, when people will be able to upload their personalities into robots, don't talk about souls.

Defining 0°

If way to the Better there be, it exacts a full look at the Worst.
~Thomas Hardy, English novelist, 1840-1928

The three degrees from $0°$ to $10°$ tend toward violence. All suffer from the old human tendency to devalue those who are not part of one's own family or tribe. Yet they do differ in how deeply they are separated from other humans, from Life and happiness. The $0°$ state of mind is somehow isolated from most other members of our species, a condition that has been described as "morally empty" and "void of feeling." Some might describe this lowest degree of awareness as synonymous with evil. However, as noted, I would bypass the age-old theological debate. Nor can we always be sure whether $0°$ is sane or insane.

The defining characteristic of $0°$ is not failure to understand others, but choosing not to care or possibly unable to care. $0°$ regards some or all human beings as its appointed prey, meant only for its own amusement or aggrandizement—or of no importance whatsoever.

Whatever the origins and motives of 0°, and whether certain individuals have genetic predispositions for their lack of conscience, here let us just say that 0° destroys others, promotes and even enjoys the destruction of others, or is utterly indifferent to the life of others.

First let us say what 0° is not. It is neither psychopathy or sociopathy, terms used to describe an individual disorder characterized by anti-social behavior and a lack of remorse, empathy, or love. Neither is 0° equivalent to extreme narcissism or other psychological term.*

Here let us simply describe the 0° disposition so that we can recognize it in action. While only a small fraction of people habitually or frequently display 0° behavior, it is a very wide-spread *potential*. Large numbers of people, sometimes the majority, may learn to display 0° towards another group designated as 'enemy.' War, after all, is murder on a larger scale. Some large-scale demonstrations of 0° greatly threaten human well-being and, it may be, our very existence as a species, as each new and improved Doomsday weapon succeeds another.

0° behavior is contagious and may characterize large groups for limited times. A decade or a generation or a century later they are no longer acting at 0°. One example: Scandinavian countries whose Viking ancestors were dreaded for their bloodthirsty raids a millennium ago but which are now among the most peaceful countries on Earth.

Not all murders express 0° but many do, especially: serial murders; 'cold-blooded' murders by what the FBI describes as 'organized killers'; assassinations, whether private or state-sanctioned; and killing during abductions for ransom or sexual purposes. It is the state of mind that produces torture, severe child and spousal abuse, and violent rape. Any of these actions can turn into physical murder, from the same dehumanizing level of consciousness.

*I explicitly remove from 0° category those on the autism spectrum who have difficulties in 'reading' others through body language and tone of voice. This is not at all the same as a lack of empathy; some suggest that autistics actually feel emotions more keenly than neurotypicals do. Autistics are not associated with any one particular disposition and many have accomplished at 45° and 50°.

Besides physical murder, there is soul-murder, described by Henrik Ibsen as killing the love of life in another person. Destruction of the victim's reason for living, capacity for joy, and basic personality structure can occur within the context of disturbed families, severe child abuse, authoritarian brain-washing, or criminal enslavement.

While the carnage of war reflects $0°$, individual soldiers do not usually operate at this degree. There is a wide range of awareness on the battlefield. Heroism—such as rescuing a wounded fellow soldier while under fire—shows the very much higher $40°$ compassion and $45°$ courage. Bonding with fellow soldiers in friendship or as a community expresses $35°$. Yet the entire war system perpetuates $0°$. Habituating soldiers to the idea of killing, by overcoming deep-seated inhibitions against murder, requires deliberate training methods. The resulting inner conflicts often lead to soldier and veteran suicides or PTSD ($15°$).

Dispositions easily spread through the culture via media. For instance, $0°$ is the prevailing state of mind among those who produce or view slasher or snuff films. Any media that dehumanizes others expresses $0°$ and this includes much of the vast field of sexual pornography. Many commercial films are dominated by shootings, explosions, and car crashes, a preoccupation that habituates people to $0°$ outlook. Similarly, some popular videogames are about nothing but destroying other entities. Although it is animated fiction, at some level the player is physically and mentally involved in the violent acts.

The viewing of actual bloodletting as a spectacle expresses $0°$, and this also applies to 'gratuitous violence' in fiction and drama. We have moved beyond gladiatorial contests, bear baiting, and other blood sports of earlier times, but people have developed a few new ones such as cage fights and rodeos, while trophy hunting and prizefighting continue. It is still considered 'sport' and/or 'entertainment' to draw blood or watch someone else doing so.

Animal cruelty is $0°$, and not only because in an individual's development it often precedes human cruelty. Deliberately inflicting pain on any sentient creature in itself shows a lack of empathy. I do not suggest that animal husbandry occurs at $0°$, because most farmers and slaughter-house workers do not deliberately inflict pain. However, the violence that is necessarily involved in meat eating is probably the main reason that many people become vegetarians.

Offering bounties for the bodies or body parts of murdered humans is 0°. Scalping, customary among warriors of some (not all) Native American tribes, was encouraged by several colonial governments who offered money for native scalps. This was directed against those Indians allied with the French during the numerous frontier wars in the 17th and 18th centuries, although those who collected the bounties made few distinctions. Both natives and colonials scalped women and children. The president of the Philippines, Rodrigo Duterte, revived this 0° mindset by offering up to 3 million pesos ($64,000) to police or military for every drug lord brought in, "dead or alive." [3]

Malice is the 0° desire to harm others, to see them suffer, to cause pain, injury or distress; it is extreme ill will or spite. (In law, malice is a wrongful act, done intentionally without just cause or excuse.) Malicious gossip or slander can ruin lives. Bullying can be so severe that it threatens the victim's physical well-being, or drives him or her to suicide. Vandalism is often a less serious 15° but at 0° it is senseless destruction of other people's possessions that ruins people's home, livelihood, or projects invested with years of work.

Recent news articles describe 0° malice in action. Courts indicted an 18-year-old Jewish youth with orchestrating more than 150 bomb threats against U.S. Jewish community centers and schools. The indictment says he was motivated by the desire to cause public alarm. Two former supervisors of a juvenile detention center in Arkansas pled guilty in federal court to repeatedly assaulting the young people in their care and falsifying documents to cover up their abuse. They often pepper-sprayed youths who were not threatening or resisting the officers, then shut them in their cells to "let them cook" instead of going through decontamination procedures. [4, 5]

Malign Indifference

> *Indifference, after all, is more dangerous than anger and hatred.*
> ~Elie Wiesel

While not actively destroying others or inciting such action, malign indifference shows cold indifference to other human life. It is dereliction of humanity. Actual examples: a gang rape in the alley outside a high school dance in 2009 involved a score of onlookers, some of them taking snapshots. In a similar case in 2012 in Steubenville, Ohio, teenagers posted photos of the rape on social media. In March, 2017 a teenage girl in Chicago was gang-raped live on Facebook. In each case, viewers did not report the assault.

In another example, Sharon Keller, presiding judge of the Texas Court of Criminal Appeals, closed the office right on time at 5:00 pm although attorneys for death row inmate Michael Richard were trying to file a stay of execution for him. Richard was scheduled to be executed at 8:20 that night. Early in the day, the U.S. Supreme Court had announced it would consider whether lethal injection is cruel and unusual punishment, and legal experts assumed that the nation's courts would wait on their decision before proceeding with more executions. Richard's attorneys were having computer problems and asked the court clerk's office to stay open a few minutes late to accept the request. Keller said "No," she had to meet a repairman at her house. She closed the office and Richard was executed at 8:20. [6]

Judge Keller, who later faced state ethics charges, had life-and-death responsibilities which she ignored. Other instances of judicial $0°$ have occurred when judges or DAs refused to review death penalty cases despite new evidence or confessions strongly pointing to the convicted person's innocence. 'Hanging judges' or prosecuting attorneys so concerned with reelection and their political reputation for being tough on crime that they railroad the accused into a death penalty are officially sanctioned serial murderers, supported by a corrupted institution. Doctors who knowingly perform needless operations, lawyers who deliberately neglect the defense of a poor person accused of a capital crime, or other dishonorable professionals whose actions endanger lives are operating from $0°$.

Malign indifference is often part of competitive business practices $(20°/0°)$ notably in the pharmaceutical industry. Martin Shkreli, as CEO of Turing Pharmaceuticals, greatly raised the price of a drug essential to the survival of many AIDS and cancer patients, with, apparently, no regrets. Shkreli indicated he would have raised the price even higher, saying "My shareholders expect me to make the most profit." Other drug-makers with Wall Street ties, such as Valeant, were following the same business model, buying older medications essential for people with certain disorders then increasing prices drastically.*

Other examples of malign indifference are the 'profits over safety' attitudes shown by company executives who deliberately cut corners or neglect safety measures, leading to deaths in mines, oil rigs, sweatshops, and neighborhoods surrounding chemical factories. If a product or process can potentially kill or injure people, it follows that failing to report negative research, or actively interfering with its publication, demonstrates malign indifference. So do policies that force people to work long, exhausting hours, especially if their lack of full attention can endanger others as well as themselves, as with medical professionals, truck drivers, and air crews. [7]

0° in History: 0° is most dangerous when it becomes established in a culture. Certain ideas and phrases carry 0° in their DNA. These 0° memes include *pesticides, ethnic cleansing, mutually assured destruction, collective guilt, collective punishment, generational curse, superior* and *inferior races, scorched earth policy, and Total War.*

History is replete with individuals and institutions showing 0°. For instance, Roman emperors Caligula, Nero, Commodus, Elagabalus, Caracalla, and Domitian reportedly murdered and raped at will, along with performing other perverse and despicable actions.

The gladiatorial contests that took place in the Roman Coliseum for 500 years had a religious component, since their religion included blood sacrifice. About half a million people—mostly slaves, convicts, and prisoners of war—and over a million wild animals died in Coliseum 'games.' So many wild animals were sacrificed in these murderous spectacles that several species became virtually extinct. Historian Keith Hopkins says "Roman commitment to cruelty (0°) presents us with a cultural gap which it is difficult to cross." [8, 9]

*Shkreli actually has fans (20°/25°): 80,000 Facebook friends and 66,000 YouTube subscribers, according to *Bloomberg News*

The 14[th]century Turkic-Mongol ruler Tamerlane conquered a vast territory from Russia to Syria to India, and was invading China when he died. Unlike his predecessor Genghis Khan, Tamerlane did not conquer to rule but to loot and pillage. He rarely set up any government in the areas he destroyed and often slaughtered most of the inhabitants. This one conqueror killed an estimated 17 million people, or about 5% of the world population at the time.

King Leopold II of Belgium made a private project of the Congo Free State, a huge area about 900,000 square miles, from 1885 to 1908. Persuading the international community that he was engaged in humanitarian work such as ending the slave trade, but actually amassing a fortune from ivory and rubber, Leopold imposed virtual slavery on the population. Under pressure, his agents used increasingly brutal means such as mutilating those who did not meet their quotas and hiring militias who committed atrocities. An estimated 10 million Congolese, half the population, died during Leopold's reign.

Nazi Germany was a "genocidal state" from 1939 until 1944; top leaders and many underlings commonly operated at 0°. As World War II wound down, Adolf Eichmann declared that he would "leap laughing into the grave because the feeling that he had five million people on his conscience would be for him a source of extraordinary satisfaction." Reinhard Heydrich ("The Hangman") was second only to Himmler in the SS, an elite army that managed the design and execution of the Holocaust. Heydrich was described by his own protégé, Walter Schellenberg, as a man with "a cruel, brave and cold intelligence" for whom "truth and goodness had no intrinsic meaning." Many believe that Hitler regarded Heydrich as his successor.[10, 11]

Heinrich Himmler,s the main architect of the Holocaust, oversaw the execution of an estimated six million Jews and at least five million other individuals including Romani (Gypsies), Soviet prisoners of war, and Polish and Soviet civilians. Himmler said: "All Polish people will disappear from the world….It is essential that the great German people should consider it as its major task to destroy all Poles." Historian Robert S. Wistrich noted that "It was Himmler's master stroke that he succeeded in indoctrinating the SS with an apocalyptic 'idealism' *beyond all guilt and responsibility*, which rationalized mass murder as a form of martyrdom and harshness towards oneself."[12]

Many fictional works depict 0° characters. Our fictional Shadow seems to be metastasizing, with uncounted villains and monsters in sci-fi and horror films; comic books and films based on them; anime, videogames; and children's toys. Apparently the glamour of psychopathic, Machiavellian, and sadistic villains is required so we can identify with the heroic characters who overcome them. But what do all these fictional villains tell us about ourselves? Is it only entertainment (25°) or are we trying to clarify our own ethics and morals?

Exterminism

Carthage must be destroyed!
~Cato the Elder, Roman Senator, 234-179 BC

Exterminism does not require evil people but only a blindness to the consequences of one's way of life. It includes those human cultural traits, ideologies, and institutions based, consciously or not, on the principle of annihilation. Edward Thompson in 1980 defined it as "those characteristics of a society—expressed in differing degrees, within its economy, its polity and its ideology—which thrust it in a direction whose outcome *must be* the extermination of multitudes." Stan Goff emphasizes "*Must be*... as in 'inevitable within the system'." [13, 14]

Historian Ronald Shaffer writes: "The memory of World War II seems to have led some air force leaders to feel that all-out annihilation war was the sole tradition of America's armed forces." Marilyn B. Young adds that "The possibility of 'obliterating everything in the enemy country, turning everything to ash' gave U.S. Air Force generals like Ira Eaker and Curtis LeMay, wholly secure in the air and able to attack any enemy at will, a sense of irresistible power." [14, 15]

Some letters to the editor call for "obliteration" "extermination," and "irradiation" (use of nuclear weapons) against enemies such as ISIS, which has committed numerous atrocities in the Middle East. These armchair belligerents do not distinguish between the terrorist army and captive people living in the conquered areas; nor do they seem aware of the far-reaching dangers of nuclear radiation to other nations. It is a reflex of rage (5°) expressed in the language of 0° exterminism. The idea of an obliterating war in the Middle East may be influenced by *Revelation*, or biblical passages in which the Israelites massacred whole cities of their enemies, down to the babes in arms and livestock.

It is often claimed that technology is neutral. Yet technologies arise from, support, magnify, and perpetuate various dispositions. Weaponry may serve empire-building 10°, exacting of revenge (5°), protecting the home (30°), or winning freedom (45°), but always carries the 0° urge to destroy. Technological warfare, in which bomber crews or those deploying drones never see their victims in person, accelerates 0°. The use of land mines, cluster bombs, or depleted uranium weapons that harm civilians for many years after the end of hostilities, appear morally 'worse,' that is, more strongly indicative of this lowest degree of awareness (0°). So do all weapons of mass destruction.*

Industrial technologies such as coal mining, lead smelting, battery recycling, tanneries, and nuclear energy production also have a strong 0° component because of the toxic substances to which they subject workers and others, and the public risks they assume. Some industries by their very nature inexorably destroy ecosystems and local communities: oil tanker with their spills; coal companies that remove mountaintops; Monsanto's toxic pollution, tropical deforestation, and other forms of ecocide.

Powerful addictive drugs have a 0° aura. Crystal meth turns users aggressive, even psychotic, as they stay awake for days on end, neglecting their children—sometimes fatally—and rapidly destroy their own health. During WWII, both sides supplied soldiers with drugs to keep them vigilant, energetic, and fearless. German troops used crystal meth; Japanese kamikaze pilots took it in high doses before their suicide

*The Union of Concerned Scientists describes U.S. plans to research a new nuclear earth penetrator that would use a 1.2-megaton weapon. According to a simulation using software developed for the Pentagon, if one of these weapons were used against the underground nuclear facility in Esfahan, Iran, 3 million people would be killed by radiation within 2 weeks of the explosion, and 35 million people in Afghanistan, Pakistan and India would be exposed to increased levels of cancer-causing radiation. http://www.ucsusa.org/nuclear-weapons/us-nuclear-weapons-policy/earth-penetrating-weapons#.WDITbk2V85s

missions. British and American military supplied soldiers and pilots with Benzedrine tablets (amphetamines) by the tens of millions.[16] The amphetamine *captagon,* used by fighters on all sides of the Syrian Civil War, is spreading to civilians in Saudi Arabia. Even more dangerous, a synthetic opioid *carfentanil,* 100 times more potent than fentanyl, and researched as a chemical weapon, is now on the illicit drug market. [17]

The multitudes subject to exterminism include wild species that humans have helped drive or are driving to extinction. Many large species of mammals or megafauna vanished at the end of the last Ice Age, around 10,000 BC. In the Americas, Australia, northern Eurasia, and large islands this extinction closely followed the spread of humans into new territories. Disappearances include the woolly mammoth in Europe and the American camel, also many bizarrely giant ancestors of modern species such as Irish elk (antlers over 6 yards from tip to tip), ground sloths 20 feet long, and 200-pound beavers and kangaroos.

The Holocene extinction continues into the 21st century as humans hunt or kill animals for many reasons. Even more destructively, ever-expanding human populations have so disturbed animal habitat that thousands of creatures are disappearing. One hesitates to mention exterminism in hunting for food or killing predators for personal security. But as the centuries flow by, human numbers grow, and the overkill continues—for table delicacies, feathers for women's hats, lamp oil, and sometimes "just for the hell of it"—one begins to see the principle at work. Many plants are also going extinct, including some that may have had great potential for food or medicine.

In 1844, three Icelandic fishermen saw the last living Great Auks. They killed both birds and destroyed their egg. In 1896, American hunters found the last remnant flock of passenger pigeons and in one day killed all 250,000 of them. Photographer Marc Schlossman notes: "Just a few decades of reckless overhunting and deforestation in the late 1800's brought the world's largest ever bird population to zero."[18]

Now humans are able to chemically destroy "multitudes" of species that bite us, carry human diseases, or compete with us for food or space. "Pests" and "vermin" include animals such as beavers or wolves that have an important role to play in ecosystems. Destruction does not require hatred, only the instrumentalism and indifference of our overly clever (20º) irrupting species. Extinction can be accomplished by transgenic organisms (Gene Drives or "gene bombs") used to destroy a competitor species or drastically reduce its abundance.

One potential target is a species of amaranth (pigweed, lamb's quarters) that has become resistant to the world's foremost herbicide, glyphosate. Pigweed now 'infests' agricultural fields in the American South, reducing crop yields. However, as Vandana Shiva, Indian scientist and eco-activist notes, related species of amaranth are raised for food in Mexico, India, China, and South America. The plant's leaves contain more iron than spinach, its grain is a rich source of calcium and protein, and amaranth flour contains the necessary amino acid lysine which is lacking in corn. This is a valuable plant. [19]

The world currently depends on just 15 crop plants for 90 percent of its food energy. The big three, rice, wheat, and maize ('corn') supply more than 42% of calories consumed by the entire human population. We are 'putting all our eggs in one basket.' To court the destruction of other food sources for the temporary profit of a few surely expresses a 0º Malign Indifference to humanity as a whole.

Besides sculpting evolution with gene drives, numerous other technologies threaten to 'get out of hand' because of greed, hubris, and limited knowledge. Swedish philosopher Nick Bostrom defines an existential risk as "one where an adverse outcome would either annihilate Earth-originating intelligent life or permanently and drastically curtail its potential." He says that except for an unlikely comet or asteroid there probably were no existential risks for humans until the mid-20th century. Now there are dozens. Some prime contenders are deliberate or accidental misuse of nanotechnology, runaway global warming, a genetically engineered 'doomsday virus,' and badly programmed Superintelligence.

Bostrom points out that past experience (30º) may not help us deal with these new threats:

> We cannot necessarily rely on the institutions, moral norms, social attitudes or national security policies that developed from our experience with managing other sorts of risks. Existential risks are a different kind of beast....We have not evolved mechanisms, either biologically or culturally, for managing such

risks… Our approach…cannot be one of trial-and-error. There is no opportunity to learn from errors. The reactive approach—see what happens, limit damages, and learn from experience—is unworkable. Rather, we must take a proactive approach [45°/50°]. [20]

Murder of Multitudes: The attempted destruction of a whole unique people such as an indigenous population, enemy civilians during war, or a racial, ethnic, religious or ideological minority has occurred many times, whether by state policy or by other groups in economic or religious/cultural competition with them—settlers, miners, rival tribes, multinational corporations. The cold-blooded, systematic killing of the Holocaust and all official genocides is clearly 0°. Many historical genocides also show aspects of 5° rage, rationalized by 20° ideology and instigated through 10° demagoguery.

To eliminate a people by crushing their culture rather than killing them outright is ethnocide (sometimes called cultural genocide). The dominant group may for instance forbid the minority group to use their own language or follow their own religious practices. While genocide kills the body, ethnocide kills the spirit. However, both may occur as part of the same process.

Yet another variant on humanity's inhumanity is ethnic cleansing, defined as the mass expulsion, deportation, imprisonment, or genocide of members of an unwanted ethnic or religious minority in order to achieve homogeneity of the dominant group. Another motivation is to take the property of the dispossessed. The term was coined during the 1990s Balkan Wars. Historians can trace the practice of removing unwanted groups from a territory as far back as the Assyrian Empire, in the 9th to 7th centuries BC.

Expulsion and deportation are sometimes thinly disguised genocide. Conditions of the flight or of the destination lead to deaths from exhaustion, exposure, and starvation, as in the Armenian Genocide (1915-1917) and the Soviet "Russification" program in the 1930s and 1940s when over three million people from ethnic minorities were sent to Siberia.

Ethnic cleansing has been employed several times in United States history, most notably the dispossession of Native Americans, about which Martin Luther King, Jr. said in *Why We Can't Wait* (1963):

> We are perhaps the only nation which tried as a matter of national policy to wipe out its indigenous population. Moreover, we elevated that tragic experience into a noble crusade. Indeed, even today we have not permitted ourselves to reject or feel remorse for this shameful episode. Our literature, our films, our dramas, our folklore all exalt it.

Less well known is the expulsion of tens of thousands of blacks from entire counties along the Mason-Dixon Line and into the Midwest, during the period from 1864 to the early 1920s, while authorities looked the other way. The "Mexican Repatriation" took place in the first years of the 1930s Great Depression, when at least a million people of Mexican descent were deported across the border, although an estimated 60% of them were actually American citizens. [21, 22, 23]

Much earlier, two 'official' genocides were the Roman destruction of Carthage in 146 BC and the Albigensian Crusade in the early 13th century (sometimes considered the first genocide of modern Europe). The first occurred because of political/economic competition; the second because of 'heresy' or religious competition. With Carthage, a flourishing city of 150,000 to 200,000 people, the Roman army demanded such harsh conditions of surrender that the Carthaginians could not realistically accede to them. The advancing Romans went house by house, systematically killing inhabitants, and then burned Carthage to the ground. The remaining residents (30,000 to 50,000 people) were sold into slavery. Legend has it that the surrounding land was salted so that it could not grow food.

The Cathars or Albigensians were a medieval Christian sect whose popularity threatened the mother church, and in 1209 Pope Innocent III declared a Crusade against them. Many of the Cathars lived in Southern France in the Languedoc, a region noted for its troubadours, high culture, and tradition of religious tolerance. An estimated half a million to a million people died in Languedoc, both Cathars and their Catholic neighbors. Voltaire said in a later century, "there was never anything as unjust as the war against the Albigensians." However, since Voltaire we have seen many more injustices and horrors. More than a dozen large-scale genocides occurred in the 20th century.*

In 2015 scholar and activist Samuel Totten listed five regions of the world as "potential genocides in the making": Burma, the Nuba Mountains in Sudan, Nigeria (with overflow into Cameroon and Chad), China (Uighurs), and Darfur, Sudan. He asks what is being done about it, and who really cares? Unfortunately, the world's political system seems to have no mechanism in place for preventing or stopping genocides. [24]

* Chronological list of 20th century genocides from *Century of Genocide*, edited by Samuel Totten, Willlim S. Parsons, and Israel W. Charny, Garland Publishers, 1997:

Indigenous Peoples, physical and cultural genocide throughout century
Hereros, South-West African tribe, most of whom were killed by a German commander 1904-1906
Armenians in Turkey
Soviet man-made famine in Ukraine
Soviet deportations of minority nationalities
Holocaust: the Jews
Holocaust: the Gypsies (Roma and Sinti)
Holocaust: disabled people
[China's Great Leap Forward]
Indonesian Massacre 1965-66
[Biafra]
Bangladesh
Burundi
East Timor
Cambodia
Rwanda
Bosnia-Herzegovina
[Sudan/Darfur 2003]

[1] "Doctor: Syria snipers targeting pregnant women and children in 'death game'," CBS News, October 16, 2013, http://www.cbsnews.com/8301-202_162-57607825/doctor-syria-snipers-targeting-pregnant-women-and-children-in-death-game/

[2] Charlie Cooper, "'Indiana Jones' of surgery' leads UK medics in war-zone training," *The Independent*, August 25, 2013, http://www.independent.co.uk/life-style/health-and-families/health-news/indiana-jones-of-surgery-leads-uk-medics-in-warzone-training-8783639.html

[3] http://abcnews.go.com/International/wireStory/philippine-president-elect-offers-bounties-drug-dealers-39503738

[4] Aron Heller, "Israel indicts teen in threat to Jews," Associated Press, April 25, 2017

[5] Amanda Claire Curcio, "Two former supervisors at Arkansas youth lockup plead guilty to abuse of detainees," *Arkansas Democrat Gazette*, April 27, 2017

[6] John Kelso, Cox Newspapers, March 1, 2009

[7] Joan Lowy, "White House delays more rest for cargo aircrews," AP, August 18, 2011

[8] Keith Hopkins, "Murderous Games: Gladitorial Contests in Ancient Rome," *History Today*, Volume 33, Issue 6, June, 1983, http://www.historytoday.com/keith-hopkins/murderous-games-gladiatorial-contests-ancient-rome#sthash.Mh1Q8sqp.dpuf

[9] Mark Cartwright, "Gladiator," Ancient History Encyclopedia, http://www.ancient.eu/gladiator/

[10] William L. Shirer, *The Rise and Fall of the Third Reich*, Simon & Schuster, 1960.

[11] MacDonald, Callum. *The Killing of Reinhard Heydrich*, The Free Press, 1989.

[12] Wistrich, Robert S. *Who's Who in Nazi Germany*, Routledge, 1997.

[13] Edward Thompson, "Notes on exterminism, the last stage of civilization," in *Peace Studies: Critical Concepts in Political Science,* Volume 4, edited by Matthew Evangelista, Taylor & Francis, 2005

[14] Stan Goff, *Energy War: Exterminism for the 21st Century,* Lulu Press, 2006   [15] Ronald Shaffer, *Wings of Judgment: American Bombing in World War II,* Oxford University Press, 1985, p. 215

[16] Yuki Tanaka, Toshiyuki Tanaka, Marilyn B. Young, *Bombing Civilians: A Twentieth-Century History*, The New Press, 2010

[17] Nicolas Rasmussen, PhD, MPhil, MPH, "America's First Amphetamine Epidemic 1929–1971: A Quantitative and Qualitative Retrospective with Implications for the Present," *Am J Public Health.* 2008 June; 98(6): 974–985.

Also
http://www.ncbi.nlm.nih.gov/pmc/articles/PMC2377281/http://tonydagostino
.co.uk/history-of-amphetamine-methamphetamine/ and
http://www.rollingstone.com/culture/news/heroin-epidemics-new-terror-
carfentanil-w438712

[18] Field Museum, Chicago, "Extinct and Endangered Birds,"
http://www.marcschlossman.com/downloads/EXTINCTION_captions.pdf

[19] Vandana Shiva, "Biodiversity, GMOs, Gene Drives and the Militarized
Mind," Common Dreams July 11, 2016,
http://readersupportednews.org/opinion2/277-75/37937-biodiversity-gmos-
gene-drives-and-the-militarized-mind

[20] Nick Bostrom, Professor, Faculty of Philosophy, Oxford University,
"Existential Risks: Analyzing Human Extinction Scenarios and Related
Hazards," *Journal of Evolution and Technology*, Vol. 9, No. 1 (2002)
http://www.nickbostrom.com/existential/risks.html

[21] Gary Clayton Anderson, *Ethnic Cleansing and the Indian: The Crime that
Should Haunt America,*   2015

[22] Elliot Jaspin, "Leave or die: America's hidden history of racial expulsions,
Statesman, July 9, 2006, http://www.statesman.com/news/news/leave-or-die-
americas-hidden-history-racial-expuls/nWR7G/

[23] Terry Gross interview of Francisco Balderrama, "America's Forgotten
History Of Mexican-American 'Repatriation,'" NPR, September 10, 2015,
http://www.npr.org/2015/09/10/439114563/americas-forgotten-history-of-
mexican-american-repatriation

[24] Samuel Totten, "A reason to care: Must act now to prevent genocide,"
Northwest Arkansas Democrat-Gazette, January 26, 2015

Chapter 5
How Humanity Becomes Inhumane

In individuals, insanity is rare; but in groups, parties, nations and epochs, it is the rule.
~ Friedrich Nietzsche, German philosopher, 1844-1900

We don't have a good definition for insanity in human individuals, much less for larger groups. However, a society that is not only destructive but also self-destructive surely fits the definition of insane.

Other living creatures obey an instinctive "prime directive" that transcends individual self-preservation. This instinctive commandment is to preserve the species. For other creatures it may be enough to lay eggs or protect nurslings until they can fend for themselves. But as a creature that has taken our own evolution so largely in our own hands, we must think ahead, not only for the lifetimes of our own progeny, but for our whole species.

For us, the prime directive requires not only physical survival, but also the preservation of our human qualities, without which we are not truly human beings—without which we could become a 0° society—a dystopia. This requires the qualities of foresight and generativity, and study of past mistakes.

In the past, various circumstances combined to break down organized societies. Many collapsed because they failed to deal with the problems they were dealt by geography and climate, including natural disasters. Some were overcome by hostile neighbors, or their own unwitting actions destroyed a natural productive base. Decline led to social chaos, desperate poverty, and often to incessant wars and conquests. It was often hard to hold on to our humanity.

Most modern societies are still overcoming wrong turns in the past such as institutionalized slavery or the caste system in India. Past wars and conquests have had enduring negative effects. Genocidal conflicts may result when empires come apart and tensions grow between ethnic and religious groups originally forced together by imperial administrations. Human societies continue to follow ideas that lead into cul-de-sacs.

Until recently enough different kinds of societies existed that failed experiments did not prevail everywhere. That is no longer the case. If the whole world becomes virtually one political or economic regime, we are in a situation of no-mistakes-allowed and no-place-to-escape. It is the danger in either a one-world government, a unipolar political world, or a shadow government of transnational corporations.

Meanwhile, nation-states continue to maintain stockpiles of doomsday weapons, quite as likely to be set off by accident as by design—although deliberate intent and pathological leaders are also possible. All the foregoing indicate deep dysfunction, if not insanity.

Certain aspects of modern world-views, ideologies, social systems, and customs tend to draw us toward a destructive and self-destructive 0° consciousness, although some also have great benefits.

- Increasing *abstraction* and *specialization*, accompanied by hyper-individualism, technological distancing, and ever-expanding scale
- The worldview of *materialism*
- Mental processes: *objectification, dehumanization*, and *demonization*
- Pernicious ideological constructions and mindsets such as *human sacrifice, racial purity*, and *useless eaters*.

Distance and Indifference

> *Complete liberty implies freedom from the tyranny of*
> *abstractions as well as from the rule of men.*
> George Woodcock, "The Tyranny of the Clock"

Several human developments increase the distance between human beings, between individuals and the whole of humanity, and between humans and the rest of life. All share a common link, which is that our ability to make abstractions has outrun our powers to understand and empathize. Abstractions can imprison us; they can lead to atrocities, wars, and destruction.

These developments may reflect an evolutionary trend. Some suggest that our cerebral cortex grew too fast (first doubling, then growing half again as large over the past 500,000 years) and that we have never been quite able to integrate the animal with the calculator.

Civilizations are built on abstractions: words, numbers, money, sovereign states. Canadian scholar George Woodcock says the modern conception of time basically separates us from earlier civilizations:

> Clock-making became the industry from which men learnt the elements of machine-making [and] without some means of exact time keeping, industrial capitalism could never have developed…. The clock turns time from a process of nature into a commodity. [With] quantity rather than quality becoming the criterion, the enjoyment is taken out of the work itself….The clock represents an element of mechanical tyranny. [1]

Other distancing factors include specialization, technologies, also the sheer numbers of human beings, and bigness in general. Even before civilizations began, *specialization* developed beyond the simple division of labor between men and women as individuals became toolmakers, shamans, warriors, weavers, or potters. Division of labor has many advantages but as the degree of specialization continues there are increasing problems, such as uneven distribution of wealth and the cost of exchange itself (transportation, advertising). At some point the rising social costs surpass the diminishing benefits.

It may be a side-effect of specialization that the human brain has been shrinking over the past 5,000 or so years. Paleoanthropologist John Hawks says measurements of early and modern skulls indicate that our brains have shrunk about 10%. Hawks says "Perhaps in big societies, as opposed to hunter-gatherer lifestyles, we can rely on other people for more things…and maybe not need our brains as much." What we gain in efficiency we may lose in adaptability. [2] Specialization has continued into the social sphere. Now people identify with their favorite music or celebrities, chosen athletic team, religious denomination, political opinions, sources of news and ideological support, and so on, to the extent that they lack knowledge of others in their community, other ideas, and other parts of the world. Schooling is based entirely on age cohorts, unlike times past when children of different ages learned and played together. We are divided into tribes without the organic ties that held ancient tribes together.

Hyper-individualism can be seen as an ultimate specialization, each person a single atom. As expressed by Objectivist philosopher Ayn Rand: "There is nothing to take a man's freedom away from him, save other men. To be free, a man must be free of his brothers. That is freedom. That and nothing else." [3] This attitude betrays some 15° confusion, since humans evolved as social animals and always require some sort of family to survive and become human beings. Here the adolescent's developmental need to individuate seems frozen in time. Meanwhile, a healthier individualism expresses itself in 50° creativity or 45° when it opposes centralized authority or rebels against blind obedience and following the herd.

Globalization can draw people closer together with international friendships, idea exchange, and cooperative efforts to solve humanity's problems. But economic globalization with its 0° commodification is a separating force, increasing the distance between consumers and those in the long supply lines of the products they buy. Owners of the ubiquitous iPhones, Smartphones, and laptops are largely unaware that civil war, rape, and slave labor were part of the package. The needed change here is more transparency (35°) allowing consumers to choose products and services based on social and environmental qualities.

Technology increases the distance between us in numerous ways. While people in less developed countries meet and greet each other on the crowded sidewalks, we in the wealthy West are enclosed in our metal and glass cages, moving faster than anybody ever did before the 20th century. Digital technology greatly expands our communication possibilities while simultaneously narrowing them as we ignore our flesh-and-blood neighbors. Toddlers and children spend great swaths of time watching screens. The ability to kill an unseen enemy by bombs and drones turns war into a matter of pushing buttons.

Add the factor of scale. How do creatures that evolved in small bands of about 30 people now wrap our minds around the existence of over seven billion neighbors? Or megacities of fifty million people? It took us many millennia just to get used to settled villages of 150 residents. In *The Human Scale*, Kirkpatrick Sale introduced the "beanstalk principle" which is: "For every animal, object, institution, or system, there is an optimal limit beyond which it ought not to grow." Based on studies by architects, anthropologists, sociologists, and others about what size groups work best, Sale suggests that the ideal or normative size of a nation is 5 million or less, a city no more than 200,000, and an elementary school under 400 students.[4, 5]

British anthropologist Robin Dunbar posited a limit, based on human brain structure, of about 150 people with whom one individual can maintain stable relationships. This is known as Dunbar's Number. For working committees, Parkinson's Magic Number is 20: fewer than 20 members will likely reach consensus, but more members are likely to end up with two permanently opposed subgroups.[6, 7]

The benefits of economies of scale in business are often greatly overestimated. .Large corporations are more inflexible when conditions change, less innovative, overly bureaucratic, and prone to excessive generosity with salaries for top executives. Smaller firms create more net jobs: by one study, over a period of three decades U.S. firms with fewer than 100 employees created about as many jobs as did the largest corporations (many of those jobs being overseas), while firms with fewer than 500 employees created most of the jobs.

Scientific Materialism

A favorite problem of Tyndall is [this]: "Given the molecular forces in a mutton chop, deduce Hamlet or Faust therefrom." He is confident that the Physics of the Future will solve this easily.
~Thomas Henry Huxley, *Life and Letters of Thomas Henry Huxley, Vol. I*

The word materialism has several meanings. First, it is a simple and widespread understanding ('common sense') that relies on the 'five senses'. Most of us live almost exclusively in this material world. The idea that reality consists *only* of what you can see, hear, smell, touch and taste is sometimes called *naïve realism.*

Second, materialism is a philosophical position claiming that matter and its motions constitute the only reality. This is actually an ancient view ('atomism') first proposed at least two thousand years ago in India and China as well as by Democritus and Epicurus in ancient Greece. Over the past few centuries materialist philosophy became the consensus view, dominant and all-encompassing. It is now known as *scientific materialism.* According to this view, physical matter alone causes all phenomena, including human thoughts and feelings. The universe is like a giant machine, and everything can ultimately be explained by physics. (Thomas Huxley parodied this view above.)

Third, money materialism is a way of life based on acquiring money and possessions. Novelist Martin Amis notes that "Money doesn't mind if we say it's evil, it goes from strength to strength. It's a fiction, an addiction, and a tacit conspiracy."

Greed is an ancient motive that has its justifying ideologies. Enclosure of the commons, like expropriation of the New World, was aided by calling it 'empty land.' Slave owners justified their use of other human beings for virtually free labor by constructing theories of racial superiority based on Bible passages or pseudo-science. Both colonial conquerors and slave-owners rationalized that they were bringing civilization and true religion to benighted peoples.

According to social theorist Max Weber, the rising merchant class in 17th century Europe found grounds for the new system of capitalism in their Protestant beliefs and work ethic. In modern America, libertarians have fleshed out the moral justifications for unregulated capitalism. Consumerism rose with colonialism, as domestic markets expanded for exotic luxury goods such as tobacco, silks, spices, and sugar. No moral justification or ideology is required for self-enjoyment and being fashionable (25°).

For all these meanings of materialism, people need to be aware of the deeper consequences. With naïve realism, problems start with the fact that not everybody perceives in the same way. For instance, some of us are color blind while a few have tetrachromatic vision and see millions more colors than the rest of us. Also, culture, language, and environment shape people's sense perceptions differently. One study found that people living in forests or rural areas have the ability to sense crooked and slanted lines more accurately than do urban dwellers. Some differences in perception involve our entire worldview:

> Modern Eastern cultures are inclined to see a world of substances—continuous masses of matter. Modern Westerners see a world of objects—discrete and unconnected things. There is substantial evidence that Easterners have a holistic view, focusing on continuities in substances and relationships in the environment, while Westerners have an analytic view, focusing on objects and their attributes. [9]

The assumption of naïve realism that everyone perceives everything alike can lead to misunderstandings and intolerance. Naive realism also contributes to a mechanistic attitude (20°) that calls itself 'practical' and 'scientific' but that actually fails to understand the complexities of modern science.

Scientific materialism introduces other difficulties, claiming that material reality as studied by science is all that really exists. Only matter matters. Surprisingly, however, matter is not yet defined. According to philosophy professor Michael Philips, "We could say that matter is whatever physicists finally decide it is. But this reduces materialism to a blank check to be filled in when physics finally closes its book." [10] A growing number of philosophers are not satisfied with an explanation that is supposed to work "in the sweet bye and bye."

Despite this absence of first principles, scientific materialism has supported three centuries of unprecedented technological and social progress as well as the political and economic dominance of those nation-states most immersed in this worldview. These apparent benefits are associated with problems, such as population growth—a sevenfold increase over two centuries—that requires ever more resources and creates ever more pollution and waste.

In a universe composed merely of things in mechanical motion, these objects—whether atoms, stars, or human beings—lose their connection. One consequence has been a general failure to see relationships in the biological world (ecology). The process of *desacralization*—divesting everything of divine, mythic, or magical significance—has also had some powerful effects. This blindness has led to the destruction of whole regions and extinction of many species. Another consequence is rampant *commodification*—the buying and selling of everything in sight. Our current economic system grows continually by finding more things to commodify, that is, to strip of individuality or spirit in order to buy and sell it.

For a century, scientific materialism has failed to explain the phenomenon of consciousness, nor does this prevailing worldview account for love and friendship, or human aspirations to create, to respect other life forms, to be better people and more heroic. Nobel-winning neurophysiologist John Carew Eccles says:

> The human mystery is incredibly demeaned by scientific reductionism, with its claim in promissory materialism to account eventually for all of the spiritual world in terms of patterns of neuronal activity. This belief must be classed as a superstition.... We have to recognize that we are spiritual beings with souls existing in a spiritual world as well as material beings with bodies and brains existing in a material world. [11]

Theistic religions are not the only alternatives to the notion that we live in a mechanical, dead universe. We have some choices here. A person can believe in love or spirit without defining or personifying it. Mystics apprehend spirit directly. Some Idealist philosophers and non-theistic spiritual traditions such as Buddhism and Taoism recognize an ideal or spiritual world. Other positions are existentialism, or an agnosticism that holds that the ultimate cause and essential nature of the universe are not only unknown but unknowable.

Scientific reductionism reduces complex interactions and entities to the sum of their constituent parts, in order to make them easier to study. This has been a very fruitful approach in acquiring knowledge

(45°).However, the idea that all life, mind, and spirit can be reduced to chemistry and physics has led to popular attitudes of "nothing but" that dehumanize humans and other living things (0°).

In recent decades, new scientific ideas and disciplines are breaking free of the reductionist straitjacket. For instance, a systems approach or *holism* is the idea that natural systems function as wholes and cannot be understood merely as a collection of parts; and the study of *emergent properties* is based on the idea that at each level of complexity entirely new properties appear—the whole is not only *greater than* the sum of its parts but *different from* the sum of its parts. These do not supplant reduction as a methodology but complement it.

However, other consequences of reductionism have to do with the third meaning of materialism. In popular parlance, those overly concerned with money or the things that money can buy are called materialists, indicating a preoccupation with material objects and considerations, while ignoring or rejecting spiritual, intellectual, or cultural values. Western society is based on economic ideas that everything is worth money and can be commodified, that is, given a price, and put up for sale. That has included owning other people (slavery), creating and patenting life-forms, and laying claim to land forms and water resources formerly regarded as part of the human commons. However any belief or practice that reduces human beings or the basics of life (water, sunshine, arable land) solely to things for sale tends to draw us down toward a 0° society.

Neither scientific materialism nor economic materialism is by itself a 0° manifestation. However, once we begin to regard living beings including humans as things it becomes much easier mentally to manipulate them, buy and sell them, or even destroy them for whatever ends we devise.

Objectification, Dehumanization, Demonization

> *All real living is meeting.*
> ~Martin Buber, Jewish philosopher, 1878-1965

Philosopher Martin Buber says *I and Thou* is a relation of two subjects, while *I and It* is a relation of subject to object. In *I and It* relations, one perceives another in terms of selected qualities, not as a whole person. Except for oneself, the subject, the world consists solely of objects. Worth less than we are, maybe worthless, these *things* do not deserve equal treatment or even humane treatment.

Feminist theorists developed the concept of sexual objectification, but the objectification process applies broadly across society and not only to the treatment of women. It relates to reductionism and commodification, to bureaucracy and 10° domination. Philosopher Martha Nussbaum lists seven features of objectification, and Rae Langton adds three additional ones:

1. *instrumentality*: the treatment of a person as a tool for the objectifier's purposes
2. *denial of autonomy*: the treatment of a person as lacking in autonomy and self-determination
3. *inertness*: the treatment of a person as lacking in agency, and perhaps also in activity
4. *fungibility*: the treatment of a person as interchangeable with other objects [people as interchangeable parts]
5. *violability*: the treatment of a person as lacking in boundary-integrity
6. *ownership*: the treatment of a person as something that is owned by another (can be bought or sold)
7. *denial of subjectivity*: the treatment of a person as something whose experiences and feelings (if any) need not be taken into account
8. *reduction to body*: the treatment of a person as identified with their body, or body parts
9. *reduction to appearance*: the treatment of a person primarily in terms of how they look, or how they appear to the senses
10. *silencing*: the treatment of a person as if they are silent, lacking the capacity to speak [12]

These objectifications characterize many aspects of public and private life in the United States, as in advertising (e.g., reduction to appearance), business practices (instrumentality), medical system (reduction to body), bureaucracies (fungibility), professional athletes (ownership), and many aspects of the 'dating game.' Objectification has long been part of the world's treatment of colonial peoples, ethnic and religious minorities, poor people, and women. Children have been greatly objectified in the past and still are even in the modern western world (e.g. denial of autonomy, denial of subjectivity, silencing).

Dehumanization is objectification plus an emotional component (5° hate), treating certain groups or individuals as less than human. During war, governments commonly depict 'the enemy' (whether soldiers or civilians) as animalistic and barbaric, with demeaning names such as 'kraut,' 'gook,' or 'raghead' so that citizens can overcome their inhibitions against mass murder. Dictatorships also use this tactic to shut down opposition within their own country, basing their propaganda on the public's previous racist, ethnic, or religious prejudices.[13]

When seeing people as despicable *things*, one can justify any atrocity. Greg Stanton describes dehumanization as the third stage of genocides such as the World War II Holocaust, the Khmer Rouge in Cambodia, Rwanda, or Bosnia. The perpetrators of genocide dehumanize targeted groups "by depicting them as animals, vermin, insects, diseases, or tumors. This rhetoric constructs a narrative which justifies the 'cleansing' of society." [14]

A further process related to objectification and dehumanization is *demonization*, or trying to make an individual or a group of people seem completely evil and satanic. Demonization requires an audience with an underlying idea of absolute evil. Sensationalist media, like melodramas, has a tendency to exaggerate goodness and badness in order to create heroes and villains. Sometimes political figures are vilified; demonization is most commonly applied to national leaders (using Adolf Hitler as a template) or to whole nations (e.g., "Evil Empire" "Axis of Evil" "The Great Satan").

One can see a progression downward from seeing a person as an object, to seeing the other as a despicable or expendable animal or disease, to seeing the person as something totally evil that must be destroyed. When human thinking has reached this point of dramatic hatred it is hard to come back up from 0°.

Human Sacrifice: The 0° custom of ritual human sacrifice was common in the ancient Near East, pre-Columbian Mesoamerica, and other early civilizations. Anthropologists and other social scientists have linked this abhorrent practice with the evolution of social stratification leading to our present complex societies. In other words, civilization co-evolved with a class system supported by human sacrifices to the gods. We must assume that eventually civilization was an improvement over the small egalitarian groups that preceded it. [15, 16]

For those groups that practiced ritual sacrifice it was necessary to please and appease the gods or spirits with human flesh, especially during times of crisis. Or they believed that human blood was necessary to nourish the crops. In some cultures, virgin daughters and first-born sons represented an especially pleasing sacrifice; it was a great honor to be chosen. In other cultures, however, sacrificial victims were those considered negligible or undesirable such as slaves, prisoners of war, beggars, cripples, and lawbreakers.

Not all human sacrifices involved religious ritual. Many lost their lives as retainer sacrifices: slaves, servants, wives, concubines, and officials who were buried along with a deceased ruler to serve him in the afterlife. Even after the custom of funeral sacrifice waned, the expectation continued in some places that new widows would die at the biers or pyres of their husbands, voluntarily or otherwise. In India, suttee continued into the 19th century, while widow-strangling in Fiji and other parts of Melanesia ended only recently.

Still other individuals were killed to consecrate buildings and bridges, buried or entombed within the foundations. It is hard to understand how or why this ancient custom began, but foundation sacrifice is found across all the continents. Legends say that thousands of people were entombed in the Great Wall of China, and the Aztecs killed thousands of prisoners to re-consecrate the Great Pyramid of Tenochtitlan in 1487.

Gradually sensibilities changed, and human sacrifices were replaced by animal sacrifices, then effigies. Wise leaders (45°) and humanitarians (40°) helped to end these ingrained customs, especially during the Axial Age (8th to 3rd century BC) a period of enlightenment

(X°). For instance Duke Xian, ruler of the Chinese state of Qin, on ascending to the throne in 384 BC immediately abolished the retainer sacrifices which had been introduced by his own ancestors.

All the major religions have long since condemned human sacrifice, yet it continued in various forms. Romans accused Carthaginians and Druids of such barbaric practices, but their own gladiatorial contests entailed both human and animal sacrifices on a grand scale. The Thuggee cult of India, worshipping the demonic aspect of the Hindu goddess Kali, for six hundred years robbed and murdered travelers, until stopped by British rulers. Aztecs and some other Mesoamerican cultures practiced human sacrifice for at least a millennium, as part of a central religious belief that all kinds of sacrifices (including animal sacrifice, breaking precious objects, self-mutilation, and self-murder) keep the Universe ongoing.

Medieval burnings of witches and heretics was another form of human sacrifice, as were brutal, public executions of even minor offenders under various legal codes. The Islamic State or ISIS, appears to have revived this human sacrifice mindset from much earlier ancestors on the Arabian Peninsula, finding sociopathic justification in the Qur'an and the Bible. In the United States, capital punishment may be another remnant of human sacrifice.

Martyrdom—suffering or death for one's religious faith—is considered a glory to God in the three Abrahamic religions. Many of us seem to take a cause seriously only with the appearance of martyrs ready to lose their own lives for their principles. Another modern echo of human sacrifice is veneration of soldiers who have died in battle, with nationalism taking the place of religion. In whatever form, the atavistic institution of human sacrifice expresses 0°.

Purity or freedom from contamination is a positive value in metallurgy, water supplies, pharmacology, and food production, where purity refers to the lack of foreign substances. Before modern genetics, plant and animal breeders understood genetic purity as trueness to type or lack of contamination by off-types. Other positive connotations of the word 'pure' are innocence, disinterestedness, intense focus, selflessness, or perfection. Problems arose from misapplying this concept to female sexual behavior, family lineage, race, and ethnicity.

Placing a very high value on young women's virginity, some conservative Christians promote purity rings, purity dances for fathers and daughters, and virginity pledges, as well as 'abstinence-only' education in public schools. While it may be a good idea to postpone adolescent sexual activity, the purity approach is linked to $10°$ patriarchal attitudes. Extreme abuses occur in cultures (Muslim, rural Hindu, or Sikh) which so prize women's chastity that they kill transgressors, usually young women. These murders are committed not only because of sexual improprieties but also from perceptions that the young women in question act too independent and 'Western.' Women are considered as the property of the family's males, a commodity $(0°)$ that can be discarded once it is found to be contaminated (impure).

The concept of purity applied to ethnic and racial ancestry is often referred to as 'blood.' American racial classification in the late 19th century and part of the 20th was based on the "one-drop rule" according to which a person with only one, distant African ancestor was considered to be black. In South Africa under apartheid, a 1950 law established four racial categories: white, mixed race or colored, Asian, and black. White officials used pseudo-scientific tests such as examining eyelids, fingernails, and gums to decide people's race. The result determined whether that person could vote, where he could reside, and whom he or she could marry.

More misuse of the concept of purity comes from analogizing animal breeding to humans, leading to excessive concern for human bloodlines, especially among the aristocracy, as though they were racehorses. A modern instance of this notion in the novel *The Da Vinci Code,* posits that the descendants of the bloodline of Jesus Christ would naturally include a number of geniuses such as Leonardo Da Vinci. However, human intelligence, character, and creativity are far more complex characteristics than those for which domestic animals are bred.

In the late 19th century, overemphasis on family heredity led to the pseudo-science of eugenics, which proposed selective breeding among humans similar to that used with animals. It led to coercive sterilizations in the United States and genocide in Nazi Germany.

Perfection, like purity, can become an antihuman attitude. Life is never perfectly balanced, never perfectly symmetrical. In a strange echo of religious asceticism, some of the individuals most devoted to technology appear to have a deep revulsion for their own physicality. It is not only a fear of death—some of them say they would actually prefer to be machines ($0°$). Did they never have much joy of their bodies through childhood play, running and swimming, or in sexual pleasures, music, making art—or do they expect to recreate these in virtual reality? Some suggest a male jealousy of the female ability to bring forth life from her womb; instead, transhumanists would bring forth superior species of life from our heads—robots and androids—or transfer our personalities to immortal storage devices; or merge ourselves with computers during the Singularity.

Useless Eaters: This is yet another insidious idea. The term implies its contrary, "useful eaters" or men who are useful to other men for their labor, taxes, tributes, or in the case of women, their sexual services. Undoubtedly every society has contained selfish, dominating, and Machiavellian people ($10°$) who saw their fellow human beings in this entirely instrumental way. Possibly this minority grew larger after villages turned into cities and people no longer knew all their neighbors by name or sight. The selfish ones exploited the useful people or despised the ones they couldn't use as they amassed wealth and power.

The 'useless eaters' notion may have come into its own in England around 1500 at the transition from feudalism to mercantile society. The great feudal lords began to enclose common lands to raise sheep for the lucrative wool market, turning arable land into pasture and tearing down cottage crofts. Small landholders and agricultural laborers lost rights such as grazing for cattle or sheep on common land, gleaning after the harvest, foraging for pigs, gathering fuel, and picking berries. These made the difference between living decently and perhaps not living at all.

Peasants, despite ancient feudal rights to the land, were forced into towns where many became beggars, vagrants, and petty criminals. One can well believe they were viewed as "useless eaters." 16th century anti-vagrancy laws allowed a person to be sentenced to two years enslavement and decreed that a third vagrancy offense would result in execution. A succession of Poor Laws mandated flogging or forced the 'undeserving poor' to leave one town for another equally inhospitable in another example of cruel hypocrisy or blaming the victim. [17]

Another great surge in the concept of the useless eater came in the late 19th and early 20th century with Social Darwinism, a peculiarly Anglo-American concept. Its basis was established by Englishman Herbert Spencer, but Americans ran with his idea of "survival of the fittest" applying it to class, race, and ethnicity/religion. Next, eugenics was developed by polymath Francis Galton (his more beneficial contributions have been overshadowed by the infamy of this one). Widely accepted, and promoted in the U.S. by many prominent people for about 50 years, eugenics led to many forced sterilizations of women who were disabled, poor, and/or minority.

Eugenics was borrowed and perverted by the Nazis, who actually invented the term useless eaters, *unnütze esser*. This notion led first to sterilization, then mass murder of the mentally ill, physically disabled, alcoholics, leftists, gay men, and eventually massive genocide of Jews, Roma, Russian POWs, Roman Catholics, Poles and other groups considered subhuman or dangerous. This horror destroyed the appeal of eugenics to the rest of the world.

In 21st century America we see another resurgence of the notion of useless eaters as part of a political ideology, especially during an economic downturn. The term 'useless eaters' has not been used, and nobody is proposing concentration camps, but there is dehumanization and blame using terms such as 'freeloaders,' 'welfare parasites,' and 'bottom feeders.'

Historically, the following groups have been condemned or treated as useless eaters: first and foremost, the poor: the unemployed, landless peasants, former slaves, vagrants, beggars, petty criminals, even former soldiers; then also the physically disabled, mentally disabled, and elderly. Death squads hired by store owners in some Brazilian cities regularly kill homeless street kids.

There is now a perfect storm of conditions that together make it rather likely that the idea of useless eaters could become more widespread and insistent. First, world population is increasing and unlikely to level off until at least 2050, at somewhere between 9 and 11 billion. That is at least ten times what it was only 270 years earlier, at the birth of the United States, nine or ten generations ago. As a result, humans are degrading resources (soil, oceans) or using them unsustainably (aquifers, Peak Oil) so that they diminish even as the number dependent on them grows.

Chronic high unemployment in many countries, especially among youths, can only worsen with automation. Climate change will create great numbers of environmental refugees in addition to refugees and asylum seekers created by wars and poor economic conditions. Anti-immigrant sentiment already exists in Europe, Australia, and the United States, and it is being exploited by demagogues.

In addition, the elderly population in most countries is increasing both absolutely and proportionally.

With only partial recognition of these looming situations, some people have subscribed to various conspiracy theories or think only in terms of scapegoats and the use of force. Unless we think ahead about the world as a whole, recognizing and dealing with changes creatively and compassionately, we may well succumb to some ideology that would rid us of the "useless eaters."

[1] George Woodcock, "The Tyranny of the Clock,"
http://www.acsu.buffalo.edu/~rrojas/TyrannyofClock.html
[2] Charles Q. Choi, "Humans Still Evolving as Our Brains Shrink," *Live Science*, November 13, 2009   https://www.livescience.com/7971-humans-evolving-brains-shrink.html
[3] Ayn Rand, *Anthem,* Cassell, 1938
[4] Kirkpatrick Sale, *The Human Scale*, New Society Publishers, 1980
[5] Kirkpatrick Sale, "To the Size of States There Is a Limit": Measurements for the Success of Secession," Middlebury Institute, February 6, 2010, http://middleburyinstitute.org/sizeofstates.html

[6] Revere, "The right (or wrong) size for a committee: less than 20 but not equal to 8," January 15, 2009 http://scienceblogs.com/effectmeasure/2009/01/15/the-right-or-wrong-size-for-a/

[7] Kevin L. Kliesen and Julia S. Maues, "Are Small Businesses the Biggest Producers of Jobs? (Chart: Average job gains (in thousands) per quarter, 1992:Q3 to 2010:Q1)" *The Regional Economist,* April 2011

[9] Paige Morris, "Culture's Influence on Perception," Chapter 3, Sage Publications, September 30, 2014, http://www.sagepub.com/upm-data/45975_Chapter_3.pdf

[10] Michael Philips, "What Is Materialism?" *Philosophy Now*, Nov/Dec 2012, http://philosophynow.org/issues/42/What_is_Materialism

[11] Sir John C. Eccles, *Evolution of the Brain: Creation of the Self,*

[12] "Feminist Perspectives on Objectification", http://plato.stanford.edu/entries/feminism-objectification/

[13] See David Livingstone Smith, *Less Than Human: Why We Demean, Enslave, and Exterminate Others,* St. Martin's Press, 2011

[14] https://sites.google.com/site/anatomyofagenocidecambodia/process/stage-3---dehumanization

[15] James Owen, "Human Sacrifice Clues Found in European Stone Age Burials, May 30, 2007, http://news.nationalgeographic.com/news/2007/05/070530-sacrifice-burial.html

[16] Joseph Watts, Oliver Sheehan, Quentin D. Atkinson, Joseph Bulbulia and Russell D. Gray, "Ritual human sacrifice promoted and sustained the evolution of stratified societies," *Nature,* April 14, 2016, http://www.nature.com/articles/nature17159

[17] https://www.marxists.org/archive/marx/works/1867-c1/ch27.htm

Chapter 6
5°Aggressive-Reactive

We are the angry mob
We read the papers every day
We like who we like,
we hate who we hate.
But we're also easily swayed.
~Kaiser Chiefs, "The Angry Mob"

Lacking impulse-control, 5° expresses fear, anger, and aggression. We share these basic emotions with other mammals (and birds) but in humans their expression is determined by culture, upbringing, and biological predispositions.

People who *habitually* act at 5° are often described as crude, hot-tempered, belligerent, scary, warlike, barbaric, or 'always ready for a fight.' They are bullies, brutes, brawlers, thugs, and enforcers. In a popular phrase, they have "too much testosterone" (medically inaccurate). One version, the A-type personality, is ambitious and impatient, with an easily triggered, underlying hostility.

Another description, the "Right Man" by Colin Wilson (based on earlier exposition by science fiction writer A. E. Van Vogt) shows a person driven by the need to always be in the right; a person whose self-esteem is so fragile that he cannot stand to lose face. He may be insanely jealous. Jealousy implies a kind of ownership (10°) of the 'loved one' that calls for a violent defense of one's 'property.' The Right Man is often a household tyrant, a domestic abuser. Van Vogt says that marriage brings out the authoritarian nature in many males.

Psychologist George Simon describes several character types that he calls aggressive personalities. These are "individuals whose overall 'style' of interacting involves considerable, persistent, maladaptive aggression." Simon says they are neglected by the official diagnostic manual of mental disorders, although posing the greatest danger to society of any. Dr. Simon lists a half-dozen distinguishing traits common to all five subtypes:

56

- They actively seek the superior or dominant position in any relationship or encounter.
- They abhor submission to any entity that one might view or conceptualize as a 'higher power' or authority.
- They are ruthlessly self-advancing, generally at the expense of others.
- They have a pathological disdain for the truth.
- They lack internal 'brakes.'
- They view life as a combat stage, with every event in life having only four possible outcomes, and their greatest desire is for the outcome "I win, you lose." [They accept win-win outcomes only with great reluctance.] [1]

Some naturally aggressive people may be prone to violent behavior (5°) while others are more strategic in taking power (10°). On the other hand, some individuals are aggressive in another dictionary sense. They are assertive and energetic but not "aggressive personalities" or "Right Men." Lobaczewski says:

> The Right Man problem is a problem of highly dominant people....Biological studies have confirmed that for some odd reason, precisely five percent—one in twenty—of any animal group are dominant—have leadership qualities. [2]

Dominant personalities who become respected leaders take a different path, focusing on the task at hand and working with subordinates rather than enforcing their own will. Natural leaders have goals other than protecting their egos.

Women are certainly not exempt from aggressive and/or violent behavior, but the temperament that often supports a 5° disposition may be over-represented among men, especially those in their teens and early twenties, the age of extreme sports, hooliganism, street gangs and soccer riots. During a long summer in Belfast, Ireland, bored youths indulged in what one priest called "recreational rioting." Anthropologist Margaret Mead said "The central problem of every society is to define appropriate roles for the men." This is especially true of the aggressive energies of young men. Throughout history they have been recruited into armies to fight each other.

Warriors or political leaders may indulge in orgies of destruction from rage, blood-lust, or grandiosity. The legendary berserkers fought in a fury-trance. When a Malaysian suddenly ran amok, his neighbors said he was possessed by a tiger spirit. Philippine President Rodrigo Duterte describes himself as a serial killer (0°/5°) saying "In Davao I used to [kill criminals] personally. Just to show to the guys [police] that if I can do it why can't you. And I'd go around in Davao with a motorcycle, with a big bike around, and I would just patrol the streets, looking for trouble also. *I was really looking for a confrontation so I could kill."* [3]

Historically, invading armies often operated at 5° in their treatment of civilians. Often soldiers were not paid except for being allowed to loot and rape. Even today, war atrocities occur. Life is cheap wherever 5° rules.

Political agents, demagogues, and propagandists who deliberately foment fear, hatred, and violence act with 0° malice to win 10° power, while followers who take the bait are often motivated by 5° fear or blood-lust. Generals and tyrants, armies and mobs have killed indiscriminately, destroying towns and landscapes like a toddler tearing down his sand-castle. Such spreading of hate accompanies social upheavals such as massacres, genocides, or fascist takeovers.

Large groups tend to converge toward lower dispositions, a problem when many of the individuals in the group are already 5° reactive. Then this 'lowest common denominator effect' can turn crowds ugly, subject to the contagion of fear and rage, reacting irrationally against bogeymen and scapegoats. Crowds are easily manipulated, as in Rwanda, where radio talk shows incited genocide. With the aid of mass media and modern propaganda techniques, crowd behavior can affect millions at once, like the "Two minutes hate" in *1984*.

Fire could symbolize 5°. Arson is a dangerous, often impulsive act, with unforeseeable and sometimes fatal consequences. Individuals may set fires for excitement, or the arsonist may make himself into a false hero by reporting or fighting the fire he himself started. Lighting a blaze in an uninhabited building to get insurance money is on the surface a rational 20° action, though 15° illegal, but fire still holds the danger of spreading to nearby buildings or injuring fire fighters.

Media express 5° when they provide or provoke a taste for blood and gore. Film critic Piers Marchant, rating film violence from bland to bloody, describes the highest intensities:

> At this level limbs are severed, heads explode, blood is everywhere, and gristle is just around the corner of any scene. [The next level] is where you want to go if dismemberment, torture, and shockingly realistic portrayals of ultra-violence are how you connect to the world around you. No judgment, but if this is your thing, you may want to investigate that a bit. [4]

Sensational news caters to the same basic emotions. Yellow journalism is well over a century old. A well-known dictum applies to the evening news on television: "If it bleeds, it leads." The Internet counterpart is fake news sites that spread paranoid fantasies, arousing fear and anger.

Customs of culture or subculture may covertly support and justify individual actions at 5° such as date rape. An individual may try to overcome his fears with a constant media diet of vicarious fear and fighting. Yet habituation and imitation only serve to addict him to violence. Whether it is catharsis or incitement depends on the individual's temperament and age, nature of the fiction, and the context.

A few years ago a topic on the talk show circuit was the "warrior gene" which is supposed to predispose one to aggression and violence. This is still a controversial theory. Since about 40 percent of us have this gene variant, it doesn't really help us to pinpoint (or scapegoat) likely aggressors. We all have an internal system that prepares us for fight or flight, but for several millions of years this instinctive way of acting has been modulated by human culture. In the wealthy industrialized nation-states, one may live an entire lifetime without experiencing a life-or-death confrontation. Exceptions are soldiers in combat, police, firefighters, or those who live in crime-ridden areas.

In extreme situations, unless specially trained to deal with such crises—and sometimes even then—we may revert to the default reactions of fear or rage. Of the two, fear is the more basic. In order to learn how to deal with fear, human beings invent ways to frighten themselves vicariously through fiction, drama, and art. More negatively, we often funnel our general anxieties into a specific fear, often involving a scapegoat or scapegoated group.

Witches and Demons and Dark Afflictions, Oh My

> *Fear is the main source of superstition, and one of the main*
> *sources of cruelty. To conquer fear is the beginning of wisdom.*
> ~ Bertrand Russell, *Unpopular Essays, An Outline of*
> *Intellectual Rubbish* (1950).

Witch hunts were not limited to 17th century Europe. In many rural and tribal cultures even today, when individuals suffer bad luck or society is under great strains, people tend to blame witches, who in the majority of cases are women. For instance, belief in witchcraft is still widespread in Papua New Guinea, where in 2013 a mob burned to death a young woman accused of sorcery.

Not all witch hunts have been directed against women, or can be explained the same way. In a study of scapegoating in Chinese history, scholar B. J.Ter Haar traces a long, orally transmitted tradition of fear. Some of the recurrent stories and rumors showed fear of the emperor himself, who was rumored to be an organ-snatcher. Or he was supposed to be recruiting young unmarried women for his harem. This last rumor caused many families to marry off their daughters in haste without careful selection of the groom.[5]

General anxieties finally coalesced around the notion of 'Dark Afflictions'—flying animals that attacked people at night and were connected with evil magic. Over several centuries the Chinese increasingly projected their fears on real individuals who were supposedly responsible for the Dark Afflictions. All sorts of marginal people, even traveling monks, were accused of being evil magicians, then beaten or killed by mobs, or taken to the local magistrate for execution or banishment. Although there are exorcism rituals in Buddhist, Taoist, and Confucian traditions, these apparently were not enough to satisfy people's fears.

Ter Haar says that many people are intolerant of ambiguity and even more so in times of stress. Rumors serve as a means of reducing anxiety and defining the object of fear. He notes "the crucial role of gossip and rumors in the interactive social process of fear, accusation and stigmatization that underlies witch hunts." Through such rumors, local anxieties and fear often lead to violent reactions such as riots, lynching, even genocide.

We need not go as far as medieval China. Today rumors can spread swiftly and widely through mass media to create public alarm over an issue believed to threaten society. The issue in a moral panic may be significant and credible, such as school shootings—or not, as in the case of the elusive satanic messages in rock and roll music.

Besides destroying lives and reputations, moral panics ignore the complexities of a situation and may divert attention from actual solutions. British sociologist Stanley Cohen described the general process. One or more groups or "moral entrepreneurs" start the panic when they fear a threat to prevailing cultural values. These anxious people identify a person or group embodying the threat: the 'folk devil' who must be restrained and punished, and who tends to be a social outsider of one sort or another.[6, 7]

Susceptibility to moral panics may be related to the kind of authoritarian upbringing that makes heavy use of fear and punishment. Societies need to educate people about how to identify and answer such hysteria at its beginnings, because the panics move very quickly.

A moral panic took place in 1980s America, spreading to several other English-speaking countries, when rumors alleged widespread satanic ritual abuse of children (SRA) in childcare centers. Evidence was largely testimony from quite young children. The most extreme SRA belief envisioned a worldwide conspiracy to abduct and breed children for ritual sacrifice or prostitution. This belief resembles the old blood libel used for centuries against Jews and similar accusations made against European witches in the 16th and 17th centuries.

Public fears are often promoted by demagogues or authoritarian rulers. As H.L. Mencken said, "The whole aim of practical politics is to keep the populace alarmed (and hence clamorous to be led to safety) by menacing it with an endless series of hobgoblins, most of them imaginary." In Egypt, the government was cracking down on religious and political opponents in 2014 when they arrested 26 men for debauchery in a televised raid on a Cairo bathhouse. Same-sex relations are not legally prohibited in Egypt but are socially condemned. In the month before the arrested men were finally acquitted, pro-government media reported on a number of threats to society from outsiders such as homosexuals, atheists, foreign plotters, and devil worshippers.[8]

In the United States, exaggerated fears about Muslim immigrants and Sharia law also show aspects of a moral panic. Most "single issue" politics thrives on fear and loathing, rumor, and demagoguery. Despite living in a high-tech society, moderns are still susceptible to the same kind of hysterias that gripped people in the middle ages. Classic conspiracy theories—those which suppose an almost omniscient, extremely powerful, and totally evil individual or cabal or alien species running things from behind the scenes—are a related phenomenon.

A Pew survey in 2013 found that a majority of Americans—especially those aged 18-29—currently believe in demonic possession. Only those over age 65 show less than a majority of believers, suggesting that the trend is growing. Even if the poll exaggerated the extent of this belief, any such widespread credulity is troubling. To some extent the growth of this idea among young people may be attributed to the popularity of stories and films about vampires, zombies, ghosts, and exorcisms. Similar ideas were also spread by evangelical books and broadcasts ranging over the 40 years between megachurch Minister John Hagee's *Invasion of Demons: The Battle between God and Satan in Our Time* (1973) and Kimberly Daniels' *The Demon Dictionary* (2013).

Ideological Demons

Propaganda ends where dialogue begins.
~Jacques Ellul, propaganda theorist

We see similar psychological mechanisms in witch hunts, hate crimes and political scapegoating. Today, the rumor-monger is often a demagogue: an effective, often charismatic speaker who gains influence by appeals to the public's passions and prejudices. In the worst cases, he may incite murder or massacre whether for political power or to express his own impulses and hostilities. With modern media, his influence is greatly expanded.

The term 'demagogue' goes back to ancient Athens, when some leaders exploited political freedom in order to garner more power for themselves (10°). In fact, demagoguery works best where people have some choice in selecting leaders and policies. Very much then rests on the knowledge and psychological maturity of the electorate, who are often bamboozled by demagogues such as Huey Long or the anti-Semitic Father Coughlin in the 1930s, Senator Joseph McCarthy in the 1950s, media personality Glenn Beck, 45th President Donald Trump; in Europe, Jean-Marie Le Pen, Geert Wilders, Matteo Salvini, and others.

The Prime Minister of India, Narendra Modi, is a right-wing proponent of Hindu nationalism (Hindutva). His controversial past involves campaign speeches in 2002 that led to attacks on Christians and Muslims that killed one to two thousand people in the state of Gujarat. Religious riots resemble moral panics, as those who believe differently become the 'folk devils.'

After Israeli Prime Minister Itzhak Rabin supported the Oslo peace negotiations between Israel and Palestinians, he was assassinated in 1995. Some blamed speeches by current PM Benjamin Netanyahu for inciting crowds against Rabin. Despite the dangers, political demonizing has become the standard for American politics today, with the man in the street repeating and embellishing the smears and insults of the paid pundits. It is no longer enough to oppose your opponent's politics: he or she is an alien, abnormal, evil liar.

The demonizing trend also applies to institutions and documents, for instance Agenda 21. This is a 1991 UN planning paper for sustainable development, 350 pages long, written in less than gripping prose. It has no force of law anywhere. Yet more than a few people believe it lays out a secret plot to impose a totalitarian world government that in the name of environmentalism will murder 90% of the world's present population. This is an extreme case of misreading and ignoring context out of fear.

The ancient habit of inventing demon-enemies is most dangerous when used to foment war. War hawks (warmongers, militarists, anyone for whom war is the first rather than the last resort) are acting at 5° or—if demagogues and propagandists—are appealing to 5° fears and hostilities. Those who do not think on their own (15°) simplify the world into a medieval morality play, a Victorian melodrama, or a videogame in which nation-states are stock characters wearing white or black hats (folk heroes, folk devils). Then they play their own fears and aggressive impulses in this game as if thousands or millions of innocent people were not involved. As an example of widespread 5° consciousness, in December 2015 a Public Policy Poll of U.S. voters found that about one-quarter of them favored bombing Agrabah—which turns out to be a fictional kingdom in the 1992 Disney film *Aladdin*. The poll may have been conducted as a prank, yet it indicated a disturbing readiness on the part of many people to commit what is, after all, mass murder. [9]

Anger, Rage, and Hatred

Anger is short-lived madness.
~Horace, Roman poet 65 B.C.—8 B.C.

Anger, rage, and hatred are quite different. Anger is a universal emotion—who among us has never been angry? It varies in intensity from irritation to rage, manifesting perhaps as a flash of heat, quickly subdued. Rage, or uncontrolled anger, is loud and violent, sometimes dangerous. Resentment or a grudge lasts longer than ordinary anger, and skirts the edges of hatred. Hatred—an obsessive anger or frozen rage—does the most harm of all because of its role in large, intra-species conflicts. Relatively few of us define our lives by personal hatred, yet most of us have the potential to act on group hatreds.

Anger has a long evolutionary history. We can identify anger across human cultures and also across species—one does not try to pet a growling dog or a cat that is switching its tail. We can equally read the signs of human anger, which mobilizes all the body's organs and muscle groups, with measurable physical effects. Anger raises the heart rate and blood pressure, also levels of hormones such as testosterone, adrenaline and noradrenaline. High levels of anger can double the risk of heart attack and destroy T-cells that are important to immune functions.

Anger is often displaced onto someone or something besides the immediate cause, or redirected as a string of taboo words. Angry individuals have been known to kick the cat or punch holes through the wall in displaced aggression. In a descent into anger I once threw a supposedly unbreakable dish at the wall (it broke). Venting anger by yelling or violence may increase it rather than relieve it.

Anthropologist Daniel Fessler notes that across cultures the causes of anger may differ but they share a common theme. "Although notions of goals, rights, property, and even the definition of a person are culturally variable, howsoever these things are defined, when they are transgressed, people react with anger." [10]

Some see a positive side to this emotion. Peter Sloterdijk, German philosopher, says that the urge to anger and aggression is as basic as the sexual urge, and that Freudians neglected "pride, courage, stout- heartedness, craving for recognition, drive for justice, sense of dignity and honor, [and] indignation" that are all connected with anger. According to psychiatrist John Nadas, "There is a close proximity of the anger circuits to the problem-solving ones. Failure to solve a problem can trigger a state of anger.... We need to understand that the anger drive is closely intertwined with the drive to succeed." [11, 12]

Thus anger may be aroused by real or perceived injury or insult to self, kin, or associates; by another's transgression of the rules of one's culture—or by wrestling with frustrating problems and situations. It all depends on how anger is handled. Too often it is misdirected to scapegoats. It may become a self-indulgent habit. When it is not acknowledged it may fester and lead to depression, an uncontrolled rage or hatred, all destructive.

Anger may be channeled into participation in body-contact sports or viewing action movies. In its more sublimated forms anger lends energy to higher degrees, helping to solve a problem or motivate creative efforts. Should we not be angry about injustice? Or war? Such angers may have motivated Pablo Picasso's painting "Guernica" or classics of literature such as *Oliver Twist* and *Les Miserables.*

Rage: Every day you read something like this in the newspaper: "[X], 35, faces criminal charges over allegations that he knocked over a trash can, threw a high chair, and assaulted an employee at a Pennsylvania McDonald's because there was cheese on his hamburger." We read that family members kill each other in arguments about what to watch on television or how to cook the pork chops; people shoot strangers for texting in a theater or playing loud music in their vehicle; caregivers shake babies to death because they are crying. We hear of 'road rage 'incidents that end in injury or death.

A growing number of other 'rages' take place on airplanes or other public places when people feel their needs or desires are not being met quickly enough. We see a growing sense of entitlement and impatience among people used to instant messaging and technological conveniences. It seems that celebrities and first-class passengers who are not used to hearing the word 'no' are among the worst offenders.

Some people are temperamentally or metabolically predisposed to rage. Therapists describe a 'hostile personality'—cynical, mistrustful, and impatient, with an intense and often explosive reactivity. Blood tests of people with a history of hostile outbursts show signs of inflammation. Low levels of the neurotransmitter serotonin are associated with aggression and anger, as well as with depression. The exact causation is unclear, but SSRI medicines are likely not the answer since they themselves have been linked to episodes of rage. For serotonin deficiency, health practitioners recommend B vitamins especially B^{12}, adequate protein, sunlight, and exercise. We note that these are the very things in short supply for incarcerated criminals who have had problems with controlling their anger.[13]

Some regularly lose their tempers but do not advance to physical assault or go to jail. Those with a habit of raging often reach positions of power and leadership if they can control their outbursts—sometimes even if they cannot. The manager who turns purple and pounds his fist on the desk may have become addicted to the physical sensation of rage, or he deliberately indulges himself in temper tantrums in order to maintain power over others.

Many drugs, including some that are commonly prescribed, can precipitate a state of rage. These include alcohol, methamphetamine, cocaine, anti-depressants, anabolic steroids, and hydrocodone. Excessive use or withdrawal of the drug or an underlying depression or other emotional disorder can intensify feelings of anger.

Rage begets rage, and it is hard not to be drawn into arguing with a hostile person. Dr. Harriett Lerner, clinical psychologist, points out that hostility spreads easily. "It takes a great deal of emotional maturity to deal with someone who is very intense and angry. The *reactivity is contagious* and you are likely to get reactive yourself."[14]

There may also be environmental triggers for episodes of violence. Research finds that throughout history, rising temperatures and declines in rainfall were "consistently linked to increased violence" both between individuals and (even more) on the scale of inter-group conflicts. This has disturbing implications for a world increasingly affected by climate change.[15]

Whatever the cause, rage means that one is controlled by something outside one's own consciousness or volition. Fessler says "In English we speak of being 'blinded by anger,' while the Bengkulu of Sumatra with whom I worked metaphorically described the state as *kemasukan,* to be possessed by an evil spirit." He says the irrationality of an extremely angry person has two components: risk indifference and disproportionality:

First, angry individuals may seek to inflict costs on transgressors that greatly outweigh the costs suffered as a result of the transgression—murderous assaults may stem from a disrespectful glance, gesture, or even a quick lane change on the freeway. Second, when attempting to inflict harm on the transgressor who elicited the emotion, the angry person often seems indifferent to the potential costs entailed by their actions. Actors may confront opponents who are much more powerful than themselves, or may risk costly social sanctions ranging from ostracism to execution. [16]

Fessler says that this desire to inflict significant harm on transgressors probably made more sense in the small, face-to-face communities that characterized most of human experience. He also says it is more of a problem for human males to control anger than for females, although both men and women are subject to excessive anger.

Among the many manifestations of uncontrolled anger are reckless driving, child abuse and spouse battering, elder abuse, disorganized murder (FBI category), fistfights, "going postal," riots, and so-called crimes of passion.

Rage motivates the form of sexual violence called 'anger rape,' in which the main motive is male hostility towards women (or one woman). The UN's large international study on rape found that forty percent of rapists said they were angry or wanted to punish the woman they raped. [17, 18]

Acts of rape or a general toleration of it in a 'rape-culture' can express several of the lower dispositions at once. The majority of rapists surveyed by the UN indicated they committed the act because of 'sexual entitlement' suggesting that a collective, entrenched form of 15° or 25° narcissism upholds these attitudes. A young American who murdered several women posted a video and a 140-page manifesto about how he hated women because they had rejected his advances, meeting approval from some commenters on men's rights forums and chat rooms who also felt they deserved sexual favors from young, beautiful women.

Few people seem aware of the prevalence of male rape victims in prisons, where the repetition and brutality of the crime constitutes 0°

torture. Some prison officials have tolerated this abuse as a sort of bribe to help control the larger and more dangerous inmates.

Rage on the larger scale, massacres and spontaneous genocides (as distinct from those that are planned in advance by a government or organized group) are often fueled by a long history of ideological hatreds. Sometimes massacres are stimulated by politicians or demagogues, but once in motion the uncontrolled violence is contagious, and people act like a pack of predators. This sort of frenzy used to be more common in wars that often involved massacres of civilians or of captured prisoners. Before the Geneva Conventions such atrocities were a regular feature of warfare. Modern wars are supposedly fought by soldiers under a discipline that restrains rage and other emotions as a threat to good order. However, many of the world's armies are not well trained, and even the most disciplined militaries are subject to lapses.

Hatred

I will permit no man to narrow and degrade my soul by making me hate him.
~Booker T. Washington

Anger is more universal than hatred. We all have the *potential* to hate but many of us do not—or at the least we sublimate it. Hatred grows when an individual makes the choice to stoke his negative emotions until they consume him. He lives constantly with his anger or resentment, and wishes other people ill. Hatred has a target, a cause.

Unfortunately, hatred easily spreads. Steven J. Bartlett lists three kinds of contagion: People who are the object of hatred usually respond by hating back. Or, one hater reinforces a fellow hater, raising the level of hatred. A third way is this: when someone associates in a friendly way with the object of hatred, he or she also becomes an object of hatred.[19]

Why hate, anyway? What do people get out of it? Bartlett lists several short-term benefits for both individuals and groups. First, hatred is a relationship, and for some people this relationship is preferable to no relationship. "No man is truly alone when he has an enemy."

Next, by the psychological mechanism of projection, a person or group can deny their own inferiority and guilt by magnifying (or inventing) the flaws and faults of others. Bartlett says, "The person who hates gains a strengthened sense of self, a self that is felt to be better, stronger, and more valuable in the contrast which hatred enables him to feel between himself and the hated other." Thus hatred helps integrate the personality and focus the identity of the individual or group.

Hatred brings a sense of community with others who share the same hatred—"a camaraderie of hatred." It also provides people with a cause around which to center their lives, allowing them to forget personal problems and disappointments. Another of the delusive benefits of hatred is that this intense experience helps people to overcome their fear of death "by absorbing their attention in their wish to bring about the suffering and death of others." But Bartlett says these psychic advantages have a terrible cost:

> Hatred is a self-incapacitating, disabling experience. [It] not only disables compassion, it also can disable the hater's cognitive functions, specifically his ability to reason....The individual who cultivates hatred does, in a certain sense, lobotomize himself.

Fanaticism

> *From fanaticism to barbarism is only one step.*
> ~Denis Diderot, French philosopher, 1713-1784

Fanaticism (5°/10°) is an extreme, obsessive, and uncritical zeal for a cause, religious or political, with an intolerance of other points of view that can lead to 0° destruction.

Some leaders promote an idealistic ideology yet turn into fanatics capable of 0° crimes such as eliminating dissenters. Often so much psychic energy (5° fear and hate) is concentrated in these ideas that they spread and persist for generations.

The media's focus on terrorist acts by Islamic extremists tends to obscure the dangers of other ideologies including super-patriotism (ultra-nationalism) and racial supremacy. Recent years have seen a resurgence of 0°/5°/10° white nationalism throughout the West, exacerbated by the 2008 recession, floods of refugees from Syria and other Mideast wars, and the election of a mixed-race man as U.S. President. Vladimir Putin apparently encourages neo-fascists, presumably to destabilize Western democracies and thus empower Russia in relative terms.

Novelist Adam Roberts describes the evolution of fanaticism: "The madman is not he who loses his reason, but he who commits wholeheartedly to one reason in place of many reasons." It usually combines a persistent rage and the power drive with an ideology of some sort (5°/10°/20°). One historical example of the kind of fanaticism that accompanies bloodshed is Tomas de Torquemada, a 15th century Dominican Friar, the first Inquisitor General of Spain. He was especially hostile to *conversos*, those Jews or Moors who professed to convert to Christianity in order to escape persecution. His name became synonymous with the cruel fanaticism of the Spanish Inquisition.

Maximilian Robespierre was largely responsible for the "Reign of Terror" after the French Revolution, during which 18,500 to 40,000 people were executed. It was a time of struggle between political factions and rampant conspiracy theories leading to violence. Despite the pathetic stories about Marie Antoinette and other aristocratic victims, most of the executed were actually peasants or workers accused of hoarding food, evading the draft, deserting from the army, and various other minor or vaguely defined crimes. Robespierre was an ideologue with a reputation for incorruptibility (45°), but his devotion to the Revolution overcame his humanity and took him down the ladder of dispositions to 0°.

The Taliban, Islamic State, and Boko Haram are the best known of current Islamist movements that demonstrate fanaticism in their religious fundamentalism, murdering those who disagree with them or who are of different beliefs, keeping women under strict control, and destroying the works of earlier civilizations.

Less violent, in Hindu India a surge of right-wing moralists take it upon themselves to police the population, attacking art exhibits, beauty salons, or individuals who show public displays of affection such as hugging, kissing, or holding hands. Vigilantism in general is 5° behavior; vigilantes are self-appointed administers of justice.

Political partisanship can approach fanaticism. When political leaders use their power to scapegoat and demonize, violence is not far behind.

[1] Dr. George Simon, Ph.D., Understanding the Aggressive Personalities, November 3, 2008, http://counsellingresource.com/features/2008/11/03/aggressive-personalities/
[2] Andrew Lobaczewski, op. cit.
[3] BBC, "Philippines' Duterte admits personally killing suspects," 14 December 2016, http://www.bbc.com/news/world-38311655
[4] Piers Marchant, "Violence on the Level," *Arkansas Democrat Gazette*, September 2, 2016
[5] Barend ter Haar, *Telling Stories: Witchcraft and Scapegoating in Chinese History,* Brill, 2006
[6] Stanley Cohen, *Folk Devils and Moral Panics*, Psychology Press, 2002
[7] Cindy Kuzma, "Sex, Lies, and Moral Panics", September 28, 2005, http://www.alternet.org/story/26131/sex,_lies,_and_moral_panics
[8] Maggie Michael, "Egypt acquits 26 of debauchery," AP, *Arkansas Democrat-Gazette*, January 13, 2015
[9] Daniel Bier, "Should We Bomb Agrabah? Sure!" Newsweek, December 22, 2015, http://www.newsweek.com/should-we-bomb-agrabah-sure-407896
[10] Daniel M.T. Fessler, Department of Anthropology, UCLA , "The Intersection of Evolved Psychology and Culture," to appear in *Missing the Revolution: Darwinism for Social Scientists,* J. Barkow, ed., Oxford University Press
[11] Peter Sloterdijk, *Rage and Time, a Psychopolitical Investigation*, translated from German by Mario Wenning , Columbia University Press, 2010
[12] John Nadas, http://www.nadasweb.com/Anger%20Insights.pdf
[13] Kathleen Doheny, "Certain Blood Proteins Higher in People Prone to Outbursts of Rage: Study finds link between levels of inflammation and explosive disorder," *HealthDay*, Dec. 18, 2013, http://consumer.healthday.com/mental-health-information-25/behavior-health-news-56/certain-blood-markers-higher-in-people-prone-to-outbursts-of-rage-683162.html

[14] Mara Estroff Marano, "The High Art of Handling Problem People," *Psychology Today*, June 2012

[15] Ajai Raj, "Feeling Hot Can Fuel Rage," *Scientific American*, Dec 19, 2013, http://www.scientificamerican.com/article/feeling-hot-can-fuel-rage/

[16] Fessler, ibid

[17] http://www.futureswithoutviolence.org/userfiles/file/Children_and_Familie s/DomesticViolence.pdf

[18] Ruchira Gupta, "India: examining the motivation for rape," January 8, 2013, http://www.opendemocracy.net/5050/ruchira-gupta/india-examining-motivation-for-rape

[19] Steven J. Bartlett, *The Pathology of Man: A Study of Human Evil*, Charles C. Thomas, 2004

Chapter 7
Revenge and Retribution (5°)

Revenge, we find, the abject pleasure of an abject mind.
~Juvenal, *Satire XIII*

Revenge, like jealousy, is an emotional preoccupation that can destroy one's personality. Captain Ahab in Melville's *Moby Dick* pursues his revenge against the white whale that took his leg, regardless of the interests of his ship's owners, the welfare of his family, the survival of his crew—or even his own.

Revenge is also powerful and long-lasting in various forms that have become institutionalized in society, responsible for many crimes and atrocities. This is the obsessive anger that animates hanging judges and lynch mobs, and in fact much of the history of criminal justice. Making a distinction between 5° revenge and 10° vengeance with its veneer of justice, Samuel Johnson said "Revenge is an act of passion; vengeance of justice. Injuries are revenged; crimes are avenged."

To begin the litany, we have a long tradition of personal combat. The 5° notion of honor is defended by physical fighting between men who are concerned with their reputation, the reputation of relatives or an inamorata, family honor, or personal vengeance because of a perceived injury or insult. These hostilities may be expressed in feuds, duels, and informal fights or brawls. A man's honor is satisfied by participation in the ordeal and especially by victory.

A blood feud or vendetta is a prolonged dispute, sometimes lasting for generations, between two families or communities, kept going by revenge and retaliation. In decentralized societies with weak governments, the vengeance of kinsmen takes the place of a legal system. Feuding has been so common among tribal societies and throughout history that it might be considered natural. (Note: this is not the same as a "war of all against all.") From the ancient Greeks and Hebrews to Japanese Samurai to 19th century Corsicans and Texans, and even today among many peoples including some in Europe and the United States, feuds are a time-honored way to handle conflicts.

In large cities and prisons, youth gangs indulge in feuds motivated by the need to defend individual and group 'honor.' Gang wars are often fueled by the perception that a group or its leader has been 'dissed" or insulted. The gang's turf is defended like the territories of warlords or the baronies and small kingdoms of former times. National honor is still a potent concept in the American South.

From the early Renaissance through the 19th century in Europe and the Americas the tendency of individual men to fight each other was codified in the duel, an agreed-upon combat with matched weapons (swords or pistols) and strict rules (the *code duello*). Originally confined to the upper classes, dueling became more widespread. It was especially frequent among military officers, in France, the American South, and South America, where it lasted into the 20th century. It was reported that the notoriously hot-tempered Andrew Jackson, before becoming U.S. President, fought more than 100 duels but killed only one man. (He was said to be a poor shot. [1]

Tens of thousands died in duels, including America's first Secretary of the Treasury, Alexander Hamilton; American naval hero Stephen Decatur; three U.S. Senators and a Representative; two of Russia's greatest poets and writers (Alexsander Pushkin and Mikhail Lermontov) ; and the brilliant French mathematician Évariste Galois who in 1832 died in a duel at the age of twenty.

Other forms of the duel occurred in other parts of the world. In the Philippines, bolo fights were once common. Meanwhile, informal disputes about women or perceived insults continue to this day in bars and streets, jungles and steppes, preceded and practiced by fights in school yards and neighborhoods that determine the 'pecking order' as well as serving to right wrongs and avenge insults of the moment.

Although we no longer recognize the code of duello, the world currently has more homicides (almost 500,000 in 2012) than war deaths (180,000 in 2014). According to the UN Office on Drugs and Crime (UNODC) men are 95% of the perpetrators and 80% of the victims. Half of murder victims are under age 30. Worldwide, guns are the weapons of choice (40%) but account for 2/3 of homicides in the Americas. [2]

The country with the greatest number of murders is Brazil, with over 50,000 such deaths in 2013. A joint report by the UN and Brazilian government on the high rate of gun violence in Brazil names factors such as widespread availability of guns, flawed police investigations, and a slow system of justice. The report says Brazilians have come to tolerate the use of guns to resolve "all sorts of disputes, in most cases for very banal and circumstantial reasons" often involving road rage, disputes with neighbors, and domestic arguments. [3]

Brazil is also the largest foreign supplier of guns to the United States, which has by far the highest rate of gun ownership (88%). The United States accounts for between one-third and one-half of all civilian-owned guns in the world.[4]

However, the highest *rate* of homicides by firearms is currently in Central America and the Caribbean: Honduras, El Salvador, Jamaica, Venezuela, and Guatemala. Contributing to these high rates are government corruption and instability, easy accessibility to guns, drug trafficking, street gangs, political coups, extra-judicial killings by police and military, and a *machista* culture that targets women.

Individually, revenge reflects 5°. When the state takes revenge as a function of its power it becomes 10° punishment or retribution. This differs from personal revenge by having a social or religious justification. Personal revenge is replaced by the idea of punishing a crime that is against the moral order, against the state, or against society.

The word "justice" usually refers to retributive justice: assigning punishment for crimes, based on a legal code. In general the process of retributive justice fits within 30° morality, but when motivated by sadism (0°), anger, or vengeance (5°); when it is set up in order to demonstrate the power of the state (10°) or is administered by a corrupt or incompetent legal system (10°/15°) then obviously it is not true justice. Additionally, the legal system in most countries is either designed to maintain certain classes of people over others, or it does so in practice.

Few parts of the world have been free of legal horrors. Throughout history, the punishment of criminals has largely occurred at 0°, 5°, and 10°. Punishments have included torture, mutilations, and general barbarity. Public executions and public displays of abused corpses inured people to the monstrousness of the legal system. Not only crimes but society's responses to them have rarely expressed our better selves. Psychologist Marshall Rosenberg, who created a widely used form of conflict resolution, says "When you have a concept of justice based on good and evil, in which people deserve to suffer for what they've done, it makes violence [against them] enjoyable."

Retribution: The Body

Instead of inflicting these horrible punishments, it would be far more to the point to provide everyone with some means of livelihood, so that nobody is under the frightful necessity of becoming first a thief and then a corpse.
~Thomas More, *Utopia,* 1516 (published 1551)

Written legal codes began over 4,000 years ago in the Middle East, such as the laws introduced by the ruler in the Sumerian city of Ur (Ur-Nammu c. 2100 BC) and other cities in the region. The Mosaic Laws appeared much later as part of the Jewish Bible rather than as a comprehensive law code, which in ancient times typically included contract law and family law as well as criminal law.

Ancient law codes used the death penalty for some crimes, proportional retaliation ("an eye for an eye") for some, and a system of fines for others. In Ur-Nammu, murder, robbery, adultery, and rape were capital crimes. Lesser crimes required fines; for instance, knocking out another man's tooth would cost a brawler two shekels of silver.

Legal scholar Francesco Parisi describes a historical progression from "discretionary retaliation" when kinsmen sought revenge, through a system of regulated, proportional retaliation ("eye for an eye") and then the commodification of the right of retaliation as fines ('blood money'). Parisi says "A system of fixed prices for specific wrongs....often produced optimal deterrence while minimizing enforcement costs." [5]

As states increasingly took over punishment, they used criminal fines for their own purposes, ending both the individual right of retaliation and the system of compensation. The victim had neither retribution nor restitution, and the state sometimes proved at least as bloodthirsty in its punishments as clans seeking their revenge. In 7th century BC, Athenian lawgiver Draco replaced the prevailing system of blood feuds with a written code of laws in which death was the penalty for every crime, including stealing a cabbage. However, a century after the Draconian Laws were passed, another lawgiver, Solon, repealed them (35° reform).

Mosaic Law included many capital crimes with a death penalty carried out by stoning, hanging, beheading, or sawing asunder. But by the first century, rabbis were making the standards of evidence so high, interpreting the ancient texts so strictly, that use of the death penalty became almost nonexistent. Unfortunately, some modern fundamentalist Christians seem to be enamored of Mosaic Law without recognizing that in Judaism, it became symbolic a long time ago.[6]

The Tang Code of Chinese law, 7th century AD, codified edicts with a long, detailed list of offenses and specific punishments. The worst crimes—"The Ten Abominations"—usually merited execution, They included plotting rebellion or treason, beating or plotting to kill close relatives, incest (with the concubines of older relatives), great irreverence (towards the emperor), and lack of filiality (such as cursing one's parents). This list reflects the very high value that traditional China placed on family (30°) and obedience to authority (15°).

Confucius had counseled mild laws and moral suasion by example of the ruler, but an ideology of 'Legalism' overcame the Confucian influence, leading to torture and many horrible punishments (0°). The Tang Code had a lasting influence on legal thinking throughout eastern Asia.[5]

Elsewhere, other versions of legalism comprise one of two longstanding but antithetical ways to deal with transgressors. For instance, John Edgar Hoover, Director of the FBI from 1924-1972, said "Justice is incidental to law and order."[6] In other words, uphold authority above all. In contrast, Thomas More, cleric and social philosopher, would deal with the underlying causes (45°) of crime (see quote above).[7]

Harsh laws and barbarous punishments appeared in English law from Anglo-Saxon times. It is said that William the Conqueror opposed taking life except in war, and ordered no person to be hanged or executed for any offense; but his views did not long prevail. English law became known as "the Bloody Code" when between 1688 and 1815 the number of crimes subject to the death penalty increased to 220, including shoplifting, consorting with Gypsies, and ""strong evidence of malice in a child aged 7–14 years of age." Faced with such extreme penalties, juries often failed to bring a guilty verdict, and reforms gradually took place (35°). Boiling alive was abolished in 1547, beheading in 1747, burning to death in 1790, and branding with a hot iron in 1829. It may have been in reaction to "the Bloody Code" that the U.S. Constitution contains an amendment prohibiting "cruel and unusual punishment."

Buddhism has always opposed execution. Since their founding in the 16th century, Anabaptists (Mennonites, Brethren and Amish) have stood against the death penalty, as have the Society of Friends. At least 140 countries have now abolished it, and in 2007 ninety-five percent of all known executions were carried out in only six countries: China, Iran, Saudi Arabia, the United States, Pakistan, and Iraq.

Judicial corporal punishment (JCP, flogging, or whipping) is another ancient bodily punishment that persisted well into the 20th century, in prisons, military settings, and shipboard. A surfeit of lashes could equal a death sentence. JCP has now been banned in most developed countries, but continues in several dozen countries in Africa, Asia, and the Near East. Since antiquity, many societies have customarily used corporal punishment (infliction of pain or harm to the body) to punish slaves, apprentices, and school students, as well as in the home with children, youths, and women. In the West, most of this is now considered illegal abuse.

Islamic Law or Sharia is a comprehensive moral-religious code including much more than criminal law. It has different interpretations in various Muslim countries, but in some the Sharia penal code includes punishments such as flogging, amputation of hands, and death by stoning—judicial punishments that have finally disappeared in Western countries. Many of the offenses subject to flogging in Sharia are sexual in nature such as adultery, homosexuality, fornication, and prostitution. Sharia punishments tend to fall much more heavily on women, and appear intended to enforce patriarchy (10°).

Some people attempt to justify harsh punishments by the biblical quote "An eye for an eye," interpreting this as a mandate. Instead the idea may have been to *restrict* vengeance so that retribution is no worse than the crime, limiting retaliation by vengeful victims or their relatives.

Early Germanic law and Brehon Law in ancient Ireland are examples of compensatory law systems. The Brehon Law replaced individual vengeance with a system of monetary compensations even in serious crimes such as murder. In contrast, the English Law that prevailed over the Brehon Law in the 17th century, as England prevailed over Ireland, relied heavily on capital punishment.

American views still seem to be colored by a long history of severe punishments in English law. Letters to the editor and blog threads often support capital punishment, with the view that the penalty should be swift and certain.

Retribution: Imprisonment

It is said that no one truly knows a nation until one has been inside its jails. A nation should not be judged by how it treats its highest citizens, but its lowest ones.
~Nelson Mandela

Some of the world's greatest people have spent time in jail. Nelson Mandela was a political prisoner for 27 years. Upon his release, he became President of South Africa, the first leader of his country to be elected in an election that represented all parts of society. He was also awarded the Nobel Peace Prize. Miguel Cervantes spent five years being held for ransom, and later spent more time locked up for alleged mismanagement of funds, during which he is said to have begun writing the first modern novel, *Don Quixote*. Fyodor Dostoevsky was imprisoned for reading and passing around writings critical of the Czar, Oscar Wilde for "gross indecency" (having a homosexual love affair). Anarchist Emma Goldman spent two years in confinement for urging Americans not to sign up for the draft in 1917.

Incarceration seems a step up from floggings and hangings, yet many prisons have been places of living death. Novelist Patrick O'Brian vividly describes Botany Bay, Australia (a penal colony in its early days) as a hell on earth, run mostly by power-seeking individuals (10°) with some acting out 0° sadism. Historically, prison management has attracted more than its share of individuals acting at the lowest dispositions. When the abuses at Abu Ghraib prison were exposed, some commentators noted that similar conditions could be found at many U.S. domestic prisons and juvenile detention centers.[8, 9, 10]

The Romans first began to use prisons as punishment, often locating them in squalid and unhealthy places such as quarries, basements, and sewer systems. Over two millennia, both guilty and innocent have found themselves in prison hells, and they still exist in modern times: Tadmur (Syria), Gitarama (Rwanda), North Korea Camp 22, Dyarkabir (Turkey), Vladimir Central (Russia), La Sante (Paris), La Sabaneta (Venezuela), Attica and Riker's Island (United States).

In contemporary America, the federal law on mandatory minimum sentences results in life sentences for many non-violent, first offenders, who are often juveniles or very young adults when their crime was committed. Most of these prisoners belong to ethnic minorities and had substandard legal representation. The idea of rehabilitation seems to have all but disappeared. Drug addicts and the mentally ill are not treated, and when an offender is released without any prospects or money in his pocket, his chances of succeeding on the outside are very poor. [11]

Solitary confinement is used in many U.S. prisons, especially to punish offenses committed within prison. An 1890 Supreme Court decision acknowledged that the practice often produces psychosis—but did not prohibit it. Instead of dungeons, the modern solitary prisoner lives in a sterile 6 foot by 9 foot cell for 23 hours a day. The United

States leads the world with about 80,000 prisoners in solitary, some for decades. Two men have each spent 40 years in solitary in a Louisiana prison for allegedly killing a prison guard. Solitary has long been known to be a form of psychological torture (0°), and could be considered as cruel and unusual punishment in contravention of the U.S. Constitution.

Whether expressed in bodily pain, death, life in prison, or surveillance, totalitarian systems of governance show the same preoccupation with punishment and total control that are reflected in the criminal justice system.

[1] Dantan Wernecke, "My God! Have I Missed Him?" teachingamericanhistory.org May 27, 2012, http://teachingamericanhistory.org/past-programs/hfotw/120528-2/
[2] UNODC, "Some 437,000 people murdered worldwide in 2012, according to new UNODC study," Press release, April 10, 2014, https://www.unodc.org/unodc/en/press/releases/2014/April/some-437000-people-murdered-worldwide-in-2012-according-to-new-unodc-study.html
[3] Simon Rogers, "Gun homicides and gun ownership listed by country," The Guardian, July 22, 2012, http://www.theguardian.com/news/datablog/2012/jul/22/gun-homicides-ownership-world-list
[4] http://articles.baltimoresun.com/1994-08-21/news/1994233019_1_handgun-manufacturers-taurus-brazil
[5] Francesco Parisi, "The Genesis of Liability in Ancient Law," *American Law and Economics Review*, Vol. 3, No. 1, Spring 2001, http://www.law.gmu.edu/assets/files/publications/working_papers/00-27.pdf
[6] "Judaism and Capital Punishment" BBC, Last updated July 21, 2009 http://www.bbc.co.uk/religion/religions/judaism/jewishethics/capital.shtml
[7] Zhangsun Wuji, *"Selections from* The Great Tang Code: Article 6, "The Ten Abominations," http://afe.easia.columbia.edu/ps/cup/zhangsun_wuji_great_tang_code.pdf
[8] Patrick O'Brian, *The Nutmeg of Consolation*, HarperCollins, 1991
[9] Human Rights Watch, "Prisoner Abuse: How Different Are U.S. Prisons?" May 14, 2004, http://www.hrw.org/news/2004/05/13/prisoner-abuse-how-different-are-us-prisons
[10] H. Bruce Franklin, "Abu Ghraib…Shocking? What Happened There Is Commonplace at U.S. Prisons," History News Network, http://hnn.us/article/8842
[11] Nicholas Kristof, "A Life Sentence for This?" *New York Times*, November 17, 2013

Chapter 8
10° Domination

Man calls it Reason—thence his Power's increased,
To be far beastlier than any Beast.
~Johann Wolfgang von Goethe, 1748-1832

There is such a thing as natural authority, as of parents with young children, or individuals with the relevant knowledge, skill, and experience to handle a given situation. There are people who are able to keep their head in an emergency, and people whose evident concern for others and relative lack of a personal agenda makes others want to follow them. Natural authority expresses higher dispositions, does not impose its authority through force, and has no lust for power.

In contrast, 10° is a ruthless drive to dominate, to own everything and run the whole show. Compared to the hot rage of the reactive disposition, power-seeking 10° is cold and takes longer to prepare actions including intimidation, seizing power, abuse of power, deception, and various forms of corruption. Very strong-willed in its attempts to control other people, 10° may express jealousy, greed, and bullying, often disguising cruelty with hypocritical sentiments. Those acting at 10° may show Machiavellian, psychopathic, sociopathic, narcissistic, and/or sadistic traits. People habitually acting at 10° are domestic tyrants and controlling spouses, schoolyard bullies, "the boss from hell," and others met in daily life. Yet some garden varieties of power are so embedded in our thinking that we hardly notice them.

Various institutions and ideologies have supported all these power-seeking mind-sets and behaviors, and they are built into social customs and institutions. In fact, this disposition underlies many established folkways, some that are as old as civilization. The majority of what is taught as history in school—the power struggles, dynasties, and wars—describes 10° in action. The state itself grew out of warfare and by definition retains the monopoly on physical force. When a country's government loses this monopoly of force it is a 'failed state.'

Top-down governance is 10°. Dictators have replaced absolute monarchs of the past yet act in similar ways. For instance the repressive regime of North Korea shows a 10° society with undertones of 5° paranoia and 0° inhumanity. However not only dictatorships but all those political concentrations of humanity that claim a *monopoly of power*—kingdoms, empires, and modern nation-states—express 10° to some degree, even if they have representative government.

War is almost always about 10° power, although it expresses many other dispositions as well. (See Chapter 18)

The most violent reaches of 10° look very much like 0°. Generally the 10° disposition claims an ideological justification because its actions are supposed to be moral, just, or decreed by God; they are committed in self-defense or in defense of kin or nation; they are in accord with nature or the arc of history; and because the end justifies the means. One could make an analogy that 0° resembles psychopathy while 10°, which always has its rationale, resembles sociopathy. Ideology or not, the dead are just as dead either way.

Greed—for land, money, or power—is an ancient 10° motivation seen in the *Epic of Gilgamesh* (2500 BC) or the *Iliad* (8th century BC) in which King Agamemnon refuses to share the spoils of war. Judas betrayed his spiritual teacher for 30 pieces of silver. In Chaucer's "The Pardoner's Tale," three young roisterers find a treasure but kill each other in their greed to possess it alone. Ironically, the Pardoner who tells the tale, for all his moralizing, is shown to be a greedy man himself. In Leo Tolstoy's story "How Much Land Does a Man Need?" the peasant Pakhom acquires more and more land until he is so stressed that he ends up underground in a patch only six feet long.

Greed drives the capitalist system, predicated on constant growth. The concept of growth conceals underlying realities of encroachment and exploitation (10°) of less developed nations by the more powerful ones, and the mining and destruction of the planet (0°). 'Free enterprise' ignores the actuality of oligopoly when up to half the American economy is composed of shared monopolies.

Ancient conquerors and modern imperialists show an overpowering drive to get bigger, to own more of the world, and to control more of the world's people. Religious and political ideologies often demonstrate a similar imperialistic urge to put everybody under one rule, one religion, or one philosophy. This sort of fanaticism could be called intellectual or spiritual greed.

Bullies and Authoritarians

The serial bully, who in my estimation accounts for about one person in thirty in society, is the single most important threat to the effectiveness of organizations, the profitability of industry, the performance of the economy, and the prosperity of society.
~Tim Field, 1952-2006, British anti-bullying activist and computer expert

Bullying is the repeated use of force, threats, or verbal abuse to impose the bully's dominance over others who are perceived as physically or socially or intellectually inferior. The school or neighborhood bully is bigger, older, or more popular than the victim, who tends to be from a dysfunctional family, less athletic, wears glasses or braces, of a different race or ethnicity, fat, stutters, takes music lessons, of a peaceable temperament, shy and introverted, unusually bright, slow learner, wears poor quality or unfashionable clothes, and so on. School bullying is said to peak in the 7th grade, when many children are reaching puberty.

At school, the persecutor may have been bullied himself, or have problems at home. But often she or he is popular, with several followers and general support of peers. Many times school authorities ignore the harassment, or don't know how to stop it, although several prevention programs have shown success. It also sometimes happens that teachers bully students. Sometimes the torment occurs in a dysfunctional family that treats one child as the family scapegoat.

Similar dynamics operate among adults who are the grown-up versions of the schoolyard bully. The adult bully usually has some hierarchical authority to back him up—he's the boss, military superior, school principal, bureaucrat, or policeman. Or he has ingrained social authority as a member of a dominant social class or as a male. Assertion of male dominance in the workplace (sexual harassment) is now a crime in the United States but has scarcely abated in the U.S. military. Women also can be workplace, schoolyard, or domestic bullies.

A physiological basis may exist for this behavior. Aggressive energy like other biological traits usually appears as a Bell-shaped Curve: at one end of the curve, some individuals exhibit very high energy and dominance, while some are very shy and retiring at the other end, and most are somewhere in between.

One of the subtypes of the aggressive personalities listed by Dr. Simon is the *channeled aggressive* who directs his energies into socially approved fields such as sports, big business, politics, or the military. Simon says they will cross acceptable boundaries when they think they can get away with it. At worst, this is a sociopath who cares only about the appearance of morality and legality. Yet many dominant children (and adults) can and often do channel their drive in ways that are socially acceptable and beneficial, from athletics to positive leadership in many fields. So the existence of individuals with unusually high levels of aggressive energy can be only a part of the bully phenomenon.

Most experts are agreed that school bullying—which has reached epidemic proportions in the United States with cyberbullying— is largely the result of dysfunctional, authoritarian, and/or abusive homes and subtle social support for scapegoating those who are different. Probably the most frightening form, from the victim's point of view, is pack bullying or mobbing. This can result in the victim's injury or death, or lifelong psychological problems. Cyberbullying often takes this form, and in the U.S. has led to several victim suicides.

Less attention is directed to bullying in the workplace, except in the form of sexual harassment. However, many European nations have passed laws to prohibit intimidation in the workplace, whether from superiors or co-workers. In France it is called "moral harassment." [1]

In the United States, small-scale tyrants are often appointed to manage businesses and agencies because of a general misunderstanding about what sort of person makes the best boss. People in positions of authority may have very large—baby-sized—egos. As executives, army generals, politicians, school superintendents, doctors, or coaches they are ensconced in social institutions such as the criminal justice system, educational system, or religious cults.

An 'authoritarian personality' may or may not act as a bully or support bullies. The term describes a more general orientation:

> A personality pattern reflecting a desire for security, order, power, and status, with a desire for structured lines of authority, a conventional set of values or outlook, a demand for unquestioning obedience, and a tendency to be hostile toward or use as scapegoats individuals of minority or nontraditional groups. [2]

Authoritarian personalities may express 5°, 10°, and 15° traits. Dominators (often narcissists) gain power because of the leader's strong will and self-confidence; or because of the apathy, confusion, or laziness of the led (15°) who interpret events by way of their own prejudices. Followers are vulnerable to 'gas-lighting' (manipulation of one's own perception so that others define our reality) and repetitive propaganda that approaches brainwashing.

Authoritarian followers give up their consciences to others. In Nazi Germany blind obedience was part of the *Führerprinzip* (leader principle), an ideology based on the philosophy of Hermann Keyserling. He said that certain individuals were endowed by nature with leadership ability, and therefore the *right* to rule. (The old 'divine right of kings' plus Social Darwinism.)

Psychology professor Bob Altemeyer extensively studied the authoritarian personality pattern and devised widely used tests that measure authoritarian traits (the RWA Scale). Authoritarians may be either a 10°/20° leader (Social Dominator or SDO) or a 15° follower (high RWA). Altemeyer identified a third type, the Double High, who scores high on both RWA and SDO scales. The Double High person has a strong drive to lead others who share the same authoritarian traits and values, and he tends to be opportunistic and Machiavellian. [3, 4]

Although Altemeyer calls his scale Right Wing Authoritarian, these folk can be or can present themselves with a range of political ideologies. Double High leaders Josef Stalin and Pol Pot were communists; Francisco Franco was a rightist; Francois "Papa Doc" Duvalier ran for office as a populist and Black Nationalist; and Robert Mugabe was first elected President of Zimbabwe as a proponent of reconciliation between the former belligerents in Rhodesia. Once elected to office, authoritarian leaders do not leave it of their own volition. Some, such as Augusto Pinochet or Idi Amin, were never elected in the first place but became leaders through a military coup. All the foregoing individuals sometimes expressed the $0°$ disposition with high levels of violence and disregard for human rights.

In contemporary America, RWAs are usually associated with ultra-conservative politics. John Dean, Counsel to former President Richard Nixon, accuses authoritarian political figures of hijacking the conservative tradition. Relying heavily on Altemeyer's research, Dean describes a number of well-known and powerful personalities as 'Double Highs' such as J. Edgar Hoover, Pat Robertson, Paul Weyrich, Newt Gingrich, Tom DeLay, Jack Abramoff, and Dick Cheney, later adding Wisconsin Governor Scott Walker to this list.[5]

Deception

[When the Indians] *grow secure uppon the treatie, we shall have the better Advantage both to surprise them and cut downe theire corne.*
~Council of State, 17th century Virginia

Lying was possible only after human creatures became able to conceive the concept of truth. Martin Buber says that "The lie is the specific evil which man has introduced into nature…different in kind from every deceit that the animals can produce." [6]

Sissela Bok, a modern authority on lying, defines a lie as "an intentionally deceptive message in the form of a statement."[7] Deception may also involve omitting information, exaggeration, equivocation, evasion, distraction, changing the subject, and even silence. It may use symbols, images, doctored photos, or heavily edited videos. All deception is intended to mislead, but its focal point is the *lie*: the intentional use of speech to represent as true what one knows to be false.

Bok points out that people will believe a lie only when most people are telling the truth (30°). The liar is a free-rider in a truth-telling society. She describes how very difficult life would be in a society where honesty was not the common practice. People would distrust each other, remain constantly on guard, and it would be hard to find out the simplest piece of information. In fact, society would likely collapse. Thus the Principle of Veracity or truth-telling benefits everyone.

Niccolò Machiavelli claimed that "Men are so simple of mind, and so much dominated by their immediate needs, that a deceitful man will always find plenty who are ready to be deceived." However, those who are themselves honest, and who have grown up in families and communities where most people are honest, are inclined to be trusting of others—which is not at all the same thing as being simple-minded.

10° disposition often employs duplicity, but devising complex forms of deception—trickery, tactics, propaganda—properly belongs to clever 20°. Those who intend to deceive know how to manipulate the emotional tendencies of others. Bok says they "can play on the biases of some persons, the imagination of others, and on errors and confusion throughout the system." She recommends looking at the ways society itself encourages deception, in order to change those customs.

According to the Oxford English Dictionary, Machiavellianism denotes "the employment of cunning and duplicity in statecraft or in general conduct." In addition to a certain shrewd strategic ability, the term describes a seemingly guiltless and facile use of deceit to further selfish personal goals. When these coincide with similarly selfish goals of one's class or nation, problems go beyond any specific lie. Buber speaks of "being a lie" and continues:

> The speaker no longer suffers merely from liars, but from a generation of the lie….With their speech they breed 'delusion' in their hearers, they spin illusions for them; in particular *they spin a way of thinking for them* which they themselves do not follow.[8]

Thus the propagandists and creators of false consciousness create lies in the deepest sense of the term.*

Cruel Hypocrisy

> *Whatever you condemn, you have done yourself.*
> ~Georg Groddeck, *The Book of the It*, 1950

In his book *People of the Lie*, psychiatrist Scott Peck describes, from his practice, several sets of self-deceived parents who dominate, thwart, and destroy the spirit and autonomy of their children while self-righteously putting the blame for all problems on the child victim. In one case the parents seem to be actively driving their child to suicide. Dr. Peck names such individuals 'people of the lie' because they absolutely refuse to admit any mistakes of their own. He also calls these persons "evil" but of course it is not our plan to attach such absolutist labels to anyone. Nor is the behavior of these parents, abhorrent as they are, necessarily the worst of the worst. Once you start calling individuals 'evil' where do you stop?

Peck believes such individuals are so enmeshed in their lies that they are incurable (by psychiatry, at least). In the cases he mentions, the self-righteous façade is the result of an ego-agreement between two people, making it stronger and thus more difficult to dislodge. A fictional example of such double-teaming by a hypocritical pair is Mr. Murdstone and his sister Miss Murdstone in Dickens' *David Copperfield*. This loathsome duo abuses the boy David and drives his gentle mother to her death by destroying her spirit in the name of uplifting her.

---

*False consciousness: 1. a Marxist theory that people are unable to see things, especially exploitation, oppression, and social relations, as they really are; the hypothesized inability of the human mind to develop a sophisticated awareness of how it is developed and shaped by circumstances; **2. any belief or view that prevents a person from being able to understand the true nature of a situation.**
http://dictionary.reference.com/browse/false+consciousness

Dickens' novels described a time and place when greed and cruel hypocrisy seemed common in positions of authority, during the brutal dislocations and injustices of the early Industrial Revolution. It was a time of middle-class striving and widespread pretenses of strict morality. His contemporary Charlotte Brontë portrays another cruel hypocrite, Mr. Brocklehurst, in *Jane Eyre*. As Master of Jane's school, Brocklehurst preaches Christian humility and asceticism for his young charges, while he and his family live much more luxuriously.

In real life, Charlotte Brontë's two elder sisters, Maria and Elizabeth, died at ages eleven and ten from tuberculosis acquired at a school where they suffered from hunger and cold, while being instructed by their teachers about hellfire and damnation. Historically, it has been only too easy for self-righteous, cruel people to find employment administering and working in orphanages, workhouses, schools, mental hospitals, prisons, and other institutions.

Maybe we should describe even garden-variety hypocrisy as 10°. Whether deception or self-deception, the aim is to protect or to advance oneself usually at the expense of others. Another very common type of hypocrisy is ideological (10°/20°), where the pretense is bolstered by thousands or millions of allies.

Corruption and Fraud

The duty of youth is to challenge corruption.
~Kurt Cobain, American musician, 1967-1994

Power corrupts, as the saying goes, and 10° is prone to corruption, a pattern of dishonest or fraudulent behavior by powerful people such as government officials or the top management of some corporation. Corruption includes double dealing, manipulating elections, diverting funds, laundering money, or defrauding investors, for instance by a Ponzi scheme. Bribery is a pervasive problem in many countries, accompanied by a lack of punishment for corrupt leaders, and public institutions that don't respond to the needs of citizens. In some cases those in power are stealing from the country they are supposed to govern—a kleptocracy.

Political corruption also happens on a smaller scale, for instance, in a small American city where public servants such as police and school teachers were expected to provide a kickback when given a job. A significant segment of society may be corrupt (Wall Street practices leading up to the 2008 economic crisis). Sometimes so much fraud and bribery goes on that one can regard the whole society as corrupt.

But what about accepted practices in the United States such as lobbying Congress and state legislatures? Although federal or state subsidies or tax breaks to specific industries may be the payoff, it is not called bribery, and the Supreme Court has now enshrined the right of corporations and unions to donate unlimited amounts of money to political campaigns, without transparency, under the name of 'free speech.' Washington D.C. and also Brussels, the center of the European Union, are infested with special interest lobbyists.

Business fraud is common in the USA. For instance, the New York Attorney General's office recently accused four major retailers of selling herbal supplements 80% of which did not contain *any* of the herb on the label. There are also bad practices in professions and trades. As a young woman I lost my first (healthy) tooth to an oral surgeon who, I later realized, had a kickback arrangement with my regular dentist. I've also in the past encountered dishonest repairmen and car mechanics.

Business professor Muel Kaptein drew up a long list of psychological reasons influencing white collar crime, two of which apply especially to 10°: He says that if corruption is already a part of the workplace, or of the employee's place of origin, people more easily become used to it and hardly see it. Second, a study shows that people who are given power tend to set rules for others that are more ethically strict than those they give to themselves. [9]

A more subtle kind of corruption uses power to benefit one's own clan or class. It includes practices deeply entrenched in a society's institutions such as racial, class, or gender discrimination in hiring, firing, promotion, and wages; persistent nepotism and favoritism in local governments and school systems; redlining in real estate or banking; or employers sharing unfair labor practices.

Transparency International compares the world's nation-states in a yearly measure of perceived government corruption (the Corruption Perceptions Index or CPI). In general, the wealthiest, democratic nations show the least public corruption. When TI surveyed people in 107 countries to prepare the 2013 Global Corruption Barometer, they found public perception of government to be low. Worldwide, people think that the five most corrupt institutions are political parties, police, public officials, the legislature, and the judiciary.[10]

TI also publishes the annual Bribe Payers Index (BPI) which ranks companies from 28 leading economies by the pervasiveness of paying bribes to government officials in foreign countries where they do business. Many companies do not include corruption prevention in their risk management strategies, nor do they have measures to protect whistleblowers. A code of ethics may be on the books but never actually used in training executives. [11]

TI's 2011 Corruption Index, based on evaluations by business leaders in thirteen countries, looked at both bribery and "state capture" (the degree to which a nation's laws have been influenced by corporations). Using this expanded definition, the survey finds oil, gas, and mining industries account for most global corruption. Also implicated are public works contracts, construction, and real estate and property development. On this scale the United States ranked as more corrupt than Canada, Australia, and almost all European countries. [12]

State capture is a more basic and lasting form of domination than bribery. Naomi Klein (*This Changes Everything*) says that many governments are so subject to state capture that they can no longer protect their citizens from corporations that threaten their homes, subsistence, and very survival. [13]

The international arms trade is one of the most corrupt industries in the world, a trillion-dollar investment in killing people estimated to account for as much as 40% of worldwide corruption (bribery). In this and many other industries, a deep structural corruption can result from the very way the industry and its products are defined. What is really being sold is not defense but overkill, threats, geostrategic dominance, or a dictator's self-image. [14]

Our entire global money system appears to be corrupt. When the world's total debt load (household, corporate, financial, and public) is over three times its GDP, one wonders if we are not all operating on some sort of Ponzi scheme.[15]

Beyond 10°

Mastering others is strength. Mastering yourself is true power.
~Lao Tzu, Chinese philosopher and poet, c. 6th c. BC

Washing one's hands of the conflict between the powerful and the powerless means to side with the powerful, not to be neutral.
~Paulo Freire, Brazilian educator and philosopher, 1921-1997

The 10° disposition is deeply ingrained in us both biologically and culturally, but many wise teachers show us how to develop past it. This requires one to go against the grain of one's culture or subculture, and demands that a person be quite honest about his or her real motives in any given situation. Besides self-mastery, one can master a craft, a skill, or a field of study. This does not limit other people's autonomy.

Also, as Freire points out, people who identify with and admire the powerful are part of the power structure. Those who ignore injustices are complicit in them. Fortunately, many people eventually see through and resist tyranny in whatever guise. The 45° disposition is especially skilled at seeing through propaganda and false consciousness, as well as being ruthlessly honest with himself or herself.

[1] Philippe Thomas, "French Law Prohibiting Bullying in the Workplace," http://www.thehrdirector.com/business-news/diversity_and_equality/french-law-prohibiting-bullying-in-the-workplace/
[2] "authoritarian personality," http://dictionary.reference.com/browse/authoritarian+personality
[3] Bob Altemeyer, *The Authoritarians*, 2006, http://members.shaw.ca/jeanaltemeyer/drbob/TheAuthoritarians.pdf

[4] Bob Altemeyer, "What Happens When Authoritarians Inherit the Earth? A Simulation," *Analyses of Social Issues and Public Policy*, Vol. 3, No. 1, 2003, http://www.overcominghateportal.org/uploads/5/4/1/5/5415260/when_rwa_inherit_the_earth.pdf

[5] John Dean, *Conservatives without Conscience*, Viking Press, 2006

[6] Martin Buber*, Good and Evil*, Prentice-Hall 1953

[7] Sissela Bok, *Lying,* Vintage Books, 2nd edition 1999

[8] Buber, op. cit

[9] Max Nisen and Aimee Groth, "27 Psychological Reasons Why Good People Do Bad Things," *Business Insider*, Aug. 27, 2012, http://www.businessinsider.com/27-psychological-reasons-why-good-people-do-bad-things-2012-8

[10] Transparency International, "Institutions perceived by respondents to be among the most affected by corruption," http://www.transparency.org/gcb2013/results

[11] Transparency International Zimbabwe (TIZ)," National Bribe Payers Index Report 2013", June 16, 2014, http://www.kubatana.net/2014/06/20/2122/national-bribe-payers-index-report-2013/

12 Susan Kraemer, "Oil and Gas Industry Leads Global Corruption Index: US More Corrupt than Qatar," CleanTechnica, May 7, 2011, http://cleantechnica.com/2011/05/07/oil-and-gas-industry-leads-global-corruption-index-us-more-corrupt-than-qatar/

[13] Naomi Klein, *This Changes Everything*: *Capitalism vs. the Climate*, Simon & Schuster, 2015

14 The Arms Trade is Big Business," http://www.globalissues.org/article/74/the-arms-trade-is-big-business#HiddenCorporateWelfare

[15] Sudeep Reddy, "Number of the Week: Total World Debt Load at 313% of GDP, "*Wall Street Journa*l, May 11, 2013, http://blogs.wsj.com/economics/2013/05/11/number-of-the-week-total-world-debt-load-at-313-of-gdp/

Chapter 9
The Long History of 10°

*The entire history of mankind is nothing but a prolonged fight
to the death for the conquest of universal prestige and absolute power.*
~Albert Camus, *The Rebel 1951*

The narratives of all civilizations to date can be written largely in terms of power struggles, greed, and corruption. Meanwhile 10° institutions that developed five or six thousand years ago still shape our present world, including the oppression of nature, female subordination, slavery, the imperial state, and oligarchy.

Agriculture and animal domestication were the first signs of human dominance over nature and commonly accepted as the impetus to civilization. However, the separation between us and the rest of the planet has grown to dangerous proportions over the past 400 years. Several dispositions contributed to the spiritual separation of humanity from the rest of nature: the short-term greed of 10°, 20° industrialism, 15° apathy and specific false notions.

Male dominance of women is a global and ancient manifestation of the 10° disposition. The social system in which the father or father-figure is the supreme authority (patriarchy) is about 6,000 years old. We note that in this hierarchical system, some men have power over other, subordinate men. Patriarchy can oppress men as well as women, but women are usually in the bottom tier of the hierarchy.

It is generally agreed that hunting-gathering cultures were more egalitarian than the pastoral and agricultural societies that began to arise at the end of the last glacial period. In the early societies, males and females had similar power. Women, through foraging, provided the bulk of the food calories while men, through hunting, provided most of the protein. However, in the new agricultural societies, women's labor was not as important as it had been before. Instead of group territory there was individual property (a 10° concept). [1,2]

Most scholars date the beginnings of the patriarchal system to about 4000 B.C. but dispute whether it replaced an actual matriarchal

96

system. Feminist historian Gerda Lerner says while no anthropological or historical evidences shows that patriarchy replaced matriarchy, such an event is reflected in Babylonian, Hebrew, and Greek mythology. Instead, there were frequent deadly clashes between the more egalitarian hunter-gatherers and encroaching states, their patriarchal system based on field agriculture and centralized power. Friedrich Engels named this the "world historic defeat of the female sex."[3],[4]

Lerner says that the commodification of women's sexuality and reproductive abilities arose about the same time as the concept of private property. 20° stands for the institutions and ideologies that support the ongoing system of property ownership. In an agricultural society, the patriarchal family structure is related to men's control of property, especially land. .Marriage was based on property relationships and women themselves have often been regarded as a form of property.

The ownership and control of land is related to the acquisition of territories through warfare, a male occupation. Among primates the physically stronger male gender evolved to protect the group. Then the rise of states constantly competing for territory and tribute greatly increased the role of warfare and with it, male power.

Lerner and others see patriarchy as the earliest, historical template for other forms of social dominance such as class: "Men learned to institute dominance and hierarchy over other people by their earlier practice of dominance over the women of their own group."

Patriarchy can be characterized by four traits. It is *male-dominated*—the most powerful roles in society are mainly held by men. It is *male-centered*—public attention is focused on men, and this focus is taken for granted. It is *male-identified*, so that personal traits and aspects of society that are highly valued are associated with men, and those valued lower are associated with women.

Fourthly, the patriarchal social system is *obsessed with control*. It ranks men high because of the idea that they are better fitted to exert control through reason, violence, or the threat of violence. Similarly, women are devalued because of their supposed lack of control and need for supervision or protection.[5]

Male dominance to the extremes of hostility and abuse of women is common the world over, especially in sub-Saharan Africa, Southeast Asia, the Middle East, and North Africa. A study for the UN estimates that one of every three women in the world will be beaten, raped, or otherwise abused during her lifetime, usually by a member of her own family.[6] Misogyny is not specific to Arabic countries or the Third World. Sexual assault is a major problem even in rich countries such as the United States.[7]

Fear of the growing education and social participation of women is a major component of religious fundamentalisms whether Islamic, Christian, Hindu, or in Orthodox Judaism.

Gendercide is the killing of victims because of their gender. In 1989 a gunman yelling "I hate feminists!" killed fourteen women engineering students at the *Ecole Polytechnique* in Montreal. In India, a particularly horrific instance of gang rape and murder led to street protests and an ongoing movement against a growing "rape culture" in which Indian officials often fail to investigate rapes or punish rapists, especially of low-caste women. Some leaders have made public statements minimizing the crime (reinforcing 10° male dominance).

India's gross demographic imbalance shows as many as 60 million women are now missing from the population because of social customs such as selective abortions of females, female infanticide, killing girls under age six through starvation, neglect and violence; dowry murders, honor killings, and witch lynching. Author/activist Rita Banerji founded the 50 Million Missing Campaign to focus on this massive tragedy. Feminist researcher Sita Agarwal claims that male dominance and hostility towards women, supported by Hinduism, has over the centuries perpetrated the greatest genocide of all times. [8, 9]

*While it is much less common, some women do abuse men or boys and it is possible for females to rape males, especially younger ones. They might be asserting their dominance (10°) for instance as female guards in a juvenile detention center; or they might be child abusers in the home. Abuse by and of either gender occurs at 10°, 5° or 0°.

Gender also contributes to victimization by war. Historical conflicts did not spare women and children, and many modern conflicts have deliberately targeted women for rape, sexual slavery, or death as in Nanking, East Timor, Bosnia, and Congo; Central American drug wars; and by the Taliban, Boko Haram, and ISIS.

Slavery

> *At the beginning of the nineteenth century an estimated three-quarters of all people alive were trapped in bondage against their will either in some form of slavery or serfdom.*
> ~David P. Forsythe, *Encyclopedia of Human Rights*, Vol. 1, 2009

Slavery is a very old and widespread institution dating back to the first wars. It developed everywhere, from China to England to the Aztecs and Mayans. Most slaves were prisoners of war; others were enslaved through debt, or as punishment for a crime. Some peasants sold themselves or their children into slavery as an alternative to starvation. At times slavery became a hereditary condition. In general the ownership and control of some human beings by others reflects $10°$ domination, but some of the practices accompanying the institution have also expressed $0°$ sadism and malign indifference.[10]

In classical times the Greek economy was entirely dependent on forced labor, from servants to secretaries, miners to business managers, with slaves being a third to one-half of Athenian population. In Sparta a large class of subjugated people, the helots, were probably the original inhabitants who became state-owned serfs assigned to individual owners. As helots outnumbered their masters, the Spartans were always wary. Secret police searched for rebellious helots and executed them. [11]

Ancient Rome also depended greatly on slaves. Roman estates were worked by synchronized gang labor, a system that reappeared many centuries later in the sugar, cotton, and tobacco plantations of the Caribbean and colonial America, and then—long after the official abolition of slavery—in prison chain gangs. Africans, Arabs, Italians, Russians, Vikings, Mongols—Muslims, Christians, Jews, shamanists—

all were involved in the medieval slave trade. Prisoners of war were always a ready source of forced labor, and in fact the word 'slave' is derived from 'Slav' because around the 9th century so many Slavic war prisoners were enslaved and sold by German Saxon rulers [12]

In Europe slavery was replaced by serfdom. Serfs were slightly freer than slaves, although bound to the land and lacking personal liberties. For instance, they required the lord's permission to marry or to change their occupation. Serfdom disappeared much earlier in Western Europe than it did in Russia, where in 1861 one third of the Russian population were serfs, numbering 23 million people before being freed by Emperor Alexander II. [13]

As serfs in Western Europe were gaining more freedom, Portuguese navigators exploring African coasts gave new impetus to the slave trade. Over a span of three to four centuries the Atlantic slave trade transported about 12 million African people to the Americas, mainly to sugar colonies in Brazil and the Caribbean. This massive commodification of human beings involved great losses of life during the Middle Passage, and then from the gang labor system on the plantations to which most were destined. [14]

Slavery still exists. An estimated 30 to 35 million people, many of them children, live in forced labor, debt bondage, coerced prostitution, as child brides, or as child soldiers. India and some African countries have the highest rates of enslavement, but Europe and the United States are also blighted. By one estimate, 60,000 people live in bondage in the United States.[15, 16] Slavery is also caught up in products that Americans buy. Anti-slavery activist Kevin Bales says that murky supply-lines make it hard for ethical consumers (35°) to make informed choices. Many slaves are employed in deforestation and other environmental destruction. Bales says that "If slavery were a country it would have the population of Canada but it would be the third-largest emitter of CO_2 after China and the United States."[17]

Slavery in general is structured at 10°, but it has often operated at 0° in terms of a trade based on kidnapping, the great loss of life that was part of the Middle Passage, the utter dehumanization of the auction block, and cruel punishments. Child slavery effectively destroys a child's human potential. One historical form of slavery—large plantations raising single cash crops such as sugar cane, rice, and indigo—operated almost entirely at 0° because of utter indifference by owners to the physical well-being of laborers, working them to death and treating them as a replaceable commodity.

Slavery and serfdom still do not exhaust the forms of labor which have put most of the world's people in bondage or semi-bondage throughout history and which to some extent still continue today. The system of voluntary indentured servitude—in which people contract to work for a specified time in return for payment of travel expenses and maintenance while working—was widely used in British colonies in the 17th and 18th centuries. About half the European immigrants to the 13 American colonies came as indentured servants.

Another half-million Europeans went to the Caribbean. A series of wars sent many Scottish and Irish prisoners of war to the sugar islands, known as death-traps. Except for POWs and convicts, the indenture system was supposed to be voluntary. Immigrants signed a contract (20°) describing the terms of employment, but some recruiting agents used deception (10°) and some people were simply kidnapped (0°). Especially in the Caribbean, work was so hard and the indentured so poorly treated, that many did not live long enough to get the freedom fee they were supposed to receive after their four or five years of servitude.

The 19th century coolie trade replaced the African slave trade, bringing several million unskilled laborers from Asia and the South Pacific to work in plantations, mines, or railroad construction in Latin America, Africa, and elsewhere. The word 'coolie' means 'bitter work' in Chinese. Although called indentured workers, most of the laborers were illiterate and couldn't read the contract that they signed with a thumbprint. A great many were totally deceived about the destination, type of work, wages, and length of the sea voyage, which took 10 to 20 weeks under terrible conditions. Both journey and work caused high death rates, and few of the survivors ever received the promised benefits at the end of their contracted time.[18]

Foreign workers continue to be abused. In November 2014 an alliance of 90 rights and labor groups called for reforms to protect 23 million foreign workers employed in the six Gulf nations of the Middle East. In countries such as Saudi Arabia and Kuwait, guest workers comprise about one-third of the population. Common complaints include conditions of "no rest periods, excessive workloads, food deprivation, and confinement in the workplace" as well as unpaid wages, physical violence, forced labor, and forced sex.[19]

Ancient and medieval armies were often manned largely by slaves or serfs. Wholesale conscription of free citizens started with the French Revolution and became the model for most nations in the 19th century. In many ways the draft resembled forced military service under serfdom except that terms were shorter and soldiers expected to be more motivated by patriotism and wages. In contrast, voluntary military enlistment has some resemblance to voluntary indentured servitude.

It is evident that most of the world's work since civilization began has been accomplished with a great deal of coercion, deception, and harsh exploitation.

The State

What are kingdoms but great robberies?
~Augustine, *City of God,* early 400s

During almost all of human existence—counting this as two hundred thousand years—people lived in autonomous bands or small villages. At the world's low population density of a few million, living from hunting, foraging, and primitive gardening, each small group necessarily governed itself. Toward the end of this period, several villages might join together in a chiefdom, although chiefs did not have absolute authority as did later kings.

Then, about 6,000 years ago, the state was invented, arising first in Egypt, Mesopotamia, and the Indus Valley. Across the continents, large aggregations of people came to live under ruling families. People were not able to maintain the old egalitarianism in a large-scale, centralized society. According to anthropologist Robert L. Carneiro, as recently as 1000 BC the Earth held about 600,000 small, self-governing communities. Mainly because of unremitting warfare or threats of war, this number has shrunk to the present number of nation-states, about 200. While some small indigenous communities still exist, they ultimately live under the power of a large political entity.[20]

17th century philosopher Thomas Hobbes proposed the idea that humans agreed in a hypothetical social contract to let one powerful authority keep everybody else from constantly fighting over resources. There's no evidence of actual social contracts in the ancient or prehistoric past, but there were important changes in human living patterns around 6,000 years ago, when the earliest proto-states developed with powerful rulers, armies, bureaucracies, and the invention of writing and systems of measurement: a living pattern we call civilization.

About 5,800 years ago there were changes in a gene that regulates smaller brains (a change often seen in domesticated forms of animals). People in these early states may or may not have had a 'bicameral mind' as conceptualized by Julian Jaynes; if the gods or rulers tell one what to do, less brainpower is needed. Perhaps this is why our brains have been shrinking.[21]

Coincidentally, 6,000 years ago is the time assigned by Young Earth Creationists to the creation by the Christian God of the Universe, Earth, and all life on Earth including humans. Based on computations derived from a literal reading of the Bible, this unscientific view is quite widely held in the United States, from 10% to 44% of the population depending on how the survey question is worded.

By further coincidence, several scholars put the development of patriarchal social structures at about 6,000 years ago. Thus field agriculture, proto-states, patriarchy, and genetic changes involving brain size are all associated with this time frame. A huge social transformation might indeed seem like the beginning of the world to those who were experiencing it (about 260 generations ago). Perhaps the changes signaled the beginning of human self-domestication.

Could the actual rise of large populations with more or less absolute rulers be seen symbolically as a tacit social contract? If so, there were still many ancient peoples in China, Ireland, or Germanic tribes where this idea did not reach.

The new kind of government in the Mediterranean world, based as it was on staple food crops, provided a surplus of food, allowing greater division of labor. Craftsmen, traders, warriors, civil servants, and others assumed their specialized roles. To keep track of things, bureaucrats developed writing and arithmetic. To glorify his regime, the ruler encouraged builders and artists to develop imposing monuments and decorative palaces. Development of the state is synonymous with 'civilization,' which makes it sound like the beginning of all human progress. Yet the state had both short-term and long-range disadvantages such as perennial war, social inequality, and new threats to human health.

Since these states grew from warfare, in most cases victorious warriors were the new rulers. Once a state developed, it tended to keep on conquering more autonomous villages, and to fight other states. Today it is still bent on conquest. As Mohandas Gandhi said, "The State represents violence in a concentrated and organized form. The individual has a soul, but as the State is a soulless machine, it can never be weaned from violence to which it owes its very existence." [22]

Early rulers were more or less absolute in contrast with the more egalitarian villages they gobbled up. Arts and sciences developed with specialization, but so did social stratification. Hierarchies arose, based on 10° domination. Throughout most of history, peasant farmers have been in the lowest class or caste.

Agriculture was not an unmitigated blessing. When a population grew rapidly, sometimes there were population crashes and mass starvation. In addition, the need for more land or better land led to wars against the neighbors. Staple crops may have lacked essential nutrients. Farming work was arduous. Archeological research indicates that as humans shifted from hunting-gathering to farming of staple crops, their physical condition deteriorated. Skeletal remains show that they became smaller and more subject to disease, which spreads more easily in dense populations. Also many common diseases such as measles, smallpox, and influenza leaped to humans from domesticated animals.[23, 24]

By mid-17th century a multitude of states—some of them quite small kingdoms or duchies—began to merge and turn into the modern nation-state. By definition, the state has a monopoly on power (10°).

Empires

> *Lust of absolute power is more burning than all the passions.*
> ~Tacitus, *Annals* 117 AD

It was a short step from state to dynasty or empire. Early centuries saw a constant struggle to control the Mediterranean world and Near East. The first empire (Akkadian) was formed about 2250 BC by Sargon the Great in Mesopotamia, followed by the Egyptian and Assyrian Empires. Other major players were the Phoenicians, Persians, Greeks, and finally the Romans, whose control lasted from 27 BC until 467 AD. About the same time as the short-lived empire of Alexander the Great, the Mauryan Empire (323-185 BC) arose in India and came to rule one-third of the world's population (an estimated 50 million out of 150 million people).

For three millennia the 10° disposition has held sway over much of the world, forcibly organizing ever larger aggregations of human beings. Whether this progression increased 10° tendencies or simply made use of them is an open question. The history of imperial conquest and colonialism is about dominators and those who lived under their oppressive rule. It was not enough to enslave or exploit people; imperialism often took the form of cultural genocide, or the extermination of native cultures and languages.

The empire model remained quite popular for several thousand years until after World War II when the British Empire broke up. Empire is now being replaced by economic globalization. Some see this as a new form of imperialism by the leading industrialized nation-states, especially the United States.

Oligarchy

Representative government is artifice, a political myth, designed to conceal from the masses the dominance of a self-selected, self-perpetuating, and self-serving traditional ruling class.
~Giuseppe Prezzolini, Italian writer, 1882-1982

Oligarchy is rule by the few, especially for selfish and corrupt purposes. An aristocratic class may rule over many serfs, as in ancient Sparta. Or one ethnic group subordinates another, as in South Africa under apartheid. Or a group of wealthy families picks one of their own or a figurehead to lead the government, as in the history of many Latin American nations. Oligarchs may be members of a royal family such as the House of Saud, of a hereditary aristocracy, descendants of a highly successful business person, or a merchant class like that which directed the oligarchic republics of Genoa, Florence, and Venice in Renaissance Italy. The term was invented by the ancient Greeks, who seem to have tried just about every political system there is. Aristotle noted that "As of oligarchy so of tyranny, the end is wealth; (for by wealth only can the tyrant maintain either his guard or his luxury)." [25]

Modern oligarchies typically show great inequalities of income. Much of Latin America as well as Russia, China, and the United States shows a high degree of income inequality, a sign of 1° economic dominance by the few. For instance, in the Russian Federation a few individuals amassed great fortunes in the wake of the fall of Communism, largely based on questionable purchases of privatized industries and corrupt relations with the government. About one-third of household wealth in Russia is held by 110 people (according to Investment Bank Credit Suisse). Income inequality *between* nations also signals 1° actions past or present such as imperialism.

Some years the richest man in the world is Carlos Slim Helu, a household name in Mexico, where he owns 200 companies. Inequality is too weak a word to describe the situation in India, where the ten richest individuals now garner about 12% of the nation's GDP—in a nation of over a billion people. The richest 1% owns over half of India's wealth (53%). According to most indices, the nations with the greatest gap between the richest and poorest are in the developing world, in Africa, Central and South America, and Asia.[26]

Just as there have been benevolent monarchs and benign slave owners, there may be philanthropic oligarchs. As individuals they may express various dispositions, including the higher ones. It is the social institution that tends to 10° dominance and greed, often accompanied by political corruption, and certainly expressing economic injustice.

A blatantly corrupt government is a kleptocracy or rule by thieves, as a dictator or a ruling class systematically plunders the nation's treasury. In ancient Rome it was the generals. Now it may be Third World dictators or 'presidents for life' such as Mobuto Sese Seko in Zaire, Suharto in Indonesia or Ferdinand Marcos in the Philippines. Mexico has had several kleptocrat presidents such as Salinas de Gortari. Or kleptocrats may be a financial elite (20°). Some suggest that the United States is this more sophisticated kind of kleptocracy. [27]

Bibliocide

Wherever they burn books they will also, in the end, burn human beings.
~Heinrich Heine, German poet, 1797-1856

Ironically, Heine's books were among 25,000 "Un-German" books burned by the Nazis in May, 1933. Bonfires of books—and sometimes the destruction of whole libraries—is an act of violent dominance of one belief over another, one culture over another. Libraries have often been the targets of brutish destruction (0°), religious fanaticism (5°), or cultural dominance (10°). Conquerors have a tragic habit of destroying the cultures and learning of those they conquer. When Rome destroyed rival Carthage in the final Punic War, besides selling surviving inhabitants into slavery, the Romans destroyed Carthage's libraries. Thus we have virtually no writings from the people who supplied the West with our alphabet.

Since then, many repositories of ancient wisdom have been deliberately burned by various invaders, Emperors, Sultans, Crusaders, and others who regarded another people's books as heretical, meaningless, or a focus of rebellion. About 1562, during the Spanish conquest of the New World, Bishop De Landa, a Franciscan monk, wrote

> We found a large number of books in these characters and, as they contained nothing in which were not to be seen as superstition and lies of the devil, we burned them all, which they [Maya] regretted to an amazing degree, and which caused them much affliction.[28]

Works of art have also been deliberately destroyed through the centuries. The Romans accused Vandal invaders of ruthlessly destroying Roman art and antiquities. In 15th century Florence, the Dominican friar and preacher Savonarola collected art objects which he "burnt as instruments of sensual pleasure and symbols of an immoral and unjust society." Conquistadors interpreted New World images as 'idols" and smashed them. Recent instances occurred at the hands of Islamic fundamentalists: first the Taliban which dynamited giant, ancient statues of Buddha in 2001; now ISIS which began to destroy Byzantine mosaics and Greek and Roman statues in Syria in 2014 because the depiction of human beings is contrary to strict interpretation of Islam. More recently ISIS destroyed ancient artifacts of Mesopotamian civilizations as 'idolatrous.' Such fanaticism cannot permit any form of expression other than its own. [29, 30]

[1] "Patriarchy," International Encyclopedia of the Social Sciences, 2008. *Encyclopedia.com.* 7 Apr. 2014 <http://www.encyclopedia.com
[2] "Women in Patriarchal Societies, The Origin of Civilization," 1992, International World History Project, http://history-world.org/Civilization,%20women_in_patriarchal_societies.htm
[3] Gerda Lerner, *The Creation of Patriarchy*, Oxford University Press, 1986, cited http://www.encyclopedia.com/topic/Patriarchy.aspx

[4] Chris Knight, "Engels Was Right: Early Human Kinship Was Matrilineal," 2012, http://www.chrisknight.co.uk/wp-content/uploads/2008/06/early-human-kinship-was-matrilineal.pdf

[5] "A Basic Definition of Patriarchy (based on Allan G. Johnson's *The Gender Knot*)," http://gray.intrasun.tcnj.edu/Coming%20of%20Age/a_basic_definition_of_p atriarchy.htm

[6] Max Fisher, "The Real Roots of Sexism in the Middle East (It's Not Islam, Race, or Hate'), *The Atlantic Monthly*, April 25, 2012, http://www.theatlantic.com/international/archive/2012/04/the-real-roots-of-sexism-in-the-middle-east-its-not-islam-race-or-hate/256362/

[7] Sexual Assault Response Services of Southern Maine (SARSSM) "Sexual Assault and Rape Statistics, Laws, and Reports", http://www.sarsonline.org/resources-stats/reports-laws-statics

[8] Sunny Hundal, "India's 60 million women that never were," August 8, 2013, http://www.aljazeera.com/indepth/opinion/2013/07/201372814110570679.ht ml

[9] Sita Agarwal, Genocide of Women in Hinduism, 1999, http://www.geocities.ws/genocideofhinduwomen/

[10] Andre Dollinger, "Slavery," An introduction to the history and culture of Pharaonic Egypt, http://www.reshafim.org.il/ad/egypt/timelines/topics/slavery.htm

[11] "Helot," http://www.britannica.com/EBchecked/topic/260582/helot

[12] "slave" http://www.thefreedictionary.com/slave

[13] "Serfdom," http://www.britannica.com/EBchecked/topic/535485/serfdom

[14] "The Trans-Atlantic Slave Trade Database," http://www.slavevoyages.org/tast/index.faces

[15] Terrence McNally, "There Are More Slaves Today than at Any Time in Human History," Alternet, August 24, 2009, http://www.alternet.org/world/142171/there_are_more_slaves_today_than_at _any_time_in_human_history/

[16] Max Fisher, "This map shows where the world's 30 million slaves live. There are 60,000 in the U.S." *The Washington Post*, October 17, 2013, http://www.washingtonpost.com/blogs/worldviews/wp/2013/10/17/this-map-shows-where-the-worlds-30-million-slaves-live-there-are-60000-in-the-u-s/

[17] Katie Herzog, "Modern-Day Slavery and Environmental Devastation Go Hand in Hand," *Grist*, January 20, 2016, http://grist.org/article/modern-day-slavery-and-environmental-devastation-go-hand-in-hand/

[18] Han Xiaorong, "Slave Trade: Coolie Trade," Macmillan Encyclopedia of World Slavery, http://facweb.northseattle.edu/cadler/Global_Dialogues/Readings/Monkey_H unting_Readings/Slave%20Trade%20Coolie%20Trade.pdf

[19] "Gulf states urged to protect migrant workers," Aljazeera, November 23, 2014,

[20] Robert L. Carneiro, "Political Expansion as an Expression of the Principle of Competitive Exclusion". In Cohen, Ronald & Service, Elman R. *Origins of the State: The Anthropology of Political Evolution,* Philadelphia: Institute for the Study of Human Issues, 1978. p. 219.

[21] Patrick D. Evans, Sandra L. Gilbert, Nitzan Mekel-Bobrov, Eric J. Vallender, Jeffrey R. Anderson, Leila M. Vaez-Azizi, Sarah A. Tishkoff, Richard R. Hudson, Bruce T. Lahn, "Microcephalin, a Gene Regulating Brain Size, Continues to Evolve Adaptively in Humans," University of Colorado
http://psych.colorado.edu/~carey/pdffiles/brainsizemicrocephalin_lahn.pdf

[22] http://www.mkgandhi.org/momgandhi/chap26.htm

[23] Stephen Shennan et al, "Regional population collapse followed initial agriculture booms in mid-Holocene Europe," *Nature Communications*, October 1, 2013,
http://www.nature.com/ncomms/2013/131001/ncomms3486/full/ncomms3486.html

[24] Mark B. Tauger, *Agriculture in World History*, Routledge, 2013

[25] Aristotle, *Politics* Book 5 Part 10, 350 BC

[26] Kevin Lincoln, "The 39 Most Unequal Countries in the World," *Business Insider*," retrieved October 6, 2016 http://www.businessinsider.com/most-unequal-countries-in-the-world-2011-10?op=1/#south-africa-gini-650-38

[27] Charles Hugh Smith, "Here's Why The US Is An Even Bigger Kleptocracy Than Greece," *Business Insider*, June 29, 2011,
http://www.businessinsider.com/the-us-is-a-kleptocracy-too-2011-6#ixzz3QzncBv00

[28] Allen Christenson, *PopulVuh: the Sacred Book of the Maya*, University of Oklahoma Press, 2012
http://www.aljazeera.com/news/middleeast/2014/11/gulf-states-urged-protect-migrant-workers-201411239393775227.html

[29] Dario Gamboni, *The Destruction of Art: Iconoclasm and Vandalism Since the French Revolution*, Reaktion Books, 1997

[30] Patrick Cockburn, "The destruction of the idols: Syria's patrimony at risk from extremists," *The Independent*, October 6, 2014,
http://www.independent.co.uk/news/science/archaeology/news/the-destruction-of-the-idols-syrias-patrimony-at-risk-from-extremists-9122275.html

Faust: Why this is hell, nor am I out of it.
~Christopher Marlowe (1564–1593). *Doctor Faustus*

Dystopia means "the imaginary bad place." It has been defined as "a futuristic, imagined universe in which oppressive societal control and the illusion of a perfect society are maintained through corporate, bureaucratic, technological, moral, or totalitarian control."[1] In other words, it is a 10° or 0° society which, although imaginary, is related to contemporary trends. Dystopian novels appeared with the Industrial Revolution, notably Mary Shelley's *Frankenstein* in 1818. Early stories prefigure fears that are growing today about technology. These techno-dystopias either increase human dependence on machines, watch everyone continuously, or mold citizens to fit the State's purpose by biotechnology or conditioning. In many such narratives dystopia follows a technological catastrophe such as nuclear war.

In "The Machine Stops," a 1909 story by E.M. Forster, most humans have lost the ability to live on the earth's surface, instead living underground, with all their needs met by an omnipotent Machine [AI?]. The 1924 novel *We* by Russian Yevgeny Zamyatin describes the nation of One State, constructed almost entirely of glass for constant surveillance of its people, who dress identically and have numbers instead of names.

Aldous Huxley's *Brave New World* (1932) depicts a society scientifically designed for hedonism and consumer consumption. The 2006 satirical film *Idiocracy* shows a devolved American society 500 years from now, when just about everyone is abysmally stupid. Culture consists mainly of advertising, while intellectual curiosity and social responsibility have disappeared. Kurt Vonnegut's *Player Piano* (1952) envisions a world ruled by computers. Each person's future is determined by tests that discourage imagination and encourage either/or, machine-thinking. (Today standardized testing dominates education in the UK, Europe, and the United States.)

Dystopian novels and films seem to appear in greater numbers each decade. The trend suggests widespread and increasing fear of the dangers both of uncontrolled technology (0°) and centralized power (10°). Many narratives depict a world of cut-throat competition (20°/0°), sometimes as gladiatorial life-or-death games.

Dystopian fictions from *We* to *1984* were 'inspired' by the oppressive rule of Soviet Russia under Stalin. However, multinational corporations also have the potential to create 'a bad place.' Many current settings involve either corporate malfeasance or total political control by mega-corporations, as in the films *Robocop, Tekken, Johnny Mnemonic, AI, Repo Man, Metropia*, and *Rollerball*. The science fiction genre cyberpunk is set in a near-future dystopian society dominated by brain-computer interface, AI, and robotics. In the cyberpunk world, giant multinational corporations (MNCs) have largely replaced governments.*

The literature of dystopia is a form of prophecy, saying not "This will happen" but rather "This will happen if people do not make radical changes." The dystopian genre itself expresses mainly 45° reason and 50° creative imagination, with a base of 40° concern for humanity.

Actual dystopias have been common throughout history. Instead of electronic Big Brother, they employed battalions of spies. Rulers claimed a divine right to rule, and regularly imprisoned or murdered relatives as potential rivals for the crown. They also dealt violently with any opposition to their authority or disagreement with their policies

*In the real world, most MNCs are invested in at least six foreign countries; they compete in oligopolistic markets (shared monopolies) and form strategic alliances with each other. Many MNCs involve telecommunications, banking, and information technology, which together form the nerve network of modern society. In the United States, the major home country of MNCs, these and other large corporations have already gained the legal status and many of the benefits of personhood and citizenship. Some observers argue that economic globalization combined with computer technology threatens the continuation of the system of nation-states under which the world has lived since the 17th century. "The Multinational Corporation and Global Governance," Indiana University. www.indiana.edu/~ipe/spero04.pdf
Historical precursors of the dystopian megacorporation included the British East India Company, Dutch East India Company, Hudson Bay Company, and the United Fruit Company.

The absolute monarch with life-and-death authority is a 10° construction which has not disappeared, but continues in the form of dictatorships. These can even become hereditary like royal dynasties (Duvaliers in Haiti or Kims in North Korea). For thousands of years, the model for most societies has been rule by one powerful ruler, his family and henchmen. Dystopian regimes of this traditional kind still exist in many places such as Uzbekistan and Zimbabwe.

If civilization is 6,000 years old, then we have tried the experiment of representative democracy (U.S. Constitution) for only about four percent of that time. Not everyone fully understands this 35°/45° system as yet, even in the U.S. Without strong traditions, knowledge, and effort, countries tend to slide back into 10° patterns.

Historian Ian Kershaw points out that on the eve of World War II, three-fifths of Europeans lived under authoritarian regimes. (And that doesn't even include the USSR under Stalin.)[2]

Authoritarian governments come in several varieties. In a police state, the government exercises power arbitrarily and makes extensive use of repressive police forces and a network of spies and informers. Examples include ancient Sparta with its secret police or *Krypteia;* Tudor England, Batista's Cuba, Chile under Pinochet, Iran 1957-1979, and Belarus today.

Totalitarianism, a 20th century phenomenon, took advantage of new technology and techniques such as advertising/propaganda, radio, television, brainwashing, and surveillance. Such regimes do what had been done earlier in history—only more thoroughly. Unlike garden-variety dictatorships, totalitarian regimes try to command every aspect of public and private life, an intimate control that suggests sadism (0°).

For instance, Nicolae Ceaușescu, dictator of Romania, tried to direct childbearing, asserting that "The fetus is the property of the entire society. Anyone who avoids having children is a deserter who abandons the laws of national continuity." Ceaușescu's police regularly took women of childbearing age from their workplaces to clinics, where government agents examined them for signs of pregnancy. But babies that were born under the rule of Ceaușescu had a high death rate because of general poverty and food shortages.

Fascism describes one-party states with a radical ideology calling for a return to traditional, patriarchal themes such as nationalism, militarism, and expansionism. The state maintains strict control over education and media. Fascism began in 20th century Italy and Germany. The latter added a fanatical racism leading to massive genocide (0°/5°). In Spain, Franco was inspired by Mussolini and adopted many of his methods, matching or exceeding the Italian dictator's brutality. Even after winning the bloody civil war he instigated, Franco executed at least a quarter of a million more people. During the 1930s, a number of Central and South American countries also had dictatorships modeled to some degree after fascist Italy.

Fascist ideologues see war and violence as creative forces, thus rationalizing both 5° aggression and 10° power drive. Another aspect of fascist ideology is exaltation of the will over reason, again a rationalization of 5° aggression. Some see the roots of fascist ideology in philosophers such as Schopenhauer, Nietzsche, Sorel, Gentile, and Strauss. Fascist constructs may be distortions of what these philosopher said, or some of their ideas may have been flawed from the beginning.[3]

Several writers describe a more subtle kind of totalitarianism disguised as a free society with the populace controlled and manipulated by propaganda and consumerism. Bertram Gross called it "friendly fascism" (1980). Political philosopher Sheldon Wolin described the United States as "inverted totalitarianism" in which economics controls politics while the public is apathetic and distracted (10°/15°/25°).[4]

An important aspect of all modern tyrannies is negative propaganda: a barrage of false or misleading information and rumors (10° deception) that appeals to lower dispositions and behaviors. War and the build-up to war are hotbeds of negative propaganda aimed at gaining citizens' support for the conflict by promoting hatred of the designated enemy. Partisan politics is a second major arena, and a number of social issues come in third. Behind the oratory of individual demagogues are political strategists and enablers of demagoguery—the masterminds of propaganda such as Joseph Goebbels or Karl Rove.

Those who produce negative propaganda typically operate at an oppositional 20° as do many of those who are receptive to it. One of the rules of propaganda (stated by Goebbels) is to present every situation in black-and-white terms, never allowing the public to think of alternatives. The propagandist also employs the 10° drive for power and the 10° lying used to gain it. The most clearly negative campaigns appeal to 5° fears and defensive violence. They target traditional enemies, instigate moral panics, and scapegoat minority populations. The result may be riots, massacres, and/or the election of strongman candidates. Another receptive audience is the 15° person who tends to obey his chosen authority and who is intellectually confused.

Other dispositions are also in play, especially with authoritarian governments. The egocentric indifference of 25° allows free rein to would-be dictators. Many at 30° and even some at 35° are hoodwinked by especially clever manipulation of their sense of duty or ideals.

For all varieties of centralized governments, the big new factor is cyber technology. Great advances in surveillance techniques create fears even among citizens of the rich Western democracies. James Bamford has been warning us about "technotyranny" for over three decades, saying in *The Shadow Factory*: "There is now the capacity to make tyranny total in America. Only law ensures that we never fall into that abyss—the abyss from which there is no return." [5, 6]

Cryptohippie—a business that provides computer security—describes an electronic police state. Eventually "the Electronic Police State destroys free speech, the right to petition the government for redress of grievances, and other liberties. Worse, it does so in a way that is difficult to identify." Cryptohippie lists nation-states advancing toward an electronic police state: North Korea, China, Belarus, Russia, the UK, and the U.S. at 6th place. Note also the "Five Eyes" or FVEY, an intelligence alliance linking Australia, Canada, New Zealand, the UK, and the U.S. Former NSA contractor Edward Snowden described FVEY as a "supra-national intelligence organization that doesn't answer to the known laws of its own countries." [7, 8]

Dystopias of all kinds tend toward 0° by their subordination of living beings to a system of control, often a bureaucratic system that reduces humans to things.

Evil on the Grand Scale

The question is not how to get good people to rule; the question is how to stop the powerful from doing as much damage as they can to us.
~Karl Popper, Austrian-English philosopher, 1902-1994

After World War II, Polish psychiatrist Andrew Lobaczewski, with other psychologists behind the Iron Curtain developed the field of ponerology, the scientific study of evil. In *Political Ponerology*, Lobaczewski describes his main concern, which is *pathocracy* or government by mentally unbalanced leaders.[9]

Lobaczewski says European civilization lacks resistance to evil because of the influence of Roman habits of legal thinking "conceived for invented and simplified beings [20°]" and indifferent to human nature and variety. Nor is Lobaczewski entirely happy with the Western psychology that developed as a science in the 1870s, because it rejected as non-scientific all previous knowledge of psychology*

Lobaczewski says that much of what we call evil has been caused by people with psychological abnormalities due to brain lesions, sometimes unsuspected and subtle; the effects of certain diseases and substances including some medical drugs; and hereditary conditions among which he includes psychopathy. Lobaczewski makes clear that ponerology should be a scientific, humanitarian, and therapeutic field that does not scapegoat those who are psychologically abnormal. He emphasizes that moralistic attitudes actually impede understanding. However, it remains to be seen how people will use this knowledge.

Others are thinking along similar lines. Barbara Oakley adds Borderline Personality Disorder as another coexisting psychiatric conditions often present in national leaders who create tyranny on the large scale. Irish psychiatrist Ian Hughes says three personality disorders account for much of the world's evil because they are often present in leaders of authoritarian regimes: Narcissistic Personality Disorder, Psychopathy, and Paranoid Personality Disorder.[10]

*Some versions of Buddhism and other Eastern religions embody more psychological knowledge. See Alan Watts, *Psychotherapy East and West*, Pantheon 1961.

The most famous example of pathocracy is Nazi Germany, whose psychopathic elite was well-studied during the Nuremberg trials. Stalin, Mao, Pol Pot, and Ceauşescu also showed signs of serious mental disorders. Inner circles in the U.S.S.R. and in Maoist China were known to contain other disturbed personalities besides the top leader. For instance, Lavrentiy Beria, head of the Soviet secret police (NKVD) under Stalin, was a sexual predator who raped numerous young women and murdered some who resisted.[11] Pathology tends to attract pathology.

Even the higher dispositions can contribute to dystopia, led by 30° fears about stability and security, or 35° desires for change which ingenuously assumes that change will be progress. The 45° struggle for independence and freedom is too often coopted by an authoritarian leader and a new form of tyranny.

[1] Terri Chung, *Dystopian Literarature Primer*, National Council of Teachers of English (NCTE),
http://facweb.northseattle.edu/jclapp/Children's%20Literature/Discussion%20Questions/Dystopias%20Characteristics.htm
[2] Ian Kershaw, *To Hell and Back: Europe 1914-1949*, Penguin 2016
[3] "Nazi Fascism and the Modern Totalitarian State,"
http://remember.org/guide/Facts.root.nazi.html
[4] Sheldon Wolin, *Democracy Incorporated: Managed Democracy and the Specter of Inverted Totalitarianism,* Princeton University Press, 2008
[5] Alexander Nazaryan, "The N.S.A.'s Chief Chronicler," *The New Yorker*, June 10, 2013, http://www.newyorker.com/books/page-turner/the-n-s-a-s-chief-chronicler
[6] James Bamford, *The Shadow Factory: The NSA from 9/11 to the Eavesdropping on America,* Doubleday 2008
[7] Cryptohippie, "The Electronic Police State: 2010 National Rankings,"
https://secure.cryptohippie.com/pubs/EPS-2010.pdf
[8] Snowden-Interview: Transcript
http://www.ndr.de/nachrichten/netzwelt/snowden277_page-2.html
[9] Andrzej Łobaczewski, *Political Ponerology: A Science on the Nature of Evil Adjusted for Political Purposes*, trans. Alexandra Chciuk-Celt, Red Pill Press, 2006
[10] Ian Hughes, "Q&A on Dangerous Personality Disorders Part 1"
http://disorderedworld.com/2014/05/17/qa-on-dangerous-personality-disorders/
[11] Ta-Nahisi Coates, "Grappling With History's Greatest Gangsters: Thoughts on Timothy Snyder's *Bloodlands,"* *The Atlantic,* January 15, 2015
https://www.theatlantic.com/international/archive/2014/01/grappling-with-historys-greatest-gangsters/283083/

Chapter 11
15° Confusion

A man who does not think for himself does not think at all.
~ Oscar Wilde

Imitation is the most basic tool of learning for social animals such as ourselves, for by it we learn to speak and behave like human beings. Yet at some point we must reach beyond those necessary role models in order to develop our full potential. Thus there is something immature, as yet unformed, about the 15° disposition, which has not developed a clear identity and agency of his own. He tends to be mentally and emotionally dependent on somebody or something else. 15° follows the crowd, a leader, rigid rules, a simplified ideology, or religious dogma.

Lacking discernment and self-insight, at 15° a person is unable to act as a true individual. In the vocabulary of mental health care, he has boundary issues or suffers from codependency. People under the sway of 15° are not very functional in society and have not had the support they needed from their culture. This lack of support may date back for generations or centuries.

It is not surprising that many of us are unable to make our own decisions, since throughout history most people's lives have been at the mercy of others. In many cultures, it was customary for parents to choose their children's mates, while each generation of males was constrained to follow their father's occupation. Few men or women were able to rise out of the family's social and economic class. The king, emperor, or sultan had life or death powers over his subjects, who suffered from his decisions to make war or to tax them into poverty in order to build extravagant monuments to himself.

In most societies, women were taught to obey their husbands without question. This is still true in many less-developed nations and among fundamentalists of several religions. Men are by nature somewhat larger with greater upper-body strength than women, and they are not physically encumbered by pregnancy, childbirth, and nursing. However, in modern conditions these physical differences have become increasingly irrelevant to the work of the world. Nor did they ever really justify subservience of half the race.

A great many of our ancestors were slaves, prisoners of war, conquered peoples, serfs, indentured servants, sharecroppers, or seamen pressed into duty aboard sailing ships. They built pyramids and cathedrals, rowed galleys, worked in the fields, marched as foot soldiers, served as maids or concubines. Few were ever expected or encouraged to think or act for themselves. It is easy to see why many people today have not fully developed their own autonomy.

For most of the world, representative democracy is very new. Even the U.S. Constitution, a model for ten generations, originally left out citizenship for women, slaves, Native Americans, indentured servants, and men without property. Many nations have attempted representative government only recently, and some have never had it. Until a democracy is well established, with supporting traditions and institutions, there is a 15° tendency to fall back into ancient forms of one-man rule. As Doris Lessing said in *The Golden Notebook*, "We all have this need for the great man, and create him over and over again in the face of all the evidence."

Obedience

When you think of the long and gloomy history of man, you will find more hideous crimes have been committed in the name of obedience than have ever been committed in the name of rebellion.
~ C.P. Snow, chemist and novelist, 1905-1980

The virtues of obedience are often promoted by authorities, whether parental, pedagogical, religious, military, or governmental. Clearly obedience has its uses in raising young children or training pets. With adults, it's a different matter. Submission to authority figures can mean that one follows the orders of a person who is operating at a very low disposition, lower than your own.

Hierarchies are created by 20° to organize people, especially men, into tiers of obedience. This is an accepted part of several important social institutions. Military organizations are notable for their strict hierarchy and discipline. 15° is often quite comfortable in institutions such as the military, bureaucracies, and large corporations because they provide a coherent structure that 15° lacks in himself. Some individuals even find a comfort in living in prison, where they have no responsibilities and most decisions are made for them.

One can submit voluntarily to the discipline of a firefighting crew or a dance troupe. Voluntary obedience by a member of a religious order or the student of a spiritual teacher can reinforce an individual's self-discipline. However, each individual must make a careful choice of whom to follow lest he or she end up in a situation like Jonestown or Heaven's Gate. *Blind* obedience is hardly a virtue.

Rote learning and strict discipline characterized education for many centuries and still do in some countries. To a lesser degree, American public schools promote 15° with emphasis on 'one right answer' and reliance on standardized testing that inhibits lateral thinking or deeper judgment.

Some 15° have so little character structure that they are on the verge of being sociopathic and 5° violent without a firm authority or a rigid religious orthodoxy to obey. They tend to think that everyone else requires the same kind of external control. These authoritarians believe in hierarchy and chains of command. They will seek and defend suitably severe and uncompromising leaders, who espouse a clear and simple ideology. Authoritarians thrive on hierarchical organizations and 'law and order.' In the most problematic situations, an individual gives up his own worldview or his conscience to another person or group.

In classic experiments by Yale psychologist Stanley Milgram in the 1960s, research subjects were directed to give increasingly strong electric shocks to others if they failed test questions. In reality, all the "learners" were confederates of the experimenters, and no electric shocks were actually given. But in the belief that they were administering painful and quite possibly dangerous levels of electricity—although in conflict with their personal conscience—six out of ten people obeyed authority.[1] These experiments suggest that the majority of people even in a democratic nation will revert to 15° disposition when directed by official authority figures. The minority who refused to cooperate in Milgram's experiment tended to be more educated, or to be expert in some field so that they felt justified in setting up their own authority against that of the experimenters.

Besides obedience to authority, there is also obedience to rules. Bureaucracy is built on the idea that rules replace individual judgments. The same mindset leads to religious dogma, red tape, and Catch-22. People who think and behave largely in terms of rules in their personal lives lack mature judgment. They do not develop the ability to see the consequences of their actions. *Unintended consequences* are associated with 15° confusion as well as with 20° ideologies.

Yet another form of obedience is excessive conformity to a group such as a business or a political party. Ideology demands that one be 'a team player' above all other considerations. Loyalty is a 30° value, but 30° maintains an individual conscience and is able to recognize when his loyalty is misplaced. Not so 15°.

Are Good and Evil 3,200 Years Old?

No one is moral among the god-controlled puppets of the Iliad. *Good and evil do not exist.*
~Julian Jaynes, *The Origin of Consciousness in the Breakdown of the Bicameral Mind,* 1976

It is possible that modern consciousness is fairly recent. I refer to the theory of the bicameral mind outlined by psychologist Julian Jaynes, using evidence from anthropology, neurology, linguistics, psychology, and ancient literature, since added to by others, especially by brain researchers. Jaynes proposes that from the beginning of Near Eastern civilizations about 9,000 BC and up until about 1200 BC, ancient people did not think as we do. Instead, in times of stress or crisis, the speech center of the brain's right hemisphere gave orders to the left—received as auditory commands from the gods or their official representatives. [2]

According to Jaynes, bicameralism characterized the earliest agricultural civilizations, theocracies with absolute rulers. This consciousness could coexist with arithmetic, building, and other practical arts (although the invention of writing may have helped undermine it). It has been called "zombie civilization." Most people in such a system would express the 15° disposition, with total obedience the norm. Jaynes says that at this stage we humans had very little sense of our own agency, no subjectivity or introspection, no capacity for moral reasoning or deliberate deception, and no sense of a unified "I." Without a modern consciousness, these ancient humans could not be said to have had free will.

Jaynes says bicameralism gradually disappeared after a series of upheavals around 1200 BC in the Mediterranean, European, and Near Eastern world—possibly more widely—known as the late Bronze Age collapse. It was a chaotic time of wars, environmental decline, and a great movement of invaders or refugees such as the Sea Peoples. Climate changes caused a 300-year drought and famines. There was possibly a pandemic, and new battle weapons and strategies.[2]

Jaynes argues that all these challenges, added to the confusion of meeting other peoples who listened to other gods, caused the disruption of the bicameral mind and the transition to modern subjective consciousness. This latent capacity, modern consciousness, was contagious. Now increasingly there was metaphorical use of language and the creation of interior space, the 'I'. The story of Eden in the second Book of Genesis relates how Adam and Eve ate of the fruit of the Tree of Knowledge of Good and Evil, after which they are driven from paradise for disobeying the word of God. Is this an allegory about the transition to modern consciousness?

However, Chinese scholar You-Sheng Li believes that modern consciousness began much earlier and that bicameralism did not characterize all civilizations. "Subjective consciousness might have first appeared with the tool explosion around forty thousand years ago and switched to the bicameral mind in early Mediterranean civilizations but not in early Chinese civilization." It may well be that bicameralism was the dominant form of consciousness in the theocratic, hierarchal societies of the Middle East that formed the Western tradition but not in other places such as northern Europe, Ireland, Russia, India, or China. [3]

Jaynes says hypnotism, schizophrenia, and religious ecstasy are modern throwbacks to this older form of human awareness. We could also note the tendency of most human beings, even educated ones in wealthy countries, to look for an authority to tell them what to do; or to believe what they hear, read, and view without critical examination. We may still be transitioning from the bicameral mind to subjective consciousness. And this has implications for our views of human agency and individual responsibility.

15° Mental Patterns

Nowhere am I so desperately needed as among a shipload of illogical humans.
~Mr. Spock in "I, Mudd," *Star Trek* Series

Insofar as people are emotional thinkers—unable to distinguish between their emotions and their thoughts—their thinking is at 15°. This is true whether a person's political orientation is Left, Right, or something else entirely. While able to handle the practicalities of a job or running a small business, in many areas of life 15° tends to think in terms of story lines, with heroes and villains, friends and enemies. She tends to personalize issues and to personify nations, states of the union, ethnicities, occupations, and other groupings of people, especially those outside her own tribe. It is not surprising that 15° is especially susceptible to conspiracy theories, which are another kind of story.

This tendency to dramatize public life and international affairs may have increased among the world's population in recent decades because of the many stories people watch on television, videos, and movies. At 15° one tends to be a creature of the media. Some find it hard to separate fiction from reality, assuming that characters on television shows are real people, not actors, or that grocery store tabloids are sources of actual news. All this is not surprising, when many people have been plunked in front of televisions sets since they were toddlers.

The preference for stories also affects public perception of the news. The first narrative created and widely disseminated by a journalist or politician to explain newsworthy events is likely to become the conventional wisdom. Later explanations may fit the facts better, but the early narrative is very hard to dislodge, especially from 15° thinking. This disposition is also prone to be captured by the anecdotal fallacy ('misleading vividness') in which one or a few dramatic incidents seem to be more prevalent than they are.

At 15° a person finds it hard to recognize figurative language, such as metaphors or personification, since he does not separate it from factual language. Although drawn to the toys of technology and the wonders of modern medicine, 15° has little capacity to think in the abstract terms of science. Traditional people at 30° may prefer to rely on their own observations, but 15° neither makes his own observations, nor does he test the received knowledge.

A 15° subculture is highly suspicious of too much learning. About this, Isaac Asimov said: "Anti-intellectualism has been a constant thread winding its way through our political and cultural life, nurtured by the false notion that democracy means that 'my ignorance is just as good as your knowledge'." Many observers believe that Americans have been 'dumbed down' over the past several decades. People read less and less, and our school children do not show up well on international tests compared with those from other advanced countries. A traditional anti-intellectualism has been joined by anti-rationalism, particularly aimed at science in the areas of evolution, climate change, or scientific findings that threaten any well-funded economic interest.

15° is highly vulnerable to manipulation by 20°, including the strategy of FUD, or the sowing of fear, uncertainty, and doubt. Citizens at 15° are the most natural audience for demagoguery. Sometimes the demagogue actually thinks this way himself.

Opinionated and defensive, 15° tends to discount other views than his own. He preemptively projects the 'tin-foil hat' label onto others, but is unable to tell the difference between 15° confusion and complex ideas at 45° or 50°. He is not likely to change his own mind or even listen to other viewpoints, but is loyal to his own fixed opinions. He may use the most tortured reasoning because the whole point is to say his piece and to win the argument however he may.

Predictably, in clashes of ideas 15° often employs the appeal to authority. He uses plenty of non sequiturs, and does not notice that he contradicts himself. Many 15° arguments resemble those of children: Other people did it first. My authority is better than your authority. If you're worried about the sea turtles, why don't *you* go and rescue them? The "arrogant ignorant." are so convinced of their rightness on various issues that they cannot actually listen and respond to the opinions of others, and discussions degenerate into 5° taunting, insults, and abuse.

Under the spell of this degree, people cannot seem to think for themselves, as if thinking is too confusing and takes too many steps. They are gullible and highly susceptible to ads, propaganda, rumors, and classic conspiracy theories.

Television and film dramas are problematic, if for instance they replace or prevent rational thought for people who are relatively uneducated or otherwise susceptible to manipulation by propaganda. Anecdotes are much more compelling than statistics. From reading or viewing genre fiction and mediocre dramas, a person may mistake the nature of his or her social context .Constant viewers of crime dramas believe themselves in greater personal danger than they are. An individual may self-dramatize or exaggerate personal events to fit some familiar narrative, or imitate the actions of television or film characters.

Gullible 15° is the natural target of advertisers. You wonder who on earth would buy a drug touted on television commercials after the announcer reports something like this: "Possible side effects include seizures, lycanthropy, bleeding from every pore, and turning bright orange." Yet 15° goes right out and buys phizelbane to cure his warts. The customer may rationalize that "the government makes them list those things" or "it's unlikely to happen to *me*." Perhaps he simply tunes out what he doesn't want to hear.

Another trait is a psychological need for a quick resolution and one right answer. The 15° person must always settle for the simplest explanation, a mental recipe, or a slogan. The constant search for a 'quick fix' to technical or social problems—the 'Band-Aid approach'—often results in unintended consequences.

Lack of mental flexibility has been called *sphexism* after behavior of the *Sphex* female wasp, which captures and paralyzes a cricket to put in the burrow with her eggs to provide fresh food for her young when they hatch. She puts the cricket on the ground by the entrance and goes into the burrow, apparently checking for intruders. However, if the experimenter moves the cricket ever so slightly, Ms. Sphex comes back out, drags the cricket back to its original position, and re-enters the burrow. This cycle can be repeated dozens of times.

Though operating far above the instinctual behavior of insects, 15° often seems stuck in a mind-set (tunnel vision) that doesn't resemble real thinking. She is so anxious to find the one and only right answer that she turns every idea into dogma. Those stuck in 15° are often hyper-partisan about chosen leaders and beliefs. While loyalty is a virtue, to continue to place faith in a man or an ideology regardless of evidence indicates 15° sphexism rather than 30° fidelity.

Attachment to one simple idea at a time allows 15° to ignore contradictions in his or her beliefs and opinions, saying yea in one breath and nay in the next without seeming to care about the discrepancy. It appears his beliefs and opinions are not held very deeply; words are used merely as game tokens.

Psychologist Robert Hare notes excessive self-contradiction in the conversation of criminal psychopaths, who apparently do not actually have a clear conception of what is true or not true. At 15° some individuals may be the gullible victim or follower of a glib and manipulative psychopath; some may be sub-criminal psychopaths themselves, perhaps part of a psychopathic subculture (5°), inclined towards violence. Attitudes are based largely on unrelated slogans, prejudices, fear, and defense mechanisms such as denial and projection.

15° may adopt a primitive ideology (myth) or take the most appealing bits and pieces of a 20° ideology for waving as war banners or bludgeoning opponents in an argument. With black and white categories, 15° constructs dramatic narratives. For instance, many

Americans see foreign nations as entities with personalities—stock characters—and current events like a Western film with its white hats and black hats. Israel is a good guy, Iran and Russia are bad guys though maybe Russia has reformed. Greece is a deadbeat that won't pay its debts. These Punch and Judy shows make few distinctions between past and present, leaders and led, or one socioeconomic class and another.

The most slavish followers of ideologies that follow from a personality cult or political religion are at 15°. Despite the spread of democracy and public education, a great many people are looking for someone to tell them how to think and what to do. 15° overuses denial as a personal defense mechanism, and some 15° ideologies are characterized by denial of well-established and accepted facts, for instance Holocaust denial or climate change denial. Fatalism, a deterministic doctrine that everything is preordained by immutable fate, promotes 15° submissive attitudes and a sense of powerlessness.

The 15° ideology of Nihilism is a rejection of all distinctions in morality or religious belief. In repudiating all previous theories Nihilism is the simplistic reverse side of dogmatic belief in one system.*

Rationalization is a common maneuver, especially in the lower dispositions. We all justify ourselves to ourselves; we need an excuse, however lame. For example, a co-worker was pilfering from our employer and also my purse before she was discovered and fired. Her defense was this: since other people had victimized her in various ways, it was only fair for her to do the same thing to us. This is the Leaden Rule "Do wrong unto others just as somebody else did wrong unto you."

Two psychologists, Lawrence R. James and James M. LeBreton, designed a system to identify aggressive personalities based on the observation that people who are in the habit of creating falsely rational defenses for their own acts are attracted to similar reasoning by others. This helps explain scapegoating and susceptibility to demagoguery.[4]

Someone acting at 5° may defend his emotional reactivity, rage and violent actions with "She asked for it" or "He was looking at me funny." This person may not be good at reading other people's faces, tone of voice, or body language. He was perhaps raised in a violent family. To people who were raised by authoritarians, the bully's 10° energy may feel like leadership. If the bully is an influential person, his rationalizations may spread to become part of the ethos, perpetuating themselves indefinitely in a cultural form of sociopathy.

In an unprovoked or "preemptive" war, nation-state X attacks nation-state Y while rationalizing that Y is getting ready to attack, and "Offense is the best defense." This is another Leaden Rule: "Do unto others before they do it to you." It assumes that everybody is out to get you (5° fears). James and LeBreton say aggressive people commonly use a justification mechanism known as the *hostile attribution bias* or a tendency to perceive hostile intent in others and to overestimate the threat of danger. Thus the aggressive ones convince themselves that their own hostile behavior is actually self-defense.

An ancient excuse, "The end justifies the means," is a 10° or 20° version of *Consequentialism:* an action is right or wrong according to whether its consequences are good or bad. This theory seems to be a minority view among philosophers. One problem is that the full consequences of an action may not be observed until long afterwards, if ever. We may not even be able to observe all the consequences, much less judge whether they are good or bad, and for whom.

Another popular ethical perspective is Utilitarianism, which resembles Mr. Spock's statement that "the needs of the many outweigh the needs of the few." It is also summarized as "the greatest good for the greatest number." This notion can serve as a rough guide, but applied rigidly (20° ideology) it can justify the tyranny of the majority. In a crisis, higher dispositions 30° and 35° may temporarily accede to distortions of utilitarianism, perhaps distracted by propaganda, or after viewing a drama with the improbable plotline that one must torture some individual in order to save a city, converting an insight about the greatest good into an evil dictum.

*Nihilism as the 19th century revolutionary movement in Russia was more complex, merging the desire for scientific rationality and social progress (20°-35°) with 5° righteous violence and detached 0° violence.

> *The root of suffering is attachment.*
> ~The Buddha

Attachment (clinging, grasping) to one thing, one idea, or one behavior may show up as an addiction, whether to substances legal or illegal, to shopping, eating, gambling, risky sex, or texting. There is even a newly recognized disorder called 'maladaptive daydreaming' in which sufferers become so addicted to (for instance) imagining themselves and their acquaintances as part of television show plots that they have no psychic energy for actual relationships.

Adam Alter, author of *Irresistible: The Rise of Addictive Technology and the Business of Keeping Us Hooked*, says that digital addictions—to cell phones, Facebook, Instagram, Snapchat, and such—are as dangerous as heroin. Gaming and Internet addiction are especially prevalent in East Asia, where it was reported in 2010 that almost a million South Korean youth were addicted. Alter notes these lonely or depressed youths are drawn to activities that don't require initiative, creative thinking, or much face-to-face interaction. In some countries the prevalence of cyber cafes contributes to the problem. China has several highly regimented treatment centers for addicted adolescents but no longer uses electroshock therapy after several teens died. (ECT is controversial but legal in Western countries including the U.S.) [5, 6]

The inability to think ahead to the next step leads to behavior that disregards consequences. The propensity to follow a stronger personality can lead 15° into crime, or to "being in the wrong place at the wrong time." This is the person who especially needs to avoid bad companions. Some commit 'copy-cat crimes.' Many petty thieves, shoplifters, check forgers, and other small-time crooks are acting at 15°. They often make egregious mistakes and are quickly apprehended. The U.S. criminal justice system tends to treat petty crime with special severity using mandatory sentence laws.[7]

People often set up pointless pranks at 15°. A high-school student attending a summer program put an envelope filled with foot-powder in a janitor's closet. On edge about white powders after the anthrax scare of 2001, officials deployed all sorts of emergency technicians and equipment, while the janitor sought medical attention. Nobody got the joke. Impulsiveness and inability to foresee consequences is typical adolescent behavior but can persist into adulthood.

Internet trolls who enjoy sidetracking discussions and annoying people are acting at 15°. They may not be capable of conducting a reasoned discourse.

Crowds often behave at 15° (and lower) as the process of *deindividuation* takes over. Sociologist Leon Mann studied how deindividuation works in "suicide baiting" when bystanders encourage a person to jump from a high building. Michael Marshall, moderator of the *New Scientist* website, said "Mann found that people were more likely to do this if they were part of a large crowd, if the jumper was above the 7th floor, and if it was dark. These are all factors that allowed the observers to lose their own individuality." Marshall adds that something similar happens with online communication. "Psychologically, we are 'distant' from the person we're talking to and less focused on our own identity. As a result we're more prone to aggressive behavior." [8]

On the larger scale, 15° is "the fog of war" and spectacularly bad decisions by military leaders such as the Charge of the Light Brigade or the Battle of Little Big Horn. It is comedies of error such as Grenada and tragedies of error such as the war in Vietnam.

The Love of Money

Acquisition means life to miserable mortals.
~Hesiod, Greek poet active between 750 and 650 B.C.

The well-known misers and money-grubbers of literature and history are often behaving at 15°. Misers are sufficiently common to have become regular characters in fiction and drama, such as Ebenezer Scrooge, Shylock, Harpagon, and Silas Marner. In Ben Jonson's play

Volpone (1606) several characters who are fixated on money have animal names as in a fable: the greedy Volpone (Sly Fox), the miserly Corbaccio (Raven), the intriguing servant Mosca (Fly), and the scavenging lawyer Voltore (Vulture). Centuries later, comedian Jack Benny got laughs from portraying a cheapskate.

Penny-pinchers include some of the world's richest men and women. Hetty Green was so fabulously wealthy that she personally bailed out the City of New York three times, taking short-term revenue bonds in repayment. Yet she lived in her office on Wall Street and cooked on the radiator to save the cost of heating an apartment. Oil billionaire J. Paul Getty was also noted for his stinginess. But some of the very rich lived frugally in order to support their philanthropy (35°).

Gambling and get-rich-quick schemes are the other side of the miser's coin. Gold rushes are accompanied by gold fever. The craze for tulips led to the first financial bubble in the 1630s—'tulip mania'. Just before the crash a rare tulip bulb cost as much as a luxurious house. Bubbles and crashes continued through history, with a housing bubble in the 2000s leading to yet another crash. The desire for sudden great wealth also continues to support lotteries, sweepstakes contests, and casinos, and allows people to become victims of a multitude of scams.

All kinds of insurance are in a sense gambling on the vagaries of fortune. The stock market is also based on gambles.

Incompetence

> *In a hierarchy every employee tends to rise to his level of incompetence ... in time every post tends to be occupied by an employee who is incompetent to carry out its duties.*
> ~Laurence J. Peter, *The Peter Principle*, 1968

Employee incompetence may result from the employee's being placed above his or her capabilities as in "the Peter Principle." On the other hand, the Peter Principle refers to *hierarchies*, which by their nature are specialized and routinized. Such posts do not call for whole persons to fill them, and they do not satisfy whole persons. Also circumstances may force people to work at employment that does not match their skills, talents, and interests—work that rather than being above their capabilities is *unrelated* to them. Many educated people have worked at low-skill jobs from economic necessity.

Actual incompetence on the job includes passive-aggressive behavior or low-grade sabotage. The personality who conveys his anger indirectly tells hostile jokes, procrastinates, deliberately makes mistakes, intentionally fails to hear or notice the targeted person, consciously misunderstands or "forgets," acts sullen and resentful, and complains of being a victim or of being cheated. Incompetence can also include petty theft and fraudulent practices. In his listing of psychological reasons for unethical business behavior, a Dutch researcher, Dr. Muel Kaptein includes one that applies especially to 15°, obedience to authority. He says that in large organizations where people feel like cogs in a machine, out of touch with leadership and goals, they are more likely to steal, commit fraud, or neglect their duties. The 15° disposition needs to relate to strong leadership.

Dr. Kaptein also says people who are tired or hungry—perhaps from skipping lunch, or eating sugary snacks for quick energy—have less self-control for resisting temptations to act unethically. 15° is already prone to confusion, and sleep deprivation or low blood sugar does not help the situation. [10]

The Dunning-Kruger effect (after researchers Justin Kruger and David Dunning) describes a cognitive bias in which people lack the capacity to properly evaluate their poor performance on a task. Because they are unaware of their incompetence, they do not take any self-improvement measures. Repeated experiments found that the poorest performers tended to overestimate their performance by roughly 30%. The researchers subsequently found that teaching specific reasoning skills to the low-performing subjects enabled them to self-evaluate themselves much more realistically and improve their performance. [11]

Individuals in high places, including leaders of nations or candidates for that post, may greatly overestimate their own abilities and powers. (Unfortunately, no mechanism exists to teach better reasoning skills and self-insight to national leaders).

Incompetence may start at the top, when industrial managers require employees to work 'fast and dirty' so that they make more goods though shoddier ones, destroying any sense of craftsmanship. The employer may be not merely incompetent, but also a 'toxic leader,' perfectionist and inflexible, who bullies, frequently loses his temper, sets people up to fail, or otherwise leaves both the business or organization worse off than before his or her leadership.

Inefficiency is often built into the system. Management operates from the top down without feedback from the people who actually do the work. The popular comic-strip "Dilbert" depicts incompetent managers who don't seem to have a clue about what their subordinates actually do. Management may set up practices that are bound to be inefficient and standards that are impossible to achieve. There may be lack of communication, micromanagement, or procedural inflexibility.

Managers often impose a new and sexier technology without analyzing the local situation. For instance, it is a given (in the U.S.) that every business and agency must operate as much as possible online. Yet expensive computer systems even at the state or federal level may be full of bugs that drive workers crazy. One branch of an agency is unable to communicate with another branch, or employees are required to take laptop applications instead of paper forms, greatly increasing the time field workers spend yet without any particular advantage.

Businesses, institutions, and government agencies that grow in size past efficiencies of scale lead to inefficiencies of 'too-bigness'. The dinosaur's small brain just cannot control the mammoth creature, which becomes top-heavy or simply loses sight of its purpose and mission.

Operating far from original intentions, many institutions continue as is through sheer inertia. Thus it seems that the rising costs of higher education in the United States reflect the creation of many well-paid administrative support positions, while academic instruction is increasingly delegated to part-time, untenured adjuncts or teaching assistants. U.S. farm subsidies, originally set up in the 1930s Depression in order to protect family farms, are now paid mostly to large corporate farms. These examples of too-bigness and inertia may be multiplied many times over, and are the special targets of 35° reformers.

Crankery

> *There exists a secret society with branches throughout the*
> *world, and its plot is to spread the rumor that a universal plot exists.*
> ~Umberto Eco, *Foucault's Pendulum*

A crank is defined as someone who holds an unshakable belief in something that most contemporaries consider to be ludicrously false. The crank latches on to some notion and holds on for dear life like a pit bull. He is prone to buttonhole people to tell them about it. Besides the unswerving nature of the person's belief, and the falsity of the belief, a third connotation of anger or irritability often attaches to the word crank.

Other people may also hold firmly to their principles or a belief-system but at higher levels of awareness, more reflective and thoughtful, and without the need to aggressively push their views on others. It is the inflexible, simplistic and dogmatic tendency, impervious to contrary evidence that indicates a 15° crank.

A person dominated by this disposition is strongly suspicious and sometimes has a paranoid personality disorder. He (more rarely she) does not trust very many people or social institutions, and feels he must rely on his own interpretations. Lacking wide knowledge of the matter at hand, he doesn't feel any obligation to seek out real evidence before coming to his conclusions, and often simply follows the opinions of someone else, perhaps a well-known conspiracy theorist such as Alex Jones, David Icke, or Jeff Rense.

'Denialists' who reject propositions strongly supported by scientific or historical evidence are often manipulated by propagandists who have their own agendas (20°). Some cranks simply enjoy holding opinions contrary to majority belief. One sure sign of crankery is belief in a number of unrelated conspiracy theories at one and the same time (e.g., Dale Gribble on the television show "King of the Hill").

But conspiracy theories are not all created equal. Although some are clearly fanciful smears aimed at politicians, while other propose an enduring, global conspiracy led by extremely powerful and totally evil entities, more credible theories draw on evidence and concern a more limited political, economic, or criminal situation.

It can be difficult to distinguish between new, divergent ideas and those that are merely eccentric and weird. There are times when the majority of one's contemporaries are wrong. Giordano Bruno was closer to the truth than those who insulted, imprisoned, and eventually burned him to death for being the first person in Europe to maintain that the Earth revolves around the Sun. People laughed at Robert Fulton's steamboat invention. Also occasional individuals with brilliant flashes of genius as well as great knowledge become attached to certain of their own opinions and ideas and promote them to the point of crankery (45°/50°/15°). One must read or listen with discernment.

Crankish opinions are sometimes held by large segments of a population. In medieval Europe most people believed in the existence of a number of monstrous creatures such as the basilisk, a reptile that can kill with a single glance. They also held many superstitious notions leading to violence against Jews and purported witches. A millennium later, several members of the Nazi hierarchy entertained pseudoscientific beliefs including a Hollow Earth, and the World Ice Theory that ice is the basic substance of the cosmos. These are but a few examples of the "extraordinary popular delusions" that dot history, including contemporary rumors or urban legends that reflect 15° gullibility. The Internet plays a large role in spreading such memes, which may also originate from deliberate propaganda.

Delusional, paranoid cults can turn into widespread and dangerous movements. In difficult times people cling to old ideas as if they were life preservers. The rapid pace of technological innovation and social change in a closely intertwined world has displaced and frightened many people, especially those acting from the confusion of 15°. This has led to "crisis cults" such as fundamentalist movements that are ostensibly religious but are actually attempts to battle modernity by reviving an older, more patriarchal and authoritarian social pattern. Such movements are often captured by narcissists and other pathological leaders, extreme nationalists, or divisive demagogues.

[1] Stanley Milgram, *Obedience to Authority: An Experimental View*. Harper and Row 1974

[2] Enrico de Lazaro, "Collapse of Late Bronze Age Civilizations Linked to Climate," *Science News*, August 15, 2013   http://www.sci-news.com/archaeology/science-collapse-late-bronze-age-civilizations-climate-change-01316.html

[3] You-Sheng Li, "Julian Jaynes' Theory of the Bicameral Mind and A Different Path to Subjective Consciousness in China," September 2008, written for The Jaynesian Newsletter; edited 15/02/2009, http://taoism21cen.com/Englishchat/essay12.html

[4] Lawrence R. James and James M. LeBreton, "Assessing Aggression Using Conditional Reasoning," http://www.psychologicalscience.org/journals/cd/19_1_inpress/James_final.pdf?q=james

[5] Claudia Dreifus, "Digital Addictions Bad as Heroin, Says Irresistible Author," *New York Times*, March 20, 2017

[6] "Treating China's Internet Addicts," PBS, January 20, 2014, http://www.pbs.org/newshour/rundown/treating-chinas-internet-addicts/

[7] Josh Harkinson, "23 Petty Crimes That Have Landed People in Prison for Life without Parole," *Mother Jones*, Nov. 13, 2013, http://www.motherjones.com/politics/2013/11/23-petty-crimes-prison-life-without-parole

[8] Michael Marshall, "Don't Flame Me, Bro'." New Scientist Blogs, November 19, 2007 https://www.newscientist.com/blog/technology/2007/11/dont-flame-me-bro.html

[9] Max Nisen and Aimee Groth, "27 Psychological Reasons Why Good People Do Bad Things," *Business Insider*, Aug. 27, 2012, http://www.businessinsider.com/27-psychological-reasons-why-good-people-do-bad-things-2012-8

[10] Daniel R. Hawes, "When Ignorance Begets Confidence: The Classic Dunning-Kruger Effect," *Psychology Today*, June 6, 2010,http://www.psychologytoday.com/blog/evolved-primate/201006/when-ignorance-begets-confidence-the-classic-dunning-kruger-effect

Chapter 12
Blame Them (5°/15°)

*Sometimes I wonder if the whole world isn't an idiot asylum for the
castaways of happier planets.*
~Malheureuse, "Four For a Cent," in *The Overland Monthly*, January
1893

Several kinds of negativism are associated with 15°, including
the tendency to feel victimized. It is quite likely that 15° *has* been
exploited, manipulated, and ill-treated as part of a generational,
historical pattern. But lacking cognitive skills or determination to mount
an effective resistance, 15° becomes a more or less irritable complainer:
a grumbler, griper, grouser, kvetcher, whiner, malcontent, sorehead,
sourpuss, or curmudgeon. (The number of words to describe this
behavior suggests its prevalence.) Or 15° succumbs to the 'kick the cat'
syndrome and picks on those in a weaker position, or simply those close
to hand.

Cynicism and a general negative view of humanity often
accompany habitual 15°: you can't trust anybody; people's actions are
always selfish; and any innovation or answer to a problem will never
work. Such cynicism leads to public corruption—with the attitude "if
everybody is cheating, I might as well too"—and towards a public
apathy that does not support or defend democratic institutions.

Mean-spiritedness, a small-minded, ungenerous and
unforgiving mind-set, is accompanied by blaming and scapegoating.
Undoubtedly this suspicion and cynicism reflects many life experiences
of 15°, and possibly an underlying depression. It is likely that 15° was
among the 40% of American children said to lack a secure attachment.

Mean

*Oftentimes, when people are miserable, they will want to make
other people miserable, too. But it never helps.*
~Lemony Snicket (Daniel Handler) American writer

Mean individuals demonstrate ill-will as a personal style and in many areas of life. The dictionary defines 'mean' as selfish, unkind, spiteful, malicious, disagreeable; and ill-tempered. One manifestation, vandalism, is motivated by a generalized hostility towards other people, their works and possessions. Mean behavior may be found at several lower dispositions, depending on people's motivations and the intensity of their actions. Envy and spite are milder forms of malice and jealousy. Activities can include malicious gossip, bullying, lies, and various kinds of manipulation. Some of this behavior is gratuitous—it does not seem to have any particular advantage for the individual.

People acting mean may have special targets (bullying) or may act in a hostile manner towards everybody. Rude and unhelpful, their idea of humor is *schadenfruede* (pleasure derived from the misfortunes of others) or practical jokes that hurt and humiliate somebody.

In the last decade American scholars have been analyzing what they call an "incivility crisis" in the workplace. In academic language this is described as "low intensity deviant behavior with ambiguous intent to harm the target, in violation of workplace norms for mutual respect." It may involve overly competitive and uncooperative co-workers who maneuver targets out of favored working conditions or benefits, humiliate them, or take credit for their accomplishments; also managers with a punitive style. Some analysts note an alarming decline in professionalism among lawyers, nurses, and college staff.

More broadly, many believe they see 'mean' increasing all over American society, in schools and public life as well as the workplace, including political debate conducted by insults rather than reasoned arguments. In a recent survey, a substantial majority of Americans say incivility has risen to crisis levels.

So what causes people to be mean? They may be angry about their life situation; defensive; judgmental; or jealous of others with more advantages. Spiteful behavior may give a sense of control over at least some part of one's life. Aggression may be a projection of the person's own feelings of inadequacy. Rudeness can become a cultural, subcultural, or family norm. Television programs that constantly show people insulting and harassing each other for laughs may be imitated by their less sophisticated viewers. After exposure to media characters who act mean, such behavior may seem normal, amusing, and even 'cool.'

Thoughtless behavior can easily slide into lower dispositions. Malicious gossip becomes a deliberate attempt to destroy another person ($0°$). People may subscribe to mean ideologies and scapegoating ($5°$). The mean person, though not the instigator of bullying or of lynch mobs, readily becomes a member of the audience or passive participant. In nations unhinged by demagoguery, by ethnic or religious violence, meanness declines further into targeted hatred.

In its most virulent form, meanness can reflect a malignant narcissism. A recurring idea to certain individuals throughout history is that one is a superior being, above all moral codes. In 1924 Chicago, two bright, well-to-do, teenage students—Richard Loeb and Nathan Leopold—murdered a younger neighbor for the thrill of it, to prove their superiority, and to 'commit the perfect crime.' Such notions get a big boost from misinterpretations of Nietzsche's writings about the 'Superman.' His ideas suffered from distorted editing by his anti-Semitic sister after his death and were further twisted to reach their most malevolent form in the Nazi movement.

Blame

A man can fail many times, but he isn't a failure until he begins to blame somebody else.
~John Burroughs, American naturalist, 1837-1921

Blaming can become a destructive habit, passed on through families where everybody projects his own deficiencies onto others. Blame serves to personalize unhappy events. It fails to look for rational ways to improve ongoing problems. The angry individual wants somebody to blame *right now*, someone he can hold responsible for a wrong or a situation gone bad.

The habit of projecting responsibility onto others may spread throughout a business or other organization, so that a *blame culture* takes root. This is a general tendency to blame people instead of trying to solve problems; a set of attitudes in an organization or subculture characterized by an unwillingness to take risks or accept responsibility for mistakes because of a fear of criticism or punishment. People blame each other to avoid being reprimanded or put down themselves.

This ancient habit of blame has an irrational effect on politics. Political reporter Chris Moody cites research showing that "voters tend to oppose incumbents when things go wrong, even if those leaders have no control over the events in question….Even a poor showing from a regional sports team can benefit a political challenger." [1]

'Blaming the victim' stems from denial of social ills, or sometimes from identification with the victimizers (as in schoolyard bullying). It even happens after disasters. Referring to British policy during the Irish Famine, Paul Krugman notes that "self-righteous cruelty toward the victims of disaster, especially when the disaster goes on for an extended period, is common in history." Some people in the United States expressed contempt for the victims of Hurricane Katrina, as though they themselves would have enough sense not to live in a disaster area. This attitude was undoubtedly influenced by the fact that many residents of New Orleans were black and poor.

Krugman points out that an economic crisis is similar to a disaster, and that many people blame the victims here too. It was true in the 1930s Depression as well as the 2008 Recession. [2]

A community may develop the custom of selecting certain individuals or groups to carry the blame for all, much as the ancient Israelites sent a goat into the wilderness to carry away all their sins. Ritual scapegoating seems to have been a frequent custom in ancient times; for instance, the ancient Greeks cast out a cripple or beggar or criminal in response to a natural disaster or an invasion. Fear is at the root of communal scapegoating. During mysterious epidemics, economic downturns, or other social stresses, the pressures mount.

As the bubonic plague decimated the population of Europe, persecutions grew of Jews and those believed to be witches. Studies of racial violence in the South between 1882 and 1930 found that as the price of cotton fell, the number of lynchings increased.[3] Another study shows that since the 1870s, a country's politics after a financial crisis are likely to take a hard right turn, toward parties that scapegoat ethnic and religious minorities, immigrants, labor leaders, and dissenters.[3,4]

Scapegoats

> *It is a principle of nature to hate those whom you have injured.*
> ~Tacitus, *Agricola*, c. 98 AD

Martin Buber wrote about how "I and It" thinking separates people, leading to fear and loathing of the other. If one blames them for whatever goes wrong they are scapegoats. If we hate and fear them as threats they are enemies, of equal power to ourselves or even magnified as a superhuman menace. If one sees them as easy marks to use as desired—manipulating them, deceiving, seducing, defrauding, robbing, even raping or murdering them—then they are prey. These are not mutually exclusive categories. Whether scapegoat, enemy, or prey, they are turned into *others* and therefore not real, bona fide people like us.

These ways to 'other' people have biological underpinnings and are deeply enshrined in social institutions and ideologies. Depending on the scale of objectification or dehumanization, the relative lack of empathy or understanding, these divisive ideas can express any of the six lower dispositions. For instance, they help the reactive individual to identify a target for his (or her) rage (5°). Blaming and bullying are related aspects of scapegoat creation. Picking on somebody else helps establish one's own superiority.

As Dwight Eisenhower said, "The search for a scapegoat is the easiest of all hunting expeditions." Scapegoat groups are usually identifiably different from the majority population because of traits such as skin color, facial characteristics, clothing, accent, gender orientation (real or perceived) or gender itself, in cultures where females are treated like a scapegoat group. Leaders may invert the true situation, claiming that the minority is trying to oppress the majority. This kind of flipping is a common propaganda device. Blaming one's victim has also been noted as psychopathic behavior.

For sixteen centuries, Jews were the default scapegoats in Christian Europe. The persistent notions that have caused so much suffering began in the second century with statements by early church fathers excoriating the Jews, who held to a rival religion at a time when Christianity was competing (20°) with several popular religions such as Mithraism and Manichaeism. In the fourth century Constantine made Christianity the state religion (10°) of the Roman Empire. The Romans then demanded that the Jews convert, or else be denied citizenship and legal protection. As the struggle continued, Jews received the label of "Christ killers" (as though Jesus himself were not also Jewish). Anti-Semitism grew from there.

To explain how entire nations can turn into blame cultures, Freud said that civilizations need to be coherent, to have a unifying story. They channel their aggression toward those people who don't fit the grand narrative—a strategy that is not effective for long. Freud notes that as scapegoats, "the Jewish people, scattered everywhere, have rendered most useful services to the civilizations of the countries that have been their hosts; but unfortunately all the massacres of the Jews in the Middle Ages did not suffice to make that period more peaceful and secure for their Christian fellows." Ironically, Freud wrote the above words *before* the Nazi Holocaust, which demonstrated anti-Semitism on the most horrific scale and with industrial efficiency. [5]

Women are an even more ancient and universal scapegoat despite the fact that women are half the human race, the objects of male desire and—so far—they are necessary for reproduction. Hatred of women reflects an ambivalence that is hard to rationalize as an ideology, which does not at all shield women from being victims of opportunity.

Scapegoat Ideologies

> *Ideas pull the trigger, but instinct loads the gun.*
> ~Don Marquis

Bigotry is a combination of 10° dominance with 5° fears and consequent projection of all negativity onto scapegoats.

For those who would conquer, exterminate, enslave, punish, sterilize, or exploit others unlike themselves, a wide variety of ideologies are available for rationalizing their behavior and were, in fact, designed for this purpose. Common ideologies involve race and economic class.

Such systems of belief can become far more complex than the simple 5° mechanism for deciding who is to blame and who is fair game. Many ideologies serve to rationalize the economic exploitation of one group by another. Both slavery and colonialism depend on the notion that some people are inferior to others. Even after the end of slavery and frank colonialism, other economic and political interests helped maintain the status quo. Over the past two centuries many influential books were published to rationalize 10° domination, with racist ideas often cloaked as science. The same ideas were used to justify cultural genocides.

Scientific racism began with *Systema Naturae* (1767) by the great zoologist Carl Linnaeus, whose animal classifications were foundational to the science of zoology (45°). But his views about humans were tragically mistaken (15°). He believed there were five human species: *Americanus, Europeanus, Asiaticus, Africanus,* and *Monstrosus*, people born with visible disabilities. Annalee Newitz notes that "In many ways, Linnaeus' system of categorizing [human] races as species has never really left us." Most people still believe that biological differences between groups of people are far greater than they are.[6]

By 1851 German philosopher Arthur Schopenhauer claimed: "The highest civilization and culture, apart from the ancient Hindus and Egyptians, are found exclusively among the white races." Schopenhauer ignored large exceptions to his rule such as the Chinese, Aztec, Incan, and Mayan civilizations, or the racially mixed yet advanced cultures of Carthage and Islamic Spain.*

It was not enough to place the 'European race' above all the others; the idea arose that certain white ethnic groups were superior to the others. A French aristocrat, the Comte de Gobineau, first developed the theory of the Aryan master race in the mid-19th century. Gobineau was the first to claim that race was the deciding factor in history.

Scientific racism was widely spread by Madison Grant's *Passing of the Great Race* (1916) which went through multiple printings and translations. Grant, a New York lawyer, not only considered the white race superior to others, but divided the white race into three subgroups: Alpines (central Europe), Mediterraneans (Southern Europe and the Middle East), and Nordics (Northern Europe). Nordics, you may have guessed already, were the whitest of the white, the *crème de la crème*. Thus 20° ideology rationalizes 10° domination.

Grant was a dedicated conservationist (35°) who helped save several animal species, founded environmental organizations, and developed the field of wildlife management. With influential friends gained from his conservation activities, including Presidents Teddy Roosevelt and Herbert Hoover, Grant was able to play an active role in forming restrictive immigration policies and anti-miscegenation laws. The Immigration Acts of 1921 and 1924 were intended to restrict immigration of Southern Europeans, Eastern Europeans, and Jews. Not until 1965 were these national quotas eliminated.

Passing of the Great Race also had a baleful influence in Germany. In a letter to Grant, Adolf Hitler called the book his "Bible." It contributed to the racist ideas already circulating in Nazi circles.

U.S. books supporting the genetic inferiority of blacks to whites continue to be published, rationalizing inequalities in economic and social success between the two groups. *The Bell Curve: Intelligence and Class Structure in American Life*, by Richard Herrnstein and Charles Murray (1994) was hugely popular though widely criticized for its poor scientific methodology.[7] The production and popularity of scientific racism appears to arise from a mixture of dispositions: scapegoats for 5° fears; 20° rationalizations for 10° dominance; and 25° (narcissistic pride in the attributes of oneself and one's group).

---

* Schopenhauer also said "Every miserable fool who has nothing at all of which he can be proud, adopts as a last resource pride in the nation to which he belongs; he is ready and happy to defend all its faults and follies tooth and nail, thus reimbursing himself for his own inferiority." Schopenhauer failed to note the possibility that "miserable fools" might adopt a similar pride in their race or civilization.

Social Darwinism

*If we do not like the survival of the fittest, we have only one possible
alternative, and that is the survival of the unfittest. The former is the
law of civilization; the latter is the law of anti-civilization.*
~William Graham Sumner, American social scientist, 1840-1910

A second focus of ideologies consists of justification for economic and class differences in the form of Social Darwinism (20°/10°) a social theory that applies biological concepts of natural selection to human society. More influential in the United States than in England, this ideology has so far lasted for about 150 years, as a rationalization of ancient attitudes. .

Social Darwinism began when English philosopher Herbert Spencer invented the phrase "survival of the fittest." Despite its popularity, this phrase is not an accurate description of Darwin's theory of evolution. Natural selection has to do with reproductive success rather than individual survival, and adaptation to specific environments rather than absolute fitness. It describes a biological phenomenon without moral implications.

Spencer's later writings became immensely popular in the late 19th century, providing a springboard for a number of related ideas, such as eugenics and *laissez-faire* capitalism (20°). For example, noted sociologist William Graham Sumner believed the state should not interfere even to regulate child labor or provide public education, that social reforms of every kind were useless and misguided.*

Eugenics was discredited because of Nazi horrors, but the Social Darwinist attitudes behind it linger. In contrast, some 45° scientists and philosophers have found quite the reverse of social Darwinism. For instance, Nietzsche says: "Wherever progress is to ensue, deviating natures are of greatest importance …. There is rarely…a physical or moral loss without an advantage somewhere else." [8]

Peter Kropotkin (1842-1921), Russian polymath and prominent anarchist, argued that "it was an evolutionary emphasis on cooperation instead of competition in the Darwinian sense that made for the success of species, including the human." Modern biologists such as E. O. Wilson would agree. Clive Finlayson, paleontologist and evolutionary ecologist, speaks of "the survival of the weakest." He refers to people who live on the edges, in marginal environments, who have to adapt constantly to variable conditions and therefore become innovators. Finlayson says they have greater long-term survival than those who are well adapted to a single, more flourishing environment.[9]

Neo-Nazism: The defeat of Nazi Germany did not end the allure of Nazism. Since World War II it has reappeared in various forms across the world from Costa Rica to Mongolia and even within Israel. While using Nazi symbols, some of these followings have little to do with historical Nazism, with a Miss Nazi beauty contest, Nazi-inspired football hooliganism, or reverence for Genghis Khan. What they do seem to have in common, besides militant attachment to their nation-state and its majority ethnic group, is a plethora of scapegoats. Some borrow scapegoats such as Jews, blacks, and homosexuals from Nazi doctrine, while others are particular to each nation's minorities and neighbors. Croatian neo-Nazis hate Serbs, while Russian neo-Nazis detest Muslims and minorities from Central Asia and the Caucasus. Mongolian targets include Chinese and Koreans. Brazilian neo-Nazis have added homeless people, prostitutes, and feminists to the list.

For those whose frustrations and poor impulse control lead to blame and rage, neo-Nazism can fulfill the function of justifying oppression and violence against whatever scapegoats fit into each culture's particular history and narrative. Neo-Nazism now appears to be scapegoat-ism, plus ethnic supremacy of whatever local group espouses it plus a few theatrical trappings from the original Nazi era—almost like sinister fan clubs.[10] If only they would learn Klingon instead.

*The much more radical early Spencer opposed private ownership of land and said that every person has a latent claim to participate in use of the Earth. He called himself a "radical feminist," supported trade unions, and advocated an economy based on worker cooperatives rather than wage-labor. The later Spencer denounced compulsory education, laws to regulate safety at work, social welfare programs, and tax-funded libraries.

Turning certain people into the 'other' serves different functions. Scapegoats receive the fear, anger, and frustrations of 5° and provide victims of convenience for 0°. Otherness is a useful idea for 10° to justify power grabs and any accompanying violence. At 15°, many will follow the lead of 10° authoritarians. Meanwhile, 20° with a more sophisticated understanding of ideology would rather spin the whys and wherefores of why we are superior and they are inferior.

Martin Luther King, Jr. had an answer to hate-filled people:

> Love has within it a redemptive power....a power there that eventually transforms individuals. Just keep being friendly to that person. Just keep loving them, and they can't stand it too long…. And by the power of your love they will break down under the load….There's something about love that builds up and is creative. There is something about hate that tears down and is destructive. So love your enemies.[11]

1 Chris Moody, "American Primitive," review of *Political Animals* by historian Rick Shenkman, reprinted from *Book Forum* by *Utne Reader*, Spring 2016

2 Paul Krugman, "Those Lazy Jobless," *The New York Times*, September 23, 2014

3 Cornelius Christian, "Lynchings, Labour and Cotton in the US South," University of Oxford, UK, 2013, https://editorialexpress.com/cgi-bin/conference/download.cgi?db_name=CSAE2014&paper_id=799

4 Funke, M, M Schularick and C Trebesch (2015) "Going to extremes: Politics after financial crises, 1870-2014", CEPR, Discussion Paper No. 10884

5 Sigmund Freud, *Civilization and Its Discontents*, 1930-31

6 Annalee Newitz, "The Nine Most Influential Works of Scientific Racism, Ranked," May 13, 2014, http://io9.com/the-9-most-influential-works-of-scientific-racism-rank-1575543279

7 For a recent study concerning the heritability of intelligence see: Scott Barry Kaufman, "The Heritability of Intelligence: Not What You Think," *Scientific American*, October 17, 2013, http://blogs.scientificamerican.com/beautiful-minds/2013/10/17/the-heritability-of-intelligence-not-what-you-think/

8 Friedrich Wilhelm Nietzsche, *Human, All Too Human: A Book for Free Spirits* (originally published 1878)

9 Clive Finlayson, *The Humans Who Went Extinct*, Oxford University Press, 2009

10 Aris Chatzistefanou, "Neo-Nazi tattoos fall out of fashion in Greece after Golden Dawn crackdown," *The Guardian*, October 21, 2013,http://www.theguardian.com/world/2013/oct/21/neo-nazi-tattoos-greece-golden-dawn

11 Martin Luther King, Jr., *Sermon Delivered at Dexter Avenue Baptist Church, Montgomery, Alabama, on 17 November 1957.*

Chapter 13
The Role of Religion

Religion is regarded by the common people as true, by the wise as false, and by the rulers as useful.
~Lucius Annaeus Seneca, Roman statesman and philosopher, 4 BC-65 AD

Rome was never noted for its spiritual achievements, and Seneca (above) could afford to be cynical. And yet no known culture has been found to be without religion, defining this in the broadest sense.

The origin of religion is a mystery. Was it a way to enforce the group's moral codes? Or to explain natural phenomena? Was it a by-product of various adaptive traits? Something to do with dopamine? One controversial hypothesis is that variants of the VMAT2 gene (the 'God gene") predispose people to spirituality. Anonymous asks, "What came first: individual religious (ecstatic) experiences, collective observances of transition situations, fear of death, ritual competence, magical coercion; mirror neurons or temporal lobe religiosity?" This list does not exhaust the possibilities.

Some nonhuman animals seem to share the rudiments of religion, such as mourning the dead (jays, elephants, giraffes, and others) or mass gatherings of creatures on the same day or lunar phase year after year. As for humans, a Pit of Bones in Atapuerca, Spain dated from 300,000 years ago suggests intentional burial of the dead by ancestral human species *Homo heidelbergensis*. We can only guess at the spiritual beliefs of early prehistoric people based on archeological findings such as burial sites or figurines of possible deities such as the Lion Man.

But here we are not concerned with cave bear cults or shamanism. What we now call 'religions' are organized belief systems that arose with the first civilizations, and especially after writing, 5,000 years ago. These early religions supported the central authority of theocratic states ($10°$) and most people probably followed them at a rote level ($15°$). Religion provided a bond between people from diverse tribes ($35°$) who were now collected together in towns and cities.

Later religions founded during the Axial Age (about 700-200 BC) were concerned with ethical values and individual conscience. These traditions include monotheism, Zoroastrianism (which influenced all three Abrahamic religions), Platonic idealism, Buddhism, Taoism, Confucianism, and Jainism. Two and a half millennia later, Axial Age beliefs are the foundation of all the major religions.

Historical religions have transformed humanity, restraining excesses of the lower dispositions while teaching expression of the higher ones. They have provided many models for aspiration. Yet religious beliefs and institutions express themselves through *all* the dispositions, including the lower ones.

The number of adherents of each religion today follows the history of conquests and empires. Christians comprise about one-third of the world's population, followers of Islam about one-fourth, while Hindus, Buddhists, and devotees of other Asian religions comprise another one-fourth. Although a few major belief systems dominate, there are today an estimated 10,000 distinct religions. Adding to this diversity, every follower of every religion may have a slightly different interpretation of it than his fellows do.[1]

Some claim the name of a religion yet barely practice the faith. Some do not profess any religion. Worldwide about 16% say they are atheist or secular. In some places they are in the majority. These tend to be richer countries and include Sweden, most of Western Europe, Canada, Australia, Korea, Japan, Czech Republic, China, Oceania, and Israel. One surprising inclusion is Ireland, long a Catholic stronghold.[2]

What Is Religion?

> *Man is certainly stark mad; he cannot make a worm, and yet he will be making gods by dozens.*
> ~Michel de Montaigne, French essayist, 1533-1592

Before describing religious dispositions, we need to define religion. The working definition borrowed here is an attempt to cover all the bases, from Amish to Zoroastrian. The definition is constrained to use qualifying words because religious beliefs are so very diverse that few generalizations apply to all.

> Religion: a set of beliefs concerning the cause, nature, and purpose of the universe, *especially when* considered as the creation of a superhuman agency or agencies, *usually* involving devotional and ritual observances, and *often* containing a moral code governing the conduct of human affairs. [Italics added] [3]

The four dimensions of religion listed are: 1) views of the universe; 2) belief in a deity or deities; 3) rites and ceremonies; and 4) morality. One could also add a fifth dimension of religiously inspired art, music, and architecture. The first dimension—"a set of beliefs concerning the cause, nature, and purpose of the universe"—belongs to mythology, philosophy and astrophysics as well as to religion. In the creation myths of every culture, and from Plato to the Big Bang Theory, people have held beliefs about how it all began and why.

The second dimension of religion is belief in a deity or deities, but this varies widely. Deity may be a person. It may be composed of interrelated entities, such as the Trinity or the composite god Atun-Ra of ancient Egypt. There may be a pantheon of personified deities as with ancient Greek, Roman, Norse, and Aztec religions.

Religious doctrine and dogma (20°) tend to *reify* the much larger but more amorphous region of spirituality (X°). Reification turns the abstract into something concrete and physical. Deities that look and act like human beings—such as the Greek pantheon—clearly show this human tendency to reify. In Christianity, many conceptions of God are colored by the famous painting by Michelangelo on the ceiling of the Sistine Chapel, in which Jehovah reaches out his hand to give life to Adam. Philosopher Christopher Ott points out that this early 16th century painting was the very first piece of Christian art to give physical form to God—and that He looks very much like the pagan god Zeus. This is a materialist conception of the same deity that the more mystical ancient Jews would not even name aloud.

While most of the world's believers may worship a personified God or gods, or intermediaries in human or animal form, those at the mystical core of all religions seek a God beyond the material world: an unknowable principle of reality (X^o). Eastern religions in particular have a more formless and philosophical conception of deity (the Absolute, Ultimate Reality, the All, the First Cause, the Ground of Being). The Buddha explicitly denied the existence of a creator deity. Jainism also does not recognize an omnipotent creator god. One of the tenets of Taoism is "there are no gods." Vedanta views all reality as a single principle, Brahman, and teaches that all that exists is divine, with the ultimate goal of each human being to manifest this divinity.

The third dimension of religion is ritual, defined as "repeatable symbolic actions involving the sacred." These may include formal prayers, fasting, communion, blessing, confession, processions, chanting, dancing, singing, daily offering of food or flowers, baptism, circumcision, christening, rites of passage at puberty, marriage, death rites, healing rituals, and seasonal observances. Scientists report that rituals of all kinds can alleviate anxiety or grief. [4]

However, rites may not be an *essential* attribute of religion, for instance, Confucianism does not have rites in the sense of religious customs. There is also a historical tendency toward interiorizing religion. J.H. Nielson notes that during the Protestant Reformation, some radical believers focused strongly on the Church Invisible and the inner light without ritual observances. Several U.S. founders subscribed to Deism, which has no rituals. Modern Quakers have little ceremony besides meeting together at regular intervals for a silent service.

The fourth dimension of religion is morality. The American public and media commonly equate religion and morality, but these are not the same thing. Philosophy professor Paul W. Diener says: "The function of religion is not to make people morally good (even if this is the result) but to provide transcendence and meaning….People who are not religious can be and often are quite moral."[6]

Many people describe their beliefs as 'spiritual' rather than religious because they find transcendence and meaning outside of established religions, often without deities or rites.

Sometimes the term 'religion' is used ironically to describe ideologies such as communism, fascism, or nationalism/patriotism; or for compulsive activities such as money-making or spectator sports. People may build their lives around them (usually at 15°, 20°, or 25°), but for the most part these faux-religions do not deal with human needs for transcendence and meaning, nor explain anything about the origin and purpose of the Universe. They may provide spectacle but are not noted for inspired creativity in religious art, music, and architecture.

While ideologies can pose as religions, religions can also turn into ideologies. As time turns, religions (also ideologies that are initially beneficent) get overtaken by people acting at lower dispositions, who misunderstand the founding ideas of their chosen belief system and who stamp it with their own personal shortcomings.

Without denying the great positive influence of religious beliefs, we must acknowledge that many people who claim to be furthering religious ideals, or who imbue an ideology with religious fervor, have been and are still responsible for a great deal of the violence and misunderstanding in the world. Religions have often provided justifications for oppressive government, wars, and the massacre and murder of minority sects and religious dissenters. Granted, the non-religious have also committed horrors. In either case, the problem is with those acting at lower dispositions, whether they reject religion or distort it to their requirements.

We begin with the negative Shadow of organized religions. The drive for temporal power (10°) has often motivated religious leaders, notably during certain eras of the long history of the Catholic Church, when popes, kings, emperors, and merchant-princes vied for authority and control of the Church's great wealth and power. The same greed operates among many popular Protestant leaders with mega-churches and broadcasting ministries.

Cruel hypocrisy and preoccupation with punishment are two other aspects of the 10° disposition that are often bolstered by religious views. Here are 'hellfire and brimstone' preachers and those who have found support in the Bible or Qur'an for war, slavery, segregation, terrorism, capital punishment, corporal punishment, or killing heretics and other selected scapegoats.

A very special case could be described as X°/0°. In some philosophies or spiritual systems, X° can become anti-life or at least indifferent to life—a 0° indifference that is neither malign nor benign but otherworldly. X°/0° is so driven toward transcendence that our shared humanity no longer means anything to him. Awareness of the Infinite becomes greater than all life on Earth. Not all mystics end up in this place but apparently some do. It may be the height of spiritual thought, or the nadir of human indifference.

Religion and the Nation-State:

Almost any sect, cult, or religion will legislate its creed into law if it acquires the political power to do so.
~Robert Heinlein, American science fiction writer, 1907-1988

Religions began with theocracies and a priestly class, and many never completely broke with the nation-state. Despite claims to universality, most modern churches identify with their own country when it is at war. Religious institutions also tend to ally with political authority or the ruling elite. As one historical example, in Latin America the church hierarchy positioned itself with the ruling class (10°) although many of the parish priests were actively sympathetic with large poverty- stricken populations (40°).

Several movements link religion and nation-state (religious nationalism 10°/20°). One example is Zionism. Rightist groups In Russia want the nation to identify more closely with the Russian Orthodox Church. Hinduism has its nationalist ideology, Hindutva, represented by the Prime Minister of India, Narendra Modi. Fundamentalist Buddhism has been involved with large-scale religious violence in Sri Lanka, Thailand, and Burma. Many Americans believe the United States was founded as a Christian nation despite statements to the contrary by early leaders. Religious nationalism became more closely tied to the American ethos (and to capitalism) during the administration of Dwight Eisenhower starting in 1953.[7]

In Europe, identification of ruler and religion was bolstered for centuries by the doctrine of the Divine Right of Kings. (In China and East Asia the Mandate of Heaven was more conditional on the ruler's behavior.) One aspect of Divine Right was that it combined apostasy or heresy with treason, making this a double crime and punished accordingly. This national religious system died out after the 17th century in Europe but the theocratic tendency is still with us, especially in the fundamentalist sects of the Islamic Middle East.

Several religious groups may compete for political dominance within a nation-state (10°/20°). Such competition has led to a variety of conflicts existing today between Muslims and Christians in Ethiopia, Nigeria, and Sudan; between the Roman Catholic Church and a popular African-derived faith called Candomble in Brazil; between Buddhists and minority Muslims (Rohingya) and Christians in Myanmar/Burma; between Hindus and Muslims or Hindus and Sikhs in India; and between the two main doctrinal groups of Islam, the Sunnis and the Shia, throughout the Middle East and western Asia. [8]

Once a religion owns a nation-state, it tends to expand itself by conquest, colonization, or missionary zeal, as demonstrated by all three Abrahamic religions. Christianity acquired a state apparatus when it became the official religion of Rome under Constantine in the fourth century. Constantine used the popular religion to create *esprit d' corps* and greater fanaticism in his army. Rome as combined empire and church forcibly Christianized many peoples.

Numerous religious wars have been fought between Christians of different beliefs as well as between Christians and Muslims. Numerous conquests, as well as slaveholding and colonialism have been justified by the claimed duty to bring Christianity to the heathens. Currently, many Christian nationalists conceive a war between the Christian West and Islam, but Western leaders no longer speak out loud of spreading Christianity as an explicit motivation for Western imperialism.

Islam, the next religion to capture nation-states, spread itself at lightning speed in the 7th and 8th centuries by conquering weak states from Spain to India, forming an empire larger than Rome's. They did not forcibly convert Christians, Jews, and Zoroastrians; instead, a policy of religious toleration (35°) reduced rebellion against political control. Non-Muslims had lesser status but were not actively persecuted. Islamic religious toleration, based on Qur'anic teachings, continued for most of a millennium (with notable lapses) and also in the later Ottoman Empire.

However, in the 18th century, a strict, fundamentalist, reform movement (Wahhabism)* began in Saudi Arabia, allying itself with the House of Saud. It is now the state religion (10°) of Saudi Arabia. The jihad against Soviet occupation of Afghanistan appears to have been the crucible for expansion of this creed. The U.S. presence in Iraq and civil war in Syria provided more opportunities. Since the 1960s, wealthy individuals in Saudi Arabia, Kuwait, and Qatar have funded the spread of Wahhabism, now dominant throughout the Arabian Peninsula and making inroads in places such as Uzbekistan, Chechnya, and India.

A minority branch of Islam (less than 5% of Muslims) Wahhabism is antagonistic to non-Muslims, Muslims of other views, many traditional Islamic teachings and practices, the West, modernism, and Enlightenment ideas. The most violent cult based on these beliefs is Islamic State or ISIS, which imitates Islamic conquests of 1,300 years ago but without any of the religious toleration. ISIS envisions the world's one billion Muslims living in one Islamic state ruled by Sharia law.

The group is unusually brutal, and will even kill fellow Muslims in the name of purifying Islam. It is as fanatic as its goals are fantastic and often operates violently at the lowest disposition (0°). Its leaders are quite clever (20°) in exploiting the social media and technology of a West that they profess to despise. Although drawing underemployed and disaffected Muslim youths from across the world to its expansive goals (10°/15°) and sadistic methods (0°), ISIS numbers at the most 200,000 militant followers.[9]

The oldest Abrahamic religion was last to acquire a modern state. Several Judean Kingdoms rose and fell between the ninth and first centuries BC, but for 2,000 years the Jews did not have a nation-state of their own and were harshly oppressed in Christian Europe. Zionism was a nationalist movement organized just over a century ago by Theodor Herzl, a secular Jew, to establish a Jewish state in the Land of Israel. It was defined according to various biblical passages as either the southern Levant or a much larger area encompassing part or all of present-day Jordan, Lebanon, Iraq, and Syria.

There were two major problems in returning to the Jewish homeland after 2,000 years. First, the region was already inhabited by others. Second, the State of Israel was founded as a tiny country in a sea of Islamic nations. In the 66 years of its existence Israel has been involved in seven wars and eight large-scale military operations. It is today a militarized state with undeclared nuclear weapons (believed to be the world's sixth largest stockpile).

Israel's continued occupation of the small area that still remains for Palestinians is the flashpoint for conflicts in the Middle East. The United States has appointed itself as Israel's protector and American leaders have long attempted, unsuccessfully, to negotiate a two-state solution between Israel and the Palestinians. Greatly complicating the future of both Islam and Judaism is the fact that about two/thirds of the world's proven oil reserves are in the Middle East. Opponents of Israel's policies claim that expansionist factions (10°) in the Netanyahu administration, Likud party, and military and intelligence establishment have a strategic plan to weaken neighboring Arab states and to expand "Greater Israel" to the most extensive interpretation of boundaries from the Old Testament (the Oded Yinon Plan).

To conflate the realm of spirit (X°) with nationalism or empire-building degrades a religion's higher teachings about peace, good will, compassion, and human unity. Such fusion of ideas has been a major cause or justification for wars.

*The term 'Wahhabism' is controversial. Adherents say it is derogatory and meaningless, preferring Salafism, a broader term with different origins.

> *If religion becomes a cause of dislike, hatred and division, it were better to be without it, and to withdraw from such a religion would be a truly religious act.*
> 'Abdu'l-Bahá, eldest son of Bahá'u'lláh, founder of the Bahá'í Faith

The very concept of heresy—religious opinion contrary to established dogma—is based on a 10° idea that one belief must dominate all others. When people start killing each other over their religious beliefs, the 5° disposition takes over. The deliberate, official disposition to punish religious heresy with torture and death is 0°.

The notion of heresy exists in several religious traditions, notably Christianity and Islam. A similar idea occurs in ideologies such as Marxism and Scientology. Heresy and treason are related because up until the last few centuries, state religions were the rule.

During the Protestant Reformation (1524-1648) the charge of heresy led to continuous wars, massacres, and executions in Europe. One figure of the times was the "Iron Duke," a noted Spanish general. His master King Phillip II of Spain gave him unlimited power to put down the Dutch revolt against Catholic Spanish rule. In six years as governor of the Spanish Netherlands the Duke ordered 18,000 executions and led brutal military operations against several cities, but never broke the Dutch revolt (45°) and was finally recalled to Spain.

Today the proclamation of religious heresy as a life-and-death matter is limited to Islam. Apostasy—abandonment or renunciation of one's religion—is also seldom punished outside of Islam. In Pakistan, vague accusations of blasphemy (insulting religion) often result in the blasphemer's death by mobs or police misconduct (5°). According to Paul Marshall, a professor in Indonesia, most of the accused belong to specific groups: Baha'i or Sufis, (two higher disposition religions that developed from Islam); either Shia or Sunni majorities persecuting the minority; skeptics, atheists, and converts to Christianity; and Muslims whose political views are different from those of the people in power.[10]

Religious Confusions (15°)

On the dogmas of religion, as distinguished from moral principles, all mankind, from the beginning of the world to this day, have been quarreling, fighting, burning and torturing one another, for abstractions unintelligible to themselves and to all others, and absolutely beyond the comprehension of the human mind.
~Thomas Jefferson, letter to Archibald Carey, 1816

People of a 15° disposition are often as confused about their religion as they are about other matters. The less they understand it, the more opinionated they are, sure that the Bible or the Qur'an supports their own social and political beliefs. They may insist on 'literalism' which in actuality is a selective interpretation that ignores context and the figurative nature of language. Regarding the practice of literalism, Joseph Campbell said: "Every religion is true one way or another. It is true when understood metaphorically. But when it gets stuck in its own metaphors, interpreting them as facts, then you are in trouble."

The three Abrahamic religions are heavily based on writings. For Christians and Jews, the Old Testament s a sacred text. Muslims accept parts of both the Old and New Testaments as divine revelation. Christians have the New Testament, Muslims the Qur'an, and Jews the Talmud and other commentaries. Varying interpretations of these texts lead to rifts and schisms and contradictions which both reflect and reinforce confusions of members. Followers who defer to those who set themselves up as religious authorities may be influenced by bizarre or nationalistic interpretations, or by leaders who preach hate and violence against other religions, including other branches of their own religion.

One part of the Christian Bible that has contributed mightily to 15° confusion over the centuries is the *Book of Revelation*. There were doubts in early centuries about the nature and authorship of this apocalyptic writing, so different from the Gospels. Revelation expresses a disdain for humanity that is almost exterminist (0°). Several church fathers expressed concerns about possible misinterpretations and abuse, and *Revelation* was the last book to be accepted into the canon (the Eastern Orthodox Church did not include it at all).

Revelation has often been used or misused by religious fanatics, leading to Millenarian movements, doomsday prophecies, and anti-Catholicism. Some Christians, in the belief that the end-times are imminent, find contemporary political significance in its bizarre imagery and violent narratives. And it has stimulated other writers and preachers to dramatic inventions such as the pre-Tribulation Rapture doctrine (created by John Nelson Darby about 1830).

Apocalyptic beliefs may be a recurring form of 5° moral panics. The foremost proponent of such ideologies today is ISIS, medieval fundamentalism with modern tech, about which Graeme Wood says:

> We can gather that their state rejects peace as a matter of principle; that it hungers for genocide; that its religious views make it constitutionally incapable of certain types of change, even if that change might ensure its survival; and that it considers itself a harbinger of—and headline player in—the imminent end of the world. [11]

Another seed of great religious confusion is the idea of Original Sin, a hereditary condition of guilt and sin. In one form or another it is part of the doctrine of most Christian sects, but reaches its most intense form in Calvinist–influenced denominations, where it is defined as total depravity and the inability even to recognize or desire good. People who learn from an early age that they are worthless, guilty, and powerless (without God) are likely to stay in thrall to those in 10° power.

A few psychologists have recently identified a Religious Trauma Syndrome, (not yet in the DSM). Dr. Marlene Winell defines RTS as "a set of symptoms and characteristics… related to harmful experiences with religion. They are the result of two things: immersion in a controlling religion and the secondary impact of leaving a religious group." She lists symptoms such as negative beliefs about one's own worth and abilities, poor critical thinking abilities, perfectionism, depression, loneliness, and information gaps. [12]

Religion in Higher Dispositions

> *Not all religion is to be found in the church, any more than all knowledge is found in the classroom.*
> ~Author Unknown

The majority of people who consider themselves religious are born into a religious tradition (30°). Their parents and neighbors worship in the same way and have never considered another spiritual path. They may be quite devout, attempting to live up to the moral code they associate with their religion. 30° Christians try to follow the ethical teachings of Jesus; they usually read the Old Testament metaphorically not literally, and pay scant attention to theological doctrines. Personal interpretation based mainly on the Gospels is one way people escape the many confusions resulting from centuries of theological accretions as churchly scholars attempted to graft a new religion (Christianity) upon an old one (Judaism).

At 35° an individual develops a more personal belief system over time. He may change churches or leave them entirely. Whether secular or religious, 35° tends to be moral and also ethical. Confucianism is basically a 35° ethical system without belief in deities, and also teaches altruism (40°) and integrity (45°).

Missionary work has two aspects: religious conversion or social and medical service. Most religions send out proselytizing missionaries, but in the past these have often expressed lower dispositions. Christian missionaries in particular were criticized for allying with colonialism, imposing inappropriate Western customs on other cultures, and paving the way for economic exploitation (10°). Anglican Bishop Desmond Tutu says "When the missionaries came to Africa they had the Bible and we had the land. They said, 'Let us pray.' We closed our eyes. When we opened them we had the Bible and they had the land."

Less than a century ago, proselytizers with destructive insensitivity to other cultures forced religious boarding schools upon children of Australian Aborigines, Native Americans, and Samis (Laplanders), in attempts to obliterate the native cultures (10°

domination/25° collective egotism). In recent years, however, Christian missions have focused on *ministries of service* such as providing health care, teaching literacy, supporting social justice, and developing small-scale industries (35° awareness and 40° humanitarianism). The Peace Corps and many NGOs are secular versions of this newer model.

Individuals at 40° care little for denomination, theology, or the letter of the law, and are more inclined to call their beliefs spiritual rather than religious. A 40° spiritual belief may express itself in devotion to God or the Good, expressing love for other human beings whatever their race or nationality, often including creatures and all nature as well.

Some religions (such as Buddhism, Jainism, and Sikhism) began as reforms of previous thinking, encouraging greater inclusiveness and 40° compassion. Quakers have long been deeply involved with social reform (35°/40°). Always a relatively small group, Quakers had much to do with ending the African slave trade and slavery in Britain and the United States. They were also active in winning rights for women, and have been tireless supporters of pacifism and anti-war movements.

One example of world-changing religion (X°) takes us back to the third century BC when Mauryan Emperor Ashoka witnessed first-hand the destruction and horrific loss of life after one of his many successful battles. Ashoka experienced great remorse and converted to Buddhism, becoming probably the most enlightened monarch the world has ever seen. Besides giving up war, Ashoka introduced the "Law of Piety" which required respect for all animate life. The Law insisted on humane and just treatment for peoples in and out of the empire, no matter how backward and uncivilized they were. "This law was to become one of the great turning points of the civilization of the East, having profound effects throughout the neighboring kingdoms, not least in India itself and in Sri Lanka, and reaching China and Greece."[13]

At 45° a person must be "true to oneself" above all, and intellectually satisfied with his profession of faith or lack of it, an attitude shown by Akbar, a 16th century Moghul ruler of India. After listening to the teachings of the world's religions Akbar declared:

Now it has become clear to me, that in our troubled world so full of contradictions, it cannot be wisdom to assert the unique truth of one faith over another. The wise person makes justice his guide and learns from all. Perhaps in this way the door may be opened again, whose key has been lost. [14]

Emperor Akbar established religious freedom in India (despite opposition from conservative Muslim clerics). In like fashion, the United States founders, with memories of religious strife in previous centuries fresh in their minds, set up a constitutional system that guaranteed religious freedom. In his 45° approach to religion Thomas Jefferson made for his own personal use a cut-and-paste New Testament titled *The Life and Morals of Jesus of Nazareth* that arranged the Gospels into one narrative but omitted any miracles.

Artists, musicians, and architects from many traditions have been inspired to create (50°) marvelous cathedrals and temples, statues and monuments, religious paintings, poetry, drama, and sacred music. Creative expressions such as Gothic cathedrals, mandalas, Khmer sculptures, illuminated manuscripts, Gregorian chants, the classical music of India, and Mozart's Requiem Mass speak universally to the human spirit (X°) whatever the individual's professed religion or lack.*

Some individuals give up the rewards of this world for a different kind of awareness. In India, an estimated four to five million holy men (*sadhus*) and holy women (*sadhvis*, about one-tenth of the total, and mostly widows) live under a strict spiritual discipline, practicing meditation and renunciation in order to reach the mystical core of religion. There are mystical strands in most religious traditions, but religion and mysticism are not the same entity, as expressed by Hafiz, a 14th century Persian poet and mystic who said "The great religions are the ships, poets the lifeboats. Every sane person I know has jumped overboard."

Mysticism manifests X°, the subject of the penultimate chapter.

*Recurring festivals of world sacred music are held in Fez, Morocco; Los Angeles; and Olympia, Washington.

[1] Pew Research Center, "The Global Religious Landscape," Dec. 18, 2012, http://www.pewforum.org/2012/12/18/global-religious-landscape-exec/

[2] Rick Noack, "Map: These are the world's least religious countries," April 14, 2015,
https://www.washingtonpost.com/news/worldviews/wp/2015/04/14/map-these-are-the-worlds-least-religious-countries/

[3] http://www.dictionary.com/browse/religion

[4] Francesca Gino, Michael I. Norton, "Why Rituals Work,"*Scientific American*," May 14, 2013   https://www.scientificamerican.com/article/why-rituals-work/

[5] Pastor Larry Peters,
http://pastoralmeanderings.blogspot.com/2011/04/ritual-without-religion-religion.html

[6] Paul W. Diener, *Religion and Morality: An Introduction*, Westminster John Knox Press 1997

[7] Kevin Kruse, *One Nation under God: How Corporate America Invented Christian America,* Basic Books, April 14, 2015

8 Center for Reduction of Religious-based Conflict,
http://www.center2000.org/

[9] Daveed Gartenstein-Ross, "How Many Fighters Does the Islamic State Really Have?" Foundation for Defense of Democracies, February 9, 2015,
http://www.defenddemocracy.org/media-hit/gartenstein-ross-daveed-how-many-fighters-does-isis-have/

[10] Terry Mattingly, "Blasphemy iceberg bigger than political cartoons," *Arkansas Democrat-Gazette*, Feb. 28, 2015

[11] Graeme Wood, "What Is Islamic State," *Atlantic*, March 2015,
http://www.theatlantic.com/magazine/archive/2015/03/what-isis-really-wants/384980/

[12] Marlene Winell, "Religious Trauma Syndrome, RTS,"
http://journeyfree.org/rts/
"Religious Trauma Syndrome,"
http://www.patheos.com/blogs/nolongerquivering/2013/03/religious-trauma-syndrome/#ixzz3PCzG0bXn

[13] Gerald Draper, "The contribution of the Emperor Asoka Maurya to the development of the humanitarian ideal in warfare," *International Review of the Red Cross*, No. 305, April 30, 1995

[14] Michael Wood, *In Search of the First Civilizations*, Random House 2013

Chapter 14

Technical 20°

Every man takes the limits of his own field of vision for the limits of the world. ~Arthur Schopenhauer, "Studies in Pessimism," *Psychological Observations*, 1851

We can thank 20° for much of the basic structure of civilization, its organization, administration, and technology. Yet perhaps civilization as we know it is not yet the peak of human development. Both 20° and civilization itself can become attached to old habits that lead to evolutionary dead-end, such as dualism. Humans have become addicted to dividing the world in two (Cartesian dualism). The roots of this habit lie deep. Human consciousness is patterned by differences— male and female, right and left, night and day. While the ability to make distinctions is basic to human thinking, people can get stuck in the either/or mode, a condition known to psychology as *splitting*.

Despite apparent oppositions in nature, most of experience is analogical rather than binary. There are many shades of gray, constant changes from one pole to the other, and almost always more than two alternatives in a given situation. Yet 20° clings to the either/or, caring little about the Tao or philosophers and their cosmic polarities. His opposites are written in stone, and he picks one side over the other. 20° often uses the metaphor of combat; this habit of itself contributes to humanity's continual history of war and lesser conflicts.

20° also greatly magnifies the role and value of competition, turning all life into games—if not wars—to be won or lost. (Games that involve ultimate power over others are played at 10°.) 29° sees interactions in terms of Win/Lose, only rarely as Win/Win. The materialist, competitive stance is especially noticeable in the modern United States, where pragmatism, instrumentalism, and theories of economic competition have developed most fully.*

---

*Pragmatism: A philosophy emphasizing practical consequences as the essential criterion of meaning or value.
Instrumentalism: A philosophy that the usefulness of ideas determines their truth.

20° believes that he has a scientific worldview but it is most likely the ideology scientism. John Michael Greer notes the difference:

> Science, at core, is simply a method of practical logic that tests hypotheses against experience. Scientism, by contrast, is the worldview and value system that insists that the questions the scientific method can answer are the most important questions human beings can ask, and that the picture of the world yielded by science is a better approximation to reality than any other.[1]

Or it is technologism, equating knowledge with technological control, assuming that every human problem has a technological solution.[2]

Another 20° habit is reductionism, a useful scientific approach (45°) that studies complex phenomena by looking at their simpler or more basic components. However, when misapplied, 20° reductionism insists that the complex whole is *nothing but* the sum of its parts. Similar attitudes are found in the larger culture. For instance, the 'reductionist fallacy' looks for a single cause to explain any occurrence, although they almost always have several contributing causes. A kind of reductionism creeps into human relationships, where party A assumes that party B has the simplest or most venial motives possible.

Two extremely influential scientists, John Watson and B.F. Skinner, demonstrate 20° reductionism. Watson's behaviorist theory dominated psychology for the first half of the 20th century. Behaviorism limits itself to the study of observable and quantifiable aspects of human and animal behavior, excluding subjective mental states such as emotions or motives. Watson famously said:

> Give me a dozen healthy infants, well-formed, and my own specified world to bring them up in and I'll guarantee to take any one at random and train him to become any type of specialist I might select—doctor, lawyer, artist, merchant-chief, and, yes, even beggarman and thief, regardless of his talents, penchants, tendencies, abilities, vocations, and race of his ancestors.[3]

Watson may have exaggerated a bit on the side of nurture, because he was arguing against eugenics. Later, B.F. Skinner (1904-1990) introduced his own theory of radical behaviorism which assumes that all animal or human behavior is determined or caused by experiences of reward or punishment. Thus there is no free will. Our actions result from our history of positive or negative reinforcement from external sources. Or as Skinner said: "What is love except another name for the use of positive reinforcement? Or vice versa."

Using animal research, Skinner showed how to create behavior change by breaking tasks into smaller parts and rewarding each small success (operant conditioning). By this means he taught pigeons to play ping-pong and cats to play the piano. His work has influenced child-rearing, behavioral therapy, management, education, and self-help. While his findings and methods have added to our knowledge, by themselves they provide a narrow view of the human being that continues into the present. A psychology professor says that every introductory textbook his department has used teaches that "dreams are meaningless by-products of brain processes" while imagination is denied or discounted simply as a source of error in memory.[4]

20° Behavior: 20° traits somewhat resemble the so-called Type-A temperament known for ambition, impatience, need for control, and the tendency to value quantity over quality. 20° is drawn not only to success but to all sorts of superlatives—the fastest, the biggest, the strongest, the newest, the loudest, and the shiniest, also exaggerated sexual characteristics, and extreme, dramatic situations affecting other people or fictional characters. If we were speaking of animals, biologists could call this a preference for *supernormal stimuli.*

20° is the more mental higher octave of aggressive 5°, with elements of 15° follow the leader and 10° authoritarianism. 20° believes he has escaped 15° confusion by denying his feelings and scorning their display in other ignoring that ambition and aggressive competition are also emotional. He considers himself an independent thinker even when he has few original thoughts. He identifies himself as rational and logical, and highly values intelligence, at least as measured by IQ tests and demonstrated in 20° pursuits. His view of intelligence is quite instrumental and spills over into educational practices in which students are force-fed information and skills like geese raised for their livers.

The modus operandi of 20° is often described as 'left-brained' or linear, or inclined to use step by step analysis rather than analogy and intuition. Linear thinking is built into our social structures and world views. We are a 'left- brain' culture, a preference which affects us all.*

One of the traits that distinguish 20° is practicality. This word has many positive associations such as dealing with reality rather than the imagined, or preferring what is reasonable and appropriate for actual use. In effect, it often means favoring short-term gain, and 'being practical' is about acquiring wealth or avoiding spending. (The more positive aspects of practicality may be found at 30°.)

Another high value for 20° is 'realism' (often this is pessimism). Anxious to avoid the 15° labels of gullibility or emotionalism, 20° may be cynical to the point of misanthropy. He is often a pseudo-skeptic, who denies minority opinions without investigating them, in contrast to the true skeptic's position of neutrality while seeking evidence.

The 20° individual aspires to be rich, admires rich people, and respects businessmen and business methods. He often identifies with owners and money managers even though he himself is a lowly paid employee. Depending on his circumstances, 20° is highly concerned either with profits, availability of good jobs, or opposition to taxes. Americans at this degree believe in the American Dream, seeing this vision mainly as individual economic success.

This degree is often compartmentalized. 20° easily becomes attached to abstract symbols that overwhelm the individual's direct observations and his empathy towards real people and other living beings. He often fails to note the contradictions in his own attitudes. He believes in competition, yet stratification of the pecking order guarantees efficiency and stability—and efficiency is a high value for 20°. So he tends to support authority, even authoritarian personalities.

*Left-brain' culture is prototypically post-17th century, post-Industrial Revolution, 20th century, Northern European, and North American

Paradoxically, while 20° is usually obedient to authority, he often is also what might be called a *vulgar libertarian*, that is, someone who believes "I should have the freedom to do anything I want to do." (Vulgar in the sense of being common and ordinary.)

We now see many Americans dividing every sort of issue into "liberal" or conservative." Categories can be useful mental tools—this book uses them liberally—but not when applied automatically and rigidly and used as short-cuts to actual thinking.

The 20° modality likes to plan ahead, to make distinctions between things, and to rank them in a hierarchy. He prefers structure and established knowledge, and is uncomfortable with ambiguity. 20° wants everything in proper order. As novelist Doris Lessing described one of her characters: "This young student…recognized that he never had a thought, or an emotion, that didn't instantly fit into pigeon-holes, one marked 'Marx' and one marked 'Freud.'"

The nature of worldviews is such that we don't realize we have them. According to authors Paul H. Ray and Sherry Anderson, about 40% of the U.S. population subscribes to the Modern worldview. "They are the people who accept the commercialized urban-industrial world as the obvious right way to live." The Modern worldview links with various ideologies and several dispositions, but its most unswerving devotees are at 20°. Its philosophical underpinnings are rigid and reductionist: the world is a closed system, composed of material objects behaving by non-varying rules (Newtonian mechanics). [5]

The Modern worldview also includes Enlightenment principles such as equality, justice, and democracy, to which 20° gives lip-service even when he promotes other ideologies that undermine them. Cynicism and materialistic values tend to trump the idealism. Enlightenment ideals are held more fully by Moderns acting at 30° or 35°.

Some at 20° consider themselves to be religious, yet do not really believe in anything beyond the material world—the world of the senses. Worship is overlaid with materiality, hierarchy, and other 20° values and characteristics. Some go to church for social and business reasons. Whatever the prevailing religion to which 20° gives lip service, he is a materialist through and through. His true religion may be the magic of technology.

Bureaucracy

> *Bureaucracy is a giant mechanism operated by pygmies.*
> ~Honore de Balzac, French novelist

20° finds a strange beauty in industrialism, standardization, mass production, and mechanization. He finds satisfaction in rationalizing (streamlining) processes and putting things into their proper categories. Thus 20° devised the first bureaucracies in ancient Sumer and Egypt. Officials and scribes oversaw the ruler's growing domain. Bureaucracy is defined as a kind of administrative system that relies on a set of rules and procedures, divided functions, and a hierarchical structure.

Government bureaucracies control and govern the production and distribution of a society's wealth. The modern nation-state cannot exist without them. However, businesses and other large social organizations are also organized bureaucratically. While 20° likes to consider himself a rebel against government bureaucracy, he tends to ignore other kinds of bureaucratic systems that are the inevitable accompaniment to large size and centralized power.

Bureaucracy's main advantage is efficiency (a 20° value) and its main disadvantage is inefficiency, as American sociologist Robert K. Merton points out:

> (1) An effective bureaucracy demands reliability of response and strict devotion to regulations. (2) Such devotion to the rules leads to their transformation into absolutes; they are no longer conceived as relative to a set of purposes. (3) This interferes with ready adaptation under special conditions not clearly envisaged by those who drew up the general rules. (4) Thus, the very elements which conduce toward efficiency in general produce inefficiencies in specific instances.[6]

In a bureaucracy, efficiency is paramount, sometimes at the cost of justice and mercy. Yet even efficiency may become lost in a welter of rules and regulations. 20° sets up bureaucracies and 15° finds comfort working in them, righteously applying rules without flexibility or imagination while the system devolves into confusion (a 'degenerated bureaucracy'). Besides inefficiency, this can result in problems such as corruption, political infighting, and a system of recruitment and promotion not based on merit. The bureaucracy becomes a sort of oligarchy (10°). Another 10° trait is the tendency of bureaucracies to grow, or as Oscar Wilde quipped, "The bureaucracy is expanding to meet the needs of the expanding bureaucracy."

The nightmare of being caught up in such a system was depicted by Charles Dickens in *Little Dorritt* with its "Circumlocution Office," and more darkly by Czech writer Franz Kafka in his novels *The Castle* and *The Trial*. In extreme cases, bureaucracy leads to treating human individuals solely as impersonal objects (0°). In the real-life horror of the Nazi concentration camps. Adolf Eichmann became the symbol of a soulless bureaucrat (0°/20°).

Deus ex Machina *(God from the Machine)*

In a technological civilization, everything becomes an imitation of technology or a compensation for the impact of technology.
~Jacques Ellul, *Perspective on Our Age*, 1981

French philosopher Jacques Ellul says the modern technological system—now only a century or two old—"eliminates or subordinates the natural world." That includes the humans who must adapt to the system. Ultimately, this becomes 0° exterminism. But is it inevitable?

Broadly speaking, technology is the application of knowledge for practical purposes, and historically involves far more than machines. We've used fire for at least a million years. Archaeologist Katheryn Twiss points out that "Every domesticated animal is a hugely complex new technology."[7] So are cassava processing, alphabets, and administrative techniques. Two ancient but still basic technologies are measurement and money. Measurement allowed our ancestors to build, to trade, and to divide common land or conquered land into private property. 20° believes that if something cannot be measured, it does not exist, or is unimportant. The measurement of time allowed industrial societies to rule our lives by the clock. And since William Playfair devised the tools of statistics in 1786, some have come to think that statistics can explain everything, from sex appeal to ultimate truth.[8]

It was probably 20° that invented money (which now makes the world go round). Surely it was 20° that invented interest (in Mesopotamia about 4,500 years ago). The same disposition invented corporations, and 400 years later it gave them personhood. Despite the abstract nature of money, interest, and corporations, the individuals most concerned with them are popularly regarded as practical, commonsense, and realistic.

Identifying himself with science, what 20° really means is technology. They are not the same entity. Science is about *understanding* the natural world (45°) while technology is about *making use of it*, which today almost always involves corporate profit. 20° identifies closely with science-and-technology (unless scientific pronouncements seem to threaten economic interests).

In modern usage, technology most often means machines and the processes related to them. Let us make a distinction between tools and technology. Tools are powered and controlled by a human being, often requiring some time for an individual to attain full mastery. Machines, on the other hand, act like magic. Tools and tool-making are 30° functions. But 30° does not model himself on his tools. Scott Russell Sanders in *The Inheritance of Tools* notes that with machines "The skill is invested in the gadget instead of the person who uses it, and this is what distinguishes a machine from a tool."

Today it is all about digital data, dubbed "the world's most valuable resource" in an article that notes tech giants Google, Facebook, Amazon, Microsoft, and Apple are the most valuable listed firms in the world. [9] (Alternatively, the world's most valuable resource is water, soil, green plants, solar radiation, the human mind, or children.)

So far, about two fifths of the world's people use the Internet and half are subscribed to a mobile phone service.[10] We employ digital technology for work and play, business and crime, research, socializing, surgery, spying, gaming, viewing pornography, and emergency rescues. The planet is plugged in, with unknown consequences.

At 20° a person may not like to hear about the disadvantages and drawbacks of any technology, as almost an attack on himself. The 20° admiration for technology is not only because of its labor-saving qualities, efficiency, and abilities that surpass those of humans—but also for its *perfection*. Some individuals at 20° take machines as their model—a kind of ideal for humans, something to emulate in our work and sports and sex lives. Machines have wide-ranging powers beyond those of 'meat' beings and they lack many of our flaws. They are cleaner, have fewer needs, think faster, and have greater physical abilities and endurance. Machines appear to be self-powered and in the primitive recesses of our consciousness they may seem to be alive.

Danger arises from the unforeseen results of scientific knowledge that is 'put to work' by others, becoming doomsday weapons or a profitable but destructive technology. The modernist 35° may interpret this as progress, but 35° environmentalists and reformers resist it because of unintended consequences (15°) that can extend even to 0° terracide (destruction of natural ecosystems or of an entire planet).

Shortcuts and the Singularity

The saddest aspect of life right now is that science gathers knowledge faster than society gathers wisdom.
~Isaac Asimov

Several shortcuts to great knowledge exist, falling under the headings of magic and technology. The potential to anger the gods was always there, and the Shadow side of great knowledge resonates through ancient myths: Prometheus gave fire and metal-working to mankind and for this Zeus arranged an eternal punishment. The Greek inventor Daedalus devised a flying machine but suffered for his cleverness by losing his son Icarus. Meanwhile, Adam and Eve were expelled from the Garden for eating the fruit of the Tree of Knowledge.

In medieval legend, Faustus traded his soul to the devil in exchange for the power of earthly knowledge. The stories end with him being carried off to Hell. Medieval wizardry has now been replaced by genetic enhancement, computer assists, and instant genius through pills. Meanwhile, science fiction, from Frankenstein's monster to cyberpunk, continually imagines or extrapolates the consequences of technologies, current or possible. The best sf is not only entertainment but it also performs a vitally necessary social function of preparing us for technological changes that are happening at an increasing rate.

Polymathic mathematician John von Neumann was first to warn that technological advances would soon provide an unprecedented crisis for humanity, in "some essential singularity in the history of the race beyond which human affairs, as we know them, could not continue." This could lead to widespread confusion (15°) and deep depression (0°).

Transhumanists actually look forward to the singularity predicted by von Neumann. The Technological Singularity is that point in time (2040?) when Artificial Intelligence (AI) is expected to surpass human intelligence. As first defined in 1990 by British philosopher and futurist Max More, transhumanism seeks "the continuation and acceleration of the evolution of intelligent life beyond its currently human form and human limitations by means of science and technology, guided by life-promoting principles and values." [11]

It is now an international movement researching technologies such as artificial intelligence, life extension, mind uploading, genome editing, bionic enhancement, 3D bio-printing, cryonics, self-replicating robots, space colonization, nanotech, and simulated reality. A number of well-known techno-futurists are investing heavily in research companies or are conducting research themselves.*

---

*Investors include multi-billionaire Peter Thiel, Eliezer Yudkowsky, Larry Ellison, Mark Zuckerberg, and Google co-founders Larry Page and Sergey Brin. Technology writer David Auerbach comments: "The combination of messianic ambitions, being convinced of your own infallibility, and a lot of cash *never* works out well, regardless of ideology…"

Transhumanism reflects 20° and 25° dispositions more than 45°. It is no coincidence that the character Sheldon Cooper, a brilliant but emotionally immature physicist in a popular television comedy, is as enamored of the coming technological Singularity as he is of fighting monsters in massively multiplayer online role-playing games.

The rest of us need to remember those three imprudent doctors—Faustus, Frankenstein, and Jekyll—and the results of their mistakes. Science writer David Auerbach notes that "If you believe the singularity is coming and that very powerful AIs are in our future, one obvious question is whether those AIs will be benevolent or malicious." Modern wizards are on the verge of developing existential threats such as weaponized nanotechnology, weaponized pathogens, and autonomous robots designed to kill humans.[12]

In a parody of spiritual transcendence, transhumanists look forward to technological transcendence and superiority to "meat puppets" (ordinary humans). Obsession with technological possibilities occurs at 20°. The prevalence of this viewpoint is increasingly important as the computer age advances. According to sociologist Richard Stivers, "Our expectations for technology have become magical and our use of it is increasingly irrational….If the sacred is ultimately that which is absolutely powerful then it was inevitable that technology would replace nature as the object of tacit veneration." [13]

A Cluster of 20° Ideologies

A reigning ideology is a little like the weather: all pervasive and virtually inescapable.
~Michael Pollan, American educator

Directing aggressive drive into mental channels, 20° is strongly attracted to ideologies. An ideology is defined here as a collection of beliefs that lend legitimacy to an individual, group, or society as a whole It is composed of both conscious and unconscious ideas, and it explains as well as motivates. 20° is the disposition most likely to develop and disseminate ideologies associated with social and economic classes, institutions, and political parties. These often include elaborate rationalizations for the status quo advantages of one group over another, justifying 5° bigotry or aggression, or acting as the mouthpiece for 10° power. Some ideologies are the result of wishful thinking.

Ideologies can be internally consistent even when they don't agree with the evidence. Internal consistency seems to lend credibility. Those who hold an ideology usually try to spread it as widely as possible, to persuade others through devising and repeating propaganda. In general, ideologizing appears to be a male preoccupation, although some women enjoy the game.

Scores of interrelated ideologies popped up in recent decades in the United States, often via the Internet, such as libertarianism, techno-utopianism, and transhumanism. These proliferating ideologies arise from a seedbed of technology worship and corporate capitalism. Highly successful men promulgate such ideas, invest in them, and serve as 20° idols. Adherents have been immersed since childhood in a culture of advertising, cyber devices, social media, Internet blogs, video games, comic book superheroes, science fiction, fantasy fiction, and sci-fi.

American libertarianism is a root ideology and has wide public support (about one-fifth of those polled and one-third of younger men).[17] Defined as "A laissez-faire political/economic philosophy that upholds individual liberties and advocates minimal state intervention," it may specially appeal to those with ancestors from the English/Scottish borderlands ('Scots-Irish' or 'Borderers') whose tradition greatly values individual liberty while distrusting formal and central governments. Libertarian theory borrows language from anarchism and classical liberalism (45°) with property rights and Social Darwinism (10°) in the subtext. Proponents and critics differ greatly on its origins, which some trace to Enlightenment thinkers, others to a 1946 arrangement with the real estate lobby by economists Milton Friedman and George Stigler. In some respects, libertarianism represents a   resurgence of the ethos of 19th century industrial capitalism (10°/20°).

However, most followers seem to be drawn, first and foremost, by the 25° individualist and egoist aspects. According to proponent David Friedman, "The central idea of libertarianism is that people should be permitted to run their own lives as they wish,".[18] The late Christopher Hitchens put it differently: "I have always found it quaint and rather touching that there is a movement [libertarianism] in the US that thinks Americans are not yet selfish enough. "

Another fairly widespread attitude/ideology, techno-utopianism (20°/35°), is the idea that technology can create an ideal society by ending resource scarcity, or that computer tech can help us achieve participatory democracy and other ideals (cyber-utopianism). Despite some very positive ventures such as Project Gutenberg, Wikipedia, online collaboration, and network sharing, we still fall far short of political and socioeconomic utopia.

In the 1930s, technocracy advocated control of society by an elite of technical experts. Decades later it enjoyed a brief revival as the Venus Project (substituting computers for experts) and the Zeitgeist Movement, also proposing scientific administration of society.

Some ideological groups teach and promote critical thinking skills a la scientism. Organized skeptics such as the Committee for Skeptical Inquiry have a strong bias toward disbelief especially of the paranormal, New Age, and religion. Rationalists (Less Wrong site) typically hold the following philosophical positions: reductionism, materialism, utilitarianism, and transhumanism.

Hypothetically, one could create Venn diagrams showing how various ideological bubbles overlap, or how many of those attracted to a certain ideology tend to be attracted to another one. Among these proliferating ideologies some are far right (10°). The neo-reactionary movement—sometimes called the Dark Enlightenment—looks back with longing at former power arrangements such as patriarchy and monarchy. It has reportedly made a few inroads in Silicon Valley with influential people such as Curtis Yarvin and Peter Thiel.

Other Internet ideologies such as the alt-right are frankly neo-fascist, anti-Semitic, anti-Muslim, and white supremacist (5°). Related ideas and movements exist in the United States, Canada and Europe, especially as a reaction to immigration, cultural changes, and the 2008 recession (high unemployment rates continue in some parts of Europe).

[1] John Michael Greer, After Progress: Reason and Religion at the End of the Industrial Age, New Society Publishers, 2015

[2] http://www.marshillonline.com/featured-articles/technologism-faith-in-technology/

[3] J.B. Watson, *Behaviorism*, University of Chicago Press, 1930

[4] Robert Moss, *The Secret History of Dreaming*, New World Library 2009

[5] Paul H. Ray, Ph.D. & Sherry Ruth Anderson, Ph.D., *The Cultural Creatives: How 50 Million People Are Changing the World*, Three Rivers Press, 2000

[6] *"Bureaucracy," New World Encyclopedia,* http://www.newworldencyclopedia.org/entry/Bureaucracy

[7] Jennifer Hattam, "Paradise Lost," *Discover*, September 2016

[8] George Woodcock, "The Tyranny of the Clock," http://www.acsu.buffalo.edu/~rrojas/TyrannyofClock.html

[9] "The World's Most Valuable Resource," *The Economist*, May 6, 2017

[10] "Internet World Stats," http://www.internetworldstats.com/stats.htm

[11] Max More, "What Is Transhumanism?" http://whatistranshumanism.org/

[12] George Dvorsky, "Ten Horrifying Technologies That Should Never Be Allowed to Exist," *io9*, Sept. 16, 2014, http://io9.gizmodo.com/10-horrifying-technologies-that-should-never-be-allowed-1635238363

[13] Richard Stivers, *Technology as Magic: The triumph of the irrational*, Continuum 1999

[14] Matt Welch, "19% of Americans Self-Identify as Libertarians, New Reuters Poll Finds: One-third of Millennials, but only one-eighth of oldsters, embrace the term." *Reason*, Apr. 30, 2015, http://reason.com/blog/2015/04/30/19-of-americans-self-identify-as-liberta

[15] David Friedman, *The Machinery of Freedom*, Open Court Publishing, 1973

Chapter 15
Competition and Capitalism (20º)

Competition brings out the best in products and the worst in man.
~Author Unknown

Competition is described as the active demand by two or more humans or other organisms for a limited resource. One widespread view claims that all life, including human society, is based on competitive struggle and self-interest, winning the game or replacing one's opposite number. An old proverb says "It's every man for himself and the devil take the hindmost." We compete with other species—predators, pests, weeds, and germs, and those that inconveniently live in places where we want sole control. We compete with other humans for jobs, sexual partners, status, and promotions. We compete as groups and sub-groups for resources and recognition, and with other nation-states in terms of global markets, resources, prestige, military preparations, and war.

In the 20º view most of life is a zero-sum game, and you must lose so I can win. Among other things this ideology justifies imperialism, 'cut-throat competition,' extreme economic inequality, and harsh domestic policies such as removing the safety net. Historically, this idea system received great impetus or justification from several 17th century philosophers and from an over-simplified and distorted view of evolutionary theory in biology. Today the competitive ideology is promoted through neoliberalism.*

Competition certainly exists in nature but does not describe every situation. Not everything is a limited resource nor is everybody in direct competition since organisms can find or create special niches. Sometimes a limited resource can be shared (35º/40º) or replaced through 50º innovation. As Serbian poet Dejan Stojanovic put it, "There is no competition of sounds between a nightingale and a violin."

*Neoliberalism: a modern politico-economic theory that favors free trade, privatization, minimal government intervention in business, and reduced public expenditure on social services.

Competition does benefit many aspects of human life. We note a more or less friendly rivalry among a dozen painters in Renaissance Florence, or 19th century French Impressionists, or among 1960s popular musicians innovating new musical forms. Competition provides a great deal of positive human expression in sports and games, which are at least as old as the human species, ranging though the dispositions to the 50° 'flow' experienced by dedicated athletes. The ancient Greeks believed that athletic talent was inspired by a god ($X°$).

But when competitiveness overwhelms other satisfactions of the game, we get cheating, sore losers, even riots. When parents of a child athlete start a fist-fight (5°) with the referee, the old-fashioned value of good sportsmanship (30°) ends.

In another arena, Loren Eiseley notes the entry of the competitive spirit in science and a resulting loss of imagination: "One of the disadvantages of big science [is] that the availability of huge sums attracts a swarm of elbowing and contentious men [20°] to whom great dreams are less than protected hunting preserves."

At some point, the competitive ethos spreads from business and sports to education and personal life. Harsh competition contributes to the civility crisis and detracts from work satisfaction. Individuals become stressed and impatient, and make decisions based on the competitor rather than their own goals. Sexual partners are rated on their 'performance' as if love is only a sport. Children become game pieces of their parent's competitiveness when young children are trained to play ball games with the same intensity as professional athletes. Little girls compete in beauty contests masquerading as seductive women. Teens compete for grades, popularity, and their ranking in the current pattern of conspicuous consumption.

Alfie Kohn writes about the damaging effects of competition on children when self-worth depends on how many people you've beaten in competitions. Hostility replaces empathy and trust, and "success comes to be defined as victory even though these are really two very different things." Kohn says that for children, there is no such thing as 'healthy competition.'[1]

Competitive Arenas

Politics is the art of looking for trouble, finding it whether it exists or not, diagnosing it incorrectly, and applying the wrong remedy.
~Ernest Benn

Some great and enduring arenas for 20° competition are economics, politics, law, and war, and the many combinations thereof.

Electoral democracy institutionalizes competition, and public life can be played as combat, with party supporters acting like warring enemies. Excessive political competition is not a new phenomenon; several American founders (Madison, Hamilton, and Washington) warned against factionalism in the *Federalist Papers* and elsewhere. However, they could not foresee the aftermath of slavery, or the magnifying effects on partisanship of modern media and advertising.

Either/or thinking is taking over the U.S, with political partisanship becoming the main paradigm in many areas of life. Mainstream media have degenerated into reporting most political news in terms of partisan and individual competition—"who's up, who's down"—and very little about actual issues and policies. This 20° consciousness has led to incivility and dysfunction in legislative bodies, as well as a belligerent public life.

While 20° expresses partisanship and politics in general, some politicians grandstand and stroke their egos at 25° and others retain their basic decency and integrity at 30°. There are always some corrupt leaders (10°) and some whose personal problems and confusion overshadow their political life (15°). When a political leader attempts to represent a larger constituency—the entire nation—at 35° it may be called statesmanship. A few national leaders throughout world history have approached a 40°/45° concern for the future and humanity as a whole. Nelson Mandela appears to be one. U.S. President John Kennedy was revered by many outside his own country because of their perception that he had this wider vision (whether or not this was true, or whether he would have made a difference had he lived longer).

The common-law legal system is patterned on opposition between defense and prosecution. However, this opposition, hedged about with laws, professional traditions, and ethical regulations, is supposed to result in an approximation of the truth—and often does. (You may say not often enough.)

War is violent competition. The 20° mindset thinks in terms of the ultimate of competition and opposing ideas. Thus we have had culture wars, cold wars, race wars, drug wars, shooting wars, water wars, resource wars, class wars, revolutions, counter-revolutions, newspaper wars, trade wars, price wars, religious wars, propaganda wars, world wars, gang wars, civil wars, total wars, limited wars, cabinet wars, perpetual wars, undeclared wars, wars of succession, wars of conquest, wars of liberation, colonial wars, guerrilla wars, proxy wars, and arms races. More abstractly, politicos declare wars against drugs, cancer, poverty, and other diseases and ills of society. We also talk about the battle of the sexes and generational warfare, and some of us carry sibling rivalry into adulthood.

Don't Be a Loser

Several studies have shown that male fans of a winning football team have higher testosterone levels after the game than the fans of the losing team.
~Barbara Oakley, *Evil Genes*

Perhaps 20° is a 'testosterone junkie.' At any rate, 20° greatly admires success of all kinds, especially victory in war and athletic teams on a winning streak. Those who once belittled Vietnam War vets as 'losers' were acting at 20°. So are those who refuse to identify with the home team unless they are winning.

One heroic model for 20° is the successful entrepreneur who has an invention or an innovative idea and carries it through to financial success: Thomas Edison or Steve Jobs or Sam Walton. The term *entrepreneur* is defined as a person who organizes and manages an enterprise, usually with considerable initiative and risk. What is at risk is money: that is, their capital or grubstake, whether it is earned, borrowed, or inherited. If the enterprise doesn't pan out, as many do not, then goodbye Charlie—you are no longer the object of 20° admiration.

Professions and businesses usually include some members who will cut corners without actually breaking laws. Such habits may lead to fraud and other white collar crime. Dr. Kaptein's list of psychologies behind unethical business behavior has several applying to 20°. A context of "Winner take-all competition" stimulates people to avoid losing, at all costs. Also, when people's actions and their moral system start to diverge, they rationalize to protect themselves from the pain of cognitive dissonance. Another situation that fosters unethical practices is tunnel vision—focusing too single-mindedly on the goal, such as sales. A fourth tendency that evokes 20° is time pressure, which studies show can undermine altruistic impulses.

Sharp business practices sometimes shade into frankly criminal enterprises. Shady businesses range from the street level (such as bootleg movies) up to securities fraud and other multi-million dollar thefts, which are seldom prosecuted because they are part of 'the system.' As defined by Howard Scott (inventor of technocracy) "A criminal is a person with predatory instincts who has not sufficient capital to form a corporation." The biggest heists often involve Machiavellian personalities who coldly deceive and manipulate others without any moral reservations (10°).

Capitalism and its Degrees

I think there has always been a huge gap between what theories of capitalism say it is and how capitalism operates out in the world,
~Naomi Klein, interview with Ana Marie Cox, June 18, 2017

Twenty degrees is the 'home base' of capitalism, describing its idealized form (free market economy), but it also appears at several other degrees. At 0° we see commodification of nature in all its manifestations from bioengineered seeds to the militarization of outer space; every kind of personal information to ownership of human beings as in slavery or prison labor.

Murray Rothbard, founder and main theoretician of anarcho-capitalism (a version of libertarianism) argues that "If a parent may own his child… then he may also transfer that ownership to someone else. He may give the child out for adoption, or he may sell the rights to the child in a voluntary contract. In short, we must face the fact that the purely free society will have a flourishing free market in children."[2]

A more common manifestation of 0° in economic life is malign indifference: selling defective products or cutting corners fully aware that this is likely to kill people. Instigating wars in order to sell weapons of war is 0°, as is war motivated mainly by acquiring or protecting foreign resources—in other words, mass murder for capital gain.

10° is economic greed and the Pac-Man tendency of capitalistic enterprises to grow ever larger, to become conglomerates, and to control more of the market. In the last half century multinational or transnational corporations have accelerated this process, with the largest of them bringing in more profits than the GDP of many smaller countries. Command economies also operate at 10° centralized power, but through a 20° bureaucracy.

Oligopoly or shared monopoly is the market structure in which a few large firms dominate an industry, making it very difficult for other firms to enter or compete. Oligopolies account for up to half of U.S. economic production and services in, for instance, cars, computers, aircraft, meatpacking, pharmaceuticals, petroleum, media, banking, and household appliances. Chains are part of the trend toward oligopoly. Ironically, the bigger and fewer the businesses, the less efficient and competitive they tend to be. Smaller businesses create more jobs. [3]

Big fish eat smaller fish, and sometimes faster, more voracious fish eat all the others. Financial speculation and manipulation can trump the whole system. In the wake of the U.S. foreclosure crisis journalist Matt Taibbi pointed out "what we've got now is a situation where there is a small class of gigantic financial companies that have put themselves above capitalism." Michael Hudson in *Killing the Host,* asserts that the more abstract, secondary, or parasitic businesses of finance, insurance, and real estate have prevailed over industrial capitalism that actually manufactures products (10°/20° over 30°?).

Hostile takeovers and union-busting are more examples of 10° behavior. When economic power translates into political power, as it usually does, the result is not only corruption but a loss of democratic government. In the U.S, well-funded propaganda insists that money is a form of political speech and no limits should be placed on its expression.

Naomi Klein first drew attention to "disaster capitalism" in her book *The Shock Doctrine*. She defines disaster capitalism as the practice by a government or regime of taking advantage of a major disaster using violent shock tactics (such as privatization of water or mass layoffs in the public sector) to impose liberal economic policies that the population would be unlikely to accept under normal circumstances. Examples are the U.S. occupations of Iraq and of Sri Lanka after the Asian tsunami. Disaster capitalism represents 10° corrupt power with elements of 0° malign indifference.

10° represents every kind of financial dishonesty and corruption as well as the Mafia, Mexican and Colombian drug cartels, and other organized crime groups. Shady businesses that involve extortion or blackmail, confidence tricks, loan sharks, racketeering, and other illegal or extra-legal activities express 10°. If using assault or execution as tactics or involved in murderous turf wars, they spin towards 0°.

When organized criminals move into various areas of legal business such as trash hauling, dock loading, and building construction, they can launder money from their illegitimate enterprises. The legitimate business may be highly profitable in itself. Or the move may be an attempt to become a respectable part of society (30°). Insofar as these owners of legitimate businesses continue to use illegitimate methods such as extortion or terrorism, they act at 10° or 0°. Their attempts to monopolize local business and to evade taxes are more blatant than similar tactics that are used by corporations widely considered to be legitimate.

The recurring business cycle of panics, crashes, recessions and depressions expresses and engenders 15° confusion. 15° also refers to repetitive and meaningless jobs, and the many who are barely interested in what they do for a living. Others are at 15° in what Marx called the *lumpenproletariat*, now known as the underclass: marginalized people on the fringes of the formal economy, often homeless or demoralized unemployed, sometimes engaged in illegal activities.*

At a deeper level, 15° refers to basic contradictions in the world economic system as described by Aldous Huxley in the utopian novel *Island*: "Armaments, universal debt and planned obsolescence — those are the three pillars of Western prosperity." Usury (interest) is an old 20° invention or deception giving the ability of reproduction to an inanimate object or abstraction. Thus money begets money over time. Meanwhile it creates debts and debtors.

Interest and debt are now bedrock to the modern capitalist system and banking industry. 'Leverage' is a form of gambling (15°) widely used in business and finances, using borrowed capital to increase the potential return of an investment. Options, futures, margins, and various derivatives and financial instruments are similarly based on guesses about the future of fluctuating variables.

The actual process of lending money at interest can involve fraud (10°/15°) and other abuses such as exorbitant interest rates that impoverish the poor. According to John Ruskin, "It is with lent money that all evil is mainly done."

20° idolizes an abstraction called the free market system based on the ideal of perfect competition.** A free market is or would be a competitive economy based entirely on supply and demand with little or no restriction from government. Yet industries and agriculture virtually never follow the four requirements of perfect competition, which are: 1.) the existence of a large number of small firms (with small market shares); 2.) All the firms make identical products; 3.) Resources are equally accessible to all firms with freedom of entry and exit out of the industry (low barriers to entry). 4.) There is perfect knowledge of prices and technology among both producers and consumers.

*However, some people in low-income areas participate in a thriving informal economy or grey market (20°/35°).
**The United States likes to consider itself the foremost champion of free markets, but *Business Insider* ranks several other nations more business-friendly.

In the real world, products are seldom identical. Money needed for advertising in order to overcome brand loyalty can be an insuperable barrier to entry into a market. The powerful effects of advertising are often based on little or no differences existing between one product and another. . For instance, all aspirin is virtually the same but some heavily advertised brands cost five or six times as much as others.

There is also the tendency for small firms to get bigger, merging with or buying off competitors, sometimes driving them out of business. Monopolies and shared monopolies have existed for centuries—the U.S. economy is about half oligopolies—and the perfect market never actually existed (15° myth).

Virtually all modern nations have mixed economies, some combination of free market and government control (20°/10°/35°). 25° represents consumer society, driven by advertising, brand identity, and pop culture. It is also planned obsolescence, the throw-away culture, and wasted resources in general.

30° stands for small-scale business, often family-run, and the self-employed. Adam Smith saw local capitalism as the basis of society in *The Wealth of Nations,* regarded as the founding book of capitalism, although modern capitalism looks completely different. Other perspectives promote a 'steady-state economy' not based on constant 10° growth that would favor smaller-scale business and 30° stability. Some economists favor 'ecological economics' to reach a steady state for the sake of 40° sustainability. [4]

The unionized working class, organized to protect the interests of its members, is 30°, with the ideal of solidarity at 35°. About one-sixth of the world's people belong to some kind of a cooperative, operating at 30°/35°/40°. (However, some very large businesses are only technically co-ops.) Product and supply chain transparency also express 35°/40° activism and generativity.

'Social entrepreneurship' is an emerging, more idealistic form of capitalism that operates at 35° or 40° depending on the relative emphasis on profit. (Some uses of the term include purely humanitarian work.) In one example, social entrepreneur Jane Chen developed a low-cost baby warmer to use in countries that can't afford incubators. Bill

Drayton helped define the term and founded an organization, Ashoka, to give support to such innovators: the Skoll Foundation gives yearly awards to the most effective efforts.

The lending of small amounts to individuals, especially women, in the developing world so they can start small-scale businesses (30°) has proved quite successful. Some of the lending institutions are motivated by humanitarian concerns (40°) while others are simply moving into a new market (20°).

The movement to forgive crippling debts of poor countries, debts run up by previous dictators, arises from a 40° humanitarianism. Another such movement for global justice is just beginning with proposals for a basic global income (UBI) that could bring the world's poorest billion into basic subsistence (40°/45°) [5] along with many other social benefits.

The Corporation

Corporation: An ingenious device for obtaining profit without individual responsibility.
~Ambrose Bierce, *The Devil's Dictionary, 1906*

Commercial corporations were invented about 400 years ago, and quickly became agencies of imperialism. The British East India Company came to rule whole nations, notably India. The institution reached another peak by about 1980 when, according to analyst Venkatesh Rao, "a significant fraction of humanity was effectively being governed by corporations." Transnational corporations continue to be more powerful than many nation-states, controlling political decisions in some countries by lobbying or bribery ('state capture').[6]

A paper trick gives the corporation its power: it is a legal entity, separate and distinct from its protected owners, with its own individual rights or personhood. This fictional being has been endowed with the rights of living human beings including free speech and the ability to exploit libel laws (UK). While usurping the rights of human beings, the corporate entity has many advantages over humans, starting with the fact that modern corporations are immortal. They have vastly greater resources for lobbying and court cases. Another advantage is that humans are unable to take corporations to court for human rights abuses because human rights law applies only to abuses by the state.

Rao says "the corporate form is ….the consequence of a social contract like the one that anchors nationhood. It is a codified bundle of quasi-religious beliefs externalized into an animate form that seeks to preserve itself like any other living creature." Not only to preserve itself but to grow. The military-industrial complex of President Eisenhower's warning is a case in point. Since his speech

the U.S. has constantly been at war or preparing for war, spending about $8 trillion dollars in the Cold War and $1.7 trillion so far in the War on Terror.

In some cases corporations dominate or are positioning themselves to dominate essential aspects of human life such as food and water. Five biotech companies, led by Monsanto, control the great majority of the world's seeds and indirectly the world's food supply. Companies such as Royal Dutch Shell, Nestle, and Monsanto are buying up groundwater rights and aquifers.

Information is also vital to humanity, yet global media have only a few owners. In the United States six corporations control 90% of media outlets: GE, News-Corp, Disney, Viacom, Time-Warner, and Comcast. As for knowledge, Internet prodigy and activist Aaron Swartz says: "The world's entire scientific and cultural heritage, published over centuries in books and journals, is increasingly being digitized and locked up by a handful of private corporations."

It is possible for a large corporation to destroy an economy. Several books accuse investment bank Goldman Sachs of being a contributing or major cause of the 2008 economic crisis. Others claim the company caused the Greek debt crisis and is trying to undermine China's economy. Matt Taibbi described Goldman Sachs as "a great vampire squid wrapped around the face of humanity."

The Union of Concerned Scientists has documented the campaign by fossil fuel companies to disinform American citizens about climate change. The world's most powerful country is also the second largest emitter of greenhouse gases and by far the largest emitter per person, but has taken weak positions during international conferences urgently trying to reach agreements on climate change. [7]

The corporate form is an instrument of domination (10°). At this point in time its trajectory may pit it against the very survival of the flesh and blood beings who invented it (0° exterminism).

[1] Alfie Kohn, "The Case against Competition," *Working Mother*, September 1987, http://www.alfiekohn.org/article/case-competition/
[2] Murray Rothbard, *The Ethics of Liberty*,
http://mises.org/rothbard/ethics/fourteen.asp,
[3] Prof. Martin Hart-Landsberg, "The Growth of Monopoly Power,"
http://blogs.lclark.edu/hart-landsberg/2012/10/18/1219/
[4] Amana Macias, "These Are the Most Business-Friendly Countries,"
Business Insider, Jan. 27, 2015 http://www.businessinsider.com/these-are-the-most-business-friendly-countries-2015-1
[5] CASSE, Center for the Advancement of the Steady State Economy
"Definition [of a steady state economy]"
http://www.steadystate.org/discover/definition/
[6] Global Basic Income Foundation, "What Is a Basic Global Income?"
http://www.globalincome.org/English/Global-Basic-Income.html
[7] Venkatesh Rao, "A Brief History of the Corporation: 1600 to 2100"
ribbonfarm,
June 8, 2011, https://www.ribbonfarm.com/2011/06/08/a-brief-history-of-the-corporation-1600-to-2100/
[8] UCS, "Documenting the Fossil Fuel Industry's Climate Deception" July 2015, http://www.ucsusa.org/publications/got-science/2015/got-science-july-2015#.V5ajNk2V85s

Chapter 16
Dispositions for War

Why do men keep making war? That is the most important question. Really, I can't think of a more important question.
~character in *New Model Army,* by Adam Roberts, 2010

We know four things about war: It is ancient. It is virtually universal among human societies. It is not an isolated event, but is prepared for by a war system around which most societies are organized. And fourth, almost all of those who directly participate in warfare have been men.

The one thing we don't know (or on which we disagree) is why wars persist. Answering this most important question could give us keys to prevent these calamities. Perhaps answers will appear as we examine various aspects of war, and how it expresses various dispositions.

Armed conflicts as we know them from history evolved from Stone Age combat, ritual warfare and periodic feuds that employed early inventions such as spear-throwers (atlatls), slings for projectiles, and the bow and arrow (all otherwise used for hunting game). Archaeologist Lawrence H. Keeley cites evidence of mass burials of individuals with weapons trauma from 24,000 years ago and possibly even earlier, adding that "Warfare is documented in the archaeological record of the past 10,000 years in every well-studied region." He also notes that 90 to 95% of known societies have been embroiled in warfare.[1]

What we now call war—involving large massed armies— appeared about 6,000 years ago. These wars began between larger settlements with central governments ($10°$). The same social structures they developed to deal with large numbers of people living together were applied to military preparations and standing armies. The civilized war system began. Ironically, modern wars began *after* human skeletons and skulls evolved to be more lightly built, less suited to close combat. Wars became more and more about strategy and weaponry.

Military historians note that "The almost constant occurrence of war among the city-states of Sumer for two thousand years spurred the development of military technology and technique far beyond that found elsewhere at the time." Ancient Sumerians developed weapons and defenses such as the mace and padded helmets and strategies such as the phalanx formation. Inventions continued to revolutionize warfare, and by 1,500 BC the war chariot and the composite bow dominated the field from Europe to China.[2] New military technology (20°) has been one of the main drivers of war ever since. Historian Matthew White says

> One contender for worst century has to be the Seventeenth. The 30 Years War was the bloodiest single conflict in Europe until World War One…The Manchu conquest of China was certainly responsible for one of the top population collapses in East Asia, while the Mughal invasion of South India caused the highest alleged body count in South Asian history…. *The primary cause of this was a quantum leap in military technology.* The development of efficient muskets and artillery was allowing entire civilizations to be brought under the command of a single dynasty, creating so-called Gunpowder Empires.[3]

Another exceptionally bloody era was the 13th century, largely because of the advanced military tactics and organization of the Mongols under Genghis Khan. In the 20th century, two world wars saw military technology grow by leaps and bounds, with rapid-fire weaponry, tanks, airpower, and nuclear bombs.

The War System

A society that is only temporarily peaceful still lives under the shadow of war.
~Joshua S. Goldstein, *War and Gender,* 2001

Prof. Goldstein says war does not represent a sudden explosion of violence; rather it is a constant potential because societies organize themselves around it. The war system defines gender relationships, is an integral part of mythology and religion, determines the direction of science and technology, and deeply influences child-raising, education, and the arts.[4] Each society uses a significant part of its resources to prepare for self-defense, building walls and fortifications, making weapons, and setting up a warrior class whose only occupation is to practice for or wage war. The very existence of preparations and trained warriors makes it more likely that war will recur.

A warrior class and its ethos may come to dominate a culture. Traditions arise: national heroes, sagas, bardic songs, codes of honor, arts and martial music, architecture, monuments and statues. Flags and national anthems become sacred symbols. History is written or rewritten along patriotic lines. Literature spins a mythical past and delineates heroes of the war system. Mark Twain blamed the Civil War on Sir Walter Scott and his romanticizing of war:

> Sir Walter Scott had so large a hand in making Southern character as it existed before the war, that he is in great measure responsible for the war....He did measureless harm; more real and lasting harm, perhaps, than any other individual that ever wrote. [5]

The classic Western movie—with its archetypal conflicts, courageous heroes, and diminished indigenous people—has played its part in constructing American war culture, as did the heroic films of World War II. The media—news, propaganda, drama, fiction, and videogames—together weave the narrative of war.

To the question, "Why do men keeping making war?" novelist Adam Roberts answers "Because it's the most immersive and intense form of grown-up play." A subset of men (5°/20°?) actually enjoy participating in war, which has a close relationship with extreme sports and body contact sports such as football. High school teams from neighboring towns engage in pseudo-wars of tribe against tribe. The metaphors of team sports transfer to patriotism and real battles. While sublimating and channeling aggressive and destructive urges of the players, they can also habituate fans to oppositional attitudes that resemble the extremes of factionalism or nationalism. [6, 7]

Both armies and team sports wear uniforms. Military uniforms are universally believed to attract women—much as large and flamboyant peacock tails attract peahens—perhaps because the youngest and fittest men are wearing them. Other purposes of the military uniform are for identification in battle, to aid in male bonding and creating an *esprit de corps* (30°), to impress the public and each other (25°), and sometimes, to intimidate the enemy.

Warriors are often fed better than the civilian population, one of the reasons not all WW I soldiers hated their service:

> If they were lucky they would avoid a big offensive, and much of the time conditions might be better than at home. For the British there was meat every day—a rare luxury back home—cigarettes, tea and rum, part of a daily diet of more than 4,000 calories….Many young men enjoyed the guaranteed pay, the intense comradeship, the responsibility and a much greater sexual freedom than in peacetime Britain. [8]

War may appeal to that part of an individual's psyche that enjoys risk and excitement (5°)—the adrenaline 'rush'. The soldier's battle high is often followed by horror and depression. Yet he goes on to fight another day, buoyed by words such as 'honor,' 'bravery,' 'manhood,' 'patriotism,' 'courage,' 'heroism,' and 'serving one's country' until finally he has experienced too much, suffering from battle fatigue or PTSD. Everyone has a breaking point, except for the two percent of us whom Frisbee describes as psychopaths who actually enjoy killing.*

Games as well as sports have become part of the war system, creating predispositions for military solutions. Today, millions of children and youths play war-like videogames, some having plots while others are mainly a shooting gallery. From 1960 through the 1990s, the Pentagon led the development of videogame technology. The first such game (*Spacewar!*) was developed by MIT grad students funded by the U.S. military, with "the navigational controls and monitor-as-sight set-up that would influence all subsequent games." [9] Meanwhile, generals attend strategy simulations that are called war games.

Throughout history, war has been almost entirely a masculine preoccupation, with women excluded from combat. Goldstein says that "For the war system to change fundamentally, or for war to end, might require profound changes in gender relations." Military heroes are almost exclusively male, their heroic traditions persisting through the centuries in male-dominated societies, motivating many to participate in war (the bards will sing about your deeds). In the evolution of our species, and the hominids and primates that preceded it, the male's very important role was to defend and protect the females and the young. But warfare has developed far beyond this, with women, children and other innocent civilians now the main victims of modern war.

Whether defenders or conquerors, great warriors represent an ideal for many males. Men of action who led vast armies into foreign lands and battles were judged by compatriots and often by later eras as heroic models for youthful aspiration. The conqueror's 'greatness' is measured by the number of square miles or kilometers he managed to subdue. Some had military genius and the skills needed to keep the conquered lands subdued, to integrate them into one empire, and rule them wisely. However, countless conquerors were distinguished mainly by their barbarism and the mountains of skulls they left behind.

Other warriors fought to defend or to liberate their land from a foreign conqueror. Conquerors/invaders and defender/liberators act in two opposing directions and are motivated differently.** But no matter the motivation, war inevitably involves the lowest dispositions in its violence. If candidates for national hero do not quite measure up, their resumes are embellished. Thus 19th century Paraguayan dictator Francisco Solano Lopez, after ruining his country and killing half its population by recklessly instigating wars against more powerful neighbors, was eventually refurbished as a national hero.

*John Horgan in *The End of War* cites two political scientists who estimate that 2% of Hutu males carried out almost all of the genocide against Tutsis in Rwanda, and that a very small percentage of men were responsible for mass killings in the USSR, China, Cambodia, Balkans, and Guatemala.

Leaders of representative governments must persuade civilian populations by integrating the war system into daily life through such means as public education and patriotic displays at sports events. Propaganda is an increasingly important part of the war system. The rise of mass media and modern advertising techniques have made possible a more sophisticated persuasiveness than ever before, manipulating people into believing that "War is peace" as in Orwell's *1984*. Those who wage imperialist and geostrategic wars prefer to pose as defenders of their own country, liberators of other countries, or saviors of freedom in general.

Often a clever 20° ruse serves to legitimize aggression. Hitler used a false flag operation, pretending an attack by Polish soldiers, to justify invading Poland in 1939 (Gleiwitz incident). Similar pretexts have been invented many times, by the Swedes to invade Russia in 1788 (Puumula incident) or the Japanese to invade Manchuria in 1931 (Mukden incident). Operation Northwoods, a 1962 plan by the U.S. Department of Defense, involved false flag operations to incite war with Cuba, but was ultimately rejected by President John F. Kennedy. Only a minority of the public ever sees through these scams; they may not learn of them for generations—perhaps never.

** Female war leaders of the past were often queens or princesses involved in defensive wars or liberation from conquerors: in 16th century B.C. the Egyptian warrior Queen Ahhotep I drove out Hyskos invaders. Queen Boudicca led first century Britons to repel the Roman legions. The Trung Sisters and Trieu Thi Trinh were, respectively, first and third century Vietnamese leaders fighting Chinese invaders. Queen Zenobia in third century Syria led a revolt against the Roman Empire. Three African defender/liberators were Kahina, a 7th century Berber queen who led indigenous resistance to Muslim Arab expansion in northwest Africa; Queen Nzinga Mbande, who held off Portuguese control of Angola for over 30 years in the early 17th century; and Nandi, a 19th century Zulu princess who fought slave-traders.
But, as Goldstein notes, historically less than one percent of soldiers have been women.

The Basics of War

It is common to imagine that, because we'd never go to war without a good reason, having gone to war, we simply must have a good reason.
~David Swanson, *War is a Lie,* 2010

It is likely that modern war began when human numbers grew to the point that territories began to overlap. Expanding towns and cities required more arable land to feed their populations. It was possible to steal the stored crops of other agriculturalists, especially after the taming of horses allowed mounted marauders to swoop in and out of a village. Civilizations with their massed armies made war on hunter-gatherers and pastoralists, as well as on each other.

To discover the most common causes of war, Keeley compared ethnographic studies of tribes, chiefdoms, and states. He found that secondary motives in tribes and chiefdoms are revenge (10°), retaliation (5°), defense (30°), personal prestige and trophies, and, for some tribes, the capture of women (5°). However, in state societies, the second most important motivation is to achieve the political subjugation (10°) of another society.[10] Keeley found that *for all kinds of societies that make war, the primary motive by far is economic gain.*

For pre-modern people, low-level conflict such as ritual warfare served to keep warriors in practice, until a shortage of game or other subsistence threat moved them to attack their neighbors in earnest. Here we see the origins of the later war system, which guaranteed that there were always men prepared to fight, whether for control of more or better land, gold and precious objects, slaves, and/or important resources or features such as a spring, a port, a fortress, or a trade route.

Among contemporary tribes, two kinds of subsistence economies stand out for their high levels of continuous warfare: animal herding and shifting cultivation (such as slash and burn). Both tend to degrade the land and thus compel people to move on into somebody else's territory. In similar fashion, the two traditional crops of the American South, tobacco and cotton, tend to mine the soil of its nutrients, forcing farmers to keep moving to better soil. One could speculate that the predominance of these two crops supported the popular 19th century belief in Manifest Destiny (10°/20°) with the subsequent western movement of slavery and the inevitable destruction of Amerindian nations.

Modern industrial civilization is coming to a similar depletion—energy resources (fossil fuels) as well as important industrial minerals such as copper, silver, zinc, indium, tantalum, and palladium. Some look forward to finding substitutes for these essentials while others want to mine the asteroids for them, but immediate resource crunches are likely to lead to covert and overt wars, and colonialism masquerading as globalization. For instance, recent wars in Iraq and Afghanistan have been linked with oil, natural gas routes, and Afghanistan's huge mineral potential; constant wars in Congo are linked with minerals such as cassiterite, tungsten, cobalt, gold, and coltan; and wars in several African nations are linked with 'blood diamonds.'

Political subjugation (a strong secondary motivation for war in state societies) is also economic—exacting tribute from the conquered or exploiting their resources while using their cheap or slave labor. But subjugation of another people leads to their desire to achieve tribal or national independence. Once started in motion, the cycle of war continues (like a larger-scale feud) through desires for revenge and retaliation. Competition for land and resources may not be the only cause of war, but it is certainly a very basic one.

More immediate motivations to declare war are found in leader's personalities and the politics of specific nation-states. Some heads of government may foment a war in order to stay in power, as the populace tends to be more unified in wartime.

War and the Dispositions

A soldier really only ever learns two things, and they are obedience and cunning, which is to say, the hunting of men little different from himself.
~Philip Baruth, *The Brothers Boswell*, 2009

Goldstein notes that war is "an extremely diverse enterprise." Clearly, many dispositions must contribute to such a complex and perennial activity. Certainly all the lower dispositions are involved, from 0° sadism toward the designated 'enemy' to 25° susceptibility to the glamour and adventurous aspects of soldiering. The higher dispositions are also involved in war as courage, idealism, and a sense of duty. Lt. Col. Dave Grossman, who studies the field of human aggression and violence, acknowledges some positive aspects to war although they are greatly over-weighted by the terrible costs:

> …the ability to recognize and confront danger, the powerful group bonding that occurs in times of stress, the awe-inspiring spectacle of a nation focused and aligned to achieve a single aim, selfless dedication to abstract concepts and goals, and the ability to overcome the powerful imperatives of the survival instinct and willingly die for others.[11]

These positive aspects, romanticized and manipulated over the centuries, have inspired many at higher dispositions—especially those who are young, idealistic, and inexperienced—to die for principles and nation even though the conflict was not inevitable; the true causes and motives of the war were not the principles for which they were asked to die; and their death would not accomplish any lasting good.

Meanwhile, throughout history a great many men really wanted no part of war and participated only because they were not given any choice. Once caught up in the conflict, their desertion might have dire social and legal consequences for them and their families. Caught in a "Catch-22," they developed friendship bonds (35°) and responsibilities toward their fellow soldiers (30°) that kept them fighting.

In historical wars until quite recent times most soldiers avoided killing another human being, often shooting their guns in the air. John Horgan cites a poll of 400 infantry companies after World War II that found only 15-20% of soldiers fired their weapons in combat. However, the military took notice. Grossman says that modern conditioning techniques are now used to overcome the reluctance to kill and that this bypassing of natural human inclinations contributes to current high levels of PTSD and suicides among American soldiers and veterans.

William S. Frisbee, Jr., U.S. Marine veteran claims in "Psychology of Killing" that "After sixty days of combat ninety-eight percent of the unit is likely to be a psychiatric casualty." The concept of 'moral injury' is new but it refers to ancient experiences. Moral injury has been defined as recurring guilt or shame caused by "perpetrating, failing to prevent, bearing witness to or learning about acts that transgress deeply held moral beliefs and expectations.[12]

In even the most warlike tribal societies, few people viewed war as more than a necessary evil. According to Keeley it was common to view the warrior who had just killed an enemy as being spiritually polluted or contaminated, in need of ritual purification and a period of seclusion before rejoining the tribe. Like modern vets, tribal warriors sometimes told ethnographers that they suffered from nightmares, usually about finding themselves alone in the midst of a battle.

While the tribe honored its warrior heroes, it did not award them their highest positions which went instead to men who were good negotiators, generous, impartial, and eloquent. When conquered by imperial powers and prevented from fighting each other, most tribal peoples said they did not miss the warfare (although they may well have disliked other aspects of colonial rule). For most such societies, warfare had become an entrenched, self-sustaining system that could only be stopped by a greater authority.

Ending War

War will never cease until babies begin to come into the world with larger cerebrums and smaller adrenal glands.
~H.L. Mencken, 1930

I disagree with Mencken. Making war is not innate, instinctual, or inevitable, but rather an ingrained habit of our race. Like a gambler who risks all he owns for a moment's rush, it is humanity's addiction.

A theory, notably expressed by Harvard psychologist Steven Pinker, is that war and other kinds of violence are declining throughout the world—and that this is because of the spread of wealth, democracy, and Enlightenment values. Pinker finds the answer to war in the modern state, Modernity, and the "civilizing process." His views resonate with the 35° optimist and believer in progress.[13]

However, some critics disagree with Pinker's basic argument that war is declining. Some argue that Pinker counts only battlefield deaths although modern wars increasingly kill civilians, and he leaves out the large-scale killing of people by their own government. There may not have been a world war for 70 years ("The Long Peace") but speaking statistically and historically, 70 years is a short period. At least 52 million people have died in military conflicts since 1945, in China, Vietnam, Congo, Iraq, Indonesia, Sudan/Darfur, Syria, Korea, Afghanistan, Bosnia, and Somalia.[14]

The 20th century by most measures was the bloodiest in human history, especially if one includes democides (mass murders by government) and imposed famines such as in Ukraine, or China's Great Leap Forward, each with death tolls in the tens of millions.

If wars and other forms of violence are *not* declining, then Modernity and Enlightenment values may not be enough to end them. Where else can we look? The dispositions most involved with ending the war system are the six higher ones.

Civilians who are taxed for wars and whose families supply the soldiers sometimes resist urgings of the state to march into war. Only by notions of duty are 30° men persuaded to leave home and family to kill other people. Inducted in youth before they are married or settled in their work, when they are at their most idealistic and easily persuaded by patriotic appeals, they lack the experience to question national policies.

But when 30° does cut through the propaganda, his basic human decency rises to the surface, for example the series of unofficial truces between British and German soldiers on the Western front in December 1914. Many exchanged gifts of food, played soccer games, and sang Christmas carols. Afterward, such fraternization was banned by military officials, although enemy soldiers still sometimes met to exchange prisoners or bury their dead.

A great deal of state propaganda is aimed at 35° who tends to be more educated and is more apt to question war and militarism and to resist specific wars—if he or she can withstand the manipulations appealing to idealism.

Meanwhile, a dedicated minority insists on the absolute necessity of working toward peace (40°) using mutually verifiable disarmament and other technical safeguards as well as non-violent strategies and the creation of a culture of peace through music, art, and social inventions (50°).

Most religions preach peace (40°) although putative followers of peaceful religions are not always peaceful. Jainism, Buddhism, and Hinduism teach peacefulness towards other humans as well as towards animals, and the Roman Catholic Church from medieval times to Pope Francis has made attempts to limit war, but both the Church and Hindu states have initiated military actions. Three sects truly dedicated to the practice of peace (40°/X°) are the historic peace churches: Church of the Brethren, Religious Society of Friends, and Mennonites. In Islam, the Ahmadiyya sect and Sufism have been associated with pacifism.

[1]Lawrence H. Keeley, *War Before Civilization*, Oxford University Press, 1996
[2] Richard A. Gabriel and Karen S. Metz, *A Short History of War: The Armies of Sumer and Akkad, 3500-2200 BC,* Army War College 1992,
http://www.au.af.mil/au/awc/awcgate/gabrmetz/gabr003a.htm
[3] Matthew White, "Selected Death Tolls for Wars, Massacres and Atrocities Before the 20th Century," http://necrometrics.com/pre1700a.htm#n.1
[4] Joshua Goldstein, *War and Gender: How Gender Shapes the War System and Vice Versa*, Cambridge University Press 2001
[5] Scott Horton, "How Walter Scott Started the American Civil War," *Harper's Magazine*, July 29, 2007, http://harpers.org/blog/2007/07/how-walter-scott-started-the-american-civil-war/
Mark Twain, Life on the Mississippi, 1883
[6] J.A. Mangan "Sport and War: Combative Societies and Combative Sports," *SGI Quarterly*, July 2006, http://www.sgiquarterly.org/feature2006Jly-2.html
[7] Steven Stark, "Drill and Kill: How Americans Link War and Sports," *Atlantic Monthly*, Sep 30, 2010,
http://www.theatlantic.com/entertainment/archive/2010/09/drill-and-kill-how-americans-link-war-and-sports/63832/

[8] Dan Snow, "Viewpoint: 10 big myths about World War One debunked," BBC Magazine, 25 February 2014, http://www.bbc.com/news/magazine

[9] Hamza Shaban, "Playing War: How the Military Uses Video Games," *The Atlantic*, Oct 10, 2013, http://www.theatlantic.com/technology/archive/2013/10/playing-war-how-the-military-uses-video-games/280486/

[10] Keeley, op. cit.

[11] Lt. Col Dave Grossman and Bruce K. Siddle, "Psychological Effects of Combat," Academic Press 2000, http://www.killology.com/print/print_psychological.htm

[12] David Koon, "The martyr of Danville Mountain," *Arkansas Times*, October 22, 2014, http://www.arktimes.com/arkansas/the-martyr-of-danville-mountain/Content?oid=3514138

[13] Steven Pinker, *The Better Angels of Our Nature: Why Violence Has Declined, Viking* 2011

[14] "War deaths since 1945," http://www.worldmapper.org/display.php?selected=287

Chapter 17
Ideological War

The war against terrorism is terrorism.
~Woody Harrelson, American actor

A man in deep despair (it is almost always a man) after losing job or a wife goes on a shooting rampage, killing not only those whom he feels have wronged him but also multiple others who are in the way and then (often) himself. He acts out of 5° rage, 0° self-loathing, and a 10° sense of power—if he can't do anything else right, he has at least the power of life and death over these unsuspecting nobodies.

Somewhere else a man or small group of men also kill strangers, more likely with a bomb than a gun. They have convinced themselves that they are heroic soldiers in an ideological war. Timothy McVeigh said he was retaliating against the government for the deaths at Waco and Ruby Ridge. Dzhokhar Tsarnaev scribbled this on the side of a boat where he lay hidden, bleeding from several gunshot wounds:

> The [Boston] bombings were in retribution for the U.S. crimes in places like Iraq and Afghanistan [and] that the victims of the Boston bombing were collateral damage, in the same way innocent victims have been collateral damage in U.S. wars around the world. Summing up, that when you attack one Muslim you attack all Muslims. [1]

Although the word *terrorism* is widely used, it does not have one agreed-upon definition, and can refer to several kinds of mass murders. Or it may refer to guerrilla wars that lie somewhere between conventional wars and terrorism, and are noted for brutal tactics on both sides. In popular usage terrorism is the systematic use of violent acts against civilians to create a climate of fear for a political objective, by those who are not regular soldiers of a nation-state. [2]

Yet the first use of this word referred to violent acts by a government against its own people—the Reign of Terror following the French Revolution in 1793-4. Tyrants have persecuted their own people for millennia, but now there is a word for such violence by governments: *democide*. Political scientist R. J. Rummel says democide includes "the murder of any person or people by a government, including genocide, politicide, and mass murder." This excludes battle deaths. [3]

Large-scale democides occurred within my lifetime in the USSR, China, Germany, Chile, Nigeria, Cambodia, Sudan, Indonesia, Iraq, Argentina, and Guatemala, with another occurring today in Syria. The latest entrant in this 0° category is Philippine President Rodrigo Duterte who compared his war against drug dealers and users to the Nazi Holocaust and said "There's three million drug addicts....I'd be happy to slaughter them." In Duterte's first two months in office, over 2,000 people were killed extra-judicially.[4]

As instruments of terror, states may use secret police such as Stalin's NKVD, East German Stasi, Shah of Iran's SAVAK, the Nazi's Gestapo, or—going back in history—the Oprichnina of Ivan "The Terrible." Abandoning secrecy, they led the Massacre of Novgorod in 1570, killing perhaps 100,000 people. A modern form of terror is perpetrated by right-wing paramilitaries that target rural villages.

Altogether, millions more have perished from state terrorism than ever did from non-governmental groups that attack civilians. However, the latter kind of terrorism gets all the press (fallacy of misleading vividness).

Terrorism has long been a part of war. Starvation sieges of walled cities and massacres of civilians occurred for thousands of years. War terrorism received new impetus with aerial bombardments in the 20th century. The airplane had barely been invented before it was used for war and soon thereafter for bombing colonial peoples trying to gain independence. Under Winston Churchill as Colonial Secretary, the RAF bombed towns in rebellious areas throughout British colonies and mandates: Iraq, Kurdistan, Afghanistan, India, Yemen, Egypt, and Somaliland. Wing-Commander Sir Arthur Harris boasted that "The Arab and Kurd now know what real bombing means in casualties and damage. Within forty-five minutes a full-size village can be practically wiped out and a third of its inhabitants killed or injured." [5]

As head of World War II Bomber Command, Sir Arthur helped make the decision to blanket-bomb Dresden, an action widely criticized after the fact. Freeman Dyson, a British physicist who worked with the RAF, said many years later, "Since the beginning of the war I had been retreating step by step from one moral position to another, until at the end I had no moral position at all."[6]

US Air Force Gen. Curtis LeMay, head of the Strategic Air Command during the Korean War (1951-1953) said later, "Over a period of three years or so, we killed off—what—20 percent of the population." The North Koreans had few defenses against carpet bombing. North Koreans remember vividly a history that Americans have forgotten, contributing to paranoia about U.S. intentions today.[7]

Terror tactics to demoralize noncombatants remain part of modern wars (the Secretary of Defense touted the 2003 bombing of Baghdad as "Shock and Awe"). One or more sides may target hospitals and first responders. If violence directed against civilians is the essence of terrorism, continued use of cluster bombs—despite an international treaty in 2008—would qualify. The United States and Russia have not signed this treaty; Russia has probably used the bombs in Syria, while U.S. ally Saudi Arabia is using U.S.-made cluster-bombs in Yemen.

Non-State Terrorism

"Because I do it with one small ship, I am called a terrorist. You do it with a whole fleet and are called an emperor."
~Pirate to Alexander the Great, from St. Augustine's *City of God,* 5th century

Or as the modern saying goes, "A terrorist is someone who has a bomb but doesn't have an air force." Although democide and war kill the most people by far, current usage focuses on relatively small, non-uniformed, loosely organized groups using violent acts against civilians to achieve goals that are nationalist, separatist, religious, or otherwise ideological. Such groups can develop into small armies or guerrillas with or without uniforms, such as ISIS, Tamil Tigers, and FARC.

In the late 19th and early 20th centuries 'terrorism' referred to attempted assassinations by anarchists and nationalists. They managed to kill U.S. President William McKinley, a Russian Czar, a French president, an Austrian empress, a Spanish prime minister, and an Italian king. Assassination of the heir to the throne of Austria-Hungary in 1914 precipitated World War I. But then the focus of terrorist actions moved away from assassination except for the Tamil Tigers. In the 1990s, the Tamil Tigers, using suicide bombers, assassinated the former Prime Minister of India, Rajiv Gandhi, and the Prime Minister of Sri Lanka, along with many other Sri Lankan government officials.

Many anti-colonial and separatist groups have enjoyed popular support, even international support for 45° goals despite 0° tactics. Globally, non-state groups using terror tactics have included the IRA in Ireland, Zionist settlers (Irgun and the Stern Gang) in the British mandate of Palestine, Basque separatists (ETA), far-left groups Baader-Meinhof (Germany) and Red Brigades (Italy), Contras in Nicaragua, Aum Shinrikyo in Japan, Hamas, Babbar Khalsa (a Sikh sect responsible for at least one Air India bombing), Chechen separatists, Puerto Rican nationalists, and AUC in Colombia, as well as Islamic extremists such as al Qaeda and ISIS.

An academic notes: "In contrast to assassination—the direct targets of [terrorist] violence are not the main targets. The immediate human victims of violence are generally chosen randomly (targets of opportunity) or selectively (representative or symbolic targets) from a target population, and serve as *message generators*.[8]

Often the message is unclear, especially when terrorist acts are committed by only one ('lone-wolf') individual or involve mental illness (Eric Robert Rudolph in the Olympics or Omar Matteen in the massacre at a gay nightclub in Orlando). Despite media focus on Islamic extremists, domestic attacks have involved white supremacists, neo-Nazis, anti-abortionists, members of the militia movement, the SLA, and the anti-technology "Unabomber."

The nature of those using terror tactics is changing. The trend is toward millenarian cults or religiously motivated groups that are more fanatic—even apocalyptic (0°)—and not averse to using WMD (Aum

Shinrikyo, al-Qaida, ISIS).[9] There is less possibility of clear-cut resolutions such as national independence or the overthrow of dictators. It is often difficult to discern the tactical advantages. Some groups may have fallen into a 0° trance, or show the same paroxysm of rage and frustration that motivates individual mass murder at 5°.

Some terrorism has no ideological roots but is simply part of a power struggle between competing warlords, drug lords, or criminal gangs. In Mexico, conflicts between rival drug cartels, combated by a corrupt military supplied with U.S. money, have led to well over 100,000 deaths and many kidnappings and disappearances. Drug cartels have spread terror throughout Central America and in Colombia.

Besides the usual violence between crime families, the Sicilian Mafia in the 1980s and '90s murdered a number of prosecutors and judges in Italy who tried to bring them to justice. There is an increasingly close connection between terrorism and organized crime, international cooperation, and various hybrids of the two such as narcoterrorism. Terrorist organizations often finance themselves through the illegal arms trade, human trafficking and prostitution, cybercrime, kidnapping, and money laundering through phony businesses or corrupt banks.[10]

We can now distinguish at least five main types of terrorism: democide, terrorism related to war, related to colonial suppression, non-state, and criminal. One clearly sees the 10° drive for power, 20° competition for ideological and political advantage, and a 5° predilection for violence. Terrorism may also sweep in those of higher dispositions, such as 30° 'serving their country' and 45° fighting for independence. Regardless of the type of terrorism or its attempted justifications, these deliberate violent *acts* occur at 0°.*

*A 1999 UN Resolution condemns terrorism as follows: "Criminal acts intended or calculated to provoke a state of terror in the general public, a group of persons, or particular persons for political purposes are in any circumstance unjustifiable, whatever the considerations of a political, philosophical, ideological, racial, ethnic, religious or other nature that may be invoked to justify them."

[1] Ray McGovern, "Boston Suspect's Writing on the Wall," *Consortium News*, May 17, 2013 https://consortiumnews.com/2013/05/17/boston-suspects-writing-on-the-wall/

[2] "Terrorism in Historical Perspective,"
http://www.digitalhistory.uh.edu/topic_display.cfm?tcid=94

[3] R.J. Rummel, *Democide: Nazi Genocide and Mass Murder*, Chapter 1, "20,946,000 Victims: Nazi Germany 1933 To 1945"
http://www.hawaii.edu/powerkills/NAZIS.CHAP1.HTM

[4] Jim Gomez, "Filipino threatens drug-user Holocaust," AP October 1, 2016, *Northwest Arkansas Democrat-Gazette*

[5] Peace Pledge Union, "Bombing from Balloons to Predators,"
http://www.ppu.org.uk/bombing/bombing-harris.html   also   http://www-tc.pbs.org/moyers/journal/01302009/bombingcivilians.pdf

[6] Freeman Dyson, *Disturbing the Universe*, Basic Books 1979

7 Blaine Harden, "The U.S. War Crime North Korea Won't Forget," *Washington Post*, March 24, 2015

8 UN Office on Drugs and Crime, "Definitions of Terrorism," June 30, 2014
http://web.archive.org/web/20070129121539/http://www.unodc.org/unodc/terrorism_definitions.html

[9] Rex A. Hudson, "The Sociology and Psychology of Terrorism: Who Becomes a Terrorist and Why?" Library of Congress, September 1999

[10] Angelina Stanojoska, "The Connection between Terrorism and Organized Crime: Narcoterrorism and the Other Hybrids"
https://www.academia.edu/2163809/The_Connection_between_Terrorism_and_Organized_Crime_Narcoterrorism_and_other_hybrids

Chapter 18
The Cult of Me (25° Narcissism)

It is not love that should be depicted as blind, but self-love.
~Voltaire

The dysfunctional condition called Narcissistic Personality Disorder or NPD is an extreme form of egocentricity that used to be called megalomania (15°). However, with 25° we are talking about a less intense but more widespread narcissism. The individual with NPD has serious trouble fitting into society, but 25° fits all too well into a consumer society that encourages shallow selfishness.

Psychoanalyst Stuart Schneiderman notes that "Narcissism, hubris, and arrogance are just different names for the same thing....an excessive love of self." Strongly favoring one's own kin, or those of one's own gender, class, race, or religion to the detriment of others is an expanded form of narcissism. So are country-club exclusiveness, or turf battles in academia, business, or government agencies.[1]

Close identification with one's group undoubtedly evolved to help human survival. But the more of us humans exist, with our great diversity and powerful technologies, the more of a problem group narcissism becomes. The self is writ large in *my* school, *my* church, *my* city, *my* state, *my* nation, *my* civilization. Nationalism/ patriotism could be viewed as a collective form of hubris, as if only our own country really counts in the grand scheme of things.

Another form of narcissism is the total preference for human interests at the expense of all other species (speciesism). As science writer Colin Tudge notes, "Present political ideologies and economic systems of the world simply do not acknowledge the existence of any species apart from our own."[2]

Collective hubris takes numerous forms. *Temporocentrism* is the common view that one's own time is more important than any other period in history. The contemporary world is the pinnacle of all history (because that's when I live). Nothing will ever replace cars, and utility companies, and nation-states, and corporate capitalism. Meanwhile, technological hubris assumes that the current state of the art approaches perfection. Combined with disregard both for other species and our own physiological and psychological limitations, this kind of narcissism threatens the whole human race from a variety of causes.

As a personality trait, narcissism is composed of self-centeredness, self-admiration, relative lack of empathy, overconfidence, and a sense of entitlement that can lead to aggressive behavior. It is one of the traits of the "Dark Triad" that may lead to callous manipulation of others. Classical Greeks used the word *hubris* to describe the arrogant, malicious aspects of narcissism. As Aristotle defined it, "*Hubris* consists in doing and saying things that cause shame to the victim…simply for the pleasure of it….Young men and the rich are hubristic because they think they are better than other people."

Or 25° may be simply shallow and manipulated by mass media and advertising, obsessed with the social media networks and digital technology that consume the waking hours of many people, particularly the young. With an egocentrism once limited to royalty and aristocrats, 25° is now widespread in the developed world and among the growing middle class in the developing world.

Where relative affluence makes it possible, some folks pursue a hedonistic, amoral lifestyle, spending their time and resources on self-entertainment and satisfying basic instincts to the fullest extent. Hedonism is a devotion to pleasure as a way of life, an obsessive drive for shallow social and sensual pleasures that are ultimately unsatisfying. For some, hedonism becomes 15° addiction.

Worldwide, the cosmetics industry is projected to rise to $265 billion in 2017. That's about $37 per person (including men, babies, and developing countries). The bodybuilding, dieting, and sports nutrition industries may surpass this amount. Worldwide, in 2013 over 44,000 plastic surgeons performed an estimated 11,599,336 cosmetic procedures. Throw in the glossy magazines, from *Vogue* to *Gentleman's Quarterly*, consisting largely of ads for what to wear from the fashion industry, and we're probably up to $1 trillion or so. It looks like we care more about how we look than, for example, climate change.

It's true that most of us given the opportunity will indulge in *some* 25° pastimes (I am no exception). However, that is not the same as spending virtually all of one's discretionary time following pop culture, adorning one's body, seeking out romantic encounters (love 'em and leave 'em), partying, compulsively following the fortunes of one's favored sports team (tribe), or indulging nonstop in social media and digital amusements. It is a matter of emphasis. The bonbons of life are not meant to be a constant diet—they have limited nutritional value.

Some examples of hedonism:

Peter Pan Syndrome
Sexual 'players'
 Debauchery
'Couch potatoes'
Gourmands
Romantic escapism
Party animals
Pornography
"Games people play"

Two classic stories about 25° hedonism are *The Picture of Dorian Gray*, by Oscar Wilde (1890), and *Madame Bovary*, by Gustave Flaubert (1856). Dorian Gray leads a life of debauchery but remains an attractive young man while the ugly consequences of his lifestyle are imprinted on his portrait. The pretty young woman Emma Bovary, dissatisfied with her mundane life as the wife of a small-town doctor, aspires to live a more aristocratic lifestyle and to experience a romantic grand passion. She ends up alone, deeply in debt after several adulterous affairs that are more tawdry than glamorous.

In novel and film, *The Great Gatsby* describes two rich and heedless hedonists, Tom and Daisy. The 1988 film *Dangerous Liaisons*, a retelling of an 18th century French novel, depicts the alliance of two aristocratic hedonists, Marquise de Merteuil and Vicomte de Valmont, who play malicious sexual games at 0°/25°.

Vanity, Vanity, All Is Vanity

What kills a skunk is the publicity it gives itself.
~Abraham Lincoln

One of our downfalls is the lure of becoming rich and famous, and the idea that everybody can receive their '15 minutes of fame.' Gossip can serve to promote 25° vanity. Self-important people do want to be talked about; for a certain kind of celebrity, it makes no difference what people say about you, just so long as they say something. An over-riding desire for fame has even led some individuals to commit crimes in order to see themselves in the headlines and on the tube.   Common manifestations of 25° vanity and egoism include:

'Bridezilla'
People famous for being famous
Snobbery
Self-righteousness
Aristocratic arrogance
Cynicism
Glory hound, hot shot
Entitlement
Know-it-all
The Meritocracy
Trophy wife (or husband)
Socialite
Social climber
'Drama queen'
Artsy (pretentious)
Lothario, playboy, man-about-town

Besides 25°, snobbism contains strains of 20° competitiveness and also 10° domination. Snobs can find countless things to feel superior about. It may be wealth or a prominent or patrician family background; it may be physical attractiveness, fashionable clothes, athletic success, house, yard, address, car, boat, popularity, academic accomplishment, IQ, university attended, or mastery of a specific body of knowledge— even cultural trivia. It may be any of these things associated with one's partner or children, friend, or acquaintance (name-dropping).

Another form of 25° reflected glory is boastful patriotism, as in a letter to the editor that said "America is the greatest country that ever existed or *ever will exist*." (Of course it is *my* country, where *I* live.)

From Jane Austen to "Downton Abbey" we learn about the snobbery of the English aristocracy, their servants, and social-climbers of the upper middle-class. But it's not only England. Parisians also have a reputation for snobbery. A British writer points out that the United States has less class mobility than Britain, but "are in denial about their privilege. The American myth of meritocracy allows them to attribute their position to their brilliance and diligence." [3]

A combination of cynicism and snobbery creates someone convinced she's superior to the general run of human beings because of her imperturbability or 'cool'. Social critic Philip Martin describes "a certain kind of postmodern sensibility, the reflexive snarkiness that finds any show of sincerity absurd." [4] The 'cool' snob has been around for centuries. 19th century author Barbey d'Aurevilly described "Dandies, who—as you know—scorn all emotions as being beneath them, and do not believe, like that simpleton Goethe, that astonishment can ever be a proper feeling for the human mind."

At 25° people may belong to a particular church because it is the thing to do, raising their status in the community. I lived in one town where people referred to a certain Episcopalian church as "Our Lady of the Cadillacs." There is also the snobbery of self-righteousness (holier than thou) that may account for Protestant churches that split apart, sometimes forming separate congregations, because of ego conflicts among the congregation more than real doctrinal differences.

Some aspects of New Age express 25°. This broad, eclectic, quite diverse spiritual movement spread in the 1970s and 1980s, mainly in the United States, other English-speaking countries, and Western Europe. New Age brought both positive and negative changes in general awareness. The particular aspects that express 25° are related to consumerism, self-indulgence, and self-dramatization. New Age also draws on 15° credulity. Yet other aspects of the movement further 35° environmentalism and social reform, 40° love, and X° spiritual beliefs.

Another expression of vanity is assuming a cleverness that one does not have, as with a character in Doris Lessing's *The Golden Notebook* who says of another: "Of course he was too stupid to make up his mind about anything without hours and hours of thought, even though the rest of us were so clever we didn't need it." Michael Dibdin describes one of his characters as "an arrogant intellectual who writes pretentious tomes on incomprehensible subjects and secretly despises his fellow man despite a shallow veneer of trendy leftist solidarity."

Pseudo-intellectuals pretend an interest in and acquaintance with intellectual matters—or the arts and culture—in order to elevate their social status. Along with this game or fantasy, 25° may subscribe to various ideologies that serve vanity or interests, but without the combativeness and preoccupation found with a 20° ideologue, 15° crank, or 10° fanatic. With 25°, it's a vainglorious show. Pseudo-intellectuals and their cousins are also known as pretentious, puffed-up, pompous, affected, high-falutin', know-it-all, blowhards, and hipsters.

Other manifestations of 25° are sensationalism and melodrama.

Indifference

The opposite of love is not hate, it is indifference. The opposite of art is not ugliness, it is indifference. The opposite of faith is not heresy, it is indifference. And the opposite of life is not death, it is indifference.
~Elie Wiesel, Holocaust survivor and writer

While 25° does not usually do anything so violently wrong, perhaps this disposition's biggest flaw is simply *not paying attention* or *not caring*. A person may be somewhat able to empathize but just doesn't bother to do so. This sin of omission allows many evils to grow, with special relevance to relationships, child-raising, citizenship, and issues that concern the whole human race. But 25° people are too caught up in their own emotions, their own sensations, their own problems and self-created problems, to care about others. One root of indifference is extreme individualism and glorification of selfishness, as in Ayn Rand's Objectivist philosophy that celebrates the individual ego, an ideology that has become especially popular among young men in the already individualistic United States.

The 25° bystander "doesn't want to get involved"—it's none of my business if my neighbor beats his wife or she abuses her child. By failure to act, 25° allows crimes and atrocities. Dietrich Bonhoeffer, a Christian theologian executed by the Nazis for his dissent, put it this way: "Silence in the face of evil is itself evil: God will not hold us guiltless. Not to speak is to speak. Not to act is to act." When conscious, deliberate, and in authority, such indifference becomes malign indifference (0°).

The indifferent citizen enables government corruption and the rise of authoritarian leaders and political groups operating at the lowest degrees (pathocracies). As Plato said, "The penalty good men pay for indifference to public affairs is to be ruled by evil men."

Wars and disasters and suffering people must fit into the 24-hour news cycle; 25° quickly gets donor fatigue. It doesn't help that the world's miseries are presented to us in a shallow and transitory way. Instead, many of the crises require deeper, more radical and longer-range 45°/50° solutions as well as 40° compassion.

The indifferent human being has no interest or desire to look ahead or think about what the future will or could be for his or her children and grandchildren. Like a small child, 25° is not ready to give up present advantages for future benefits. Cynicism is often conflated with being sophisticated. It gives one an excuse for not acting. But one hardly needs an excuse—there is a world of distractions out there.

Britt Stevens describes modern culture as follows:

> Our civilization understands itself not as a product of history and maker of future history but as a facilitator—like a big shopping mall with a legal system—of individuals doing what pleases them so long as they do not interrupt others doing the same and disturb the peace. [5]

Whatever people say they believe, their actions speak louder than words. Or as James Frick, a college educator said: "Don't tell me where your priorities are. Show me where you spend your money and I'll tell you what they are." Here are some U.S. and world priorities:

Weapons: World military spending in 2015 was $1.6 trillion. The United States spent 37% of that, almost $600 billion. (10°/20°)

Sports: In 2015 the U.S. 'golf economy' generated about $70 billion of goods and services. The U.S. Department of Defense maintains 234 golf courses across the world. In four-fifths of the states, the highest paid public employee coaches either football or men's basketball; the highest paid public employee in the United States is a football coach in Alabama (20° idols).

Prisons: The United States spends $80 billion a year to incarcerate prisoners. It now holds one-fourth of the world's inmates. A recent federal report showed that since 1980, the amount that states and local governments spent on prisons and jails increased three times faster than spending on public education. (10°/15°) [6]

[1] Stuart Schneiderman, "How to Cure Narcissism, Hubris, and Arrogance," http://stuartschneiderman.blogspot.com/2010/09/how-to-cure-narcissism-hubris-and.html
[2] Colin Tudge, *The time before history: 5 million years of human impact*, Simon & Schuster, 1997
[3] Richard V. Reeves, "Stop Pretending You're not Rich," *The New York Times,* June 10, 2017, https//:
www.nytimes.com/2017/06/10/opinion/Sunday/stop-pretending-youre-not-rich.html?emc=e
[4] Phillip Martin, *Arkansas Democrat Gazette,* June 5, 2016.
[5] Britt Stevens, foreword to Pentti Linkola, *Can Life Prevail*, English translation, Integral Tradition Publishing, 2009
[6] Emma Brown and Danielle Douglas-Gabriel, "Since 1980, spending on prisons has grown three times as much as spending on public education," July 7, 2016,
https://www.washingtonpost.com/news/education/wp/2016/07/07/since-1980-spending-on-prisons-has-grown-three-times-faster-than-spending-on-public-education/

Chapter 19
Consumer Society and Conformity (20°)

*A fellow who is ashamed merely of shabby clothing or modest meals is
not even worth conversing with.*
~Confucius, Analects 4.9

The USA, epicenter of 25°, spreads popular, commercialized culture across the globe and is also distinctive in the persistence of social patterns carried over from public high school. Ralph Nader remarked, "We have the most prolonged adolescence in the history of mankind. There is no other society that requires so many years to pass before people are grown up."[1] Many expressions of 25° resemble adolescent behavior and would seem more appropriate in that stage of life.

Modern American teenagers are a rather new phenomenon. Many traits that we associate with adolescence are not typical of youth in previous centuries and other cultures. I personally experienced the birth of this phenomenon, graduating from high school just before the post-World War II discovery of adolescents as a separate market and target for advertising. The teen-age drive for conformity and ownership of socially indispensable things was still dormant. The term 'teen-ager' was itself a product of this postwar period.

25° culture is dependent on novelty and change: the top ten hits of the day, what is trending, the news cycle, fads and fashions, bestsellers, latest slang, and other passing fancies spread by memes. People bond through rumors and gossip, with Twitter and texting replacing the phone, emails, water cooler and back fence as the main venues.

A number of critics describe an increasing narcissism in American society, calling it an 'epidemic' that began to blossom in the 1970s. Some blame a custom of over-praising that spread from therapy for people with low self-esteem—people who needed reassurance—to everyone. Constantly telling people that they are special and wonderful may lead them to feel entitled and overconfident. Another contributing cause is the self-promotion required to get ahead in a competitive job market, during an era of increasing income inequality.[2]

Consumer Society: Media

It is hard to contend against one's heart's desire; for whatever it wishes to have it buys at the cost of soul.
~Heraclitus, Greek philosopher, 535-475 B.C.

Advertising, media, and the new social networks spread this new narcissism with TV commercials, radio ads, digital ads, spam, junk-mail, telemarketing, newspaper and magazine ads including glossy magazines that contain more ads than copy, neon signs, billboards, and more. Advertising is a $171 billion industry in the U.S and $517.7 billion (over half a trillion) worldwide.

At one time the description in, say, the Sears Roebuck catalogue (a fixture in small town America) was just that—a neutral description of the item for sale. But more and more, advertising became a scientifically researched technique for deceptive persuasion. The most expensive television ads in the last decade included a $33 million two-minute commercial for Chanel beauty products, featuring actress Nicole Kidman. That is only the production cost and doesn't include the network's hefty price to air the ad. [3]

We must also take into account the public relations industry that puts its spin on celebrities, events, and issues for those who can pay for it. PR is increasingly influencing the news. As daily newspapers lay off journalists during economic hard times, they replace investigative reporting with self-serving handouts. Robert McChesney, co-author of *The Death and Life of American Journalism*, says: "What we are seeing now is the demise of journalism at the same time we have an increasing level of public relations and propaganda."[4]

In the United States, elections hinge on which candidates have the most money for television campaign ads, as well as the type of presentation and how it is likely to be received. Politics has become the province of television networks, spin doctors, polling companies, and advertising experts.

Some aspects of consumer society are:

Constant distractions, Fashion and fads, Infotainment and 'fluff' news;
A fetish for the latest, newest, and most novel;
Manipulation by supernormal stimuli;
Conformity;
Living vicariously through celebrity idols;
Self-indulgence; Luxuries become necessities;
Indifference to the future; Planned obsolescence, 'throwaway'
mentality, waste;
Popular culture crowds out serious culture

An early critic of consumer culture, economist Thorsten Veblen, described how the "conspicuous consumption and conspicuous leisure" of the wealthy had become the basis of social status in America (*The Theory of the Leisure Class,* 1899). Examples are Rolex watches, diamonds, fur coats, and luxury cars.

Vance Packard, in *The Hidden Persuaders* (1957) later explored the use of psychological techniques in advertising. Motivational research reaches deep into the human psychological makeup, including instinctive responses. A supernormal stimulus is an exaggerated version of a stimulus to which there already exists a response, for instance sexual attraction. But real women cannot compete in attractiveness with the exaggerated curves of photo-shopped models. In another case of manipulation, videogames are designed to be so addictive that players play continuously for days and collapse from lack of food, water, and sleep before they will stop. At least three fatalities have been reported.[5]

Eliezer Yudkowski (artificial intelligence theorist) says: "Our limited willpower evolved to deal with ancestral temptations; it may not operate well against enticements beyond anything known to hunter-gatherers." In terms of brain chemicals, willpower is an exhaustible pool and often helpless against scientifically created inducements based on supernormal stimuli. [6]

In *The Wastemakers* (1960) Packard brought the idea of planned obsolescence to public attention. By producing consumer items for short-term use, businesses sell more goods but use up resources more rapidly. A recent example of conspicuous consumption and planned obsolescence is the wedding custom called 'trash the dress' in which the bride deliberately ruins her wedding gown after the ceremony, although it is probably the most expensive garment she will ever buy. In the past this dress had great sentimental value, often handed down to her daughter. The new trend began in imitation of high-fashion advertising photography that is meant to draw attention through shock-value.

Commercialism has moved deeply into 30° traditions such as family holidays and personal milestones—birthdays, graduation, and nuptials. The average wedding now costs more than a hybrid car.

A response to conspicuous consumption and planned obsolescence came in the 1980s, when 'sustainability' became a buzzword. In 1987 the Bruntland Commission of the UN defined sustainable development as "development that meets the needs of the present without compromising the ability of future generations to meet their own needs." (40° generativity)

The Pleasure Market

We are the slaves of objects around us.
~ Johann Wolfgang Von Goethe, 1749-1832

As the spice trade so greatly influenced ancient and medieval worlds—it was the first driver of globalization, inspiration for explorers and motivation for colonizers—so in more recent times certain trade goods transformed the world again. In the 18th century, British colonies provided a brisk trade in several new commodities, all of which are more or less addictive: sugar, tobacco, opium, whiskey, and rum. Meanwhile, the Dutch and their colonies ruled the coffee trade.[7]

Luxuries were often produced with slave labor. The sugar industry in particular was dependent on slavery from the end of the middle ages to the abolition of slavery in the mid-19th century. Sugar also fueled the growth of modern capitalism. "The sugar-slave complex was not only an example of capitalism but a pioneer of that system."[8]

Many of these new luxuries had destructive social or environmental effects. For instance, the 19th century opium trade in China, forced open by British military actions (10°), is estimated to have created 12 million opium addicts. The whole country's standard of living went down as a result. Late 19th century trade in the feathers and wings of snowy egrets—for fashionable women's hats—brought that species to the brink of extinction. More recently, the taste for caviar threatens all 27 species of sturgeon with extinction; and some species of sharks are at risk because of the Chinese appetite for shark fin soup [9]

Whether for adornment or food, any wild animal that draws the attention of the crowd is in danger. French scholars say "the human predisposition to place exaggerated value on rarity.… probably drives the entire market for wildlife based luxury goods."[10] The desire to consume what is rare speaks of 25° self-absorption and thoughtlessness.

Heedless exterminism is also driven by trophy-hunting, a custom invented during the Victorian heyday of the British Empire but currently accelerating. Almost two million animal trophies have been exported across borders in the last decade (2004-2014) with at least 200,000 of them from threatened species such as the American black bear, mountain zebra, leopard, and African elephant. The recent surge of trophy hunting is led by well-to-do American, German, and Spanish hunters willing to risk an animal's extinction for the sake of décor. [11]

Entertainment

He enjoys true leisure who has time to improve his soul's estate.
~Henry David Thoreau

Once upon a time, the whole community gathered in an amphitheater to watch the performance of a tragedy by Aeschylus or Sophocles—it was a religious experience (X°) as well as entertainment. It is also counted as entertainment when men gather to watch a fight to the death between roosters or between dogs (5°) or when they watch humans pummel each other online. Whatever we call entertainment, consumer society has a lot to choose from.

Most of us crave stories like a vitamin, and stories include news, gossip, history, religious narratives, political ideologies, anecdotes, jokes, and conspiracy theories. When they depict complex characters with mixed motives, stories and dramas further social and psychological learning (35°), help to develop 40° compassion and 45° idealism, and broaden the substratum of experience that underlies 50° creativity. In contrast, narratives composed of deadly conflicts between 'good' and 'bad' stock characters reflect 5°/15°/20° mindsets.

However, after a hard day's work, not everyone looks for a great novel with ambiguities, anti-heroes and unhappy endings. Commercial fiction and films are attractive precisely because the consumer knows just what to expect— they have become traditions (30°). Readers and moviegoers feel comfortable with the often predictable plots and cliché dialogue. Today the world of genre novels and genre films itself becomes simplified into comic books and video games. Constant consumers of these genres are likely feeding their 5°, 15°, and 20° dispositions with explosive action, pointless plots, and dualistic ideas about us and them.

Film critic Judith Hess suggests that genre films are popular and financially successful because they temporarily take people's minds off social and political conflicts. For instance, lavish and light-hearted musicals were very well attended during the dark days of the 1930's Depression. "Genre films are nostalgic….their social structure posits some sort of movement backward to a simpler world. [They] reject the present and ignore any likely future."[10]

Zombie Ideas and the Status Quo

When the highest value in a community is loyalty to the greater cause,
meaning the continuity of the status quo, all means to this end are
imbued with religious significance, and are thereby [seen as] justified.
~Pearl Abraham, *"Hasidic Noir,"* 2004

The current state of affairs—the way things are now—is a comforting place. Prevailing conditions may not be wonderful, but many of us overrate the moment in fear of unknown alternatives. 15°, 20°, 25°, and 30° may be attached to the existing order or worldview. Old ideas that do not really accord with people's experience may still take a long time to die out. The Norwegian dramatist Henrik Ibsen described them as "ghosts" (the title of one of his plays).

> It's all sorts of dead ideas, and lifeless old beliefs, and so forth. They have no vitality, but they cling to us all the same, and we can't get rid of them. Whenever I take up a newspaper, I seem to see Ghosts gliding between the lines...And then we are one and all, so pitifully afraid of the light [11]

A century later, economist John Quiggins described "zombie ideas" that refuse to die despite the evidence against them.

One general belief that upholds the status quo is the assumption that the world is fundamentally just, and that people generally get what they deserve. This "just-world hypothesis" has been studied by social scientists since Melvin J. Lerner introduced it in the 1960s. He was trying to explain why people often accept social customs and political regimes that produce suffering. Why put up with these dysfunctions?

Lerner and later researchers also observed a widespread tendency to blame or devalue victims, including those who have been injured by rape, traffic accidents, domestic violence, illness, poverty, even victims of natural calamities such as earthquakes or hurricanes.

We can see on every side that life is not always fair, and virtue is not always rewarded. So how do we explain away this evidence? There are several strategies, rational and irrational. One accepts that the world is not always just, one tries to prevent injustice, or one denies it or tries to explain it away by blaming the victim. Lerner says that the prevailing belief in a just world is vital to a person's mental health—a 'positive illusion.' It makes us feel that the world is predictable, that we have some power to influence the future; and it encourages us to work toward goals.

Researchers have found stronger belief in a just world among those who also measure high on scales of right-wing authoritarianism and among members of certain Christian religious groups. In one cross-cultural study of students in 12 countries, belief in a just world was weaker among those living in countries with authoritarian leaders, where most people were relatively powerless. In the United States, African Americans have the lowest levels of belief in a just world. [12]

Another common idea is that the truth always lies in the middle between two extremes. As expressed by the centrist U.S. President Dwight D. Eisenhower: "Extremes to the right and to the left of any political dispute are always wrong." However, the world is not as simple as all that. Objectivist philosopher Ayn Rand said, "There are two sides to every issue: one side is right and the other is wrong, but the middle is always evil." The world is not that simple, either.

Babbitt, Mrs. Grundy, and Gossip

The ideas of order that the culture industry inculcates are always those of the status quo.
Theodor W. Adorno, German sociologist, 1903-1969

The deep desire to conform that drives 25° mass culture, advertising, and propaganda is depicted in the 1922 novel *Babbitt* by Sinclair Lewis. George F. Babbitt is a well-to-do realtor in Zenith, a fictitious mid-sized American city quite consumed with boosterism—excessive enthusiasm for its own growing prosperity and industrial progress, a kind of religion for the up-and-coming middle-class.

To the critic H.L. Mencken, George F. Babbitt was an archetype of conformity. "It is not what he [Babbitt] feels and aspires that moves him primarily; it is what the folks about him will think of him. His politics is communal politics, mob politics, herd politics; his religion is a public rite wholly without subjective significance."[13]

Finally realizing that his life-style is shallow and unfulfilling, Babbitt's efforts to rebel and achieve a more satisfying life ultimately fail, adding a note of tragedy. Spanish philosopher and social critic Jose Ortega y Gasset might have been speaking about the inhabitants of

Zenith when he said "The mass crushes beneath it everything that is different, everything that is excellent, individual, qualified and select. Anybody who is not like everybody, who does not think like everybody, runs the risk of being eliminated. [14]

A best-seller in the Twenties, *Babbitt* is now a classic. The word Babbitt entered the dictionary: "A narrow-minded, self-satisfied person with an unthinking attachment to middle-class values and materialism."

Another perspective on conformity is provided by Mrs. Grundy, a minor character in an 18th century play who personified the conventional and prudish members of society who enforce 'respectability.' Herbert Spencer said "The tyranny of Mrs. Grundy is worse than any other tyranny we suffer under." The Victorian Age is long past, but Mrs. Grundys are still imposing their version of morality using the fear of what people will say [15]

Conventional morality and manners are often imposed through the medium of gossip, defined as idle conversation (often rumors) about the details of other people's personal lives. To some degree gossip serves as an informal network of information about the community—who has married, died, or been born—and evolutionary biologists see it as an aid to social bonding and community cooperation. But when it is based on misinformation, focuses on scandals, and circulates at the speed of light via social media, it serves less beneficial purposes, becoming malicious gossip or spreading rumors that start moral panics.

Nationalism—Hubris?

The ultimate in selfishness is to care only for the protection, preservation and multiplication of one's own body. By body I mean all that is related to your name and shape--- your family, tribe, country, race, etc. To be attached to one's name and shape is selfishness. A man who knows that he is neither body nor mind cannot be selfish, for he has nothing to be selfish for... To be selfish means to covet, to acquire, accumulate on behalf of the part against the whole.
~Sri Nisargadatta Maharaj

According to the ancient Greeks who named it, *hubris* is an exaggerated pride and arrogant self-confidence, over-ambition and presumption toward the gods, that eventually leads to the hero's ruin. Hubris often indicates a loss of contact with reality and an overestimation of one's own competence, accomplishments or capabilities, especially when the person exhibiting it is in a position of power. Today hubris may characterize either individuals or groups.

Attachment to one's extended family, region, and traditions (30°) stabilizes individuals and societies, and is generally a healthy attitude. But narcissistic self-love cannot see beyond the limits of its race and ethnicity, language, civilization, religion, class, technological know-how, and nation-state. These external attributes become part of the 25° person's ego, and he includes them in his self-love.

I believe that Americans as a whole suffer from a dangerous form of hubris and collective narcissism based on our commanding position of wealth and military power, science, and technologies. The arrogant assumption that we are the best that ever was (or could be?) is underlain by persistent Social Darwinism and profound ignorance of history. Nationalism aka patriotism is a collective form of 25° and a dangerous ideology that often leads to war. This belief system brings forth extremely strong emotions, yet has existed no more than four centuries in its modern form of devotion to the nation-state.

A nation-state is not the same thing as a *nation,* which is an ethnic community united by common descent, culture, history, and ancestral territory, and sufficiently large to hold or desire to hold their own territory, to gain independence from, or to win greater autonomy within, a nation-state. Many ethnic nations do not have their own state, for instance Tamils, Sami, Kurds, Romani, Basques, Yoruba, Palestinians, Uyghurs, Tibetans, and Chechens. In fact hundreds of stateless nations exist, many with secession movements.[16, 17]

The urge of a large cultural collective for independence or greater self-determination is a 45° desire, but in seeking it people sometimes resort to terror tactics at the lowest dispositions, or fight guerrilla wars, which typically involve a great deal of brutality on both sides.

On the other hand we have the nation-state, resembling a nation in its relative homogeneity, common history and traditions, but often includes several ethnic groups or nations. The nation-state has a sovereign government that controls a defined territory with boundaries delineated on maps; it is the ultimate authority in that territory, with a monopoly on the use of force. Though ancient and medieval models exist, most scholars say that the era of modern nation-states arose around the time of the French Revolution (1789) or the Treaty of Westphalia (1648). Others say that England and the Dutch Republic were modern nation-states by 1600. In any case, within the last 400 years.

Nationalism in the modern nation-state becomes somewhat more abstract and formal than with nations; perhaps to compensate, these nationalists may impose arbitrary restrictions on the ethnic nations within their boundary, or may enforce an ideological conformity (10°) to replace the organic unity of a nation. Everybody now has to speak the same language, or subscribe to the same religion. The majority culture is the only acceptable culture. Nationalism in modern nation-states can express a range of dispositions:

- 5° displays xenophobia, jingoism, and enemy-thinking. He promotes and instigates aggressive wars and invasions.
- 10° supports conquest and imperialism. He identifies patriotism as support for one's country's wars—past, present, and proposed.
- 15° exhibits mindless flag-waving, conformity to patriotic symbols, and shows ignorance, with distorted ideas, about other nation-states and his own.
- 20° asserts the interests of his country as separate from that of other countries or from the common interests of all countries. There is competition for national pride (e.g., space exploration, tallest buildings, biggest army, etc.)
- 25° shows excessive pride in his country, with the belief that it is better and more important than all other countries (ego-identification and snobbery). U.S. historian Crane Brinton (1898-1968) spoke of U.S. patriotism as a religious ideology: "The ritual surrounding the flag, patriotic hymns, the reverent

reading of patriotic texts, the glorification of national heroes (saints), the insistence on the nation's mission, the nation's basic consonance with the scheme of the universe—all of this is so familiar to most of us that…we never even notice it." [18]

- 30° holds a conventional patriotism: devotion and loyalty to his country and willingness to serve it (by fighting) without questioning the reasons for war. But he is also capable of disillusionment.

- 35° has pride in his nation's positive principles and accomplishments such as representative government, freedom of speech, public education, equal rights, religious tolerance, public parks, universities, etc. He may express patriotism by participation in community improvement, nature conservation, environmental activism, and/or social and political reforms.

- 40° is a global citizen; in his own country, patriotism is devotion to the welfare of inhabitants and the land itself. He or she is dedicated to peace.

- 45° expresses patriotism by deep reform efforts, responsible dissent, and leadership in support of freedom and justice.

Thus nationalism, or patriotism, means many things, but tends to be captured by the lower dispositions.

[1] Ralph Nader, speech at Harvard Law School February 26, 1972

[2] Jean M. Twenge, Ph.D., and W. Keith Campbell, Ph.D., *The Narcissism Epidemic,* Free Press, 2009

[3] Patricia Laya, "The Most Expensive Commercials of All Time," *Business Insider*, June 20, 2011, http://www.businessinsider.com/most-expensive-commercials-2011-6?op=1

[4] John Sullivan, "True Enough," *Columbia Journalism Review*, May/June 2011 http://archives.cjr.org/feature/true_enough.php

[5] Caitlin Gibson, "The Next Level," *Washington Post*, Dec. 7, 2016 http://www.washingtonpost.com/sf/style/2016/12/07/video-games-are-more-addictive-than-ever-this-is-what-happens-when-kids-cant-turn-them-off/?utm_term=.4d90d92ace5a

[6] Elie Yudkowski, "Superstimuli and the Collapse of Western Civilization," Less Wrong (blog), March 16, 2007, http://lesswrong.com/lw/h3/superstimuli

[7] Producer/Director Sarah Barclay, "Addicted to Pleasure," BBC documentary-series, shown on AETN, October 2014

[8] "Capitalism and Slavery," *Macmillan Encyclopedia of World Slavery*, 1998, *World History in Context,* www.contextworld.com

[9] William Sauder, "How Two Women Ended the Deadly Feather Trade," *Smithsonian*, March 2013, http://www.smithsonianmag.com/science-nature/how-two-women-ended-the-deadly-feather-trade-23187277/?no-ist

[10] Agnes Gault, Yves Meinard, and Franck Courchamp, "Consumers' taste for rarity drives sturgeons to extinction," *Conservation Letters, A Journal of the Society for Conservation Biology,* Vol. 1, Issue 5, pages 199-207, December 2008

[11] Damian Carrington, "Millions of Animal 'Trophies' Exported across Borders," *Guardian UK*, June 14, 2016, https://www.theguardian.com/environment/2016/jun/14/millions-of-animal-trophies-exported-across-borders-figures-show

[12] Judith Hess, "Genre films and the status quo," Jump Cut, A Review of Contemporary Media, No. 1, 1974, http://www.ejumpcut.org/archive/onlinessays/JC01folder/GenreFilms.html

[13] Mrs Alving, Act II, Ghosts

[14] "Just-world hypothesis," http://en.wikipedia.org/wiki/Just-world_hypothesis

[15] H.L. Mencken, qtd. Linda de Roche, *The Jazz Age*, ABC-CLIO 2015

[16] Jose Ortega y Gasset, *The Revolt of the Masses*, 1930, The History Guide, Lectures on Twentieth Century Europe, http://www.historyguide.org/europe/gasset.html

[17] Herbert Spencer, "On Manners and Fashion" *Essays on Education* 1861

[18] James Minahan, *Encyclopedia of the Stateless Nations*, Greenwood, 2002

[19] Mark's Lists, "Stateless Nations," http://www.markslists.net/geography/statelessnations/index.html

[20] Crane Brinton, *The Shaping of Modern Thought*, chap. 5, Prentice-Hall 1963, 2nd ed.)

He who cultivates the inferior parts of his nature is an inferior man.
He who cultivates the superior parts of his nature is a superior man.
~*I Ching*, hexagram 27

Chapter 20
30° Mr. and Mrs. Everyman

The people yes
The people will live on.
The learning and blundering people will live on.
They will be tricked and sold and again sold
And go back to the nourishing earth for rootholds…
~ Carl Sandburg, excerpt from book-length poem "The People Yes"

Most human beings work, marry, and raise a family. While this is a common social expectation, it is really quite an accomplishment, always requiring some degree of selflessness, foresight, and patience. As Francis Bacon said some centuries ago, "Wife and children are a kind of discipline of humanity." Of course husband and children are also a kind of discipline of humanity. So is the necessity to earn a living, whether one is married or single.

Family life and work make the world go round. And so the majority of us are found most of the time at 30° where we have a job, take care of our children, say hello to our neighbors, mow the lawn, and generally abide by the rules of society. We are kindly disposed towards our kin, the people who live near us, those like ourselves (our tribe), and a few objects of charity. Here also is the beginning of unconditional love (especially in caring for young children).

Buber said: "The two basic qualities on which men's common life rests are good will and loyalty or reliability." These are 30° values. There are a great many decent people among us, doing the best they can. This may take years of sacrifice to care for a house full of children or an ill or disabled family member. Sometimes it requires sticking with a bad marriage or an uncongenial job for the sake of others. There are many kinds of love and commitment, and many unsung heroes.

Even certified heroes that make it into the newspapers, people who pull others from burning buildings or floodwaters, often say "I'm no hero." Never did it before, may never do it again. They just do what needs to be done. Duty—one's responsibilities and moral obligations—is at the core of 30° even if its people do not use the word. It is generally defined by one's culture. It is not the blind obedience of 15° nor yet the self-defined integrity of 45°. Morality comes to flower with 30°, while ethics is linked more with 35°, 40°, and 45°.

Family Comforts

Call it a clan, call it a network, call it a tribe, call it a family.
Whatever you call it, whoever you are, you need one.
~Jane Howard

In China, the oldest continuous civilization, family has always been of fundamental importance. Many people have a connection with the deep past and knowledge of ancestors as far back as 40 generations. Worldwide, family is the great bulwark against despair and chaos. Strong women, in particular, keep it all together. Many social and economic forces are working against the family (both extended and nuclear versions), and it is often overlooked in national policies that emphasize economic issues, yet this basic social institution remains as necessary as ever. The *I Ching* says "When the family is in order, all the social relationships of mankind will be in order."

The modern family is not always in order. Some families are rent with constant bickering (20°); others spend most of their free time vegetating in front of a TV set (15°). Some families are ruled by a domestic tyrant, male or female (10°) and some by violence and abuse (5°). Yet most families, however constituted, are functional and supportive, and parents take their responsibilities seriously.

Tolstoy said "Happy families are all alike; every unhappy family is unhappy in its own way." With 30° we are talking about a reasonably happy family, living up to the standards of their society. Some families are neighborhood models, their house and yard the neighborhood hangout. Parents may actively support children's interests in art, music, sports, games, natural science, scouting, and community activities (35°). The family may be an ideal society in miniature, promoting the self-actualization and happiness of all their members (40°).

Marriages (with or without children) also range from mismatched pairs who can scarcely speak to each other without fighting, or cold marriages of convenience, on up to truly wedded bliss and couples who live happily together for as many as sixty years. They may appear to enjoy an almost telepathic communication (X°).

While 30° puts high value on both marriage and traditional gender roles, this disposition is not prone to moral panics or harsh punishment of those who diverge.

Work

In order that people may be happy in their work, these three things are needed: They must be fit for it; they must not do too much of it; and they must have a sense of success in it.
~John Ruskin, art critic and social thinker, 1819 - 1900

To Ruskin's three qualities of good work we, living a century and a half later, might add that the work must be perceived as having some value in itself. Also, if paid work, it should provide a decent living.

Work spans a wide variety of awareness. Cut-throat competition and office politics drag people down to 20°. Monotonous work on an assembly line, performed only for a paycheck, tends to pull one into a 15° trance as in Chaplin's silent film *Modern Times*. A tyrannical boss is acting at 10°. A disgruntled or fired employee sometimes 'goes postal' at 5°. Work done under direct coercion—building a pyramid or breaking up rocks on the chain gang—might engender hopelessness with an intermittent rage or desire for vengeance. We don't know much about the inner lives of such individuals, as historically they rarely had the opportunity to express their feelings directly in art or literature.

Visiting Mexico City some decades ago, I daily passed a young beggar sitting on a blanket with his cup of coins. He looked about ten years old but because of malnutrition may have appeared younger than his years. Morning, noon, and evening he was there, and I have never seen an individual look more deeply unhappy. Throughout history countless children have been exploited, their nature thwarted, as in the early Industrial Revolution when children as young as eight attended machines for most of their waking hours. Today across the world there are many child laborers, child soldiers, and child prostitutes.

Even among adults, working for wages is seldom fulfilling in itself. Many people find that the main satisfaction of their job comes from social interaction with their co-workers, who become like a second family (30°). Some enjoy performing technical skills, and a few are fortunate to find work they actively enjoy. According to surveys, most people in the United States and strong minorities almost everywhere would prefer to be 'their own bosses.' In self-employment 30° develops the problem-solving attitudes and abilities that in lower dispositions tend to be swamped by emotional needs.

The master craftsman, like the Stone Age makers of axes that were more beautiful than they needed to be, has fulfilling work at 35°. Healing, intellectual, creative, or spiritual work may be accomplished at other of the higher degrees.

Dangerous work entered into for the public good—for instance fighting forest fires or rescuing people from disasters—often involves 40°/45° heroism. Police work across the world ranges from 5° use of excessive force or 10° coercion, bullying and corruption, to 40°/45° rescues, emergency medical assistance, and heroism "beyond the line of duty." Probably most of it occurs at 30°, based on protection of families. The idea of community policing, in which police develop partnerships within the community and work to prevent problems, is a 35° model.

Teaching

> *No one has yet fully realized the wealth of sympathy, kindness and generosity hidden in the soul of a child. The effort of every true education should be to unlock that treasure.*
> ~Emma Goldman, anarchist writer, 1869 –1940

Some biologists believe that the reason that humans developed full-blown culture while the higher apes did not is that we learned to teach each other on a regular basis. Teaching has always been an important part of the parenting role (30°) and it even precedes humanity, since many animals have to be taught to survive. For instance, pied babbler birds in southern Africa actively teach their fledglings to forage. Cheetahs train cubs in hunting skills over an 18-month period. Young orangutans stay with their mothers until they are seven or eight years old, learning how to build a sleeping nest and how to recognize over 300 different edible plant species. [2,3]

Humans have the longest childhood because we have the most to learn. A child learns about the basic structure of the world and acquires most of her language skills within the home before she is old enough to go to school. Even then the majority of learning occurs informally, outside of school hours, in family and neighborhood (30°).

In modern industrialized countries, the learning period lasts at least 18 years after birth (both informal and formal instruction). Without knowledge from the past we would be helpless creatures. Human cultures have always provided for the preservation of specialized knowledge through teaching and apprenticeship. Dispositions especially involved in preserving human knowledge are 30° (traditional knowledge), 35° (mastery of skills), and 45° (search for truth).

Various aspects of education express all the higher dispositions. The *profession* of teaching is at 35° but the *act* of teaching must involve elements of 40° love or else it is nothing but drill (15°) or even 10° dominance. Without love, all education becomes a mechanistic addition of information, never fully integrated with the personality. With it, children flower into whole human beings. Teaching occurs at all ages, and the proverb "Each one teach one" which began among African-American slaves forbidden to read, now symbolizes an international literacy movement in which ordinary people teach each other.

Honor is a concept with several quite different meanings that run the gamut of dispositions from 0° to 45°. Family honor is very important in several cultures that believe honor depends on the behavior of the family's women. What are called 'honor killings' occur when family members agree to the murder of another family member, almost always a woman, whom they believe has brought disgrace to the family by offenses such as objecting to an arranged marriage, asking for a divorce, having illicit sexual relations, or having been raped. This custom violently enforces a primitive patriarchal code, and while it has to do with family, it expresses 0°.

The 5° view of honor, reflecting masculine personal pride, drives fist fights, dueling, and vendettas. The 10° sense of honor is an aspect of power. Show the 10° individual respect due to his aristocratic birth, his rank or position of authority—or else somebody will face the consequences. Authority figures don't need to enforce their honor by personally fighting those who fail to bow deeply enough—instead they can arrest, imprison, torture, execute, or send offenders to Siberia.

20° honor depends on winning. Social reputation and the trappings of status are important to a 25° who is a stickler for titles and protocol. The corner office, the key to the executive washroom, the snappy salute are all-important. In general, lower dispositions view their personal worth and status as dependent on how others see them.

By contrast, the 30° ideal of honor is simply basic human decency. It is a personal code that includes positive guidelines and it also lists actions that one simply does not do, a standard below which one refuses to fall. It may include self-admonitions such as "a day's work for a day's pay," "women and children first," "honesty is the best policy," "leave other men's women alone," "don't kick a guy when he's down," "serve your country when it calls," and "Do unto others..." World religions and ethical systems have at least two dozen versions of the Golden Rule. Societies can barely function without it.

30° maintains vestiges of medieval chivalry in the notions of fighting fair and respecting those weaker. This code applies to women as well as men; for instance, I would give up my seat on the bus to either a man or woman on crutches or one carrying a baby. People generally seem to make an intuitive assessment of who is in the weaker position.

When 30° goes to war, it is to defend home and family, even if national leaders are planning conquest. Clever propaganda manipulates 30° in various ways by twisting basic, traditional values, for instance, exploiting the 30° natural sense of loyalty in order to support corrupt leaders. Honor is often associated with patriotism. Pacifists and others who strongly oppose certain policies of their own country on principle (45°) may be accused of being unpatriotic. Mark Twain, an outspoken anti-imperialist during the Spanish American War (but eminent enough to escape repression for his views) defined patriotism differently:

> Each man must for himself alone decide what is right and what is wrong, which course is patriotic and which isn't. You cannot shirk this and be a man. To decide against your conviction is to be an unqualified and inexcusable traitor, both to yourself and to your country, let men label you as they may.[1]

To basic human decency 35° adds professional ethics, active citizenship, and the satisfaction of doing something really, really well without shortcuts such as performance-enhancing drugs or plagiarism.

Honor at 45° includes the further refinements of intellectual integrity, self-insight, and a more complex philosophy that searches ways to deal with the complications and contradictions of the human condition—when, for instance, serving your country or doing your job conflicts with other basic values. Thus Edward Snowden is deemed a traitor at 20° or 30° but a whistleblower hero at 45°.

Such contradictions are difficult for many to resolve. This means that 30° also includes the 'walking wounded,' for whom the rules they live by don't seem to work very well. They went off to war as they were expected to do and now they suffer from PTSD precisely because they are decent people with a conscience and the ability to mourn and feel guilt. Or they want to earn a living but there no jobs are to be had.

During the Great Recession that began in 2008, unemployment rates in countries such as Spain and Greece reached rates even higher than in the U.S. at the peak of the Great Depression in 1933. In other countries unemployment rates seem always to be at similar high levels. People who can't get work to feed their families feel shame, despair, and anger. Nothing in the prevailing economic theory of neoliberalism gives them any support or hope. Thus the 30° basis of society erodes.

Then there are the effects of 10° customs and institutions that tend to drag individuals into lower dispositions. Decent people who live in a corrupt society find themselves making compromises and devising all sorts of stratagems just to survive day-to-day. For instance, there is a   whole subgenre of Italian fiction about principled detectives who must thread their way through a society that has never quite recovered from its corrupt fascist past and Mafia influence.*

For Better or for Worse

According to Father's lexicon, people who started on a job and didn't stay at it for 50 years were "quitters." If you stayed 20 years and then shifted to more congenial work you were a 'drifter'.
~Richard Bissell, *My Life on the Mississippi, or Why I am not Mark Twain*

At 30° people tend to persevere at whatever they're doing and to put a high value on loyalty and 'stick-to-it-iveness.' They are likely to accept whatever society has to offer, and to exhibit a certain stoicism. Having achieved a responsible adult life, 30° is inclined to rest on its laurels and to scorn others who don't place job and family as their *summum bonum* or highest good. For all its virtues, this degree has a somewhat limited horizon. It can be rather smug and unimaginative.

*Examples of detectives in this subgenre are Donna Leon's Commissario Brunetti, Andrea Camilleri's Inspector Montalbano, Michael Dibdin's Ispettore Aurelio Zen, Timothy Williams' Commissario Piero Trotti, and others

Scottish philosopher David Hume identified three powerful human inclinations, to favor those who resemble us, who are related to us, and who live nearby. These natural biases are noticeable at 30°.

This disposition also tends to be pretty practical, although not with the competitive, industrial focus of 20°. At 30° one tries to get good grades in school for the sake of family pride and for the diploma or degree that provides entry to a good job—but there is not much enthusiasm for ideas. Because of limited interest in the world beyond family, work, and neighborhood, 30° produces only a nominal citizen and even less of a world citizen. 30° keeps the human race going, but doesn't take it forward. That remains for other degrees to do.

Lower dispositions for one reason or another fail to see other humans as unique individuals, but 30° with its family focus does recognize people it is close to—even pets—as *persons*. Recognizing individuality is a great leap forward for inclusiveness. This disposition also believes in equality as a general value.

A frequent 30° flaw, perhaps related to being so involved with children, is a tendency toward sentimentality (excessive expression of shallow emotions). Strong family orientation can lead to problems such as nepotism and clannishness. Besides actual kin, 30° tends to identify with 'people like us' and the status quo. Sometimes this produces a "good ol' boy network" or excessive attachment to one's own religious sect or ethnic group to the exclusion of other kinds of people.

The criminal family such as Mafia-type organizations arises from too strongly favoring family over community:

In areas historically affected by a strong presence of Italian organized crime…mistrust towards the state amplified the role and the power of the family….The state was often seen as a greedy and hostile entity imposing taxes without providing services, and the extended family was considered the only reliable point of reference….leading to actions for the benefit and aggrandizement of the family and its members, even to the detriment of the community. That overpowering sense of family, which has been romanticized in cinema and literature, is a formidable obstacle to the normal evolution of the community. [4]

Similarly the 16th century Borderer's identification with his clan customs of feuding and reiving. But for the most part, the bond with family, tribe or village is beneficial.

Some 30° conceptions and institutions are: band of brothers, village, workingman, labor unions, kindergarten, and home. When these are extended universally, they become 40° concepts as in The Family of Man, the Commons, Global Village, and Mother Earth.

Peasants

The earth is the earth as a peasant sees it, the world is the world as a duchess sees it, and anyway a duchess would be nothing if the earth was not there as the peasant sees it.
~Gertrude Stein, modernist author, 1874-1946

Those living in modern industrial countries tend to think of peasants as poor people who lived in European medieval times. 'Peasant' is sometimes used as a mild insult, as if most of us were aristocrats, although almost all of us are only a few generations removed from small farmers and herders. Even today, nearly half the world's people are small family farmers. By some estimates, small family farms produce as much as 70% of the world's food.[5, 6]

At the inception of the United States, Thomas Jefferson had a vision that America might become an agrarian republic, a land of yeoman farmers, which is to say small landholders or prosperous peasants. These citizens would be self-sufficient, independent, and therefore resistant to tyranny. However, the nation did not develop that way and today the United States has only about two million farms.

City dwellers or not, the peasant life still has a pull on us. Many of us are attracted to 'old-timey' music and paintings of thatch-roofed cottages surrounded by chickens and a cow or two. The head may call it 'kitsch' but the heart resonates with this rustic picture. Recurring back-to-the land movements, such as in late 19th century England, many countries during the 1930s Depression, and 1970s America, are manifestations of the urge to return to an ancient template.

Peasant societies are based more on cooperation than are urban societies which have a money economy that promotes 20° competition. Small landholders usually have well developed social support networks, and the community takes care of those who have a poor harvest or who suffer other hardships (35°).

Small farmers tend to be conservative (30°), loyal to inherited power structures despite their own low status within the social hierarchy. Even now in the United States, rural states in the South and Midwest tend to be more politically and socially conservative than urban areas. In states such as Illinois and California, politics is defined by the fact that rural areas vote directly counter to the large cities.

The traditional peasant sees no point in producing more than can be stored and consumed locally. However, the West in its wisdom thinks they would be better off growing cash crops for export to affluent nations. Powerful leaders from Josef Stalin to western neo-liberal institutions such as the World Bank have tried to move peasants and small farmers into an industrial framework (20°) whether it be large collective farms or Western-style mechanization and a global money economy. Modernization (20°/35°) is supposed to increase food production and end poverty, but in the process chemical farming delivers many toxins to the environment, increases corporate control, and is unsustainable in the long run because of its dependence on oil.

World trade policies have not so far worked as promised to alleviate poverty. According to the World Trade Organization, "Current trade liberalization rules and policies have led to increased poverty and inequality." [7] Modernization is also destroying an ancient way of life. Spreading industrial capitalism on a world scale disrupts traditional social patterns and forces landless peasants into wage labor. In this modern enclosure process many who have lost their land move to the slums surrounding megacities in the Third World.[8]

Today's peasants, along with indigenous peoples, still struggle to have their voices heard on the world stage. In a symbolic protest, Spanish shepherds once a year drive their flocks through Madrid to assert ancient droving rights dating back at least seven centuries. A more far-reaching effort to support "people of the land" is mounted by La Via

Campesina, an international agrarian movement formed to defend peasants and small-scale farmers from the dominance of a corporate food system and "depeasantization." The organization claims that "Sustainable peasant and family farm agriculture can feed the world."[9]

Traditional Knowledge comprises the kind of local knowledge passed down orally, often in the form of story-telling or ritual, about technologies for hunting and agriculture, ecological knowledge, astronomy and celestial navigation, midwifery, herbal healing, and similar lore. TK has often been ignored or belittled by colonists or city folk who assume that their more generalized knowledge covers all situations. However, we still use TK even in modern America. For instance, most of us know how to read a large, dark rain cloud and other signs of local weather patterns. We look to the robin as harbinger of spring. We drink peppermint tea for our indigestion.

In others ways we think like our rural ancestors did. We still use the distilled wisdom in sayings such as the following:

Live and let live.
Slow and steady wins the race.
You reap what you sow.
There's no place like home.
A man's house is his castle.
Better to be safe than sorry.
Don't outdrive your headlights.
Make hay while the sun shines.
Don't rock the boat.
Keep your nose clean.
A rolling stone gathers no moss.
Blood's thicker than water.
When in Rome, do as the Romans do.
Honesty is the best policy.
Don't look a gift horse in the mouth.
In time of test, family is best.
You can't keep a good man down.

30° is the repository of folk wisdom because after all they/we are the 'folk.' Peasant wisdom is based on the ability to gain knowledge and understanding through personal observation. Since this knowledge may be passed down through generations of experience without formal education, it may lead to a deep distrust of 'book learning' and all secondhand information. Journalist Simon Carr reports a conversation with a Russian peasant who cautiously answers questions as follows: "I do not talk of what I have not seen," and "If a person has not been there he cannot say anything on the basis of words."[10]

The Internet may be increasing the divide between experience-based peasant wisdom (30°) in contrast to learning based on words and abstractions (20°/45°). A 2011 Harvard study indicated that our dependence on cyber knowledge has rewired our brains, suggesting that when we want information, instead of working it out based on what we already know, we think first about how we can find it online. "We are becoming symbiotic with our computer tools, growing into interconnected systems that remember less by knowing information than by knowing where the information can be found." [11, 12]

An ethnographer working with peasant farmers in Belize says most of them "believe that someday all the trappings of the modern world will crumble and that people in the future will need to remember the ways of the past in order to survive in this post-capitalist world." [13]

In fact, this prediction is a distinct possibility.

Conservatism

There are three classes of men: the retrograde, the stationary and the progressive.
~ Johann Kaspar Lavater, Swiss poet, 1741-1801

Expressing the "stationary class" of humanity, 30° is basically conservative and conventional. By 'conservative' we do not refer to political conservativism but rather the conservatism of habit. Actually most people are conservative about most things, most of the time. We form routines and resist change. We fix the same breakfast every day, take the same route to work, watch the same TV programs every week, and stay with the same partner for years. We conform to social norms, but not necessarily to the fads and fashions of consumer culture.

This generalized, customary conservatism saves energy, reduces stress, and adds stability to our lives and to society. It is beneficial unless it invades all our thinking processes to become an unthinking sphexism, as in the quip by Alfred E. Wiggam: "A conservative is a man who believes that nothing should be done for the first time." Or 19th century observer Alexis de Tocqueville: "I cannot help fearing that men may reach a point where they look on every new theory as a danger, every innovation as a toilsome trouble, every social advance as a first step toward revolution, and that they may absolutely refuse to move at all."

Another reason to separate conservatism (defined as the tendency to prefer an existing or traditional situation over change) from political conservatism is confusion about the latter term as applied to United States politics today. For instance, one might regard social institutions such as Social Security (about 75 years old) and Medicare (almost 50 years old) as the existing, traditional situation—the status quo. This would mean that those who don't want drastic changes in these programs are acting in a conservative way, and those who want radical changes are not conservatives but something else.

In another example, conservationists are often found trying to protect a distinctive natural area from human encroachment, that is, to preserve the natural status quo. But conservation is not currently part of U.S. political conservatism.

Historians Will and Ariel Durant defended our customary conservatism by tacitly comparing new ideas with biological mutations:

> Out of every hundred new ideas ninety-nine or more will probably be inferior to the traditional responses which they propose to replace. No one man, however brilliant or well-informed, can come in one lifetime to such fullness of understanding as to safely judge and dismiss the customs or institutions of his society, for those are the wisdom of generations after centuries of experiment in the laboratory of history. [14]

By "traditional responses" the Durants refer to folk culture—the traditions of a relatively small community, adapted to the particular bioregion that these people inhabit. These folkways include traditional arts, lore, tales, music, dance, food, and customs related to courting, raising children, farming, tools, and more. Even in modern, heterogeneous societies many of us continue to celebrate religious and other traditions that connect us with humans past and present and with the land and seasonal cycles (for instance, Thanksgiving as harvest festival and Easter as spring/fertility celebration).

Spiritual teacher Thich Nhat Hanh notes "When we respect our blood ancestors and our spiritual ancestors, we feel rooted…. Learning to touch deeply the jewels of our own tradition will allow us to understand and appreciate the values of other traditions, and this will benefit everyone."[15]

We need to distinguish between the stabilizing benefits of tradition on one hand and mindless clinging to the past on the other, although both express 30°.

[1] Mark Twain quote,
http://web.mit.edu/norvin/www/somethingelse/twain.html
[2] Lisa G. Rapaport, "Parenting Behavior: Babbling Bird Teachers?" *Current Biology*, http://www.cell.com/current-biology/pdf/S0960-9822(06)01986-5.pdf
[3] *Nature,* "Animal Childhood," co-production of THIRTEEN Productions LLC and BBC in association with WNET, viewed on PBS May 13, 2015
[4] "Europol, Threat Assessment: Italian Organized Crime," The Hague, June 2013
FILE NO: EDOC#667574 v8,
https://www.europol.europa.eu/sites/default/files/publications/italian_organis ed_crime_threat_assessment_0.pdf
[5] According to La Via Campesina, "The figure "nearly half" is composed of "1.5 billion peasants on 380 million farms; 800 million more growing urban gardens; 410 million gathering the hidden harvest of our forests and savannas; 190 million pastoralists; and well over 100 million peasant fishers." One could add one billion slum dwellers (landless peasants).
http://viacampesina.org/downloads/pdf/en/paper6-EN-FINAL.pdf

[6] Benjamin E. Graeb et al, "The State of Family Farms in the World," World Development, Vol. 87, November 2016, p. 1-15 http://www.sciencedirect.com/science/article/pii/S0305750X15001217

[7] "Trade Liberalization Statistics," http://www.gatt.org/trastat_e.html

[8] Olivier De Schutter, "Responsibly Destroying the World's Peasantry," June 4, 2010, http://www.project-syndicate.org/commentary/responsibly-destroying-the-world-s-peasantry#VHXw5fgotLW4bkwZ.99

[9] Priscilla Claeys, "From Food Sovereignty to Peasants' Rights: an Overview of Via Campesina's Struggle for New Human Rights," http://viacampesina.org/downloads/pdf/openbooks/EN-02.pdf

[10] Simon Carr, "There's a Lot in Peasant Wisdom," July 13, 2009, http://www.independent.co.uk/voices/commentators/simon-carr/simon-carr-theres-a-lot-in-peasant-wisdom-1743376.html

[11] Bryce Emley, "How Google flushes knowledge down the toilet," August 18, 2013, http://www.salon.com/2013/08/18/how_google_flushes_knowledge_down_the_toilet/

[12] Betsy Sparrow, Jenny Liu, Daniel M. Wegner, "Google Effects on Memory: Cognitive Consequences of Having Information at Our Fingertips," *Science Express*, July 14, 2011, www.sciencexpress.org/

[13] [4] Erik Nathaniel Stanley, *Native Soil: An Ethnography of Value Among Masewal Peasants of Cayo, Belize*, Florida State University, 10-28-2005, http://diginole.lib.fsu.edu/cgi/viewcontent.cgi?article=4814&context=etd

[14] Will Durant, Ariel Durant, *The Lessons of History*, Simon and Schuster, 2012

[15] ThichNhatHanh, *Living Buddha, Living Christ*

Chapter 21
Comparisons, Combinations, and Interactions

You become like the five people you spend the most time with…Choose Carefully.
~Anonymous

Since humans learn so much by imitation, even into adulthood we look for role models, although those we pick reflect patterns already formed and forming. For instance, a model for 5° may be a bully or authoritarian leader; 40° most admires someone like Jane Goodall or the Dalai Lama; 25° would imitate a celebrity of her own gender who is 'hot'; and the hero for 30° is Grandpa on his mother's side. Some pick fictional characters to emulate.

It is ancient folk wisdom that like attracts like, as with a school of fish or an oak grove; and now science finds that not only do stars cluster but so do galaxies. This principle of clustering applies to human behavior, whether a gang of thieves, a social clique, a pathocracy, or a gathering of highly creative people in the same place and era, as in ancient Greece, Renaissance Florence, or 1920s Harlem. To some extent dispositions are contagious, though not so much so as memes, the more discrete cultural elements that are also spread by imitation.

Not only are like minds and like dispositions attracted to each other, but those who live in the same communities, speak the same languages, and attend the same churches or temples tend to share certain dispositions. Although each person typically exhibits many dispositions, one or two patterns may predominate in individuals, cultures, and eras.

People all too readily misunderstand and stereotype those who are 'coming from' other mindsets, with misunderstandings especially frequent in lower dispositions that are deficient in empathy. In a novel set in medieval times, "It was the difference between them that Robert thought in hierarchies, and Rhisiart thought in blood-ties, high and low of one mind and in one kinship." Robert clearly sees his world in 20°

terms, while Rhisiart is deeply traditional, part of family and clan (30°). In the story, tragic events ensue from this difference in basic outlook.[1]

Shakespeare scholar Ian Johnston suggests that the division of drama into comedy and tragedy reflects two basic ways of experiencing life. "The comic vision celebrates the individual's participation in a community as the most important part of life." (30°/35°/40°) In contrast the tragic vision explores the individual's "desire to confront the world on his own terms....Tragic heroes are passionately egocentric and unwilling to compromise their powerful sense of their own identity in the face of unwelcome facts." (25°/45° and sometimes 5° fanaticism). [2]

Relationships between individuals with different disposition patterns can become quite complex. Sometimes the higher awareness informs the lower awareness; or the person acting at his worst drags the other down to this more cynical worldview and less ethical behavior. Or both of these effects may happen in different areas of their life together.

There are complexities within each individual. The unconscious defense mechanism of *compartmentalizing* is how a person tries to avoid the confusion and anxiety of holding conflicting emotions and beliefs. For example, in one area (say, family) an individual operates at 30° and in another area (business) at 20° cut-throat competition. He may contribute generously to charity (35°) and at the same time subscribe to 10° ideologies about how criminals need to be speedily executed without appeals. Speaking of such compartmentalization, Ken Hughes, a Nixon scholar, says "There are different Nixons for every occasion." To some degree, this could be said of us all.

I can see the full range of dispositions in myself. Although my 0° is sublimated, and my 5° losses of temper are relatively rare, they exist and I cannot disown them. It is likely that creative people such as actors and novelists are more in touch with their own spectrum of possibilities than is the average person, and this may be an important part of their creativity. At the same time, deeply loving people acting at 40°/X° may accept the full range displayed before them and forgive all.

At 10° or 0° a person usually fails to understand those operating in higher dispositions, believing that either they are hypocrites putting on a show of love or altruism to cover their real motives or that they are fools, natural-born suckers to manipulate or dominate.

At 15°, individuals tend to misunderstand a lot of what goes on in the world. When this degree predominates, people are functionally illiterate, not very observant, or their reasoning powers are underdeveloped. They are easily manipulated by charming psychopaths acting at 0° or 10°, or by authoritarian propaganda with the same effect. 15° holds a great deal of fear and anxiety. She is afraid of the anger of 5°, the bully-power of 10°, and the cleverness of 20°.

15° strives to live up to 20°, 25°, and 30° values, that is to say, his aspirations are to make and spend money and have a family. But 15° is not a very good parent, having had poor role models. Two people who develop a relationship at 15° may produce a dysfunctional family.

A 15° or 20° ideologue assumes that anyone who doesn't agree with him is another ideologue with the opposing viewpoint. He cannot think out of his either/or stereotypes, nor imagine the existence of quite different perspectives. For ideologues, the world appears to be composed of other ideologues.

Both 15° and 20° tend to think in terms of tit for tat, that is, retaliation seems to be justice. On the other hand, 10° wants to crush designated enemies so that there is no more cycle of retaliation; and 5° rage would obliterate them.

Many people are quite incurious about what goes on around them unless it impinges directly on their personal life. This is especially true of 15° and 25°, sometimes also of 30° when overly wrapped up in family, work, and daily routine.

Love comes in many forms. An individual may manifest numerous lower and higher aspects of love in a single lifetime—or in a single day. The ability to compartmentalize makes it possible for a hitman or a guard at an extermination camp, acting at 0° in his working life, to come home to pat his dog and play with his children at 30°. Love equals lust for 5°, or it easily turns violent. At 10° an individual possesses and rules the loved one. Dysfunctional relationships cluster at 15°. The 20° marriage partnership is conventional and convenient, while 25° expresses vanity through association with the economic success, talent, or beauty of spouse (Trophy Wife) or children (my son the doctor).

In the lower dispositions, men are likely to pick a life partner mainly for her erotic appeal, then find themselves with a mate who is not only incompatible but also selfish, irresponsible, or mentally disturbed. Women, even at 30° or 35°, may be vulnerable to charming, manipulative men behaving at very low levels of awareness, or to angry, abusive 5°.

Lower dispositions tend to see other people instrumentally, as victims, love objects or possessions, competitors, cash cows, servants, subjects (as of royalty), underlings, suckers, prey, audience, fans, enablers, scapegoats, enemies, etc. With 20°, there is a tendency to see other people solely as members of a category rather than as unique individuals. With 25°, others very often become counters or tokens in whatever life games one is playing.

Truer expressions of love—enduring affection and concern for the welfare of another—usually begin with 30° and throughout the higher dispositions.

Those who tend to act in lower dispositions do not care anything about future generations or at most, nothing beyond getting their own children out of the nest and into gainful employment. They have a bare minimum of the *generativity* trait that we humans need in order to replace the instinctual programs of less-aware creatures. But by 30° most people are, at the least, very concerned with the future of their extended kin.

At 20° a person overvalues the importance of competition and financial gain, and greatly undervalues the unpaid work which is part of family life (30°) and of community service (35°). This often means that men do not value the work that women do in the home. (Standard economic theories ignore the value of such unpaid work.) Women acting at 20° may nag or goad their husbands to earn more money. 20° does not understand those who choose careers in the arts, teaching, or other vocations that are not highly paid, and may strongly oppose such career or marriage choices by their own children.

Various 20° ideologues dislike science because it does not support their economic interests or theological beliefs. Meanwhile, 20° advertising and PR for technological innovations claims the mantle of disinterested science, and promotes the concept that scientists are modern wizards. Debunkers at 25° turn science into dogma (10°) in order to prove their own superiority to the gullible 15°.

Acting from mixed motives leads to mixed results. Take for instance Jestin Coler, a leading entrepreneur of online fake news during the 2016 American presidential campaign. Most of his fake news domains targeted Trump supporters (although Coler himself is a registered Democrat) because, he says, liberals are not so easily fooled. The sites had abundant traffic and earned a great deal of money through ads, but Coler suggests he has a 35° motivation to educate the public:

> The whole idea from the start was to build a site that could infiltrate the echo chambers of the alt-right, publish blatantly false or fictional stories, and then be able to publicly denounce those stories and point out the fact that they were fiction…. We have a whole nation of media-illiterate people. Really, there needs to be something done [3]

Yet Coler did little to denounce his own work or educate the public, perhaps more motivated by 20° profits and 10° pleasure in manipulating people: "I do enjoy making a mess of the people that share the content that comes out of our site." False stories went viral because they supplied part of the public with the "red meat" of fear, anger, and conspiracy theories (5°/15°). The effect on election results is unknown.

The character Wally in the "Dilbert" comic expresses 15°/20° saying "Meetings used to be frustrating and boring until I *gamified* that situation…Now I try to *win* meetings by criticizing co-workers, offering no ideas of my own, and leaving without any new task." [4]

Twenty-five degrees may scorn the natural conservatism, homespun values, and family responsibilities of 30°, which for him embodies 'middle-class morality' and 'middle-brow' tastes, a boring and unimaginative life-pattern. From 30°'s point of view, 25° is irresponsible and selfish—and 'needs to grow up.'

In an example of conflict between 25° and 30° values, a visitor to my home admired a large 1890 tintype on my wall and wanted to know my price. (She knew that I was in straitened circumstances). I explained that it was my grandparents' wedding picture, a priceless possession. Yet it was 'perfect for her décor' so she persisted in asking me how much I would take for it. But who sells their own grandparents' wedding picture? Not me, anyway.

The natural tendency of 30° is to trust institutions. This allows subtle manipulation by those acting at lower dispositions, such as the common practice of planted newspaper stories by PR firms, or the CIA (10°/20°). Also, 30° attempts to keep to the middle of the road. "Seek moderation in all things." An imbalance in 35° or 45° intellect tends to 20° mechanical or categorical thinking. Imbalance in 45° courage might lead to 10° fanaticism. Imbalanced 40° could become 25° sentimentality or 15° gullibility. An unbalanced 50° tends toward 25° artiness or publicity-seeking.

30° sees higher degrees as models of aspiration or else as people exhibiting unrealistic, selfish, and ultimately irrelevant behaviors. Everything is seen through the filters of family, earning a good living, and obeying the rules of society. Henry David Thoreau describes the view of practical 30° or mercenary 20° toward a nature-loving 40° or X°: "If a man walks in the woods for love of them half of each day, he is in danger of being regarded as a loafer. But if he spends his days as a speculator, shearing off those woods and making the earth bald before her time, he is deemed an industrious and enterprising citizen."[5]

A popular slogan is "Think globally, act locally." 40° or 45° is more likely to think globally, while 35° has a greater commitment to acting locally. Bioregionalism, a modern movement to recreate 30° traditions, traditional knowledge, and connection with the land, also encompasses 35° communitarianism and environmental ethic, 40° universality and generativity, 45° scientific knowledge, and X° nature spirituality. But it has little appeal for the lower dispositions, and mainstream media have generally ignored it.

Several writers have attempted to distinguish between shades of green, that is to say, between different kinds of environmentalism; others have surveyed the wider range of attitudes toward nature and the environment. We might compare these as follows: *Light Greens* see protecting the environment primarily as a personal responsibility through consumer choices, recycling, and personal conservation (30°/35°). Like a good soldier, 30° carpools or puts out his recycling bin. *.Lite Green* refers to greenwashing and to marketing practices appealing to those with the shallowest commitment (20°/25°).

Public Greens focus on neighborhood and community issues such as trails, parks, real estate development, and water treatment (35°). Bright Greens work through large environmental organizations and are often techno-optimists (20°/35°). *Bright Greens* protesting or bringing lawsuits against corporate polluters need 45° background to make their case legally and in the court of public opinion. Lester Brown of Worldwatch Institute is one 45° analyst/theorist with a world-wide 40° perspective. Others are scientists, journalists, or dedicated citizens.

Deep Greens have a biocentric perspective (45°/X° Deep Ecology). Some Earth defenders have become martyrs (40°). Chico Mendes died defending the Brazilian rainforest and the peasants who draw a living from it. Indigenous activist Berta Caceres, who opposed a hydroelectric dam, was murdered in Honduras. Former employees of the dam's construction company and military officers are currently on trial for the crime.

Monkeywrench Greens actively resist the destructive industrial system, occasionally employing lower disposition violence (intended against property not persons). *Dark Greens*, looking toward a civilizational collapse in the not too distant future, are downshifting and going off the grid as much as feasible. Unlike Survivalists, they work together to serve as models of resilience for society (35°/40°/45°).

Creative Greens are coming up with many new ideas to help save Earth, from using canine teams to help save endangered wildlife, to the Solar Bottle Bulb, a plastic bottle filled with water and bleach, which stuck into a hole drilled in the roof, makes a 40 to 60- watt lamp (invented by Brazilian Alfredo Moser, used in over a million homes).

Kari McGregor, Australian sustainability activist, notes that all shades of green are needed to reach different segments of the population (50° synthesis). Meanwhile, those (dubbed 'Browns') who are quite uninterested in environmental issues, or oppose environmental measures for allegedly interfering with economic health, apparently comprise the attitudes of about one-third of Americans, ranging 15°/20°/25°. [6, 7].

At the deeper level of worldviews, people tend to think of the world as either cyclical or linear. Indigenous cultures and Asian philosophies have found more cycles than do we in the fast, linear culture of the United States, which leads to entirely different behaviours. A permaculture site (permaculture is an agriculture based on working with natural cycles) describes the differences: "Societal consequences of viewing a through a linear filter include alienation from Nature, production systems which consume more energy than they return, and a compulsion to respond to Life's inevitable ebbs and flows with manipulative, often violent attempts at unilateral control (seen in both individuals and societies)." [10°] [8]

[1] Ellis Peters, *The Benediction of Brother Cadfael,* 1992
[2] Ian Johnston, "Dramatic Structure, Comedy and Tragedy," excerpt http://www.siue.edu/~ejoy/eng208NotesOnComedyAndTragedy.htm
[3] Laura Sydell, "We Tracked Down a Fake-News Creator in the Suburbs. Here's What We Learned," NPR "All Things Considered," November 23, 2016,
http://www.npr.org/sections/alltechconsidered/2016/11/23/503146770/npr-finds-the-head-of-a-covert-fake-news-operation-in-the-suburbs
[4] Scott Adams, "Dilbert," August 18, 2017
[5] Henry David Thoreau, "Life without Principle," 1863
[6] Kari McGregor, "What Shade of Green Are You?" Generation Alpha, 2014? http://www.generationalpha.org/shades-of-green/
[7] Elizbeth Palermo, "50 Shades of Green? Environmental Attitudes Vary Widely in US," Live Science, December 9, 2015
https://www.livescience.com/53022-american-enviromental-attitudes.html
[8] "Linear vs. Cyclical Paradigms and Permaculture Mind," (Perma)Culture and Sanity, http://permaculture-and-sanit.com/pcarticles/linear-vs-cyclical.php

Chapter 22
35° Good Citizens

In the long history of humankind (and animal kind, too) those who learned to collaborate and improvise most effectively have prevailed.
~Charles Darwin

The 35° disposition is relatively recent, speaking from the long view of our species. When people settled in towns and cities, the constant, complex human interactions required new behaviors. 35° grew along with civilization, very involved in the organization of society and the forms of fellow-feeling, establishing friendship bonds and assuming responsibilities to people beyond family and immediate neighbors, beyond 'people like us.' Also at 35° one has obligations to one's craft or profession.

The development of morality and ethics has a long history. We are hard-wired for most of it: altruism and cooperation, a sense of fairness, taking care of infants, pair-bonding, caring for ill, injured, and aged. Note that all of these behaviors have pre-human antecedents.

The concept of the Common Good first appeared at 30° but as a more tribal notion. Then 30° learned about the Golden Rule and "Love thy neighbor" and established norms such as: don't lie, don't speak ill of others, keep your promises, take care of those who depend on you.

These are excellent rules, but sometimes situations arise where they don't apply, or perhaps one contradicts another, or one must think farther ahead. The intricacies of interpersonal relationships and how to apply ethical principles to the whole community or nation, becomes the work of 35°. Many ethical principles appear at 35°.

However, ethics is far from the only expression of this disposition. Some of the areas, behaviors, and qualities that demonstrate 35° awareness are:

Charity	Justice
Civic Participation	Neighborhood
Community	Pay it forward
Conversation	Philanthropy
Cooperatives	Professionalism
Comradeship	Rites of passage
Democracy	Scouting
Environmentalism	Teaching
Equality and Equity	Teamwork
Friendship	Theatre
Hospitality (ancient sense)	Volunteering

Some of the above are more aspirational and abstract; some need a little explanation. For instance, *hospitality* evokes the image of a welcoming host or hostess who throws a good party, but in many ancient societies hospitality was an essential value that ensured the welfare and even the survival of neighbors and travelers. To the ancient Greeks, hospitality was a divine right. In East Indian tradition, "the guest is god." Hospitality remained important in early modern Europe, and is still a high value in many traditional societies such as the Pashtuns and Maoris. The older and broader meaning expresses 35° awareness

Conversation is a true exchange of thoughts rather than alternating monologues. At 45° there is dialogue, as in Socratic dialogue, in which a focused conversation becomes intellectual exploration.

Theatre arose long ago out of community rituals. The earliest recorded theatrical event (around 2000 BC) was the story of the God Osiris, performed every year at festivals in ancient Egypt. The first *written* dramas were performed annually in ancient Greece beginning in the 6th century BC, with the entire community as their audience. Greek drama formed the basis for the entire Western tradition of theatre.

The link between theatre and 35° awareness? Drama is the preeminent community art, drawing everyone together in a discharge of emotions (laughter or tragic catharsis) with a healing and unifying effect. For both performers and audience the dramatic experience encourages development of fellow-feeling, with a strong element of 40° empathy and, with the greatest plays and actors, 50° creativity and X° realizations.

Friends and Comrades

*Friendship is the hardest thing in the world to explain. It's not
something you learn in school. But if you haven't learned the meaning
of friendship, you really haven't learned anything.*
~Muhammad Ali, professional boxer, 1942—2016

Humans are not the only ones to form friendships. Field research has demonstrated that animals of several species such as horses, monkeys, elephants, dolphins, and hyenas may form long-lasting bonds with certain others of their kind. Other animals appear to recognize these special relationships. Friendship ensures greater reproductive success and longevity for its participants. Also, inter-species friendships have been well-documented in both wild and domesticated animals. [1]

Humans have many different kinds of friends, ranging from drinking buddies or people we hardly know on Facebook to others we have known since elementary school, and even some for whom we would lay down our life. With some, friendship is a strategic alliance (20°); it may be somebody with whom we enjoy pastimes (25°); or it may be an association built solely on similar interests or proximity as neighbors or workmates. While 30° has friends, family usually comes first. At 35° friendship is a closer and more committed relationship.

Aristotle in the Nichomachean Ethics divided friendship into three kinds: the pleasurable, the useful, and the perfect. The last is what we think of as true friendship, in which someone wishes the best for the other person for his own sake. Aristotle compares it with what mothers feel toward their children (40°).

Then there is *comradeship* or group friendship often noted among men in armies and other dangerous and isolating occupations such as ocean sailing and firefighting where men form an artificial community (30°/35°). This behavior is probably as old as humans and their cooperative hunting. Women's work relationships and mutual support are equally important but less celebrated. Through most of our existence women worked together to provide the major part of the human diet (caloric) and practiced collective child-raising. This team spirit can occur apart from war and dangerous occupations, and expand to all, women as well as men. Working people in labor unions and dedicated activists working in a common cause often develop such solidarity and camaraderie.[2] However, when any group develops an *esprit d' corps* that is exclusive and elitist it becomes less like 35° friendship and more like 25° snobbery or even 10° power lust.

Liberal Education

A liberal education...frees a man from the prison-house of his class,
race, time, place, background, family and even his nation.
~Robert M. Hutchins, American educator, 1899-1977

Operating at 35° a person is likely to have had some sort of liberal education, even when most of his or her education was training for a craft or profession. In some cases, the individual is self-educated through reading. A common misconception is that a liberal education is only about the humanities, therefore it is useless or impractical in the 'real world.' However, the traditional meaning of the term has to do with acquiring a basic knowledge of many fields of study, including mathematics and the sciences for personal growth and all-round mental fitness. Mortimer Adler, a well-known educator, spelled this out:

> The liberal arts are traditionally intended to develop the faculties of the human mind, those powers of intelligence and imagination without which no intellectual work can be accomplished. Liberal education is not tied to certain academic subjects, such as philosophy, history, literature, music, art, and other so-called 'humanities.' In the liberal-arts tradition, scientific disciplines, such as mathematics and physics, are considered equally liberal, that is, equally able to develop the powers of the mind. [3]

The idea is that the liberally educated person not only gains knowledge but *learns how to learn*; learning skills are transferable, giving the necessary grounding to master any specialized field one wishes. Besides a basic acquaintance with all the major fields of human study, a liberal education is intended to give a deepened sense of values and ethics, and a readiness to participate in the larger community. The idea is often traced back to ancient Greece when education for freemen was intended to produce well-rounded citizens. Broadly educated students with a liberal education also develop their physical skills, not so much to excel in public performances but rather for overall fitness.

Respect for Reason

> *In a republican nation, whose citizens are to be led by reason and persuasion and not by force, the art of reasoning becomes of first importance.*
> ~Thomas Jefferson, 3rd President of the United States

Although not always intellectual, 35° prefers civil, reasonable discourse, and can discuss an issue without always trying to win the argument as does 20°. She looks at diverse sources of information, not just those she agrees with. In an era dominated by mass media, advertising, and propaganda, it is a crucial skill for people to watch, listen, and read messages critically rather than to swallow them whole. This skill is called *critical literacy.* It needs to be taught to children as soon as they are able to read, watch television, or use the computer.

Critical thinking (CT) is a somewhat different ability. It is self-guided, disciplined thinking that attempts to be fair, open-minded, and informed by evidence. Critical thinkers (35° and 45°) question all sides of an issue and are willing to be wrong. They look for their own biases and recognize contradictions even in their own thinking. Like critical literacy, CT needs to be emphasized much more in American schools (I don't know about other countries) and presented more widely to adult citizens in adult education courses, on television, and in videos.

Most at 35° maintain a scientific viewpoint, that is, a respect for scientific knowledge and processes. They may be in a technical field. Sometimes there is a thin line between 35° attitudes and a more doctrinaire 20° faith in current science-and-technology. This sometimes shows up as exaggerated futurism (technological utopia). [4, 5]

Another pitfall to which 35° is prone is a special form of egotism first noted by the Spanish philosopher Jose Ortega y Gasset as part of "the barbarism of specialization." Ortega says that since about 1890 "a type of scientist unparalleled in history" has taken intellectual command in Europe [and the United States?]:

Only acquainted with one science [he] proclaims that it is a virtue that he takes no cognizance of what lies outside the narrow territory....He is a learned ignoramus...with all the petulance of one who is learned in his own special line....In politics, in art, in social usages, in the other sciences, he will adopt the attitudes of primitive, ignorant man, but he will adopt them forcefully....This very inner feeling of dominance and worth will induce him to wish to predominate outside his specialty. [6]

(The egotism of the specialist applies to other than scientists.)

Although priding himself on dedication to reason, 35° is still susceptible to well-crafted propaganda. As a 10°/20° character in a Regency-era novel says: "It's all in the way you phrase things. Good of the realm and all that rot. It's the earnest, honorable ones who are the easiest to manipulate."[7] According to Noam Chomsky's propaganda model, there are two main targets of propaganda: the general public and the political elite that includes many acting at 35°. Indoctrinating them to continue the status quo involves massaging reality so that it fits 'the party line' along with persuading or marginalizing those who oppose a given policy. Even the well-educated 35° can be manipulated.

Yet another pitfall for 35° comes with membership in the meritocracy, a system in which people supposedly advance because of their abilities and effort (merit) not because of their money or social position. Marianne Cooper notes that "Americans' support for meritocratic principles has remained stable over the last two decades despite growing economic inequality, recessions, and the fact that there is less upward mobility in the United States than in most other industrialized countries."[8]

Onward and Upward! Or Not

It would be advisable to think of progress in the crudest, most basic terms: that no one should go hungry anymore, that there should be no more torture, no more Auschwitz. Only then will the idea of progress be free from lies.
~ Theodor Adorno

Of all the dispositions, the greatest believer in progress is a 35° who is happy and confident after having had a secure attachment in childhood, feels good will towards most others, and has no serious problems with health or finances. Naturally optimistic 35° sees the foundations of here and now as basically sound, although needing a tweak here and there. He works for reforms—not for fundamental change. This more Panglossian version of 35° believes that civilization (Western civilization), modernity, science, representative government, market economies, modern technology, and the Internet all combine to make everybody's lives infinitely better than ever before in history.

35° differs from the 20° techno-utopian in that he has a broader focus, is more concerned with society's welfare, not so ideological, and more capable of changing his mind. After discovering the Janus face of modernity, some acquire a deeper sense of urgency and commitment to action. They express the ethical aspects of 35° in social engagement. They may be dedicated activists, convinced of the need for reforms, in the sense of making things better. (More recently the word 'reform' has been used to describe any political and institutional change even when there is broad public disagreement about the likely consequences.)

Nation-states have at times made extreme changes by force. Most such drastic reforms are initiated at lower dispositions, although sometimes 35° is persuaded by words like 'modernization' and 'progress.' The 'Great Leap Forward' was Mao's campaign to reform China by changing its economy from agrarian to industrial. This plan was implemented with brutal violence and far too rapidly, costing at least 18 million human lives, perhaps up to twice that many.

'Social engineering' acquired negative connotations because of intensive campaigns by authoritarian governments such as Mao's. On the other hand, most government policies and laws seek to change behavior. For instance, penalties for crimes and misdemeanors are intended to discourage them. Philosopher Karl Popper attacks social engineering when it is based on an ideological blueprint and superimposed on an existing society, but he approves of a more piecemeal approach, which works on the small scale and on specific, urgent evils. Based on trial and error, he says that piecemeal social engineering allows people to learn from their mistakes and it is compatible with democracy.[9, 10]

Yet even piecemeal social engineering can run into problems. It may begin nobly but then proceed from low motives such as 10° power drives or ideologies based on racial or class superiority/inferiority. The would-be improvement may suffer from overly simple, mechanistic ideas (20°) or from the 25° drive towards conformity. Enthusiasm for improving society needs to be tempered by humility and historical understanding of what can go wrong with such plans. One has to know when an experimental idea is in fact an experiment, and not let bureaucratic inertia carry it forward forever.

One historic example of progress gone wrong is the pseudo-science of eugenics, a plan for improving the human race very popular in the United States from the turn of the century through the 1930s. It still survives in pockets of 10° ideology. Another seemingly good idea that did not work out is solitary confinement, first proposed by Quakers and Anglicans in the early 19th century as a humane alternative to the brutal prisons of the time. The idea was that prisoners could reside in a clean and quiet environment while seeking penitence from their Lord. Instead, many of the prisoners went mad. Now it is the ministers and other human rights advocates who are trying to *end* the practice.

Four areas of reform that are fairly straightforward and which clearly relate to 35° are first, ending political corruption involving bribery, fraud, cronyism, nepotism, and similar practices. The second involves political reforms that increase government transparency and public participation. The third area encompasses a number of economic and social actions that support 35° values such as equal opportunities and religious tolerance. Fourth, reform is needed to combat the inertia involved with institutions and laws that outlive their functions or turn their mission into something else entirely.

Utopianism

Utopia is nothing more than a truth that the world is not yet ready to hear.
~Yann Arthus-Bertrand, French photographer, 1946--

Several dispositions (35°, 40°, 45°, 50°) contain a bright streak of utopia. Visions of a better world go back into antiquity and are implicit in the narratives of nations, cultures, and subcultures for instance the Garden of Eden, Heaven, Paradise, Arcadia, or "the City upon a Hill." The Bible tells of the Sabbatical Year and Jubilee Year when debts are forgiven, slaves and prisoners freed, and land is redistributed. This in turn was probably based on earlier Mesopotamian traditions in which the government periodically issued edicts that cancelled debts.

Utopian threads run through myth and fiction, such as the medieval myth of the Land of Cockaigne or the popular 1933 novel and film *Shangri-La*. The central worlds of the Star Trek Federation are utopian. Modern science fiction is more likely to describe dystopias.

Unfortunately, many political writers equate utopia with the failures of 20th century communist states, as if Marxism were the only utopianism. The narrow definition of utopia ignores a long tradition of literary utopias (45°/50°) such as *New Atlantis* (Francis Bacon, 1625), *Herland* (an early feminist utopia by Charlotte Perkins Gilman, 1915) and *Ecotopia* (Ernest Callenbach, 1975). Ideals can and do influence cultures and movements without being applied as a rigid 10° template. Utopian ideals of world peace, social justice, or harmony with nature are strong motivators, e.g., the "I Have a Dream" speech of Rev. Martin Luther King, Jr. At 35° utopia links with reformist enthusiasm.

Justice has several meanings, and is far more than the punishment of crime. The ideas of fairness, impartiality, equity, moral rightness, and the assignment of merited rewards and punishments are all implied in the term justice, which is defined rather differently in every society. Notions of fairness are so ancient that they predate the human species and have been found among primates and canines. (Try giving a treat to one of your dogs and not the other, and you will encounter something that looks very much like righteous indignation.)[11, 12]

The earliest written legal codes appeared in the Middle East as early as 2300 BC, and one of the first was far more than a penal code; it was also concerned with social justice. In a Mesopotamian city the Code of Urukagina exempted the city's widows and orphans from paying taxes, and cleared debt obligations for indentured citizens forced into living as debtors because of grain taxes, or from suffering theft or family murder. The ruler Urukagina appears to have been a social reformer (35°) who came into power following a corrupt ruler. During the Old Babylonian period (2000-1600 BC) governments periodically issued *mesharum* edicts cancelling debts, along with other poor relief. The biblical sabbatical and jubilee years are an adaptation of this idea (which has been largely ignored in Christian tradition). [13, 14]

Justice has three major facets: retributive, restorative, and distributive. We have already discussed retributive justice, which expresses 10° desires to punish wrongdoers. *Restorative justice* comes from a different place. It focuses on the needs of both the victims and the offenders, as well as of the surrounding community, rather than on punishing the offender or applying abstract principles of law. Its focus is on repairing the harm (35°/40°). [15]

Restorative justice involves all the stakeholders in a cooperative process that may include mediation between the victim and the offender, to find agreement on how to "make things right." Or the discussion may take place in circles or conferences involving families, law officers, and concerned community members as well as victim and offender—these models were adapted from peacemaking courts used in Maori and Native American cultures.

Community support groups help the victim through crises brought on by the crime, which may be psychological or economic, while others advocate for the victim's rights. Other programs assist former prisoners to reintegrate into the community. Such reintegration not only helps the former prisoner and his family, but has been shown to greatly reduce further crimes (recidivism).

Distributive justice, the third type of justice, is distinctively 35° and concerns the just allocation of society's goods, to everyone's advantage. However, the proponents of social and economic justice differ on how to achieve it. Several criteria may be used to judge fairness, such as equity, equality, and need, or some combination of these. John Rawls says that distributive justice limits the influence of luck; others are more concerned about a fair process of exchange.

Questions of distributive justice are involved in many important issues such as land reform, gender equality, world and national income inequality, affirmative action, social safety nets, and reconstruction after war or natural disasters. For instance, addressing the issue of inequality, UK economist Sir Anthony Atkinson proposes a "participation income" for people who actively engage in society by going to school or caring for children; granting a minimum inheritance amount for every citizen reaching adulthood—paid for by a wealth tax; and several other researched ideas (45°) that might lead to 35° reform.[16]

Land reform has been a recurrent theme ever since ancient times. Rulers, priestly castes, aristocrats, the Church, colonial powers, and finally corporations all amassed huge tracts and monopolized land (10°) in country after country. In an early example of land conflicts, agrarian reforms introduced by Tiberius Gracchus led to the civil struggles that ended the Roman Republic. During some centuries, the Church owned a fifth or more of Europe and Latin America.

Colonial rulers of several South American countries owned the majority of land. Salvadorans believed that 14 families owned virtually all the country. The world's first corporations, the East India Company and the Dutch East India Company—arms of their respective nations— laid claim to whole countries. When empires broke up in the 20th century, many of the new nations quickly instituted land reform. Large popular movements for land reform by landless peasants have occurred in countries such as Brazil, South Africa, and India.

Concentration of land-holding occurred in the English Isles from which most white Southerners came. After the Civil War, sharecropping and tenant farming replaced slavery with a new form of serfdom. By the Depression years, nearly half of white farmers and three-fourths of black farmers did not own any land. Land ownership continues to decline, especially among African-Americans.

Tools and Skills, Artisans and Professionals

Professionalism is a frame of mind, not a paycheck.
~Cecil Castle

Our genus (*Homo*) describes us as tool-makers. Humans and proto-humans have been making tools for at least 2.6 million years. There is evidence that tool-making helped shape the evolution of the human hand. Our ancestor *Homo erectus* made Acheulean axes, many of them so symmetrical and beautiful to a modern eye that several archaeologists consider them works of art:

> Such is the perfection of the carving on some hand axes that they give the impression that the artist took great pleasure in them *per se*....in our heart of hearts we are sure that they were searching for beauty, aesthetics, as they could have achieved the same efficiency with cruder pieces. [17]

At 35° the artisan masters the necessary skills and creates objects far beyond simple adequacy. For countless centuries the artisan produced articles both useful and decorative. But less than two centuries ago, hand tools and simple machines began to be replaced by more complex machines, at industrial scale production. Already by the 1850s Henry David Thoreau announced "Lo! Men have become the tools of their tools," indicating a regression to 20°.

Today the master craftsman is a person highly skilled in his or her craft, who in many places and in associated trades still follows the training route from apprentice to journeyman to master. The training itself is supposed to instill   professionalism, a term that besides skill denotes good judgment, honesty, responsibility, and courtesy.

In fields that require academic training and often concern human relationships (such as teaching, medicine, and law) professionalism means that an individual conforms to the technical and ethical standards of that profession, and acts in a courteous, conscientious, and efficient manner. Yet difficulties may occur within professions because of their insular outlook. The professional may jealously guard her professional turf, or become closed to new ideas and techniques outside of her invested tradition. Speaking of Washington insiders, Thomas Frank speaks of a "meritocratic elite" who do "what professionals always do: defining the boundaries of legitimacy." Frank says the 'Washington consensus' is "an ideology of the professional class." There are undoubtedly other forms of ideology (20°) among other professions.

[1] Robert M. Seyfarth and Dorothy L. Cheney, "The Evolutionary Origins of Friendship," *The Annual Review of Psychology*, 2012, 63:153-77
[2] James Smith Page, "Is Mateship a Virtue?" *Australian Journal of Social Issues*, 2002, http://eprints.qut.edu.au/3567/1/3567_1.pdf
[3] Mortimer Adler, "What Is Liberal Education?" http://www.ditext.com/adler/wle.html
[4, 5] Recent technological predictions are variously attributed to Udo Gollub, the CEO of 17 Minute Languages or to the CEO of Daimler Benz (not named or quoted directly, but he is Dieter Zetsche).
https://www.linkedin.com/pulse/must-read-article-how-our-lives-change-dramatically-20-delahunty
https://www.ferrarichat.com/forum/threads/must-read-article-on-how-our-lives-will-change-dramatically-in-20-years-by-ceo-of-mb.557096/
[6] José Ortega y Gasset, *The Revolt of the Masses*, (1930) W.W. Norton 1994
[7] C.S. Harris, *Where Shadows Dance*, 2012
[8] Marianne Cooper, "The False Promise of Meritocracy," *The Atlantic Monthly*, December 1, 2015, https://www.theatlantic.com/business/archive/2015/12/meritocracy/418074/
[9] Karl Popper, *The Open Society & its Enemies* volume I, *The Spell of Plato* (1945)
[10] Gordon Marshall, "Piecemeal Social Engineering," *A Dictionary of Sociology 1998*. 11 Aug. 2015 <http://www.encyclopedia.com>
[11] Sarah F. Brosnan, "Nonhuman Species' Reactions to Inequity and their Implications for Fairness," *Social Justice Research*, Vol. 19, No. 2, June 2006, http://www2.gsu.edu/~wwwcbs/pdf/Brosnan%20SJR%202006.pdf
[12] Stuart Wolpert, "Brain reacts to fairness as it does to money and chocolate, study shows," UCLA Newsroom, April 21, 2008, http://newsroom.ucla.edu/releases/brain-reacts-to-fairness-as-it-49042?link_page_rss=49042
[13] International World History Project, "The Reforms of Urukagina," http://history-world.org/reforms_of_urukagina.htm
[14] J.J.M. Roberts, The Bible and the Ancient Near East: Collected Essays, Eisenbrauns 2002, https://books.google.com/books?id=5IXecSZOcS8C&dq=Akkadian+mesharum+edicts&source=gbs_navlinks_s
[15] Christopher Bright, "What Is Restorative Justice?" Prison Fellowship International, Copyright 1997 http://www.restorativejustice.org/university-
[16] Anthony Atkinson, *Inequality: What Can Be Done?* Harvard University Press, 2015
[17] Sara Reardon, "Stone tools helped shape human hands," *New Scientist*, April 11, 2013, http://www.newscientist.com/article/mg21829124.200-stone-tools-helped-shape-human-hands.html#.VCNLUE3QcqQ

Life's most persistent and urgent question is, "What are you doing for others?"
~Martin Luther King, Jr.

Many other creatures display concern for their own kind—calling when they find food, or giving a warning cry even though it draws a predator's attention to themselves. Older females help with the young among elephants and cetaceans. Elephants and some primates aid their elderly. There are also documented instances of interspecies altruism, such as a goat that guided a blind horse, or dolphins that herded pilot whales stranded on a New Zealand Beach and led them to deeper waters. Or, indeed, dogs that save members of their human family from poisonous snakes, fires, drowning, or human attackers. [1,2,3,4,5]

Kindness and altruism are in our genes, and are essential characteristics of humans in all cultures; however, at 40° loving-kindness becomes dominant. Love here is unconditional love, maternal love, brotherly love, *agape*—loving-kindness for all humans, everywhere, and for members of the animal kingdom too. It is the special disposition of those who devote their lives to healing, peacemaking, and humanitarian work. Here too are those heroes who protect or rescue others at risk to their own lives. They are volunteer firefighters; they rescue others during floods; they are members of MAG (Mine Advisory Group) who go to the sites of recent wars to remover leftover explosives. In Syria, they are several thousand volunteer first responders known as the White Helmets.

Heroism may last minutes or an entire lifetime, during which an individual reaches the heights of 40° selflessness.

Numerous good Samaritans rescued Jews from certain death in the Holocaust. The official list of "Righteous among the Nations" recognizes 24,356 such individuals, about half of them women. Diplomatic officials from many countries issued visas and false papers, each man allowing tens of thousands of Jews to escape. Individuals hid families in their apartment, farm, church, or convent. A concerted effort by the people of occupied Denmark saved almost all of their resident

Jews by secretly ferrying them to Sweden. Albania, a predominantly Muslim country, saved almost all of their Jewish population.

Conventional thinking misunderstands empathy—a principal trait of 40°—-mistaking it for sympathy. Elizabeth Young-Bruehl wrote, "The usual, indeed, the clichéd way of describing empathy as 'putting yourself in another's place' seems to me quite wrong. Empathizing involves, rather, putting another person in yourself, becoming another person's habitat." [6]

As revenge occurs at 5° and institutional retribution at 10° so forgiveness transcends them both at 40°. Some people take very seriously Christian admonitions to forgive, for instance the relatives of the nine victims of a 2015 shooting in a South Carolina black church, and Amish families who help support the widow and children of the man who killed five of their children in a 2006 school shooting.

A key aspect of 40° is 'the universal language' of music, a capacity that has been with us for at least 40,000 years—the age of the oldest known musical instrument, a flute made from a vulture bone. Who knows how long humans were singing, drumming, and dancing before that? The evolutionary origin of music is a mystery. Researchers have recently discovered that the brain has a separate neural pathway for music similar to the one for language—attesting to its importance. A massive international gene sequencing project found that the same genes control the development of bird songs and human speech. Some scientists suggest the possibility that early hominids including Neanderthals sang rather than spoke. Neuroscientist Josef Rauschecker says, "There are theories that music is older than speech or language. Some even argue that speech evolved from music." [7,8]

Numerous studies show how music enhances brain functions. Playing an instrument.

> engages practically every area of the brain at once — especially the visual, auditory, and motor cortices....Playing music has been found to increase the volume and activity in the brain's corpus callosum—the bridge between the two hemispheres—allowing messages to get across the brain faster and through more diverse routes. This may allow musicians to solve problems more effectively and creatively, in both academic and social settings. [9]

According to Ludwig von Beethoven, "Music is the mediator between the spiritual and the sensual life." We know that music has healing power and the ability to bring a community together. It is a vital part of many kinds of religious observances. Music also requires empathic communication between performers, between performer and audience, and—according to the work of Manfred Clynes—between performer and composer. Music belongs to all the dispositions but I propose that its home base is 40° because of its universality.

We Are One

> *Let us have but one end in view, the welfare of humanity; and let us put aside all selfishness in consideration of language, nationality, or religion.*
> ~John Comenius, Czech philosopher, 1592-1670

Admonitions to practice loving-kindness are found in all world religions, whose followers say they believe in acceptance, trust and forgiveness—although they may not display these virtues consistently. Some religions put human unity at the very center of their beliefs; for instance, the first principle of Baha'i is "The Oneness of the World of Humanity." The religion's founder Bahá'u'lláh said "So powerful is the light of unity that it can illuminate the whole earth."

Ubuntu is a Zulu and South African ethical concept that translates literally as human-ness. It joins together all those positive qualities at the core of what it means to be human, and recognizes that we are all connected: "I am what I am because of who we all are." The Ubuntu idea has been taken in several different directions. Some propose smaller, more closely-knit communities on the model of early and indigenous cultures, as a bulwark against corporate power and large-scale power generally. "If it's not good for everyone, it's no good at all."

Scientific research finds that altruistic behavior benefits the loving person physically as well as emotionally. At 40° all personal relationships achieve a higher vibration, expressed in the Hindu greeting:

Namaste [I bow to you]. I honor the place in you in which the entire Universe dwells, I honor the place in you which is of Love, of Integrity, of Wisdom and of Peace. When you are in that place in you, and I am in that place in me, we are One.

Human unity and universal loving-kindness encounter many obstacles of ingrained customs, institutions, and ideologies. The lower dispositions tend to scoff at 40° as naïve or simple-minded or to suspect it of hypocrisy. They may take advantage of 40° openness. A Sufi saying says "When a pickpocket looks at a saint, all he sees are his pockets."

Another recurring problem is that 40° sentiments can be counterfeited by those, such as sociopaths, who are operating at lower dispositions. For instance, imperialism (10°) has often been rationalized as concern for those who are conquered. Rudyard Kipling wrote of "The white man's burden," the supposed humanitarian responsibility of Europeans to govern and impart their civilization to nonwhite colonists. The execrable King Leopold of Belgium pretended humanitarian motives for annexing the Congo, while as many as half the population died under his rule. War, slavery, and female subordination have also been rationalized. But we are learning to see through these ruses.

Of course 40° has no monopoly on either love or altruism. At 30° people may be somewhat suspicious of strangers and those unlike themselves, but they do believe in the Golden Rule and are capable of unconditional love for family members. Meanwhile, 35° includes the whole community in her purview, and considers tolerance a virtue. Acting at 40°, individuals not only tolerate but love their neighbours. They are able to transcend nationalism and social differences, fully realizing that unity does not require sameness.

Universal loving-kindness may be harder to sustain in large-scale urbanized cultures based on materialism and competition, yet 40° endures and the number of its followers may actually be increasing.

Human Rights

Some values must be universal, like human rights and the equal worth of every human being.
Bjorn Ulvaeus, Swedish musician, 1945—

The notion that *human beings have inviolable rights simply because they are human beings* gradually developed over many centuries, then more clearly during the Renaissance, becoming central to the 18th century Age of Enlightenment. The beginnings of the idea were linked with the conduct of war.

One line of thinking began in the 17th century with John Locke's idea that individuals possess natural rights beyond any granted them by the government under which they live. The idea of universal human rights lay behind both the American and French Revolutions, expressed in landmark documents such as the 1776 American Declaration of Independence, the 1789 French Declaration of the Rights of Man and Citizen, and the Bill of Rights (ratified 1791). Thomas Jefferson was crucially involved with all three of these documents and the spread of this 40° concept despite the fact that he owned slaves (10°) and had an ambiguous relationship (15°) with one of his female slaves.

Further evolution led to the formal abolition of slavery in the 19th century and widespread acceptance of universal suffrage, including women's suffrage, in the 20th. While expressing 40° identification with all humanity, to uphold human rights also requires a supporting civil and legal framework (35°/45°). After the horrors of two world wars, the Universal Declaration of Human Rights declared in 1948 that every human being is entitled to life, liberty, personal security, equal worth, freedom from arbitrary arrest or exile, a fair trial, freedom from torture and degrading treatment, and several other rights. International human rights law is based on the idea that these rights are universal.[10]

Many writers, artists, and performers have been devoted to social justice and furthering human rights, for instance Victor Hugo in the 19th century. He strongly opposed the death penalty. In his famous novels *Les Miserables* and *The Hunchback of Notre Dame,* about poor and marginalized people, Hugo also advocated for a more representative government and freedom of the press. Hugo expresses his own integrity when his character Jean Valjean says "You ask me what forces me to speak? A strange thing: my conscience."

Amnesty International, founded in 1961, is the foremost nongovernmental organization that seeks to prevent human rights abuses, including imprisonment and torture by governments across the world. Amnesty also opposes capital punishment. In the United States, the Innocence Project is the best known of several organizations that seek to overturn wrongful convictions.

Healing

In nothing do men more nearly approach the gods than in giving health to men.
~Cicero, Roman statesman, 106-43BC

Healing by its nature involves an empathic connection between healer and patient. It is an ancient occupation among humans, already glimpsed among other animals: dolphins nudge injured members and newborns to the water's surface, and Canada geese care for injured members. Prehistoric people used herbalism and trephination (surgical drilling of a hole in the skull as emergency treatment for a head wound). Egyptian papyri of the 2nd millennium BC documented surgeries and medical texts by the famous physician Imhotep. Schools of medicine developed in ancient Babylonia, India, China, Greece, and Rome.[11, 12]

In the aspirations of their working life, doctors and other medical workers express 40° compassion backed up by a large 45° knowledge base. Medicine has the oldest code of professional ethics (35°), the Hippocratic Oath. After almost two and a half millennia it is still used by medical schools across the world for their graduating students. Some schools prefer the Oath of Maimonides, a 12th century Spanish Jewish physician and philosopher, which reads in part:

May the love of my art motivate me at all times, may neither avarice or miserliness, nor thirst for glory or a great reputation engage my mind; for enemies of truth and philanthropy could easily deceive me, and make me forget my lofty aim of doing good…. Endow me with strength of heart and mind, to serve the rich and poor, the good and the wicked, friend and foe and that I may never see in the patient anything else but a fellow in pain.[13]

Other healing practices exist such as acupuncture, therapeutic massage, or herbalism. Within families a great deal of informal healing takes place, of both body and psyche, also at 40°. Environmentalists try to protect a community's health from toxic pollution (35°/40°). Others attempt to heal the Earth itself, in the restoration of damaged ecosystems.

Healers do not always live up to their aspirations. Scientific reductionism (20°) leads some practitioners to a sterile specialization that ignores the actual person before them. Psychiatrist Mariquita West describes medicine as "95% compassion and commonsense, and then 5% expertise," but with some specialists, it seems to be 95% expertise. The practice of medicine may have a significant 20° business aspect with endemic problems of 10° corruption because of the involvement of insurance companies, drug companies, and for-profit hospitals.

On the other hand, some medical people are doubly 40°, both healers and humanitarians. Doctors without Borders (*Médecins Sans Frontières*) is an international medical humanitarian organization that gives emergency aid "to people affected by armed conflict, epidemics, healthcare exclusion and natural or man-made disasters." MSF epitomizes 40° selflessness, adding a large dose of 45° courage since the healers often work in areas of armed conflict.

As a volunteer over the past 25 years, Venetian Dr. Gino Strada has performed 30,000 surgeries inside war zones such as Afghanistan and Sudan. Through his foundation Emergency he has founded 47 non-profit medical centers, one of which is a world-class cardiac hospital in the Sudanese desert. Emergency's hospital in Sudan is so clean that infection rates aren't just lower than in hospitals in the UK and the US, they're "lower by a power of 10." [14]

Yet a third such example is the organization Mercy Ships. For four decades it has operated hospital ships to serve developing nations. One such ship, Africa Mercy, is the largest non-governmental floating hospital in the world. The entirely volunteer crew is made up of 400 people from 45 different nations.

Humanitarians

> *My true religion is kindness.*
> ~14th Dalai Lama

We read biographies of great humanitarians such as William Wilberforce, Harriet Tubman, Albert Schweitzer, Eleanor Roosevelt, and Martin Luther King, Jr.; we hear of performers such as Sting or Bono or Angelina Jolie who use their success and resources to help heal the world; but all around us are altruists relatively unknown and unsung. I know scores of them in my own community. You too probably know people who work for peace, protect the environment, foster and adopt neglected children, go to foreign countries to share their professional skills, and in many other ways express 40° love in their daily lives.

In some cases they are activists who combine compassion with 45° courage and knowledge. The person acting at 40°/45° tends to be more deeply committed to a cause than at 35°, often leading others and starting movements. It takes great determination to keep to one's purpose in the face of defeats. An activist says

> At times we feel outnumbered in our attempts to improve the world—to brighten and beautify, to preserve and heal and do what's best for humanity. Selfless efforts can start to feel beleaguering, discouraging, even pointless with so little support. It is at these times I remind myself that I would rather be the last Good Samaritan standing than to join the ranks of selfish multitudes creating misery. [15]

The career of violinist Rachel Barton Pines demonstrates 40° both as humanitarianism and music, as well as the 45° courage to rise above severe personal obstacles. As a highly talented child musician she had to overcome her family's poverty and periodic homelessness. When she was twenty a subway car closed on her violin strap and dragged her along the platform, resulting in the loss of her leg. Throughout these obstacles and setbacks she has continued a brilliant musical career while also educating and aiding young musicians in developing countries.

International humanitarian standards and law add legal and intellectual underpinning to ideals to create lasting traditions (30°) of humane behavior. Or as the African proverb says, "If everyone helps to hold up the sky, then one person does not become tired." We see the effect of humane standards during another of those startling contrasts between lower and higher dispositions, taking place off the Mediterranean coasts as boats with Syrian and other refugees encounter rough seas. To get the most possible money from desperate people, traffickers overload some decrepit freighter, point it in the direction of Italy—and then abandon the ship to its fate (20°/0°). Many ships have capsized, and thousands of women, children, and men have drowned.

The Italian Coast Guard has been involved in many rescue actions not because they are all heroic individuals—although some undoubtedly are—but because they are part of an international standard of humanitarian behavior (40°) and a professional ethic (35°) that is encoded in the rules of various coast guards and sea-going vessels.[16]*

A similar story has unfolded on the coasts and islands of Greece, where the small coast guard is supplemented by fishermen who have been rescuing refugees from various conflicts for a decade. A Greek army sergeant who personally saved 20 people from a capsized boat conveyed the sense of 30°/40° duty and humanitarianism, saying, "Life is difficult for them, and it's difficult for us but at the end of the day, we are all people, we are all human, we should all help each other." This is an enduring ethos. [17]

Terrible circumstances caused by war, tyranny, poverty, and environmental degradation have led to growing numbers of displaced people and refugees throughout the world—65 million at last count.[18] Their movements into other countries may be resisted strongly, even violently, by those acting at lower dispositions. The reaction to large immigrations often produce far-right politicians and governments (5°). Yet international humanitarian law and norms serve to undergird people's better impulses and expand 40° realization of human unity. Standards in warfare have been recognized since ancient times, and rules of war were applied during the late medieval period, when sieges of cities were more common than pitched battles. According to the chivalric code, attackers were required to attempt a truce or settlement before the siege began (based on Deuteronomy 20:10–12). The Code

*More recently a new Italian government is less inclined to support rescues.

required surrender under honorable terms, such as allowing safe conduct for civilian inhabitants of the Castle.

The medieval Catholic Church developed the Just War doctrine that has dominated political thinking in the Western world for about 1,500 years. Intended to limit wars only to those with just cause such as self-defense, the doctrine had the opposite effect. With no commitment to peace, nation-states were more concerned about how to justify wars than how to prevent them. Armed conflict was usually the first option, not the last resort. The Vatican seems to be rethinking the ancient doctrine. An April 2016 conference hosted by Pope Francis and Pax Christi International recommended rejection of Just War doctrine and a new encyclical that is committed to the nonviolence of Jesus.

International treaties on the conduct of war began mid-19th century and resulted in the Geneva Conventions—four treaties and three protocols now accepted by virtually all nation-states. The 1949 Convention imposes rules to protect civilians, prisoners of war, sick and wounded soldiers, and medical and humanitarian workers. The 1925 Geneva Protocol, after the horrific use of poison gas in World War I, banned chemical and biological warfare. Of course there have been many violations of all these rules but undoubtedly fewer instances than if the laws had not existed. The ultimate goal of such agreements is to create a conscience for the whole human race.

Nonviolence and Peacemakers

Peace hath higher tests of manhood
Than battle ever knew.
~John Greenleaf Whittier. American poet 1807-1892

Peacemaking is healing on a larger scale. Despite their often dramatic stories, peacemakers are not nearly as well-known as are the conquering heroes. The lives of many old and new peace heroes call for the modern equivalent of sagas and songs. They includ Fridjof Nansen, Yitzhak Rabin, Ashoka, Deganawida, Lalla Aziza, Leynah Gbowee, and a great many others who dedicated themselves to stopping conflicts.

To pass along tales of peacemakers is but one of myriad ways to replace the ancient mindset of war with a Culture of Peace.

Some heroes have simply refused to kill. According to scholar Stan Hoig, a Cheyenne peace chief was required "to be a man of peace, to be brave, and to be of generous heart. Of these qualities the first was unconditionally the most important, for upon it rested the moral restraint required for the warlike Cheyenne Nation." An old trader, witness to the 1864 Sand Creek Massacre, recounts that the peace chief White Antelope, when he saw government soldiers shooting into the lodges at women and children, made up his mind not to live any longer. White Antelope stood in front of his lodge with his arms folded across his breast, singing the death-song: "Nothing lives long," he sang, "only the earth and the mountains."[19]

In struggles to overthrow tyrannical governments, conquerors, or overbearing majorities, groups seeking freedom or autonomy gain more local and international support when they do not use the same indiscriminate violence used in wars of state versus state. Creative, non-violent tactics (40°/50°) are often successful. Many nonviolent actions were involved in the struggle for American independence from England. For instance, colonists refused to buy goods imported from Britain, an action that spurred local industries. They did not cooperate with unjust laws, and almost unanimously failed to pay the Stamp Tax. In the decade before 1776, acts of civil disobedience along with the building of a parallel society led to virtual independence before the war broke out.

Gene Sharp, three-time nominee for the Nobel Peace Prize, has documented scores of countries where people have nonviolently overthrown dictators or foreign occupiers. The book and film *A Force More Powerful* describes the history of successful use of nonviolent resistance. Some national heroes whose words and actions have inspired and helped unify a nation to throw off its conquerors without leading an army are Mohandas Gandhi, Nelson Mandela, Jose Marti, Thomas Paine, Vaclav Havel, and Lech Wałęsa. [20, 21]

Since 2007, the Global Peace Index (GPI) attempts to measure the relative peacefulness of the world's nations and regions, or in my terms, it helps to gauge the relative influence of 40° disposition among political leaders, nations, cultural institutions, and eras. Unfortunately, the 2016 Index found continuation of a decade-long trend of deteriorating peacefulness, driven by conflicts in the Middle East and Africa. [22]

Biophilia

I am life that wants to live, in the midst of life that wants to live.
~Albert Schweitzer, Alsatian physician, humanitarian, and philosopher, 1875-1965

Humanitarianism encompasses more than working for the welfare of one species, even if it is our own. Most of us realize that human welfare is intimately linked with, and depends on, the health of the whole of life. Many are greatly distressed that we are losing so many familiar creatures in the ongoing extinction crisis, as well as thousands of plants and animals we never knew. The higher dispositions are allied in efforts to keep the planet healthy and as many as possible of its interrelated organisms in existence. The spirit of the whole finds creative ways to reverse the destruction as 45° science joins 40° generativity and empathy, and 35° activism stimulates the 30° sense of responsibility. Meanwhile, 25° may become 'Green' because it's trendy. Whatever the motivation, we need them all because life on this planet is in trouble.

Hypothesizing that humans have an instinctive bond with other living things, biologist and theorist Edward O. Wilson coined the term *biophilia* to describe "the urge to affiliate with other forms of life". As scientific hypothesis it is new, but biophilia describes an ancient connection that undoubtedly goes back to the very beginnings of the human race—a time when nobody would have questioned that humans were part of nature. Wilson has since called for humans to set aside half of the Earth's surface for other species. [23]

You can see young children are instinctively drawn to other living things. Many people rescue injured or orphan animals, caring for them until they are able to live in the wild. Some have made this bond the theme of their adult lives, studying wild animals even as they live with them, with a special blend of 40° empathic identification, 45°

scientific detachment, 30° patience and endurance, and sometimes a heavy dose of 45° courage. All this is often joined with 35° mastery of photography and 50° inventiveness.

Three pioneers in this field are noted for their scientific work as well as for protecting three species of great apes—our closest living relatives. Jane Goodall spent decades in the jungle observing and interacting with chimpanzees. She discovered that they were making tools (adapting a stick to fish for termites) thus forcing a redefinition of humans as the only tool-makers. Dian Fossey formed a similar bond with mountain gorillas and lost her life attempting to protect this severely threatened species. Birutė Galdikas spent 40 years in Indonesia studying orangutans along with her conservation efforts to preserve the forests essential to their survival.

Korean photographer and naturalist Sooyong Park spent six months a year for several years alone in a concrete bunker in the subzero temperatures of Siberia in order to study and photograph Siberian tigers. Only a few hundred of these magnificent creatures are left in Russia, China, and North Korea. Park says,

> When I follow the tracks of a Siberian tiger in the wild, I can sense when a tiger is nearby. I can't see him, but he can see me. Of course, he can kill me. But he doesn't. He watches me. I carry no gun and do not smell of metal or death. I love Siberian tigers because they make me feel humble. And when I am humble, I can let go of my ego and love all living things. When I feel compassion for other lives, I am happy.[24]

Naturalist Joe Hutto lived with mule deer for seven years and spent 18 months with a flock of wild turkeys he raised from eggs. The latter experience was recreated in a film, *My Life as a Turkey*. Working at a lion sanctuary near Johannesburg, Kevin Richardson has slept next to and played with lions he has known since they were cubs. He has also made documentaries with hyenas, leopards, and cheetahs to change awareness of these creatures and publicize their endangerment.

Biophiles may identify not only with animals but also plant life and whole ecosystems. Julia Butterfly Hill lived for two full years in a 600-year-old California Redwood tree "Luna," successfully keeping it from being logged. Protecting nature can be very dangerous work. In the last decade, over 1,000 wildlife rangers who were defending elephants, rhinos, and other creatures have been killed by poachers. [25]

Scientists, inventors, and entrepreneurs are finding ways to further life. David Vaughan, a marine biologists, worked out a quick-grow technique for corals to restore dying reefs that provide habitat for tens of thousands of marine species. Eco-entrepreneur Shubhendu Sharma developed a way to enable a native, self-sustaining mini-forest to grow almost anywhere, at ten times faster than the normal rate of growth. The tiny forest, as small as 1,000 square feet, may be in a backyard, an industrial park, or a schoolyard. Afforestation provides sanctuary and food for wildlife, improves local air quality, and as the concept spreads, helps slow climate change.

Pope Francis described environmental destruction as a sin. The leader of Orthodox Christians, Bartholomew I, is known as the Green Patriarch because of his support for ecology. Buddhism has always emphasized interconnection and the web of life. Meanwhile, countless nature-lovers watch and feed the birds and other animals in their backyards, plant flowers to support the butterflies, bees, and hummers, spare garter snakes, and stop their cars to help turtles cross the road.

Other 40° concepts are generativity, sustainability, global citizenship, the Commons, and the ethic of sharing scientific knowledge.

Generativity

Let it be such work as our descendants will thank us for.
~John Ruskin, English social thinker, 1819-1900

The word *generativity* is underused and usually relegated to individual psychology. Yet this capacity needs to spread because it has the power to save us all. Generativity is a concern for the next generation or generations. It is a desire to make a difference, to create positive changes that will outlast one's lifetime.

According to psychologist Erik Erikson, generativity is a stage of psychosocial development in middle age, associated with becoming a grandparent. This is similar to becoming an elder in indigenous cultures. Many Native Americans consider eldership to begin around age 55. However, an entire community may be committed to 'Seventh Generation' thinking. This is the belief, inspired by the laws of the Iroquois Nation, that decisions should consider the impact on people seven generations hence "even those whose faces are yet beneath the surface of the ground–the unborn of the future Nation." This is also a way of paying respect to our parents, our grandparents, and our ancestors of the past 10,000 generations of *Homo sapiens.*

In First Nations, elders are the repositories and transmitters of the tribe's cultural and philosophical/spiritual knowledge. Elders model and teach what it is to be a human being.

> Elders should be role models for everyone else.... teachers to the grandchildren and all young people because of their wisdom.... advisors, law-givers, dispensers of justice....Elders should be teachers for every one of the past history of Innu people [and] of values important to Innu to be passed on from generation to generation....[26]

Some anthropologists believe that longevity—more humans living past age 30—was key to the surge in human cultural progress 30,000 years ago. Grandparents gave us an evolutionary advantage. (It's called the 'Grandmother Hypothesis').[27] One also sees generativity beginning at much earlier ages—sometimes in adolescents who work zealously to make their community, world, and planet a better place. Traditionally, adolescence has been a period of idealism, creativity, and the desire to contribute. Rites of passage channeled this tendency.

The concept of environmental sustainability depends on widespread generativity. Sustainability is defined as "the rates of renewable resource harvest, pollution creation, and non-renewable resource depletion that can be continued indefinitely."[29] Sustainability absolutely requires foresight (45°) as well as concern for future generations, which brings it into direct conflict with the capitalist economic goal of continuous growth and expansion (10°).

One tradition of generativity is *tikkun olam*, a concept in Judaism (but not in Orthodox Judaism) that many modern Jews define as constructive behavior and acts of kindness performed to perfect or repair the world. The phrase is found in the Mishnah, a body of classical rabbinic teachings 2,000 years old. Today *tikkun olam* often refers to social policy that protects the vulnerable and disadvantaged.

Generativity is one of the hallmarks of the adult human being. While 30° expresses generativity in concern for the future of the family and individual family members, 35° expands this caring to the entire community. The aboriginal elder adds a spiritual dimension at 40°, with concerns about future generations and the whole of humanity. All the higher degrees express generativity in one way or another, and according to psychoanalyst George Vaillant, this expression of generativity is essential for our own mental health. As Dr. Jonas Salk said, "Our greatest responsibility is to be good ancestors."

The Commons

None ought to be lords or landlords over another, but the earth is free
for every son and daughter of mankind to live free upon.
~Gerard Winstanley, a leader of the Diggers, 1609?-1660?

English-speaking peoples recently celebrated the 800th anniversary of the Magna Carta, with its guarantees of individual freedoms such as "No freeman shall be captured or imprisoned…except by the lawful judgment of his peers or by the law of the land." What has been largely forgotten is that much of the charter concerned property matters related to royal encroachment on forests and other common land. These important rights were drawn together in a separate document, the 1217 Charter of the Forest, likewise ignored today. The *Carta de Foresta* states: "Henceforth every freeman, in his wood or on his land that he has in the forest, may with impunity make a mill, fish-preserve, pond, marl-pit, ditch, or arable in cultivated land outside coverts, provided that no injury is thereby given to any neighbour." [29]

About all we have left today of common lands are public parks and wildlife preserves. The original conception of the commons was rooted in prehistory when people lived without the notion of private property. For many centuries it was about village traditions (30°) of sharing use of the common lands to pick berries, gather firewood, let animals forage, and other such uses vital to subsistence living. Spurred by increasing enclosure (privatization), the Diggers expressed a larger 40° conception that speaks of all people and the whole earth.

Enclosure began the process that we now call globalization, which is basically a 10° concentration of economic power. Not only land but virtually every physical aspect of the known universe is now an object for money-making privatization, including wave frequencies, human DNA, and extraterrestrial phenomena, also mental phenomena such as names, ideas, and music.

The idea of the Commons has great relevance today, when the actuality is so rapidly disappearing. It is also closely related to sustainability, which is about long-term sustenance for all people rather than short-term benefits for a few.

The Internet has vastly expanded the scope and potential of the Commons, especially as it relates to the ownership of mental constructs. The Internet tends to decentralize and democratize society. It is a vital part of the new sharing economy. Some related 40°/45° ideas are free sharing, open source, collaborative efforts such as Wikipedia, and the Creative Commons. An international movement exists to keep the Internet free and accessible to all. In Iceland it took the form of the "Pirate Party," which has won several seats in the European Parliament.

Another extension of the Commons is Basic Income, based on the ancient idea that all inhabitants of Earth have common ownership of it. Over the past four centuries the intuition of common ownership has developed into increasingly concrete plans. Today the idea of a basic income unconditionally granted to all on an individual basis without means test or work requirement is being proposed quite seriously by social scientists, economists, religious leaders, and members of parliaments. Experiments are underway in Finland, East Africa, Switzerland, Netherlands, Canada, India, and Oakland, California.[30]

Global Citizens

Who is a wise man? He who learns from all men.
Simon ben Zoma, Jewish philosopher, 1st-2nd century, *Ethics of the Fathers*

Socrates said: "I am not an Athenian or a Greek, but a citizen of the world." His contemporary Diogenes said the same. However, for a millennium or two the idea seems to have faded. Perhaps the notion of a world citizen was absorbed by overarching entities that claimed universality such as the Roman and Islamic empires or the Catholic Church. Perhaps other-worldly demands took precedence: St. Paul said "Our citizenship is in heaven."

When next we hear of world citizens it is from Francis Bacon (1561-1626), who defends hospitality, saying, "If a man be gracious and courteous to strangers, it shows he is a citizen of the world, and that his heart is no island cut off from other lands, but a continent that joins to them." By Bacon's definition, many ancient peoples and contemporary traditional peoples who put a high value on hospitality to the stranger have an intuitive understanding of world citizenship. (Today, large numbers of refugees from war, unemployment, and environmental stresses are putting the ancient value of hospitality to the test.)

A century after Bacon, French lawyer and philosopher Charles de Montesquieu described his allegiances more plainly: "I am a citizen of humanity first and by necessity, and a citizen of France second, and only by accident. " Thomas Paine said, "The world is my country, all mankind are my brethren and to do good is my religion." Some describe Benjamin Franklin and Thomas Jefferson as citizens of the world.

Socialist Eugene V. Debs—who won 6% of the vote in the 1912 presidential campaign—was imprisoned for sedition after public speeches against the draft during World War I. Debs said in his defense "I have no country to fight for: my country is the earth, and I am a citizen of the world." A few modern political and religious leaders such as Dennis Kucinich, Mikhail Gorbachev, and Pope Francis clearly show the global perspective. [31]

Throughout the 20th century an assortment of people from many walks of life declared themselves as world citizens such as Albert Einstein, World Heavyweight Champion George Foreman, tennis great Arthur Ashe, and actress Blythe Danner, who points out that "citizens of this earth" have an obligation "to leave the world a healthier, cleaner, and better place for our children and future generations" (40°

generativity). Lebanese-French author Amin Maalouf poetically expressed the ideal: "I come from no country, from no city, no tribe. I am the son of the road... all tongues and all prayers belong to me. But I belong to none of them."

To the 40° idea of human unity, citizenship adds social and political responsibility. A *citizen* is committed to informing herself and participating in constructive action for the good of all. Today the idea of world citizenship (now more likely to be called global citizenship) has acquired new vigor. It is a response to economic globalization and to world-wide threats that cannot be dealt with by nations acting alone.

Some academics talk about "governance without government." Oran Young, Professor Emeritus at the University of California, describes "the remarkable degree of stability or order that exists in international society, despite the absence of conventional governmental agencies at the international level."

Note that the momentum for world citizenship is *not* based on some hypothetical world government. (The UN is of course not a government because it has no military of its own, nor a monopoly of force.) Proposals for world government, although motivated by 40° desires for peace, may also express 15° naiveté or 35° utopianism. It is unlikely that contemporary nation-states, highly armed and obsessively pursuing their own geostrategic interests at 10°, would form a just and peaceful world government. Any such attempt is likely to be dominated by a superpower such as the United States or a bloc of nations.

Rather than a political organization, the Global Citizens Movement (GCM) is a socio-political process or shift in values among many people (especially 35°, 40°, and 45°) across national borders. Orion Kriegman of the Tellus Institute describes this as follows:

> The emergence of a global identity is a new implicit social contract in which increasing numbers of people understand themselves practically and aspirationally as global citizens. They share the broad values and principles that would underlie a transition to a just and sustainable planetary society, such as human rights, freedom, democracy, pluralism, and environmental protection. This new global identity need not subsume or eliminate subglobal or group identities. [32]

Already scores of international organizations bring together professionals such as civil engineers, microbiologists, chefs, or animation artists. World Wildlife Fund, Greenpeace, Rainforest Action Network, and World Watch Institute have an international or global perspective or membership. Global Citizens focuses on ending world poverty.[33] Student exchanges and other less formal cooperation among the world's people also further the sense of global citizenship. For instance, the Olympic Games are intended to "contribute to building a peaceful and better world by educating youth through sport practiced without discrimination of any kind and in the Olympic spirit, which requires mutual understanding with a spirit of friendship, solidarity and fair play." Even tourism allows people to get to know their counterparts in other countries and perceive their commonalities.

[1] Laura Zuckerman, "Seeing-eye sheep, goats guide blind horse," Reuters, May 23, 2011 http://www.reuters.com/article/2011/05/23/us-horse-blind-idUSTRE74M4G720110523

[2] "Animal Odd Couples," http://www.pbs.org/wnet/nature/episodes/animal-odd-couples/meet-the-odd-couples/8025/

[3] "Orphaned animals who were adopted by a different species," https://www.thedodo.com/inspiring-animal-families-958705512.html

[4] "Dolphins to the Rescue—Again!" http://www.science-frontiers.com/sf035/sf035p09.htm

[5] Charles Q. Choi, "Selfless Chimps Shed Light on Evolution of Altruism," Live Science, June 25, 2007, http://www.livescience.com/4515-selfless-chimps-shed-light-evolution-altruism.html#sthash.Y7B8HUq9.dpuf

[6] Elizabeth Young-Bruehl, "The Biographer's Empathy with Her Subject.

[7] *Karl Leif Bates, "Genes Tell Story of Birdsong and Human Speech," Duke Today,* December 11, 2014, https://today.duke.edu/2014/12/vocalbird

[8] Steven Mithen, *The Singing Neanderthals: The Origins of Music, Language, Mind, and Body,* Harvard University Press, 2007

[9] Maria Popova, "How Playing Music Benefits Your Brain More than Any Other Activity," https://www.brainpickings.org/2015/01/29/music-brain-ted-ed/

[10] The Universal Declaration of Human Rights (abbreviated), http://hrlibrary.umn.edu/edumat/hreduseries/hereandnow/Part-5/8_udhr-abbr.htm

[11] Jenni Irving, "Trephination," Ancient History Encyclopedia, May 1, 2013, http://www.ancient.eu/Trephination/

[12] Jan van der Crabben, "Medicine," Ancient History Encyclopedia, August 5, 2011, http://www.ancient.eu/medicine/

[13] "Jewish Medical Ethics: Oath of Maimonides," http://www.jewishvirtuallibrary.org/oath-of-maimonides

[14] Carole Cadwalladr, "Meet Gino Strada, Unsung Hero to the Poorest Victims of War," *Guardian,* July 13, 2013, https://www.theguardian.com/global-development/2013/jul/14/gino-strada-emergency-giles-duley

¹⁵ Richelle E. Goodrich, *Making Wishes: Quotes, Thoughts, & a Little Poetry for Every Day of the Year*
¹⁶ Alan Cowell, "Another rescue unfolds in rough seas off Italy," *The New York Times,* reprinted *The Arkansas-Democrat Gazette*, January 3, 2015
¹⁷ Helena Smith, quoting Antonis Deligiorgis, in "Stories of 2015: the heroism of a Greek soldier who pulled refugees from the sea," *The Guardian*, December 23, http://www.theguardian.com/world/2015/dec/23/saved-greek-soldier-eritrean-refugee-from-sea-antonis-deligiorgis-wegasi-nebiat
¹⁸ Camila Domonoske, "Refugees, Displaced People Surpass 60 Million for First Time, UNHCR Says," June 20, 2016, https://www.npr.org/sections/thetwo-way/2016/06/20/482762237/refugees-displaced-people-surpass-60-million-for-first-time-unhcr-says
¹⁹ Stan Hoig, *The Peace Chiefs of the Cheyenne*, University of Oklahoma Press, 1980
Also see "The West: Episode Four (1856-1868) Death Runs Riot," http://www.pbs.org/weta/thewest/program/episodes/four/whois.htm
²⁰ Peter Ackerman, *A Force More Powerful*, Palgrave Macmillan, 2000. For film see http://www.aforcemorepowerful.org/films/afmp/
Also see http://www.yesmagazine.org/people-power/10-everyday-acts-of-resistance-that-changed-the-world
²¹ Gene Sharp, *Dictatorship to Democracy:A Conceptual Framework for Liberation,* 4th U.S. Edition, Albert Einstein Institution, 2010, http://www.aeinstein.org/organizations/org/FDTD.pdf
See also: Albert Einstein Institution, "198 Methods of Nonviolent Action," http://www.aeinstein.org/nonviolentaction/198-methods-of-nonviolent-action/   and Global Nonviolent Action Database, http://nvdatabase.swarthmore.edu/browse_methods
²² "Global Peace Index 2016" http://reliefweb.int/report/world/global-peace-index-2016
²³ Edward O. Wilson, *Biophilia,* Harvard University Press, 1984
²⁴ Simon Worrall, "Beauty of Siberian Tigers," *National Geographic,* October 25, 2015, http://news.nationalgeographic.com/2015/10/151025-natural-history-siberian-tiger-siberia-poaching-russian-mafia-ngbooktalk/
²⁵ Global Conservation, "Park Rangers on the Frontline Being Killed at an Astonishing Rate from India to Thailand to Africa," March 31, 2016 http://globalconservation.org/news/park-rangers-frontline-being-killed-astonishing-rate-new-solutio/
²⁶ Statement by the Innu delegation from Sheshatshiu Native Canadian Centre of Toronto, April 27, 1989, qtd. S.M. Stiegelbauer, Ontario Institute for Studies in Education of the University of Toronto,"What Is an Elder? What Do Elders Do? First Nation Elders as Teachers in Culture-based Urban Organizations." *The Canadian Journal of Native Studies* XVI, 1 (1996):37-66, http://www2.brandonu.ca/library/cjns/16.1/Stiegelbauer.pdf
²⁷ Robin McKie, Science editor, "Wisdom of grandparents helped rise of prehistoric man," *The Guardian*, July 23, 2011, http://www.theguardian.com/science/2011/jul/24/prehistoric-man-helped-as-elderly-survived
²⁸http://www.thwink.org/sustain/glossary/EnvironmentalSustainability.htm
²⁹ "Henry III: Charter of the Forest," http://www.constitution.org/sech/sech_045.htm
³⁰ *"About Bien,"* http://basicincome.org/

[31] Mikhail Gorbachev, http://www.kosmosjournal.org/contributor/mikhail-gorbachev/

[32] Orion Kriegman, with Franck Amalric and John Wood, "Dawn of the Cosmopolitan: The Hope of a Global Citizens Movement," March 9, 2006, http://citeseerx.ist.psu.edu/viewdoc/download?doi=10.1.1.495.5577&rep=rep1&type=pdf

[33] https://www.globalcitizen.org/en/about/who-we-are/

Chapter 24
45° Seeking Truth and Freedom

Persons with weight of character carry, like planets, their
atmospheres along with them in their orbits.
~Thomas Hardy, English novelist, 1840-1928

The 45° disposition has three main facets. The first consists of those qualities of integrity, honesty, and determination often described as 'character.' At 45° people work at making their actions consistent with their beliefs. When acting here, people are described as 'honorable' and 'principled,' and others look up to them as heroic models or wise leaders. Often 45° is a professional: academic scholars, jurist, writer, minister or other religious leader, but especially those who are noted for their wise perspective and disinterested advice. On the other hand, 45° may be a minority of one who is persecuted for holding to his or her principles.

The second major 45° aspect concerns the life of the mind, intellectual curiosity and truth-seeking. This is the degree of philosophy and pure science, encapsulated in the ancient rules of logic and the scientific method. People acting here are greatly responsible for expanding human knowledge and outlook.

With a view larger than one's own country and century, 45° is relatively free of the world's dogmas and doctrines. He 'thinks for himself' and faces the truth no matter how distasteful it is because intellectual honesty requires it. But just as parents may be irritated by preschool children who constantly ask "Why?" so is 45° often misunderstood by society, especially those not in the habit of questioning the status quo or looking deeply into things.

A third aspect of 45° is love of freedom. Individuals acting here defend and work towards personal autonomy and participation in governance. They also struggle against the shackles of the mind. This should not be confused with the more selfish forms of personal liberty, or the state propaganda that paints every war as a defense of freedom. Other dispositions—and other animals—share a resistance to physical constraints, invasion of personal space, or seizure of one's possessions. That is not what we mean here by the love of freedom.

Asserting one's will like a two-year-old, or rebelling against authority like an adolescent, although necessary stages of human development, do not describe 45° dedication. Aggressors at 10°, ideologues and propagandists at 20°, the self-centered at 25° may claim to be motivated by a desire for freedom, but 45° envisions and works for an expanded freedom for everybody, and has initiated and led many historical advances in human rights and political freedoms.

This more complex disposition developed along with civilization and writing, and is relatively new in evolutionary terms. People look widely to find positive 45° role models in fiction, drama, history, or contemporary life. One popular model is the character Atticus Finch from *To Kill a Mockingbird* (1960) by Harper Lee. A fair and honorable man, Atticus has insight and empathy, freedom from conventional prejudices, and the courage of his convictions. However, Lee later published an early book in which Atticus is a much less appealing character with racist attitudes (10°). Devotees of *Mockingbird* were deeply disappointed, many refusing to read the new book, their dismay emphasizing the importance of such role models.

The Courage of One's Convictions

Common experience shows how much rarer is moral courage than physical bravery. A thousand men will march to the mouth of the cannon where one man will dare espouse an unpopular cause.
~Clarence Darrow, *Resist Not Evil*

Quite a few people acting at 45° have died for their principles. Others suffered exile, imprisonment, or loss of reputation or employment. Regardless of the possible risks, 45° simply feels compelled to stand up for his beliefs or in defense of others. And very often, his or her dedication forces change. Yet we must distinguish between true convictions and dogmatic prejudice or personal advantage that may also raise a stout defense. Needless to say, a strongly-held belief that rests on scapegoating others does not qualify. One may be a hero for a misguided cause. "Just because a man has died for it, does not make it true" said Oscar Wilde. A 45° moral conviction is based on a broad perspective and founded on a great deal of personal reflection. It is quite likely to be a minority opinion.

We have no way to know how far back in history or prehistory some humans held principles for which they were willing to risk injury or death. An early dramatization of moral courage is the ancient Greek play *Antigone* by Sophocles (441 BC). After Antigone's brother Polynieces is killed in battle, the king, seeing him as a traitor to Thebes, forbids a proper burial for him on pain of death. When Antigone commits civil disobedience by burying her brother, claiming that divine law is higher than man-made law, she pays with her own life.

Of the countless people who have suffered for their principles we note only a handful. Suffragettes Emmeline Pankhurst in Britain and Americans Alice Paul and Lucy Burns were imprisoned many times and brutalized because of their demonstrations to gain the vote for women. Native American activist Richard Oakes was at various times tear-gassed, jailed, beaten to a coma, and finally shot to death at the age of 30, but he did accomplish several goals in his short life. He developed the curriculum for the first Native American studies department in the nation, at San Francisco University. Protests he led at Alcatraz Island are credited with changing the US government's position from Indian [tribal] termination to self-determination.

Despite the American public's negative view of politicians, some do act on principles. Republican Bob Inglis, a six-term U.S. Representative from South Carolina, lost his bid for Congress in 2010 after reversing his position on climate change. Inglis realized the risk to his political career, but briefings with scientists and discussions with his children had convinced him that this was the right course.

Representative Barbara Lee of California was the only member of either house of Congress to vote against the Authorization for Use of Military Force (AUMF) on September 14, 2001. She regarded the resolution as overly broad, giving too much power to the president to initiate military conflicts. For her stance, she was widely insulted and received so many death threats that she needed 24-hour bodyguards. Since then her warning that the AUMF would be used as a "blank check" seems prophetic, as presidents Bush, Obama, and Trump have used it to justify many military actions around the globe that were unrelated to the 9/11 attacks that the AUMF was supposed to address.

Another often vilified group is lawyers. Yet many real-life lawyers and judges have been persecuted—for upholding the law or defending dissenters—by criminal gangs, vigilantes, or even their own governments as in China where the government has detained several hundred lawyers known as 'rights defenders.' [1]

The *pro bono* tradition, in which attorneys are ethically obliged to take on cases without charge for the public good has played an important role in U.S. Supreme Court decisions such as Brown v. Board of Education, Loving v. Virginia, and Miranda v. Arizona. [2]

Civil disobedience, the refusal to obey a law that one believes is morally wrong, has probably occurred throughout history whenever an individual or group simply refused to follow laws that went against their beliefs and deep-seated interests. The 45° concept of civil disobedience as a right and a duty was developed by Henry David Thoreau in 1849 and has since spread widely, notably in the movement for Indian independence led by Mohandas Gandhi and the U.S. civil rights movement led by Rev. Martin Luther King, Jr.

Among many successful examples are the Singing Revolution of 1987-1991 that led to the independence of Estonia, Latvia, and Lithuania; the nonviolent 1919 revolution by which Egyptians gained independence from British occupation; tax resistance and work stoppages in contemporary China to protest government injustices and malfeasance; the anti-apartheid movement in South Africa..

Telling the truth in the public interest also requires courage. *Whistleblowers* expose corrupt, unjust, and dangerous practices from a position inside a business or a government agency. In the early days of U.S. history, two naval officers, Samuel Shaw and Richard Marven, revealed to the public that the commander-in-chief of the Continental Navy was torturing British POWs. This led to the first whistleblower protection law, passed by the Continental Congress. Yet today's laws still have weak areas. Many countries have no laws to protect whistleblowers while some, such as Australia, have passed laws that actually criminalize them. [3]

Even with protective laws, and certainly without them, telling the truth can lead to death, imprisonment, or exile. We note the fates of Karen Silkwood, Chelsea Manning, Julian Assange, and Edward Snowden. Jeffrey Sterling, who helped a journalist expose a risky and ill-conceived CIA covert operation in Iran, spent years in prison despite a serious heart condition. After 9/11 the U.S. government stepped up prosecution of people in the intelligence and national security community who spoke out against agency abuses, for instance John Kiriakou and Thomas Drake, who blew the whistle on torture and secret domestic surveillance, respectively. In Israel, Mordechai Vanunu spent 18 years in prison, including more than 11 in solitary confinement, for divulging facts about Israel's secret nuclear arsenal. Many Israelis consider him a turncoat but international supporters see him as a whistleblower for worldwide peace.

Investigative reporters also face increasing risks since the turn of the previous century when 'muckrakers' took on corporate monopolies, political machines, and social ills. Muckraking led to a great many reforms (35°) that included child labor laws, shutting down Standard Oil's monopoly (10°) over the oil industry, the NY Tenement Act that forced landlords to install hallway lighting and toilets, and passage of the Pure Food and Drug Act of 1906.

Today, investigative journalists and war correspondents are often government targets, with more than 1,000 casualties since 1992. Several dozen journalists have met mysterious deaths since Vladimir Putin took power in Russia, while Turkey, Iran, and China are noted for the high numbers of journalists they have imprisoned. [4]

Free Minds

The man who invented the wheel was an idiot. The man who invented the next three was a genius.
~Sid Caesar, American comedian

The predominance of 45° in a life often indicates a professional, a scientist, a journalist, perhaps a public intellectual—but expression of this degree is by no means limited to the credentialed or the well-known.

Although a person who tends to study, reflect, and speculate, 45° has a certain general curiosity and breadth of interests not always found in academic settings. He or she might be a comedian or court jester, a truck-driver, a nurse.

Careful observation is the bedrock of 45° knowledge. Jean-Henri Fabre, "the father of modern entomology," first carefully studied the insects of his back yard. Not only scientists and detectives but many other good observers make it a habit to experience the world directly, without the blinkers of other people's words and ideas pre-defining what one sees and hears. As Charles Darwin said "It is a fatal fault to reason whilst observing."

To observation add the habit of reflection, which comes more easily in quiet and natural surroundings, away from constant socializing or electronic distractions. It helps 45° to have a childhood with freedom to explore, in which a child's experiences and interpretations are respected—not immediately corrected into conformity. The more rounded vision of 45° is nourished by learning more than one language, living abroad, or leisurely travel. A diverse set of friends or a broad range of interests and skills also help to achieve a larger perspective.

To reflection is added openness to ideas, even if they seem to oppose one's own. At 45° a person does not attach her ego to her personal opinions. She can and does change her mind. Another 45° quality is *discernment*, the intuitive ability to know what is real and good, to tell the difference between truth and fiction, to discriminate between the genuine and the phony. Discernment is a necessary ingredient for wisdom.

Another 45° trait is *foresight*. It first made a rough appearance at 10° as cunning or Machiavellian strategy solely to further self or cohorts. 15° has little sense of the consequences of his actions, and many who act at 20° or 25° do not care about environmental or social consequences—only personal consequences. Global markets and changing technologies have popularized business forecasting (20°/35°) but it is only incidentally concerned with human welfare rather than profit. At 30° people primarily use foresight to serve the future of their own families; otherwise they are likely to look to the past (tradition) for guidance.

As a tendency to look forward for the whole community, actual foresight begins at 35° where it is often linked to scientific methods, environmentalism, or social and political reforms. At 45° foresight comes to full flower, with a larger context: civilization, the whole human race, the planet. An essential part of this process is reviewing experience— one's own and the larger history. If one does not know the past, it is difficult to navigate the future.

Reason and Enlightenment

> *A wise man is not governed by others, nor does he try to govern them; he prefers that reason alone prevail.*
> ~La Bruyère, *Characters*, 1688

A modern individual who generally operates at 45° may not be a scientist, but he or she usually has a scientific world view, and tends to reach conclusions by using logic, critical thinking, and the scientific method. As it developed fully in the 17th century, the scientific method is a model of 45° thinking, a form of problem-solving that observes phenomena, makes a hypothesis about those observations, and then tests this hypothesis by experiments. After a hypothesis is verified by repeated experiments, it becomes a generally accepted theory.

Sometimes new research and new interpretations can transform the field in a scientific revolution. Other dispositions may resist such drastic changes of worldview, but 45° is either leading the advance or at least open-minded about it.

While pure science and the scientific method are at 45°, individual creative scientists such as Isaac Newton or Nikola Tesla may be working at 50° and possibly X° (since the *concepts* of science are not themselves material).

Philosophy is the pinnacle and playground of 45° reason. Philosopher Richard Bradley says "Philosophy is 99 per cent about critical reflection on anything you care to be interested in." This deeper kind of thinking about every conceivable subject underpins every civilization. According to British philosopher Alfred North Whitehead

A philosophic outlook is the very foundation of thought and of life. The sort of ideas we attend to, and the sort of ideas which we push into the negligible background, govern our hopes, our fears, our control of behavior. As we think, we live. This is why the assemblage of philosophic ideas is more than a specialist study. It moulds our type of civilization. [5]

Another essential 45° field of knowledge is history, the narrative of all our pasts, which began with pictographs and tales told around the campfire. Oral traditions were replaced by written narratives beginning in ancient China and Greece. Historical memory is greatly dependent on libraries and universities, which have been storehouses of and seedbeds for all the complex ideas and techniques known to humankind. These 45° institutions are almost as old as writing itself. The first known library consists of the Ebla tablets, a collection of 20,000 clay tablets in cuneiform script from ancient Syria dated to around 2350 BC. A century later, the first known center of learning was Shangyang in China.

An Indian university, Taxila, flourished from 600 BC to 500 AD, with thousands of students coming from Babylon, Greece, China, and Syria to study the Vedas, mathematics, philosophy, languages, medicine, archery, warfare, astronomy, commerce, music, dance, and the occult and mystical sciences. Nalanda, another early Indian university, had an astronomical observatory, a huge library known as the "Mountain of Knowledge," and 300 lecture halls.

Today it is estimated there are at least 26,000 institutions of higher learning across the world, and several hundred thousand libraries.

The Struggles of Reason

> *No, no, you're not thinking; you're just being logical.*
> ~Niels Bohr, Danish physicist, 1885-1962

Human knowledge does not advance along a straight and smooth road. 45° dedication to the search for truth faces obstacles from both without and within. Numerous 10° dominators—tyrants, conquerors, and religious authorities—have tried to smother ideas and knowledge they didn't like. Sometimes scholars are persecuted by those acting from malicious envy or personal ambition (15°/ 20°). Among such victims were two Islamic physician polymaths of the medieval period. Because of his advanced thinking and fame, Rhazes was arrested and beaten with his books until he was blind. The prominent physician and philosopher Abumeron Avenzoar was forbidden to write or teach, ending up his days as a manual laborer.[6]

In the 16th century, astronomer Giordano Bruno and physician Michael Servetus were burned at the stake for their dissenting views. In the 20th century, Russian botanist, geneticist, and plant explorer Nikolai Vavilov starved to death in a gulag despite his brilliant research on plant diversity. For ideological reasons, Stalin preferred the pseudoscientific theories of Trofim Lysenko, an obscure but ambitious agronomist.

Ideological or personal hostility are not the only problems. Scientists, historians, and other scholars undergo constant stumbles and controversies. They struggle with nationalism and other kinds of bias, with 25° vanity and 15° intellectual confusion. Scholarly research may suffer from personal rivalries and turf battles, also provincialism and other narrow perspectives. The pioneer light researcher Dr. John Ott and Elaine Morgan's aquatic ape hypothesis have been ignored because they came from outside the academic world.

Even highly educated people are unlikely to know much about the history and culture of other civilizations than their own, and this seems to be especially true of modern Americans. Thus a great deal of research and many broad generalizations about human beings have been based only on modern American subjects (often male college students).

Another difficulty is the "Idea Entropy" that results from misusing the ideas of seminal thinkers by oversimplifying and distorting them—turning them from 45° or 50° insights into 20° rigid and exclusive ideology. There is a story that Karl Marx, exasperated by some of his followers, exclaimed "I am not a Marxist!" A number of other thinkers could with justice have said something similar.

Many unexamined assumptions and fallacious ideas derive from ossified scholarly traditions and 15° dogma. In 1620 Francis Bacon described four categories of these persistent though outmoded fixations, calling them idols. In "Idols of the Theatre" he says:

In my judgment all the received systems are but so *many stage-plays*, representing worlds of their own creation after an unreal and scenic fashion. Nor is it only of the systems now in vogue, or only of the ancient sects and philosophies that I speak; for many more plays of the same kind may yet be composed and in like artificial manner set forth. [Nor] do I mean this only of entire systems, but also of many principles and axioms in science, which by tradition, credulity, and negligence have come to be received. [7]

The classic example of servile obedience (15°) to established authority is the millennia-long deference to everything Aristotle said. A few minutes' observation would disprove claims such as that males of all species have more teeth than females. In a modern example of conceptual limitations, Joshua Goldstein notes that 'Realism' is the dominant conceptual system in the field of International Relations, conceptualizing war and peace in terms of 1) territorial states operating as autonomous actors, 2) states rationally pursuing their own interests and 3), an "anarchic" system of sovereign states. He says these concepts about rational and autonomous actors are a poor fit for observed reality. [8]

Anthropologist Richard Rudgley notes that at least 95% of the human story occurred in prehistory, yet historians write about ancient Egypt and Mesopotamia as if they rose out of a vacuum. Psychologist James Hillman criticizes the assumptions of standard psychotherapy:

It makes every problem a subjective, inner problem. And that's not where the problems come from. They come from the environment, the cities, the economy, the racism.... architecture, school systems, capitalism, exploitation. Psychotherapy theory turns it all on you: *you* are the one who is wrong. [9]

Modern (neoclassical) economics works from an outmoded paradigm (15°/20°) according to growing criticism from many directions. Critics say it is based on a mythically rational economic man and relies heavily on mathematical models that do not describe reality. It is "an ideology masquerading as scientific theory" according to the New Economics Working Group. [10]

Another issue is that specialization can stymie creative cross-fertilization of ideas. Scientist-essayist Loren Eiseley blames academic enforcement of disciplinary boundaries (in the name of professionalism) for a loss of imagination in science: "Some minds exhibit an almost instinctive hostility toward the mere attempt to wonder."

There are nonscientists at 20° and 35° who all but worship science—its knowledge, methods, and practitioners. Many restrict the term science to lab sciences—not field sciences—and assert that experiments are the entire story. On the other hand, 45° understands the subtleties and limitations recognized by eminent scientists themselves. Albert Einstein: "The whole of science is nothing more than a refinement of everyday thinking"; Stephen Jay Gould: "Science is all those things which are confirmed to such a degree that it would be unreasonable to withhold one's provisional consent"; and rocket scientist Wernher Von Braun: "Research is what I'm doing when I don't know what I'm doing."

Freedom

The people never give up their liberties but under some delusion.
~Edmund Burke

Several freedoms are vitally important to 45°: intellectual freedom; national struggles with conquerors and colonial rulers; the overthrow of oppressive governments; struggles of slaves, serfs, and women oppressed by long-standing customs and institutions; and the historical acquisition of civil liberties that allow self-governance.

A surprising degree of intellectual freedom and creative thinking existed 2,500 years ago At least three known ancient cultures gave free rein to their thinkers: China, India, and Greece. At this early period philosophers were laying down worldviews that served as the basis for how billions have perceived the world since then. However, this was not an absolute or permanent freedom. Socrates was condemned to death for impiety and corrupting the youth. In China, the era of open speculation was followed by Qin emperor Shihuang who in his zeal to suppress all opposition burned most of the important books and buried alive about 460 intellectuals.

In India, the great ideas of Hinduism were undermined by caste stratification and oppression of women. In the 15th and 16th centuries India revived a tradition of religious dissent. Teachers and philosophers such as Ramananda, Kabir, and Guru Nanak rejected caste and other Hindu orthodoxies.

In the West, intellectual freedom began to flourish again in the Renaissance. The Low Countries (now Netherlands, Belgium, and Luxembourg) have a long tradition of religious toleration and intellectual openness, with thinkers such as Desiderius Erasmus, Baruch Spinoza, and Hugo Grotius. Their intellectual freedom attracted immigrants from many parts of Europe, including English dissenters such as the Pilgrims, Jews from Portugal and Germany, and several noted philosophers. French-born Rene Descartes lived in Holland because of its freedom of expression, and the English political thinker John Locke took refuge there when he was persecuted by King James II. John Amos Comenius, an educational reformer and religious refugee from Czechoslovakia, spent his final years in Amsterdam.

Philosopher Bertrand Russell said "It is impossible to exaggerate the importance of Holland in the seventeenth century, as the one country where there was freedom of speculation." It was also the center of European publishing, with several hundred publishers in Amsterdam.

In Europe women began to be publicly recognized as intellectually capable. A few women were admitted to universities in 17th century Spain, Netherlands, Sweden, and Italy, with two receiving doctorate degrees. In 1732, the first woman appointed to teach at a university was Laura Bassi, at the University of Bologna.

The world's scientific community has an ethic of sharing information, although this sometimes conflicts with an identification with national interests. Intellectual freedom also concerns the free dissemination of information, which in modern times largely means freedom of media. Freedom of the press was such an important idea to the founders of the American Republic that they enshrined it as part of the First Amendment to the Bill of Rights. Thomas Jefferson wrote to John Tyler in an 1804 letter:

> No experiment can be more interesting than that we are now trying, and which we trust will end in establishing the fact, that man may be governed by reason and truth. Our first object should therefore be, to leave open to him all the avenues to truth. The most effectual hitherto found, is the freedom of the press. It is, therefore, the first shut up by those who fear the investigation of their actions. [11]

Currently, continued free access to the Internet is an important issue across the world. The inventor of the world wide web—Sir Tim Berners-Lee—warns of challenges to its continued existence as a platform for humanity's benefit, such as loss of privacy and gaming of the system in order to spread misinformation and propaganda.

Freedom and Autonomy

> *As long as but a hundred of us remain alive, never will we on any conditions be brought under English rule. It is in truth not for glory, nor riches, nor honors, that we are fighting, but for freedom—for that alone, which no honest man gives up but with life itself.*
> The Declaration of Arbroath (Scottish independence), April 6, 1320

Free agency whether for nations, classes of people, or for individuals may be the most basic right after life itself.*

It has taken a long time for civilizations to realize this truth in their institutions, and the struggle is certainly not over yet.

Basic concepts of freedom and justice grew for many centuries, in philosophical and spiritual ideas of the Axial Age and in documents such as the Magna Carta; they developed more fully in Western Europe during the 17th and 18th century Enlightenment.

We could call this set of ideas the 'anti-10° factor.'

*Libertarians recognize life and liberty as basic freedoms, but their insistence on the primacy of property rights, while overlooking the history of property acquisition and institutionalized privileges, muddies the waters considerably. (10°/20°/45°)

Ideals of freedom such as national self-determination, civil liberties, representative government, and personal autonomy, so often taken for granted in the West, are widely flouted in most of Asia and Africa. In the world as a whole, freedoms may be slipping, at least temporarily. Freedom House says that 2016 was the "10th consecutive year of decline in global freedom."[12] Note the difference between human rights (40°) and civil liberties (45°). Human rights are universal, inherent rights of all human beings. Civil liberties are individual rights protected by law from unjust interference by government or others.

For millennia human groups have struggled to defend or regain their lands and autonomy from conquerors. As far as we know, the first empire in history was the Akkadian state that rose to its height around the 23rd century BC., one of countless times that 10° asserted the dominance of one group over another. Those conquered—torn from their own folkways and languages, their labor exploited, and treated as inferiors or slaves—inevitably struggled to regain their former liberty.

In the early 1800s, inspired by the American War of Independence, Simon Bolivar and others drove the liberation of a dozen former Spanish and Portuguese colonies in Latin America, while in Europe the Greeks and Serbs finally threw off the yoke of the Ottoman Empire. After each of the two world wars, a number of former colonies became independent states—three dozen after WWII.

Struggles to attain national freedom, although motivated at 45°, may manifest at lower dispositions (e.g., a war for independence might turn into guerrilla warfare with atrocities on both sides).However, nonviolent revolutions are becoming more frequent, and allow a new nation to start up without a legacy of hatred and violence.[13]

Most countries have experienced periods of oppression by tyrants or corrupt elites (10°) and misrule has resulted in hundreds of revolutions or civil wars. The earliest recorded popular rebellion was in 2380 BC in the Sumerian city Lagash, when people deposed the king and put a reformer on the throne. Ancient Greece recorded several civil wars to overthrow despots and unjust rule. The Peisistratids, a family of tyrants, were dislodged from Athens in 510 BC only after four years of strife and after the Athenians solicited aid from a Spartan army.

Today, as with revolts against conquerors, in many cases oppressive regimes can be dislodged by nonviolent means (45°/40°) as described in the article "History Is a Weapon: Strategizing for a Living Revolution," by civil rights activist George Lakey. [14]

One type of struggle develops because conquerors combined two or more distinct language groups or ethnic nations in one colony that later became a nation-state. A common solution to this problem is for the two groups to form separate countries. Americans tend to assume that secession is necessarily linked with war, but there have been many peaceful secessions, even here. Kentucky, West Virginia, Maine, and Vermont were formed from other states. To formalize the right to negotiated secession, the treaty establishing the European Union has a provision for member states to withdraw from the EU.*

Oppressed Classes

Silence never won rights. They are not handed down from above; they are forced by pressures from below.
~Roger Nash Baldwin, co-founder of ACLU, 1884-1981

Another form of oppression involves people subordinated by historical institutions: slaves, serfs, peasants, low castes in India, and women. The quest for autonomy has sometimes led to armed rebellion. Several large-scale slave rebellions occurred in ancient Rome between 135 and 71 BC (the Servile Wars) and in many places since, until formal slavery ended 150 years ago. The most successful slave revolt (Haiti, 1791-1804) resulted in the founding of a new, independent country.

As for serfs and peasants, feudalism was a widespread institution in the ancient Near East and Asia, but we are more familiar with it from medieval Europe. Peasants owned their own land, while serfs were bound by hereditary obligations to the manor (typically a small-holding of between 1,200 and 1,800 acres). Serfs had to work for the lord at whatever he job he assigned them; bonded or indentured peasants had to work on the lord's farms for a living; free peasants could choose their business (but had to pay taxes to the lord). Typically, free peasants ('freemen') were a small proportion of the peasantry.

A long history of mostly unsuccessful peasant rebellions dates back to ancient times (Yellow Turban Rebellion in China, 184 AD). The English Peasants' Revolt in 1381 resulted in greater rights for serfs—soon revoked by Richard II. Demands in the German Peasant's War (1524-25) were abolition of serfdom, relief from heavy taxes, the right to fish and hunt, liberty to choose their own pastors, and restoration of common lands. Of an army of 300,000 peasants, about one-third died, especially in harsh reprisals after their military defeat. Russia, where serfdom lasted longest, had hundreds of peasant revolts in the 18th and 19th centuries until the Czar officially freed 23 million serfs in 1861.

Supported by Marxist ideology and nationalist sentiments, 20th century peasant revolutions succeeded in Mexico, Russia, China, Algeria, Cuba, and Vietnam. They successfully ended serfdom but typically resulted in another form of authoritarian government.

The human group that has taken the longest to gain autonomy is the female gender, half the human race. Most freedoms were gained in the last two centuries as part of the general spread of Enlightenment values (45°/40°/35°/30°) and from several eras of organized, cooperative actions (feminism). This struggle is by no means complete, especially in less-developed countries, and continues as both a general humanitarian concern and as national movements led mainly by women.

Truth(s)

The greatest enemy of any one of our truths may be the rest of our truths.
~William James, American philosopher, 1842-1910

Is truth one of two choices—like True/False questions? Is there one truth or different truths for different people? How simple things would be if there really were just one clear Truth. Philosophers, preachers, lawyers, and politicians would be out of a job.

*Examples of peaceful secession: Belgium from the Netherlands (1830), Ecuador and Venezuela from Gran Colombia (1830), Iceland from Denmark (1874-1918), Norway from Sweden (1905), and Malta from Britain (1964). In 1991, as the Soviet Union suffered economic collapse, it dissolved into 15 separate countries.

Different truths coexist within each individual. We are operating by body wisdom, aware of our thirst, aches and pains, sexual attractions, or deep fears. At a deeper level of physiological processes, networks of cells communicate their own truths.

Another aspect of instinctual truth is intuition, described by some as a 'gut feeling.' Intuition consists in part of nonverbal abilities such as reading micro-expressions and rapidly combining a multitude of sensory impressions. We note the hostility of an associate even during a discourse about the abstract and abstruse. Difficulties occur because people differ widely both in their ability to intuit and to separate their intuitions from their personalities and prejudices. While 20° denies the existence of intuition, 25° may exaggerate her personal claim to having this gift. The highly intuitive tend to congregate at 40°, 45°, 50°, and X°.

Reification is the human tendency to turn the abstract into something more concrete, treating a concept as if it has a real existence. When used consciously (personification) it is a literary device. At 15° it is a fallacy in reasoning. At 5° it incites rioters by personifying evil as the current scapegoat. At 50° reification creates gripping stories and fantastical worlds and at X°, mythic and poetic truth.

Confusion between various levels of abstraction leads to many common cognitive errors and mutual misunderstandings. One person cites government statistics while the other one claims he saw a person buying sirloin steaks with food stamps. They are not on the same page. In general, only the higher degrees can manage the necessary gear-shifting between sense experiences and ideas.

For many, truth is not an important concept. Words are simply tools for personal deception or domination or marketing (0°/10°/20°) or ammunition for winning the argument (5°/20°). When Arnold H. Glasow said "The fewer the facts, the stronger the opinion" he was probably thinking about 5° to 20° disposition.

15° may believe truth resides with a particular leader or group. Or she finds the entire Truth within the pages of one holy book. This disposition reads its holy book literally. At 20° the Truth is one of two sides (the opposite of something else). 20° believes in a materialist universe (but he may distrust science, and he often distorts facts). Above all, 20° finds Truth in his chosen ideologies.

Truth for self-centered 25° is first, 'Is it good for me?' Second, it is social conformity and the conventional wisdom or perhaps the opinions of a particular subgroup or clique.

Folk wisdom and common sense provide much of the Truth at 30°, along with "Do unto others" morality. 30° tends to follow the crowd but has more respect for facts than does competitive 20°, and little attraction to ideologies.

Many at 35° accept scientific materialism as a worldview, and find Truth in the greater good (utilitarianism). If not this ethic, 35° will have another, because this is an ethical disposition.

The Truth for compassionate 40° is Love (philia or agape), loving-kindness, peace, and unity of all humanity or all life. 40° apprehends truth through the heart. In contrast, the more intellectual 45° has a deep commitment to ideas and principles, rising above the identifications of nationality and religion by a path that owes more to reason and judgment than through love and intuition as with 40°. There are, however, many 40°/45° fusions.

For 50° the Truth may be creative flow, an intensely pleasurable, effortless, yet focused state of mind that may synthesize a multitude of values and perspectives. When fully absorbed in whatever one is doing, it is easy to achieve peak performance. In the physical realm, athletes call this 'being in the zone.' [15]

X° goes beyond both the animal and the abstract, and is often expressed as paradox. Swami Vivekananda said, "Truth can be stated in a thousand different ways, yet each one can be true." 20th century quantum physicist Niels Bohr said, "The opposite of a correct statement is a false statement. But the opposite of a profound truth may well be another profound truth."

[1] "China rounding up rights lawyers," *Northwest Arkansas Democrat Gazette*, July 19, 2015
[2] "Ten Hero Lawyers Who Helped the Poor and Marginalized," http://www.online-paralegal-programs.com/hero-lawyers/

3 Tiffany Ap, for CNN, "'Whistleblowers' challenge Australia's law on reporting refugee conditions," July 1, 2015, http://www.cnn.com/2015/07/01/asia/australia-border-force-act/

4 Committee to Protect Journalists, "1083 Journalists killed since 1992," http://www.cpj.org/killed/

5 Alfred North Whitehead, *Modes of Thought*, Macmillan 1938, p.87.

6 Steven I. Hajdu, "Persecution of Noted Physicians and Medical Scientists," *Annals of Clinical and Laboratory Science,* Summer 2007, vol. 37 no. 3, 295-297, http://www.annclinlabsci.org/content/37/3/295.full

7 Francis Bacon, *Novum Organum*, 1620

8 Joshua Goldstein, op. cit.

9 Scott London, "On Soul, Character and Calling: A Conversation with James Hillman" http://www.scottlondon.com/interviews/hillman.html

10 Garry Jacobs, Mark Swilling, Winston P. Nagan, Jamie Morgan, Barry Gills, "Quest for a New Paradigm in Economics - A Synthesis of Views of the New Economics Working Group" *Cadmus Journal*, May 24, 2017 http://cadmusjournal.org/article/volume-3/issue-2/inside-issue

11 Thomas Jefferson, "To Judge John Tyler, Washington, June 28, 1804 "http://www.let.rug.nl/usa/presidents/thomas-jefferson/letters-of-thomas-jefferson/jefl164.php

12 "Freedom in the World 2016," https://freedomhouse.org/report/freedom-world/freedom-world-2016

13 Gene Sharp, *The Politics of Nonviolent Action*, Porter-Sargent, 2003

14 George Lakey, "History Is a Weapon: Strategizing for a Living Revolution," 2002, http://www.historyisaweapon.com/defcon1/lakeylivrev.html

15 Mihaly Csikszentmihalyi, *Flow: The Psychology of Optimal Experience*, Harper 2008

Chapter 25
The Creative Human (50º)

Creativity is a survival instinct.
~Tom Ardavany American writer and film director

Humans appear to have been creative from the very beginning. Some stone carvings are so old they may have been made by other human species than our own. By at least 40,000 years ago our immediate ancestors were moved to create art and music. Cave art in El Castillo, Spain, is the earliest known and possibly made by Neanderthals. From the same period, flutes of bird bone and mammoth ivory have been found in Germany. A few millennia later artists at Chauvet Cave in France show superb mastery of line and the illusion of movement in hundreds of animal drawings.

Our ancestors invented nets, baskets, fish hooks, bone needles, and shoes in this same early period. They watched the stars, the phases of the moon, the patterns of nature, and seasonal changes with a far more intimate understanding than do most moderns, who are usually indoors. Long before the invention of writing, many cultural inventions had already been diffused across large regions of the world—for instance boats, pottery, and the domestication of animals. [1]

We can only make educated guesses about what prehistoric people knew, thought about, and aspired to be, since we are limited to fragments of material objects that have survived time's erosion. Yet it is clear that humans have always wanted not only to improve their lives but also to make them meaningful.

At 50° one may develop new kinds of processes, make existing objects more functional, or create something beautiful or interesting, whether an object, a dance movement, or a pattern of sounds. Creative imagination also combines ideas or human relationships in new ways, seeing everything from a different perspective. At 50° a human being is powerfully motivated to experience, to learn, to grow in understanding, to make something new, and to give back. This is the disposition for creating art, solving problems, and living life to the utmost.

Psychologist Abraham Maslow notes that western culture often defines creativity in a very limited way, applying it only to certain arts or theories; to products rather than processes. Instead, he describes a self-actualizing creativity—an openness to experience—that expresses every psychologically healthy person, whatever his special talents: "I learned that a perfect tackle could be as esthetic a product as a sonnet and could be approached in the same creative spirit….A first-rate soup is more creative than a second-rate painting." [2]

Creativity involves curiosity, ingenuity and imagination, play, humor, and daily problem-solving. This disposition is possible for all, not just a few prodigies.

Individuality

At bottom every man knows well enough that he is a unique being, only once on this earth; and by no extraordinary chance will such a marvelously picturesque piece of diversity in unity as he is, ever be put together a second time.
~Friedrich Nietzsche, German philosopher, 1844-1900

Since the beginning of our race 50,000 years ago, an estimated 108 billion of us have been born, no two exactly alike, even identical twins. Humans, like snowflakes, are one-of-a-kind. Geneticists point out that every person has the capacity to generate 10^{3000} eggs or sperm each with unique sets of genes. Put these genes together in an act of reproduction and "the likelihood of anyone else with your set of genes in the past or in the future becomes infinitesimal." [3]

Human experiences are similarly unique, and whatever we have of free will leads us to different choices and decisions. Yet many human institutions tend to treat everyone the same: bureaucracies and schools; military, industrial and commercial systems; statistics and experimental protocols. This is not 30°/35° egalitarianism but 20° reductionism. The human spirit invariably spills out of these rigid containers.

One's own life story is a creation of sorts. The term *self-actualization* was introduced by psychologist Abraham Maslow to describe the final level of psychological development achieved after basic physical and social needs are met. Maslow saw it as full realization of each person's potential to be fully alive and to find meaning in life, an ideal state that may be achieved through creative work, autonomy, spontaneity, the search for knowledge, contributing to society, being at peace with one's conscience, and deep understanding of reality (wisdom). Following Maslow, Kurt Goldstein says that self-actualization is our master motive and our most basic drive.

Maslow: "Self-actualization is the intrinsic growth of what is already in the organism, or more accurately, of what the organism is." Carrying this idea further, Jungian therapist James Hillman points to the ancient, widespread idea that every person is born with a *daimon* or guiding spirit (Plato), second soul (Inuits and Australian aborigines), spirit animal (indigenous), guardian angel, or genius. He says this calling to a unique fate is more concerned with the soul's evolution than with an individual's conscious plans. The soul's lot is not known ahead nor predestined—only necessary. To discover our calling we should look at our lives "with the imaginative sensitivity we give fictions." [4]

Our unique fates form the basis for democracy, says Hillman: "What is the basis for the claim 'All Men are created equal'? We are equal because each brings a specific calling into the world."

Divergent Thinking

> *There are always possibilities.*
> ~Mr. Spock

Creativity involves divergent thinking, the exploration of many different alternatives and potentials. It is "what if?" Other elements are flexibility, fluency, complexity, curiosity, originality, imagination, elaboration, and risk-taking (Leslie Owen Wilson 2004). Creative individuals may have a deep craving for beauty or the form that perfectly fits its function.

Two useful models are *tinkering* and *bricolage*. A tinker (or tinkerer) works in an unskilled or experimental manner, making small changes in order to improve, adjust, or repair something, while a 'maker' is somebody who likes to create things in their spare time, maybe combining art and electronics. Garage mechanics as well as artists might be characterized this way. Tinkering is above all informal and open-ended; it resembles play.

Applied science often requires on-the-spot adjustments, like those performed by *Star Trek's* redoubtable engineer Scotty. In *Intelligent Tinkering*, ecology professor Robert J. Cabin offers restoration ecology as an area well-suited for multidisciplinary tinkering similar to the careful trial-and-error strategies used by indigenous peoples, hobbyist mechanics, and inventors. His title comes from Aldo Leopold's classic *Sand County Almanac*: "To keep every cog and wheel is the first precaution of intelligent tinkering."[5]

The second model for creativity—*bricolage*--comes from a French word meaning 'odd jobs' or DIY. A *bricoleur* is a handyman, a jack of all trades, one who is able to make something from whatever materials are at hand, such as pieces left over from other projects. An exemplar of this was the television character MacGyver, noted for his ability to devise emergency solutions using only his Swiss Army knife, duct tape, and everyday items, described by fans as 'MacGyvering.'

The ideas of creating from diverse sources and making do with what is at hand have spread to fields such as postmodern literature, 'entrepreneurial bricolage,' computer software, and academic research that mixes different methods and approaches. Examples are junk art, mixed media, mashup music, the use of found objects as musical instruments, and improvisational theater.

Readiness to experiment and to find new uses for the familiar spur creativity. On the other hand, some cultural attitudes discourage it, such as mistaken notions that creativity is only about the arts, or that 'geniuses' are the only creative people. Societies that are more insular and hidebound ($20°/25°/30°$) tend to discourage novel ideas and look askance at the often eccentric people who come up with them.

To Be or Not to Be Creative

I saw the angel in the marble and carved until I set him free.
~Michelangelo

One or two options satisfies most people. We are trained in convergent thinking—one right answer. This may make it hard to understand highly creative people who have certain traits that set them apart and may even make them seem deranged to the less imaginative. According to a landmark study by psychologist Frank X. Barron:

> The common traits that people across all creative fields seemed to have in common were an openness to one's inner life; a preference for complexity and ambiguity; an unusually high tolerance for disorder and disarray; the ability to extract order from chaos; independence; unconventionality; and a willingness to take risks [and make mistakes]. [6]

Creative people are sometimes perceived as selfish—and sometimes they are—because of a compulsion to perfect their creations that may eclipse their social interests or obligations.

A recent study indicates that Americans have been declining in various aspects of creativity since the early 1980s, beginning in childhood. Eric Weiner says that in the U.S, "the exact year when a child's creative-thinking skills plateau [is] the 4th grade." In an ideal world, children are allowed to explore, try out new things, learn for themselves, and develop at their own pace. But entire societies seem to be trying to speed-up children's development with the excuse that this is needed for international economic competition (20°). Emphasis on standardized testing (also 20°) leaves little time for creative pursuits. [7]

In contrast, children don't enter school until age seven in countries such as Finland and Sweden, yet they catch up by age ten with their peers who were taught to read at five or six, and then they show greater reading comprehension. We need to keep in mind that life is not a race, and human beings have inborn time tables. [8]

Play (50°) is absolutely essential to healthy development of children and to creativity in both children and adults. While early formal instruction cuts into play time, an even more pernicious trend encourages very young children to watch television and videos, to play with smartphones, and generally to depend on looking at screens for their entertainment and learning. A related block to children's creativity is the lack of unstructured playtime outdoors (see Richard Louv in *Last*

Child in the Woods (2008). For the past generation or two, children are staying indoors more and more. Louv says that the ensuing "nature deficit disorder" contributes to childhood obesity, attention disorders, and mood disorders, as well as a loss of imagination.

Outsiders

Human salvation lies in the hands of the creatively maladjusted.
~Martin Luther King, Jr.

As individuals, creative people have often started out as outsiders for one reason or another, such as physical illness or poverty or family dysfunction. In order to make sense of diverse experiences they are forced to think outside of the box, tending to see the world from more than one perspective. Some statistical data supports a link between foreign birth and creativity. In the United States, foreign-born residents are about two and a half times more likely to hold patents and almost twice as likely to win a Nobel Prize. [9]

Contact with foreign cultures stimulates creative ideas and behaviors. Historical nations that conducted widespread trade, picking up new ideas from other peoples, often experienced a surge of creativity (a Golden Age). The European Renaissance flowered after increasing trade with Islamic culture, while Calcutta flourished from about 1840-1920 as the more ancient culture absorbed European culture. Also, eras of religious toleration often coincide with a flourishing of the arts and sciences, such as in 17th century Amsterdam.

People of ethnic and religious minorities often struggle to maintain their own culture and individuality within the dominant culture, but having two simultaneous perspectives facilitates creative insights and understanding. A person might also have this creative double vision because of divergent gender orientation. Someone like Gloria E. Anzaldúa, a lesbian Chicana scholar, may live in multiple worlds. Her *Borderlands* examines the many dimensions of *la mezcla* or hybridity.

Another kind of outsider is the person whose brain is wired a bit differently. Medical science and psychology have tended to pathologize human differences, yet there is evidence that those diagnosed with

Asperger's, bipolarity, or dyslexia can claim a higher frequency of creativity than neurotypicals. Weiner notes that creative people tend to be physiologically more sensitive to stimuli, with at least a touch of synesthesia (a neurological condition in which stimulation of one sensory or cognitive pathway automatically leads to experiences in a second pathway). Renowned biologist George Church ascribes his creativity and scientific achievements to his narcolepsy, with most of his visionary ideas occurring at the beginning or end of a narcoleptic nap. Church says, "I think we should be embracing [neurodiversity] a whole lot more than we are right now. My guess is that we need more high-functioning autistics or more OCDs....Being different at all allows you to think out of the box." [10]

A few creative individuals are found at the anti-social end of the spectrum, yet an individual's immorality, crimes or psychosis do not necessarily taint his creations. For example, the Renaissance artist Benvenuto Cellini was an aggressive and disputatious man (5°) who committed murder, but this did not affect the exquisite nature of his sculptures. The Italian painter Michelangelo Merisi da Caravaggio was another brawler who killed someone. Both committed their crimes in the context of 16th century Italy, a tumultuous period.

Arguably, some creative productions are themselves malign (0°/50°) such as the writings of the Marquis de Sade, or pro-Nazi films by Leni Reifenstahl. However, many creations considered immoral or degenerate in one society have been accepted by another society or another generation. Satire, disturbing art, and discordant music are often created with the intention of reflecting society back to itself (35° or 45° social criticism). One example is offensive comedy ala Lennie Bruce, George Carlin, Roseanne Barr, or Richard Pryor.

Creativity that is harnessed to another disposition expresses this as much or more than it does 50°. For instance, invention purely for profit is 20°/50°. Creativity becomes cleverness. Groups and institutions are more likely than are individuals to tie creativity to lower dispositions, for instance by promoting the invention of new weaponry, new means of surveillance, and new propaganda techniques. Much current information regarding creativity seems related to developing or harnessing creativity for the purposes of economic competition

(20°/50°) or advertising (25°/50°) rather than furthering the aims of higher dispositions.

Clusters of creative people occur when the talented come together to find kindred spirits for friendship, to compete (sometimes fiercely), to learn from each other, and to build on each other's work. These clusters include what are called 'Golden Ages,' which have often appeared in the long ranges of history, or more narrowly as in "the Golden Age of Hollywood" or of children's fiction, variety shows, French cinema, science fiction, television, or other fields of endeavor. Dean Keith Simonton, who pioneered the study of Golden Ages, first noted the effect. Eric Weiner's *The Geography of Genius* describes several such historical aggregations from ancient Athens to Silicon Valley, with insights gained by traveling to their locales.[11]

Creative scientists and notable scholars often congregate in certain university departments, which fact when publicized tends to attract especially talented students to them.[12] Gay men, frequently found in artistic pursuits, tend to gravitate to cities with a thriving arts community, where people are more open and accepting of differences.

Anglo-American popular music, and the African-American traditional music on which it is largely based, have manifested numerous clusters of musicians with distinctive styles, such as New Orleans, Memphis, and Chicago jazz; Liverpool pop and rock; Detroit Motown; and hip-hop from the Bronx. Nashville has long been the center of country music. Experimentation and constant reinvention has occurred in the field of popular music (spreading to classical music) over the past 60 years or so due to many new technologies of sound engineering such as multiple sound tracks, electric guitars, looping, synthesizers, and digital recording from laptops.

In 2004 the government of Hong Kong commissioned a research group to study creativity, create a Creativity Index, and to devise a framework for making a world city more hospitable to creative efforts. Weiner notes Danilevsky's Law (from a 19th century Russian theorist) that says people are more likely to reach full creative potential when they belong to an independent nation, even if it is small. [Perhaps especially if it is small?]

The Multiply Abled

A human being should be able to change a diaper, plan an invasion, butcher a hog, conn a ship, design a building, write a sonnet, balance accounts, build a wall, set a bone, comfort the dying, take orders, give orders, cooperate, act alone, solve equations, analyze a new problem, pitch manure, program a computer, cook a tasty meal, fight efficiently, die gallantly. Specialization is for insects.
~Robert Heinlein, *Time Enough for Love, 1988*

Certain individuals are so driven by curiosity and the desire to master as many skills as possible that they stand out in their era as 'universal geniuses.' Others of us are, perhaps, simply highly versatile. Some of the multiply-abled are more noted for their knowledge (45°) others for their inventions and creations (50°). The person of many talents has been admired as polymath, as Renaissance man or woman, and most recently, as the Competent Person described above by science fiction writer Robert Heinlein.

The word 'polymath' is Greek for 'having learned much.' We speak here not of dabblers and dilettantes but of people who have attained mastery in several fields. The Egyptian physician Imhotep was the first polymath recorded to history, almost 5,000 years ago. Multi-talented people began to appear regularly among the ancient Greeks. Several historical eras teemed with polymaths, such as the Islamic Golden Age (about 750 AD until the Mongol conquest in 1258) and Renaissance Italy from the 15th to 17th centuries. Two great polymaths, Su Song and Shen Kuo, were almost contemporaries during the Song Dynasty in 11th century China. Two others, Thomas Jefferson and Benjamin Franklin, were United States founders.

You would think that the modern increase in knowledge would make it extremely difficult to master more than a single field; yet a great many polymaths and versatile, multi-talented people exist today. For instance, Manfred Clynes, an Austrian-Australian-American concert pianist, musical theorist, neuroscientist, inventor, and poet. Clynes invented the inertial guidance system for aircraft at age 15 and later the CAT computer and color ultrasound—40 patents in all. He also founded the field of Sentics, the scientific study of emotions.

The late Maya Angelou survived poverty, racism, and childhood rape to become a famous poet, also singer, dancer, author, professor, editor, lecturer, and civil rights leader. Angelou acted, wrote, directed, and produced plays, movies, and public television programs, and mastered five foreign languages.[13]

The ideal of the 'Renaissance man' was once proposed as a conscious model for everybody (or at least men of a certain social class) to develop all potentials—intellectual, athletic, artistic, and political—to the extent possible in a single lifetime. The model was developed by 15th century Italian humanist scholars such as Leon Battista Alberti and Giovanni Pico della Mirandola who believed that most people have an unlimited capacity for self-development. Alberti—author, architect, painter, poet, priest, mathematician, linguist, philosopher, and cryptographer—said "A man can do all things if he will." Pico was a polymath with a prodigious memory and epic ambitions remembered for his "Manifesto of the Renaissance" in which he defends the human search for knowledge against clerical criticism. [14]

Another Renaissance humanist, Baldassare Castiglione, scholar of classic literature, poet, soldier, and diplomat, described the ideal of the age in *The Book of the Courtier* (1528). This became the popular model across Europe and in England for several centuries thereafter. The courtier or gentleman is moral as well as multi-talented; he is calm and self-composed; and he accomplishes all that he does with a certain casual grace or *sprezzatura*. Or in modern terms, he is *cool*.

Attractive as it is, this model does not fully represent the mature human being, as it says little about family and intimate relationships or about spiritual development beyond obedience to the Church. *The Courtier's* ideal is a young man who has yet to acquire the wisdom of experience (45°). And although Castiglione said "Everything that men can understand can also be understood by women," the Renaissance man *was* usually a man, and one with advantages of birth allowing him to develop his talents. Castiglione's book suggests that while a man of humble birth could achieve the ideal state, it was much less likely.

A modern version is known mainly as a modern fictional hero, the Competent Person, or Jack (Jacqueline) of all trades who excels at everything they put a hand to. Warrior heroes of the past now give way to the individual distinguished by the *breadth* of his or her abilities, including the everyday practical. The Competent Person appears in fiction as Jeeves, James Bond, Yoko Suno, Batman, Jamie Fraser, Heinlein characters such as Jubal Hashaw, and many others.

However you name it, some people are unusually versatile. Dave Baldwin, a major league baseball player with a unique pitching style, retired from baseball to earn a PhD in genetics and M.S. in systems engineering. He is also an accomplished painter. Another athlete, Justin Tucker, kicker for the Baltimore Ravens, is a trained opera singer who can sing in seven languages. Queen Margrethe II of Denmark, besides writing and translating in Danish, French, English, Swedish and German, is a noted painter, illustrator, and costume designer, added to the knowledge of history, economics, law, politics, and military science necessary to being a monarch.

A polymath may or may not be a 'genius' (a word that is poorly defined and greatly overused; for instance, some use it to mean a person with a high IQ who may not have actually accomplished anything). Philosopher Arthur Schopenhauer described the difference between talent and genius as follows: "Talent hits a target no one else can hit. Genius hits a target no one else can see."

Universal Education

Education is not the filling of a pail, but the lighting of a fire.
~William Butler Yeats, Irish poet, 1865-1939

For centuries, a major drawback to realizing our creative potential has been long hours of back-breaking labor and lack of leisure time for most of humanity. This is no longer true for perhaps half of the world. A second obstacle has been lack of opportunity to gain an education, sometimes outright withholding of literacy from slaves or women. In 1800, it is estimated that only 12% of the world's people could read. Some countries have had "Each one teach one" campaigns that increased literacy very rapidly, but historically, the major social institution devoted to knowledge is universal education. Of course literacy, knowledge, and creativity are quite different things, but since the invention of writing, the creative person who lacks this skill is increasingly handicapped.

Karl Marx said that in an ideally constructed world, everyone would be able to self-actualize to the fullest extent possible, expressing his or her own genius—"Every man a Goethe." This is also the ideal of a universal education for all the children of the world. (However, this brave ideal goes by the off-putting name of 'compulsory education.')

Schooling began with the invention of writing some 5,000 years ago in the Near East. A limited number of boys learned to read and write in preparation for work as scribes and bureaucrats. Ancient schools in India and China taught upper-class boys a variety of subjects including both practical and liberal arts. Royalty and nobility continued to have the benefit of some broader education through the centuries; however, women, peasants and tradesmen seldom learned to read and write before the 17th century. Today about 84% of the world's people are literate (although that may include many who are functionally illiterate). Two-thirds of the illiterate are women, most of whom live in South and West Asia, Sub-Saharan Africa, and the Arab States. [15]

[1] Brian Hayden and Suzanne Villeneuve, "Astronomy in the Upper Palaeolithic?" *Cambridge Archaeological Journal*, 21, pp 331-355, September 20, 2011,
http://journals.cambridge.org/action/displayAbstract?fromPage=online&aid=8384192&fileId=S0959774311000400
[2] Abraham Maslow, "Creativity in Self-Actualizing People,"
http://academic.udayton.edu/LawrenceUlrich/LeaderArticles/Maslow%20Creativity%20in%20SA%20People.pdf
[3] Robert Plomin, John C. DeFries, Valerie S. Knopik, Jenae Neiderheiser, *Behavioral Genetics* 6th Edition, Palgrave Macmillan, 2013
[4] James Hillman, *The Soul's Code*, Warner Books 1996
[5] Robert J. Cabin, *Intelligent Tinkering: Bridging the Gap between Science and Practice*, Island Press, 2011
[6] Carolyn Gregoire and Scott Barry Kaufman, "Creative people's brains really do work differently," *Quartz*, January 4, 2016,
http://qz.com/584850/creative-peoples-brains-really-do-work-differently/
[7] Kyung Hee Kim (2011). The creativity crisis: The decrease in creative thinking scores on the Torrance Tests of Creative Thinking. Creativity Research Journal, 23, 285-295.

[8] Sebastian P. Suggate,*, Elizabeth A. Schaughency, Elaine Reeseb, "Children learning to read later catch up to children reading earlier," *Early Childhood Research Quarterly*, April 2012

[9] James Witte, "Build Bridges, Not Fences: Thirty Percent of U.S. Nobel Laureates Are Foreign-born, March 13, 2013, http://www.huffingtonpost.com/james-witte/nobel-laureates_b_2458128.html

[10] Sharon Begley,' "A Feature, Not a Bug": George Church Ascribes His Visionary Ideas to Narcolepsy,' *Scientific American*, June 9, 2017, https://www.scientificamerican.com/article/ldquo-a-feature-not-a-bug-rdquo-george-church-ascribes-his-visionary-ideas-to-narcolepsy/

[11] Eric Weiner, *The Geography of Genius*, Simon & Schuster 2016

[12] For instance, http://www.usnews.com/education/best-global-universities/mathematics

[13] "Polymaths Today: Nerds of a Higher Caliber," http://timeblimp.com/?page_id=203 http://www.achievement.org/autodoc/page/mus0int-1

[14] Giovanni Pico dellaMirandola, Oration on the Dignity of Man, http://vserver1.cscs.lsa.umich.edu/~crshalizi/Mirandola/

[15] Max Roser (2016) –"Literacy", https://ourworldindata.org/literacy/

Chapter 26
Spirit (*X°*)

Care I for the limb, the thews, the stature, bulk, and big
assemblance of a man! Give me the spirit.
~William Shakespeare, Henry IV, Part II

We here define spirit as the soul or psyche, essence or animating principle of an individual, group, or culture (*ethos*). Or even of a time-frame (*zeitgeist*). As broadly as possible, we could define spirit as all the non-material aspects of human experience. James Hillman speaks of "the spirit of a place, the quality of a thing, the soul of a person, the mood of a scene, the style of an art." [1]

Note that our subject is *not* institutional religion, which is quite recent compared to the whole human story. Neither is X° completely described by what many call spirituality. It is true that most of the original founders and greatest teachers of historical religions inhabited regions of X°. So have many aspiring followers within the limits of their understanding and ability. However, X° religion or spirituality constitutes only part of the total realm of spirit.

Note too that science, while tracing some of the components of spirit, is still light years away from explaining most of what makes life worth living.

All our human values involve spirit. It exists in friendship, in the many faces of love, in devotion to God or Good or Truth. Non-material human aspirations and expressions includes qualities such as courage, a sense of place (30°/X°), charisma, imagination, intuition, workmanship, and a desire for perfection.

Spirit also encompasses ideas, theories, models, metaphysics; Logos itself. It is about evolution, chaos theory, the Big Bang, and emergence. It is what Johannes Kepler knew about the music of the spheres, and what modern physicist James Hopwood Jeans meant when he said: "The universe looks more and more like a great thought rather than a great machine."

Wisdom involves spirit. The ability to discern or judge what is good, true, and lasting is based on experience and learning. Though commonly associated with age and experience, wisdom is sometimes acquired early and many older people never gain it. This quality is especially associated with 45° but the connection with X° is this: No matter how much knowledge one has gained, a person is not *wise* unless devoted both to the furthering of life and to truth. These non-material values are implicit in the term.

Pure mathematics, as practiced in ancient India or Greece, by a Newton or Leibniz, Leonhard Euler or Alexander Grothendieck, is X°. Albert Einstein said: "Pure mathematics is, in its way, *the poetry of logical ideas.*" Gregory Bateson spoke of "that *world of rigorous fantasy* we call mathematics." Perhaps that explains how a mathematician wrote *Alice in Wonderland.*

X° is the awe and wonder we feel confronted with something much larger than ourselves: a sky full of stars, an ocean crashing against the rocks, the history of life, patterns of existence. It is the mystery of lightning, striking the Earth eight million times a day. It is the unexplained and that which only pretends to be explained by assigning it a word. Matthew Hutson describes "The experience of encountering something so vast—in size, skill, beauty, intensity, etc.—that we struggle to comprehend it and may even adjust our worldview to accommodate it."[3]

Arts, poetry, and music express X° spirit speaking through the perception of beauty and the desire to create it with metaphor and analogy, surprise, symmetry, asymmetry, color, harmony, rhythm, melody, flowing lines and soaring forms.

Spirit is the Tao: equilibrium turning into creative movement; potential energy into kinetic energy; yin into yang and back again.

X° is the brute devotion of one creature for another, whether kin or not, or even of the same species. It is the visionary imagination of a Nikolai Tesla, and the prodigious creative outpouring of a Wolfgang Amadeus Mozart. All the higher dispositions partake of spirit in forms such as 30° love of family and devotion to perceived duty, and 35° desire to make friends and to cooperate. Spirit is 45° courage and dedication to truth, and the mystery of 50° creative impulse.

Spirit extends unconditional love beyond the baby at the breast, beyond familiar loved ones, to all humanity; it refines and focuses 40° loving kindness into entire lives dedicated to peace and serving others.

Mythology is a manifestation of X°. Bill Moyers calls it "an interior road map of experience." Mythologist Joseph Campbell made it his life work to find "the commonality of themes in world myths, pointing to a constant requirement in the human psyche for a centering in terms of deep principles." [4]

And there are fictional or mythical entities who take on a life of their own. They come out of books or oral traditions; they are beloved characters: Santa Claus, superheroes, Coyote, Anansi, and the tens of thousands of deities that were ever worshipped by any people anywhere.

Numerous human belief systems past and present express spirit: animism and neo-animism, shamanism, pantheism, paganism, Eastern mysticism, mystical traditions in Christianity, Judaism, and Islam, transcendentalism, various idealist philosophies, nature mysticism, Deep Ecology—and more. X° has variously been called Christ consciousness, Buddha consciousness, and Cosmic Consciousness. It is the Dreamtime of Australian Aborigines who call it the 'all-at-once,' the realm of gods and ancestral beings.

To do any justice to these many manifestations of spirit would require several books by several people more learned than I, so what follows is only a tiny and fragmented sampling of X°.

More than One Consciousness

Now I do not know whether it was then I dreamt I was a butterfly, or whether I am now a butterfly dreaming I am a man.
~Zhuang Zhou, Taoist philosopher, 370-287 B.C.

Spirit recognizes spirit in others—even in the nonhuman.

We could view X° consciousness from many directions, such as animal sentience; *umwelt*; and altered states of consciousness.

So, do animals have consciousness? *Animal Ethics* says that only beings with a centralized nervous system (and a brain of whatever size) can be sentient, that is, able to have positive and negative experiences. The author concludes that until the problem of consciousness is clearly solved, "we should act on the assumption that any animal with a centralized nervous system may be sentient....and so we should give them moral consideration." [5]

Animals with a central nervous system include cephalopods and insects, creatures with behavior more complex than most people realize. Australian researchers note that structures in the insect brain perform functions similar to those of vertebrate brains, and propose that "the insect brain also supports a capacity for subjective experience." Ingenious experiments recently found that honey bees understand the concept of zero and can count to four. Bees use symbolic communication in the 'waggle-dance.' [6,7]

Night-flying moths may also lay claim to sentience, their intelligence honed over millions of years by evading the sonar of their chief predator, bats. Like butterflies, some moths migrate long distances, making complex decisions about when to launch, in which direction to fly, and with what speed during changing conditions. [8,9]

German biologist Jakob von Uexküll (1864-1944) defined *Umwelt* as the perceptual world in which a particular organism exists and acts as subject—an environment-world where only certain markers stand out. Naturalist writer Barry Lopez observes that "The worlds they perceive, their *Umwelten*, are all different." If we suppose that only vertebrate, cephalopod, and arthropod species have *Umwelten*—that alone would result in over a million different worlds. The number still doesn't account for differences between subspecies, families, and so on; or the possibility that plants might also have sentience. [10,11,12]

Then there are differences between individuals. An owl's *Umwelt* clearly differs from that of a horse; it is also probable that Owl A perceives its environment with slight differences from Owl B, since its experiences are not exactly the same. In the case of humans, we know that with any two individuals, though of the same species, culture, and even family, each lives in a different universe. Now we are talking about billions of worlds—and without ever leaving the Earth.

We (humans and creatures) have more than one mode of being. Of several altered states of consciousness, dreaming is by far the most common, a nightly occurrence humans share with almost all mammals and birds, and quite possibly with reptiles. Dreaming began early in evolution. It seems quite important, for when experimentally prevented from dreaming, humans start to go mad. During dreaming the whole brain is active, from brainstem to cortex. [13, 14]

John Lennon pondered "Who's to say that dreams and nightmares aren't as real as the here and now?" Lucid dreaming—during which some people are able to maintain conscious awareness and even change the direction of their dream, has been associated with bursts of gamma waves, the fastest kind of brain waves, only recently discovered. [15]

Anthropologist Richard Rudgley says that dreaming shows that humans have a natural predisposition to altered states whether induced by meditation, fatigue, ritual solitude in isolated places, illness, darkness and acoustic resonance in caves, sensory deprivation, music, dancing and drumming, or intoxicating substances. The ancient Vedas of India spoke of meditation 3,500 years ago. There is archeological evidence of the use of psychoactive substances such as mescal, opium and *amanita muscaria* for many millennia. Rudgley says that the art and religious experiences of many cultures have been permeated by images from altered states. [16]

Robert Moss, Australian historian and "dream archaeologist," says dreams have been of great importance to many cultures. In ancient Egypt advanced dream practitioners guided and healed people at temples, and also developed conscious dream travel. The *Muqaddimah*, a 14th century classic by Muslim historian Ibn Khaldun, describes dreaming as one of six essential conditions for human society along with such basics as geography and food supply.

Moss says that among most indigenous peoples dreams mean that we are either traveling or receiving travelers from elsewhere. Dreaming is a social activity: people are likely to wake up during the night to discuss their dreams, and sometimes two or more people dream interactively. Many make a distinction between personal dreams and 'Big dreams' that concern the whole tribe. Moss says among indigenes, "Dreamers are speakers for the earth and travelers between the worlds. They connect us with the web of life in an animate universe, with the ancestors, and with the needs of the whole." [17]

I know nothing but the holiness of the heart's affections and the truth of the imagination.
~John Keats, English poet, 1785-1821

Poetry was once deeply important to every society when epic poems such as Gilgamesh, the Mahabharata, the Iliad, or the Edda expressed each nation's basic values, its national spirit. Percy Bysshe Shelley wrote that "poets are the unacknowledged legislators of the race." Today, poetry appears a minor part of most people's experience, often misunderstood as something that rhymes.

Some of what aspires to be poetry is Hallmark sentimentality filled with 15° clichés; some of what you may hear at a Poetry Slam is 25° adolescent ranting. For many, popular song lyrics are the only poetry they know. Nevertheless, fine poets exist in the 21st century, writing in every language.*

There are still people for whom true poetry is central to their lives, although they are not as numerous as in previous centuries. Poet and editor Robert Lee Brewer says "[poetry has] helped me deal with anger, frustration, heartbreak, headache, hopelessness, isolation, depression, and more. It's helped me be human. That's the true value of poetry as far as I'm concerned. Everything else is icing."[18]

Australian philosopher Tim Rayner notes that "Poets and oracles transmitted cultural wisdom that functioned as social cement. The function of poetic truth was cultural mnemonics—it held society together." If modern society has given up poetry for demonstrable truth, yet Rayner says "poetic truth never really went away. We experience poetic truths in the course of our daily lives. We use poetic speaking to articulate truths that have profound implications for our personal, social, cultural, and political lives." And, we add, our spiritual lives [19]

*For instance (in English) Carolyn Forche, J.S. Prynne, Kei Miller, Natasha Trethewey, W. S. Merwin, Claudia Rankine, Don Paterson, Gregory Pardio, Alice Oswald, Brenda Shaughnessy, Sherman Alexie, Sharon Olds, Kevin Young, Charles Simic, Ricky Laurentiis, Marie Howe, and others.

> *Become the sky. Take an axe to the prison wall. Escape.*
> ~ Jalāl al-Dīn Rūmī, 13th century Persian poet, scholar, and Sufi
> mystic)

> *Sell your cleverness and buy bewilderment.*
> ~Rūmī, translated by Edward Henry Whinfield
> (http://www.quotegarden.com/rumi.html)

We could begin with the early origins of the religious, or spiritual, impulse in the ancient and widespread beliefs of animism, wherein all natural things such as animals, plants, rivers, storms, and mountains have a spirit or soul, and are in effect deified. Pantheism sees divinity as the totality of everything in the Universe—one Oversoul (per Emerson) not separate souls as in animism. Native American religions combine animism and monotheism (the Great Spirit).

Within the Abrahamic tradition, 17th century Jewish philosopher Baruch Spinoza and 20th century Christian theologian Paul Tillich also expressed an expanded conception of God. Tillich said: "God does not exist. He is being itself beyond essence and existence. Therefore to argue that God exists is to deny him."

Mysticism is the experience of direct union with ultimate reality; belief that direct knowledge of spiritual truth can be attained through intuition, contemplation, and self-surrender. It plays an important part in world religions but is not itself a religion; there are mystics who do not hold to any named religion, and ordinary people who have isolated moments of mystical realization, most often in nature.

Mysticism should not be confused with the occult or New Age. It has nothing to do with channeling, Tarot, astrology, or magic. W.T. Stace, Princeton philosopher and early scholar of mysticism, although not himself a mystic, described mysticism as "the apprehension of an ultimate non-sensuous unity in all things." Finding the mystical experience in all cultures, Stace considered it part of human nature. He notes that ecstatic mysticism calls into question the assumption that awareness only exists with data processing.[20]

Mysticism is often associated with East Asian religions such as Hinduism, Sikhism, Buddhism, and Taoism that teach about self-realization as knowledge of the true self beyond delusion and beyond identification with material phenomena. It is realization of one's own divinity, or God-realization. Eastern enlightenment is an individual journey, an *involution* that follows physical evolution. This is the inner path of the human soul to the Self, as it dissolves the multitudes of *sanskaras* or psychological imprints that cloud our view of reality. For Zen Buddhists, sudden enlightenment is possible, awakening to the reality beyond logical thinking and the spider web of words. Other traditions say the process takes thousands of successive reincarnations.

Christianity also has a long tradition of mystics, from Hildegarde of Bingen and Francis of Assisi to the 20th century Simone Weil and Thomas Merton. Islam has its mystical branch—Sufism—and a tradition of mystical poets such as Rumi, Hafiz, and Shirafi. Jewish mysticism was expressed in Ezekiel's visions and the medieval Kabbalah, the philosophy of Moses Maimonides, and Hasidic Judaism. Medieval German theologian and mystic Meister Eckhardt said, "Theologians may quarrel, but the mystics of the world speak the same language."

Novelist Tom Robbins notes that "Religion is nothing but institutionalized mysticism. The catch is, mysticism does not lend itself to institutionalization." It does not even lend itself to definition. Like a wild songbird in a cage, capture destroys it. As the first few degrees express the negative human Shadow, so the very highest awareness appears in an illuminated area, with brightness that blinds the naked eye. Sometimes it is hidden behind clouds of false interpretations. Or it is like the sky itself, which appears blue to human perception although scientists tell us the sky actually has no color of its own.

Mysteries

Of all obstacles to a thoroughly penetrating account of existence, none looms up more dismayingly than 'time.' Explain time? Not without explaining existence. Explain existence? Not without explaining time.
~John Archibald Wheeler, American physicist, 1986

Göbekli Tepe, a site in what is now Turkey, has hundreds of pillars two and three times as tall as a man, arranged in circles, on the top of a mountain ridge. It is 13,000 years old, built long before we think people should have been capable of building it. In 2016, scientists discovered 18,000 new species of animals and plants, some quite strange. Other recent discoveries are anomalous phenomena such as quasicrystals or localized magnetic sites. There are undoubtedly many more but anomalies are often ignored or discounted by 20° gatekeepers.[21, 22, 23, 24]

As a college student in 1948 I met several bright young men who were sure that knowledge was then at its apex; everything of importance was already discovered (25° *temporocentrism*). This was before the double helix and molecular biology, the birth control pill, satellites, the Internet, decoding of the human genome, solar cells, the discovery of four extinct human species,* and nanotechnology, among much other new knowledge and transformative technologies.

It seems that every question answered brings up a host of new ones. Many scientific mysteries are yet to be solved. In biology, for instance, we do not understand the reason for biological aging, how and why sexual reproduction began, why we dream, the function of most DNA, the rapid diversification of multicellular life about 500 million years ago (the "Cambrian Explosion"), and the origin of life itself.

But the greatest of mysteries is consciousness. For a generation a debate has raged among philosophers and scientists about what consciousness is and whether we will ever find out (sometimes called the Hard Problem). Philosophers such as Colin McGinn say that no matter how much scientists study the brain, the mind is fundamentally incapable of comprehending itself. Some neuroscientists are much more sanguine. In their search for the neural correlate of consciousness (NCC) they have found some pieces of the puzzle, for instance, that an abstract concept can be encoded in a single neuron. [25]

Homo habilis, 1960; *Homo floresiensis*, 2003; The Denisovans, 2010; *Homo naledi*, 2013

Other, quite new lines of inquiry focus on gamma waves; or on the cerebellum or "little brain" which some researchers think plays a large role in human consciousness (and X°). The long-underestimated cerebellum contains more neurons than the rest of the brain put together, and constantly communicates with the cortex and other parts of the brain.

Some, such as philosopher David Chalmers and neuroscientist Christof Koch, have begun to consider a viewpoint long neglected in the West: *panpsychism,* the idea that everything in the universe might be conscious or potentially conscious.

Post-material Science

If you want to find the secrets of the universe, think in terms of energy, frequency and vibration.
~Nikola Tesla. 1856-1943, Serbian-American inventor and physicist

Energy, frequency, and vibration—they are subjects of science but are they themselves *material* phenomena? As for cycles, they may be thought of as waves of very long frequency. Indigenous cultures and Asian civilizations are more attuned to thinking in terms of cycles.

Light sometimes acts as a wave, sometimes as a particle; physicist Niels Bohr saw this "duality paradox" as a fundamental or *metaphysical* fact of nature. We use electricity every day, yet electrical engineer William J. Beaty says that electricity has so many contradictory definitions that the term is meaningless.[26]

Then there is 'psi' or ESP. Many psi phenomena could have natural explanations. We know that sharks and some other fish (also dolphins and bees) can detect electrical fields; and that about fifty species of birds, mammals, reptiles, and invertebrates use the earth's weak magnetic field for navigation. Humans can detect polarized light with the naked eye and it is plausible that humans have other natural abilities yet to be discovered. [27]

ESP or extrasensory perception is defined as "perception or communication outside of normal sensory capability." But how do we define 'normal'? Ancient peoples did not have a word for 'blue' and may not have been able to see it. The rainbow doesn't have seven colors—we think it does because we have only a limited number of words for describing the colors we use. It now seems that an unknown number of women and a few men have a fourth cone in their retinas, and in some cases are able to see millions more colors than the rest of us.[28, 29, 30]

Only about one in 10,000 people has perfect pitch (absolute pitch) according to a study at the University of California. Perfect pitch is not 'normal' yet it exists. An estimated one in 2,000 experiences synesthesia, a neurological phenomenon in which stimulating one sensory or cognitive pathway leads to production of a sense impression in a second pathway. It is often linked with creativity.[31, 32]

45°, 50°, and X° are open to the possibility of receiving information through currently unrecognized senses or the mind directly. In general, moderns, with a world view of scientific materialism, tend to dismiss all other ways of knowing, past or present. Yet a number of great thinkers have not done so. Carl Jung said, "I simply believe that some part of the human Self or Soul is not subject to the laws of space and time." Two noted physicists—Freeman Dyson and Brian Josephson—believe in the existence of ESP. Dyson says "Paranormal phenomena are real but lie outside the limits of science." Because they tend to be accompanied by strong emotions, they are "inherently incompatible with controlled scientific procedures." Josephson has said that telepathy exists, and he thinks quantum physics will help us to understand it.

Philosopher Thomas Nagel challenges scientific materialism as the basic assumption of modern science:

> The scientific outlook, if it aspires to a more complete understanding of nature, must expand to include theories capable of explaining the appearance in the universe of mental phenomena and the subjective point of view in which they occur—theories of a different type from any we have seen so far....Mind, I suspect is not an inexplicable accident or a divine and anomalous gift but a basic aspect of nature that we will not understand until we transcend the built-in limits of contemporary scientific orthodoxy. [33]

An expanding field of post-materialist science leads to growing debate about whether science is ripe for another drastic paradigm change like the Copernican Revolution was in the 16th and 17th centuries. This revolution would be about human consciousness; the new paradigm would give equal primacy to mind and matter.

[1] James Hillman, *The Soul's Code*, Warner Books 1996

[2] Erin Reeves, "Charles Ludwidge Dodgson," April 1, 2008 http://math.ucdenver.edu/~wcherowi/courses/m4010/s08/erdodgson.pdf

[3] Matthew Hutson, "Awesomeness is Everything" *Atlantic Monthly*, January/February 2017

[4] Joseph Campbell, *The Power of Myth*, Apostrophe S. Productions 1985

[5] Animal Ethics, "The problem of consciousness," March 24, 2014 http://www.animal-ethics/org/problem-consciousness/

[6] Andrew B. Barron and Colin Klein, "What insects can tell us about the origins of consciousness," *Proceedings of the National Academy of Science* Vol 113, no. 18, May 3, 2016 http://www.pnas.org.cotent/113/18/4900.full

[7] Sam Wong, "Bees are first insects shown to understand the concept of zero," New Scientist, August 4. 2017, http://www.newscientist.com/article/2142884-bees-are-first-insects-shown-to-understand-t...

[8] Joseph Stromberg, "How One Moth Species Can Jam Bats' Sonar Systems," *Smithsonian,* September 20, 2013, http://www.smithsonianmag.com/science-nature/how-one-moth-species-can-jam-bats-sonar

[9] Cell Press, "High-flying Moths Don't Just Go with the Flow," *Science News,* https://www.sciencedaily.com/releases/2008/04/080403131936.htm

[10] Jakob von Uexküll, *A Foray into the Worlds of Animals and Humans*, University of Minnesota Press, 2010

[11] Barry Lopez, *Arctic Dreams,* 1986

[12] Josh Gabbatiss, "Plants Can See, Hear, and Smell—and Respond," BBC, January 10, 2017   http://www.bbc.com/earth/story/20170109-plants-can-see-hear-and-smell-and-respond

[13] MIT News, "Animals have complex dreams, MIT researcher proves" January 24, 2001 http://news.mit.edu/2001/dreaming

[14] Amana Onion, "Birds Practice Singing in Sleep," ABC News, October 26, 1998   http://abcnews.go.com/Technology/story?id=119843

[15] Emily Underwood, "Do sleeping dragons dream?" *Science*, Apr. 28, 2016, http://www.sciencemag.org/news/2016/04/do-sleeping-dragons-dream

[16] Richard Rugley, *Essential Substances*, Koansha Internatonal, 1994

[17] Robert Moss, *The Secret History of Dreaming,* New World Library 2009

[18] Robert Lee Brewer, "What Is the Value of Poetry? *Writer's Digest*, April 16, 2014 http://www.writersdigest.com/whats-new/what-is-the-value-of-poetry

[19] Tim Rayner, "Socrates as Social Entrepreneur: What Is Poetic Truth?" Philosophy for Change, May 1, 2012 https://philosophyforchange.wordpress.com/2012/05/01/socrates-as-entreprcneur-a-five-part-series/

[20] "Mysticism Defined by W.T. Stace" http://www.bodysoulandspirit.net/mystical_experiences/learn/experts_define/stace.shtml

[21] "A Timeline of Fossil Discoveries," Australian Museum, https://australianmuseum.net.au/a-timeline-of-fossil-discoveries

[22] "Magnetic Anomaly Map of the World" https://ccgm.org/en/maps/113-carte-des-anomalies-magnetiques-du-monde.html

[23] Michael Brooks, "13 things that do not make sense," *NewScientist*, March 19, 2005 https://www.newscientist.com/article/mg18524911-600-13-things-that-do-not-make-sense/

[24] Michael Brooks, "13 more things that do not make sense," *NewScientist,* September 2, 2009, https://www.newscientist.com/article/mg20327245-800-13-more-things-that-dont-make-sense/

[25] Oliver Burkeman, "Why can't the world's greatest minds solve the mystery of consciousness?" *The Guardian,* January 21, 2015

[26] William J. Beaty, "What Is 'Electricity'"? ©1996, http://amasci.com/miscon/whatis.html

[27] Juliette McGregor, "Polarised light and the super sense you didn't know you had," *The Conversation*, June 30, 2015 http://theconversation.com/polarised-light-and-the-super-sense-you-didnt-know-you-had-44032

[28] Kevin Loria, "No one could describe the color 'blue' until modern times," Business Insider, Feb. 27, 2015 http://www.businessinsider.com/what-is-blue-and-how-do-we-see-color-2015-2

[29] Veronique Greenwood, "The Humans with Super Human Vision," *Discover Magazine*, June 18, 2012

[30] Kimberly A. Jameson, Susan M. Highnote, and Linda M. Wasserman, "Richer color experience in observers with multiple photopigment opsin genes," https://www.ncbi.nlm.nih.gov/pubmed/11495112

[31] Oliver Sacks; Schlaug; Jancke; Huang; Steinmetz (May 1995). "Letters: Musical Ability" *Science*. 268 (5211): 621–622.

[32] Siri Carpenter, "Everyday Fantasia: the World of Synesthesia," Monitor on Psychology, APA, March 2001, Vol 32, No. 3 http://www.apa.org/monitor/mar01/synesthesia.aspx

[33] "Thomas Nagel, The Core of 'Mind and Cosmos'" August 18, 2013, https://opinionator.blogs.nytimes.com/2013/08/18/the-core-of-mind-and-cosmos/

Chapter 27
Bootstrapping

When we do something several times it forms a habit. Continue with that habit for a long time, and it becomes your character. Continue with that character and eventually, perhaps in another life, it comes up as instinct.
~Swami Satchidananda, *The Yoga Sutras*

Things are looking up. We no longer beat horses to death, or hang people for penny theft. The majority of countries have at least some pretense of representative democracy. Eighty-six percent of the world is more or less literate, and legally, women can vote in all but one country. In many ways, general awareness is increasing—but is all this happening fast enough? Can our social evolution keep up with our destructive side? I suggest we concern ourselves with the welfare and survival of the human creature. Put simply, how do we get from the lower dispositions to the higher ones—more of us, more of the time?

It's best to take a broad view here, as if we were visitors from one of Jupiter's moons. Human dispositions are now mainly expressed in civilizations: complex societies characterized by urban centralization, rule by a small elite, and expansionism (10°); specialization with social stratification, writing and other symbolic communication (20°); and a new sense of separation from and domination over nature (0°/10°). Civilizations have also developed arts, sciences, philosophies, and ways of living together that express the higher dispositions.

Civilization, an approximately 6,000-year experiment out of the 300,000 year lifetime of humanity, represents only two percent of our total development as Homo sapiens.[1]

Despite wars and plagues, human numbers have risen continually, and dramatically so over the past two centuries when world population increased seven-fold. Population is expected to grow quite a bit higher before leveling off. As a consequence of this human irruption, many other species are disappearing (the Sixth Extinction). Human technologies are changing the Earth's geology and climate, creating existential threats to human and other life.

War has been a constant through history, giving full rein to 5° aggression and anger, 10° will to dominance, and 0° indifference to other human lives. As burgeoning numbers of humans fought for control they continually invented new weapons and strategies (20°); this stimulated technology of all kinds, for better and worse.

We are not yet out of this phase of humankind. Large-scale wars between nation-states have come to a standstill for 70 years because the use of nuclear weapons threatens everyone. But it is an uneasy peace that may not last. Accidental war is quite possible. Meanwhile, many smaller wars combine to kill millions of people with conventional weapons.

Since civilization began, one-man rule (10°) has prevailed in most times and places. Only within the 20th century did representative government (35°) and associated democratic institutions become at all widespread. Yet 10° behaviors and ideologies are still extremely powerful in all kinds of societies, as reflected in the nation-state system, war system, prisons, economic oligarchy, corrupt governments, and the continuing subordination of women in many countries.

Higher dispositions have always existed among us. Without 30° we could not have survived as a mammal whose offspring depend on parenting for longer than any other creature. At some point in our early evolution, humans became a truly eusocial animal or "super-cooperators" in E.O. Wilson's word. Eusocial creatures live in multigenerational communities, practice division of labor, and can altruistically sacrifice some personal interests to group welfare (35°).

The first written records of humanitarian, philosophical and religious thinking (40°/45°/X°) appeared about three thousand years ago in the *Vedas* and the *Egyptian Book of the Dead*. Zoroaster and Moses were leading figures. Further development led to the Axial Age (eighth to third century BC) with its great flowering of philosophical and religious thought, graced by leaders including Buddha, Confucius, Socrates and other Greek philosophers; biblical prophets Elijah, Jeremiah, and Isaiah; Mahavira (founder of Jainism); and others.

This was indeed a pivotal time, and we are still spinning out many of those Axial Age ideas. Yet this 3,000-year era of recorded philosophical and spiritual thought represents only about 1% of the history of *Homo sapiens*. It is not surprising that despite these philosophies, religions, and ethical systems, we are still not very good to each other, especially *en masse*.

Current members of our species boast of singular achievements, and of the high standard of living available to half the human race. The 20th century produced technological wonders, but progress in human relationships—not so much. Some things improve while others stay the same or regress. For example, although we abolished slavery as an institution, there are now more human beings in slavery than ever before in history. Many others toil under such dismal conditions that they might as well be slaves. Hundreds of millions of us live in deep poverty and die young. The gap between the richest and poorest is, in fact, growing.

Until the day dawns when humanity kicks its ancient habit of warfare, we cannot claim to have progressed very far. Some of the things we currently do—or fail to do—make it a real possibility that our species might extinguish itself. Or we might survive for a time in a totalitarian dystopia, a mere shadow of our potential humanity.

Civilization and centralized power changed human behavior for both better and worse, increasing some prevailing tendencies while decreasing others. According to biologist E.O. Wilson, we are "a dysfunctional species [with] Paleolithic emotions, medieval institutions, and god-like powers."

Environmental sociologist William R. Catton points out that our cultural heritage was formed at a time when "carrying capacity exceeded the human load"—when there were a lot fewer people. Humans are now not only rapidly increasing in numbers but are also consuming resources and impacting the environment at a far faster rate. Yet most of the cultural heritage persists, increasingly out of step with population growth and technological change.[2, 3]

Computer scientist George Mobus says humanity as a whole faces an urgent need for further evolution of our species toward sapience. He believes this evolution may even require a change in our DNA:

The brain capacity for wisdom…was a relatively new emergent capacity coupled with symbolic thinking and language and second order consciousness (conscious of being conscious) for early *Homo sapiens*. But it was evolved, as Catton notes, to meet the needs of the late Pleistocene existence of our small group-oriented species. It is not, on average, up to the task of modern complex society….Our species is simply not sufficiently wise …to deal with the world we have created. [4]

Unlike Mobus, I believe it is possible for humanity to develop this emergent capacity for wisdom without either waiting for biological evolution or else tinkering with our genes (which would be very unwise). Instead of stumbling blindly into looming disasters, we could give this old civilization a new lease on life. But developing this wisdom requires a large and conscious effort, the courage to face our current reality, and the will to do what is needed as quickly as possible. We urgently need to rein in our numbers, our consumption habits, and our technologies. There is evidence that this consciousness raising has already begun.

Which dispositions are increasing or decreasing? This would be important information for bootstrapping, but one can only make rough guesses. I see 35° and 45° growing because a greater proportion of individuals are able to educate themselves, with leisure to reflect. Far more live autonomously, under representative governments, especially compared with the preponderance of serfs, slaves, indentured servants, voiceless women, and landless tenants of only two centuries ago. Yet, there are many new distractions; and during the last century propaganda and other manipulations have grown more sophisticated so that reason has to thread its way through mazes that older generations were spared.

40° has been growing too, as part of what Steven Pinker calls the "Humanitarian Revolution" of the last few centuries that "saw the first organized movements to abolish slavery, dueling, judicial torture, superstitious killing, sadistic punishment, and cruelty to animals, together with the first stirrings of systematic pacifism." [5]

There is growing admiration and encouragement of 50°, although much of it focuses technology, business, and entertainment.

20° is widespread in the United States and other industrialized nations, also among the new middle class in developing countries and wherever people are striving in a Hobbesian world of "all against all." Its ideologies are powerful. Another disposition that undoubtedly draws in more people than in previous history is 25°, especially in wealthier countries that can support a consumer culture. Meanwhile, 30°, which in all times and places forms the bedrock of human experience, continues to be the most prevalent disposition, expressing the basic concerns of the majority of humans. However, family is not as close and interconnected as it once was, and work is often unsatisfying. In many case people can't find work of any kind to provide for their basic necessities.

Lacking measurement tools, we can only speculate about the everyday awareness of the average human being today. Those who tend to act out the first four dispositions 0° through 15° are *possibly* one-fourth of us. We guess that another fourth usually behave at 20° and 25°, manipulated by false consciousness, advertising and ideologies.

Those acting habitually at lower dispositions are not actualizing their full potential as human beings. Many need psychological help, but this help is in surprisingly short supply even in developed nations. Everybody deserves loving acceptance and a good childhood, but many people fail to get their birthright. An estimated 40% of infants in western societies begin life without a secure attachment to a caregiver.[6]

The dead hand of the past impedes us. Like arterial plaque, an accumulation of ideological and institutional sludge slows the flow of creative spirit. It is composed of malign notions and customs bound together with a startling lack of foresight or generativity.

On the individual scale, there are many ways to teach living skills, such as CBT or positive psychology, or training people to be more optimistic. It is possible to unlearn addictions, which the Canadian neuroscientist Marc Lewis says are always a "response to some degree of psychological suffering….Studies show that even rats will voluntarily withdraw from narcotics when their environments become more livable." Methods exist to help people better connect actions and consequences. There are also ways to teach empathy.[7, 8]

As long as therapeutic help is linked to profit-making, or is barely available in poor countries, it will not be deployed on the large scale, with the necessary imagination. We need new paradigms for therapies and also for how to make them more available.

As Maslow said, individuals attempting to self-actualize must first meet basic human needs such as food, shelter, security, and a sense of belonging. People who are starving or fleeing bombs do not write symphonies or invent new kinds of solar cells. Meeting basic human needs is obviously a major part of raising human consciousness as a whole. (Which comes first, the chicken or the egg?)

Another key is to focus on children. Too many childhoods are wasted as child laborers, child soldiers, child brides, and street nomads. Even in rich countries many of the young are not loved or treated as every child deserves. One very favorable sign is that fifty-two countries (most in Europe and Latin America) have now banned corporal punishment both at home and at school. The great majority of children, however, live in large countries such as the United States, Russia, China, and India that still retain physical punishments for the young.

Cultural Creatives

> *Be the change you want to see in the world.*
> ~Mahatma Gandhi

Social scientists Paul H. Ray and Sherry Ruth Anderson write about an emerging subculture that embodies values and concerns of the higher dispositions in general. These individuals are reframing changes brought about by the many new social movements and consciousness trends that appeared over the past half century. 'Cultural creatives' have appeared sporadically throughout history, but since the 1960s they are becoming much more widespread. In 2013, Ray and Anderson estimated that there are currently 80 million CCs in the United States, 90 million in Europe, and 25 million in Japan, or roughly about 35% of adults in all the developed countries. Ray says:

> We were beginning to build a picture that showed people who were the best informed and were trying to put together a better

picture of the world around them than they were fed from the media with their fragmented factoids; people [who] were concerned about developing themselves over their entire lifetime and not just freezing themselves into one way of life in their twenties. [45°, 50°] [9, 10]

Many had been active in the social movements of the '60's and '70s, but the CC movement is more about transforming consciousness with 'Green' values, personal authenticity, holism, spirituality, natural healing, social responsibility, and the importance of women. CCs appreciate diversity and are good at synthesizing information. The core group or creative leading edge includes many writers, artists, musicians, psychotherapists, holistic practitioners, and other professionals who pass on new ideas and insights. A larger group of people around them are in the process of becoming aware of these messages and changing their lifestyles, a process of change that Ray says takes about ten years.

Although there are almost as many CCs as Moderns, the media and business world has tended to ignore them. However, a U.S. marketing analysis identifies a certain demographic as LOHAS (Lifestyles of Health and Sustainability). This group is claimed to represent over 30% of the consumer market—worth $290 billion. Repeated surveys show them willing to spend or refrain from spending in order to further their values (ethical consumers 35°). [11]

The Long View Grows Shorter

Discoveries of truth form legacies that can be built upon for generations.
~Criss Jami, *Venus in Arms,* 2012

Some believe that positive advances can happen only individual by individual. While acknowledging individual responsibility, we can at the same time attend to physical problems, social circumstances, and above all customs, ideologies, and institutions that breed low awareness with the resulting misery. It is not an either/or but a both. History tells us that broad social adaptations have already occurred many times. Now we need to modify ourselves more consciously and more globally.

This transformative project appears less 'utopian' and more doable if we look at human history in terms of human generations. Here the past does not seem so foreign and remote. Most of us have personally known four or five generations in our own families. My own knowledge dips back through three centuries into the 1880s, with stories my grandmother told me. Memory extends yet further back with genealogical research and tintypes of an even earlier generation.

From the individual's perspective, changes can occur quite rapidly. For instance in the course of a single lifetime my contemporaries and I have adapted to the changes wrought by the 1930s economic depression, World War II, nuclear weapons, the civil rights movement, the sexual revolution, environmentalism, and the computer revolution, among other events. Historians point to the sudden realization that slavery was immoral and the rapid spread of abolitionist thinking, between 1760 and 1800, in England, France, and the American colonies.

We see the American Revolution began only nine generations ago, and a mere 88 generations have passed since the date assigned to the birth of Jesus of Nazareth. Even the beginning of arable farming 12,000 years ago was only about 520 generations back. This all reminds us that humans are a young species that has made enormous changes in a relatively short period of time. And we can do so again.*

CPTSD

Even our misfortunes are a part of our belongings.
~Antoine de Saint-Exupéry, *Night Flight*, 1931

One understanding that might help us in attempting to bootstrap the entire human race is that not only individuals but whole nations may become traumatized. Most of us are familiar with the syndrome PSTD suffered by combat veterans and those who have survived mass killings, domestic abuse, accidents, and natural disasters. The Mayo Clinic defines PTSD as: "a mental health condition that's triggered by a terrifying event—either experiencing it or witnessing it. Symptoms may include flashbacks, nightmares and severe anxiety, as well as uncontrollable thoughts about the event."

A traumatized person may suffer from other conditions. A long-lasting PTSD results in "hostility and mistrustful attitude toward the world, social isolation, a feeling of emptiness and hopelessness, irritability, and estrangement." Some people suffer not only from a single horrible event but a continuing series of them. This Chronic or Complex Post-Traumatic Stress Disorder may occur with combat veterans, hostages, and victims of torture or child abuse, among others.[12, 13]

People suffered from PTSD long before it was named. Our early ancestors experienced horrors—erupting volcanoes, wildfires and floods, earthquakes, attacks by monstrous animals and by other humans. Historical traumas included plagues, famines, wars, enslavement, and genocide. All these events left their mark, especially on the most sensitive such as children. For example, the Black Death killed an estimated 75 to 200 million people in 14th century Europe and Asia, with 30-60% of people dying. Imagine losing your whole family, neighborhood, or village while not knowing what caused the plague, how to prevent or treat it, or when another wave of illness would strike.

Terrifying events lived on as images in people's minds, in the way they raised their own children, and in art, ritual, and stories that they passed on to following generations. We need not assume anything mysterious to call that a collective unconscious. In fact, intergenerational traumatization has been demonstrated in another species. After mice were sensitized to a chemical smell by electric shocks the fear reaction (shuddering) lasted through two more generations, even to those conceived by in vitro fertilization. The cause could be epigenetic modifications that alter the *expression* of genes but not their actual sequencing. However, more experiments are needed to convince skeptical biologists that this is the mechanism involved.[11]

*Traditionally the length of a generation was assumed to be about 25 years in historical times and 20 years in prehistory. However today in the industrialized countries generations are getting closer to 30 years or more. The prehistory estimate may also be on the low side. Following the lead of several anthropologists, I take the long-term length of human generations to be 23 years, meanwhile keeping 25 years for historical times and 30 years for the projected future.[1, 2]

Nations or subcultures that have suffered from a total defeat, cultural genocide, or persistent discrimination may become demoralized and vulnerable to widespread depression (15°), for instance high rates of alcoholism among Native Americans and also among Russians after the breakup of the Soviet Union. Sometimes traumas occurred with such intensity or in tandem, over such a long period of time that they overcame the culture's ability to rebound. In this case, whole cultures as well as individuals may continue to suffer from historic traumas from which they have not fully healed. This has variously been called collective, complex, chronic, or cultural PTSD—or CPTSD.

In the last two decades, researchers have created models of how an unresolved trauma is passed from one generation to the next, calling it historic trauma transmission (HTT). Major focus has been on the Indigenous people of the North American continent who of all contemporary peoples have suffered from the longest, most unremitting succession of traumatic events. This began 500 years ago with the introduction of diseases unknown to them, for which they had no immunity: measles, influenza, bubonic plague, yellow fever, cholera, malaria, and the most destructive, smallpox. An estimated 90 to 95 percent of the population died within two generations, including the leaders and healers who might have helped people to cope. Epidemics continued to break out across the continent. [12]

These devastating illnesses were followed or accompanied by warfare and conquest, slavery, famine, and starvation. Even after several centuries of such experiences, when after 1892 the fighting ended and the indigenous peoples were rounded up, another period followed of forced assimilation (cultural genocide).

The knowledge gained from this focus on the Aboriginal people of North America and other continents can also be applied to numerous other peoples who may have suffered—and may still be suffering—from some version of CPSTD. Are large populations still feeling the psychological effects of slavery in the United States, of Ottoman rule in Europe, or of European rule in Africa? Do the Jews and the Palestinians both suffer from CPTSD? Do wars ever end?

We need many more committees of reconciliation, more grief counselors—or what new kinds of therapeutic tools and institutions would help to heal nations and peoples? Let's work on inventing them. There is a lot to do, on every scale, in every field.*

Mass Consciousness-Raising: Some of us practice ancient spiritual traditions, benefiting both individuals and society when people (usually college-educated and middle-class) overcome adolescent self-centeredness and raise their awareness through spiritual practices. This is important and necessary self-work. However, we have an urgent need for raising consciousness more widely. So far, consciousness-raising has been applied to specific practices of social discrimination. Not much is said anywhere about helping collectivities—cultures, subcultures, nation-states—to reach higher levels of awareness.

Is it even possible to raise consciousness as a whole, a broader change, on a much larger scale? Some nations have attempted it. For instance, a number of small countries and Pacific islands have abolished their armies, some in their constitution, thus averting growth of the war system. Examples are Liechtenstein, Costa Rica, and Samoa.

The first and so far only nation on Earth to make happiness the official goal of public policy is Bhutan, a quite small, poor country in Asia. In the 20 years since, Bhutan has doubled life expectancy, enrolled almost 100% of its children in primary school and overhauled its infrastructure. Bhutan has pledged to remain carbon neutral and to keep at least 60% of its land in forest for all time.

Kerala is a larger polity, a constituent state of India with the population of California. Despite a per capita annual income of about $300, Kerala has a very low infant mortality rate and its literacy rate is among the highest in the world. Its people live nearly as long as Americans or Europeans. Keralans show a high degree of political participation. While statistics do not show anything directly about the range of dispositions in Bhutan or Kerala, they definitely suggest a high degree of 40° generativity and 35° citizenship.

As we look at Western and U.S. politics and ideologies in the year 2018, the lower dispositions appear to be rampant. Nor is the rest of the world progressing. Only imagine the possibilities if our collective will could trigger a transformation, minimizing hate and violence, increasing the absolute and proportional numbers of reasonably contented and cooperative people. I look forward to the possibility of actualizing the known potential of human beings to be happy and wise.

*Recemt decades have seen a resurgence of Native American arts, one way that indigenous people can heal themselves from CPTSD.

[1] Recent fossil discoveries suggest humans may be over 300,000 years old. http://www.msn.com/en-us/news/science/oldest-homo-sapiens-fossils-ever-found-push-hum
http://www.smithsonianmag.com/science-nature/scientists-just-sequenced-the-dna-from-a-400000-year-old-early-human-180948055/

[2] William R. Catton, *Overshoot: The Ecological Basis of Revolutionary Change*, University of Illinois Press, 1982

[3] William R. Catton, *Bottleneck: Humanity's Impending Impasse,* Xlibris, 2009.

[4] George Mobus, "Bottleneck by William Catton - A Review," *The Oil Drum*, November 24, 2009, http://dev.energybulletin.net/node/50821

[5] Steven Pinker, *The Better Angels of Our Nature*, Viking, 2011

[6] B. Rose Huber, 'Four in 10 infants lack strong parental attachments," Woodrow Wilson School of Public and International Affairs, Princeton University, March 27, 2014 https://www.princeton.edu/news/2014/03/27/four-10-infants-lack-strong-parental-attachments?section=topstories

[7] Marco Visscher, "Optimism is More than Positive Thinking, *Optimist,* Fall 2015

[8] Marc Lewis, *The Biology of Desire*, quoted by Elleke Bal, "Unlearning Addiction," *Optimist*, Fall 2015.

[9] Paul H. Ray and Sherry Ruth Anderson, *The Cultural Creatives*: *How 50 Million People Are Changing the World,* Harmony Books, 2000;

[10] Lisa Reagan, "Same Planet, Different Worlds: "How Cultural Creatives Are Transcending Alienation and Isolation to Bring Forward The Practical Wisdom of Conscious Living: An Interview with Social Scientist, Paul Ray, PhD," September 15, 2013, http://kindredmedia.org/2013/09/same-planet-different-worlds-how-cultural-creatives-are-bringing-forward-the-practical-wisdom-of-conscious-living/

[11] http://www.lohas.com/new-cultural-creatives-survey

[12] Iva Nemčić-Moro, Tanja Frančišković, Dolores Britvić, Miro Klarić, and Iva Zečević, "Disorder of extreme stress not otherwise specified (DESNOS) in Croatian war veterans with posttraumatic stress disorder: case-control study," *Croation Medical Journal*, August 2011, NCBI, http://www.ncbi.nlm.nih.gov/pmc/articles/PMC3160697/

[13] "Complex PTSD," U.S. Department of Veterans Affairs, PTSD: National Center for PTSD https://www.ptsd.va.gov/professional/ptsd-overview/complex-ptsd.asp

[14] Ewen Callaway, "Fearful memories haunt mouse descendants: Genetic imprint from traumatic experiences carries through at least two generations," *Nature*, Dec. 1, 2013, http://www.nature.com/news/fearful-memories-haunt-mouse-descendants

[15] Cynthia C. Wesley-Esquimaux, Ph.D. and Magdalena Smolewski, Ph.D., "Historic Trauma and Aboriginal Healing", The Aboriginal Healing Foundation, 2004, http://www.ahf.ca/downloads/historic-trauma.pdf

INDEX

Magna Carta · 280, 298

malice · 25, 58, 78, 137

malign indifference · 26, 27, 98, 182, 183, 213

Maximilian Robespierre · 71

mean-spiritedness · 136

mechanical tyranny · 40

Médecins Sans Frontières · 271

Mercy Ships · 271

meritocracy · 211, 257, 264

military technology · 190

missionaries · 159

mixed economies · 185

mixed motives · 6, 220, 248

modern nation-states · 83, 225

Modern worldview · 167

monopolies · 83, 111, 185, 290

monopoly of force · 82, 283

moral absolutes · 11, 12

moral harassment · 85

moral imagination · 2, 3

moral injury · 197

moral panic · 61, 62

moral relativism · 12

moral universalism · 12

morality and ethics · 2, 4, 252

Mrs. Grundy · 223

muckrakers · 290

multinational corporations · 33, 111

mythology · 320

N

naïve realism · 43, 44

national shadow · 18

nationalism · 51, 63, 70, 113, 151, 152, 155, 191, 226, 268, 294

natural authority · 82

natural biases · 236

nature deficit disorder · 310

negativism · 136

neoliberalism · 177, 235

neo-Nazis · 70, 145, 204

Nihilism · 126, 127

nonviolent resistance · 275

O

obedience · 41, 77, 86, 118, 119, 120, 121, 131, 196, 229, 295, 314

objectification · 39, 47, 48, 55, 140

Oded Yinon · 155

oligarchy · 104, 105

oligopoly · 83, 182

operant conditioning · 165

Original Sin · 13, 18, 158

P

panpsychism · 327

paradigm change · 328

paradox · 303, 327

pathocracy · 9, 115, 116, 244

patriarchy · 79, 95, 96, 102, 107, 175

peacemakers · 274

peasants · 54, 71, 98, 237, 238, 242, 250, 262, 300, 301, 316

perfection · 52

permaculture · 251

planned obsolescence · 184, 185, 217, 218

poetic truth · 302, 323

polymath · 13, 53, 144, 313, 314, 315

pragmatism · 163

prime directive · 38

Principle of Veracity · 88

priorities · 214

private property · 96, 170, 280

pro bono · 289

professionalism · 137, 263, 296

progress · 44, 103, 116, 127, 144, 171, 198, 222, 257, 258, 259, 279, 333

propaganda · 3, 48, 58, 62, 86, 88, 93, 112, 113, 124, 127, 134, 140, 174, 180, 183, 191, 199, 216, 222, 234, 246, 256, 257, 286, 298, 311, 334

propaganda model · 257

pseudo-intellectuals · 212

pseudo-skeptic · 166

psychopath · 11, 15, 16, 19, 125

PTSD · 24, 192, 197, 234, 338, 339, 342

purity · 39, 51, 52

Q

quick fix · 124